# Colonial

## STATE FO

## MID-NINETEENTH

D0760596

Traditional historical approaches to state formation dwell on legal and constitutional developments that theoretically subjected government to the control of citizens. This collection of essays departs sharply from that traditional approach. Its authors focus on the practices – administrative and economic as well as legal – by which citizens came under the control of the state.

Included are studies of the law of associations, the bureaucracy of public schooling, and the establishment of police forces. Other contributions focus on the railway construction boom, the revolution in government finances, the post-Rebellion transformations effected by the Lower Canadian Special Council, and the utilitarian inspiration of changes in imperial administration. One paper examines the entire process of state formation from the point of view of gender, while another discusses the issues raised from a Maritime perspective.

The articles offer, for all their diversity, a common challenge to what might be called the liberal myth of the liberal state. State formation, they suggest, was a powerful and wide-ranging shift that involved far more than a simple 'growth of government.' As against those who take at face value the nineteenth-century rhetoric of 'limited government' and *laissez-faire*, the contributors point to the unprecedented expansion of state institutions and the increasing attempts at government supervision of civic life.

ALLAN GREER is associate professor, Department of History, University of Toronto. He is the author of *Peasant, Lord, and Merchant: Rural Society in Three Quebec Parishes, 1740–1840*.

IAN RADFORTH is associate professor, Department of History, University of Toronto, and author of *Bushworkers and Bosses: Logging in Northern Ontario, 1900–1980*.

# Colonial Leviathan

## State Formation in Mid-Nineteenth-Century Canada

Edited by
ALLAN GREER
and
IAN RADFORTH

UNIVERSITY OF TORONTO PRESS
Toronto Buffalo London

© University of Toronto Press 1992
Toronto  Buffalo  London
Printed in Canada

ISBN 0-8020-5931-7 (cloth)
ISBN 0-8020-6871-5 (paper)

Printed on acid-free paper

**Canadian Cataloguing in Publication Data**

Main entry under title:

Colonial Leviathan

ISBN 0-8020-5931-7 (bound) ISBN 0-8020-6871-5 (pbk.)

1. Canada – Politics and government – 19th century.
2. Political socialization – Canada.  I. Greer,
Allan.  II. Radforth, Ian Walter, 1952–

FC472.C65 1992    320.971    C91-095116-0
F1031.5.C65 1992

This book has been published with the help of a grant
from the Social Science Federation of Canada,
using funds provided by the Social Sciences and
Humanities Research Council of Canada.

The multitude so united in one Person, is called a COMMON-WEALTH, in latine CIVITAS. This is the Generation of that great LEVIATHAN, or rather (to speake more reverently) of that *Mortall God*, to which wee owe under the *Immortal God*, our peace and defence. For by this Authoritie, given him by every particular man in the Common-Wealth, he hath the use of so much Power and Strength conferred on him, that by terror thereof, he is inabled to forme the wills of them all, to Peace at home, and mutuall ayd against their enemies abroad.

Thomas Hobbes, *Leviathan*

Government is a contrivance of human wisdom to provide for human *wants* ... Among these wants is to be reckoned the want, out of civil society, of a sufficient restraint upon their passions ... The inclinations of men should frequently be thwarted, their will controlled, and their passions brought into subjection.

Edmund Burke, *Reflections on the French Revolution*

The bourgeoisie has at last, since the establishment of Modern Industry and of the world market, conquered for itself, in the modern representative State, exclusive political sway. The executive of the modern State is but a committee for managing the common affairs of the whole bourgeoisie.

Karl Marx and Friedrich Engels, *The Communist Manifesto*

# Contents

# Acknowledgments

———

Preliminary drafts of most of the essays in this book were first presented at a workshop, 'Social Change and State Formation in British North America,' held at the Univerity of Toronto in February 1989. The workshop format proved to be a highly successful one that encouraged genuine exchange and lively debate. We want to thank all who attended and especially those who made formal presentations: professors Ramsay Cook, Susan Houston, Daniel Salée, and Reg Whitaker. We would also like to take this opportunity to thank those who made the workshop possible: the Social Sciences and Humanities Research Council of Canada, Conference Grants Program; Professor Joan Foley, Provost, and the Department of History, University of Toronto. Finally, we are grateful for the support and encouragement consistently offered by Gerry Hallowell, Laura Macleod, Beverly Johnston, and Margaret Allen of the University of Toronto Press.

# Contributors

---

**Peter Baskerville** recently published *The Bank of Upper Canada.* He is chair of the Department of History, University of Victoria.

**Lykke de la Cour**, a doctoral candidate in the Department of History at the University of Toronto, specializes in the history of the medical regulation of women.

**Bruce Curtis** teaches in the Department of Sociology, Wilfrid Laurier University. His most recent study, *True Government by Choice Men? Inspection, Education, and State Formation in Canada West* will appear shortly from the University of Toronto Press.

**Jean-Marie Fecteau**, professeur au département d'histoire, Université du Québec à Montréal, est spécialiste d'histoire du droit et du contrôle social au Québec au XIX^e siècle. Il a publié notamment : *Un nouvel ordre des choses: la pauvreté, le crime, l'État au Québec de la fin du XIX^e siècle à 1840* (VLB 1989).

**Allan Greer**, an associate professor of history at the University of Toronto, is the author of *Peasant, Lord, and Merchant: Rural Society in Three Quebec Parishes, 1740–1840* (University of Toronto Press 1985) and of a forthcoming study of popular participation in the Lower-Canadian Rebellion.

**Douglas McCalla** is the author of *The Upper Canada Trade, 1834–1872: A Study of the Buchanans' Business* (University of Toronto Press

1979). He teaches in the Department of History at Trent University and is completing a study of the economic history of Upper Canada/Ontario to 1870.

**Cecilia Morgan** is a doctoral candidate at the University of Toronto. Her research examines the language of gender in Upper-Canadian religious and political thought.

**Michael J. Piva** is an associate professor at the University of Ottawa. His study of Canadian government finances in the mid-nineteenth century is soon to be released by the University of Ottawa Press.

**Ian Radforth** teaches in the Department of History at the University of Toronto and is the author of *Bushworkers and Bosses: Logging in Northern Ontario, 1900–1980* (University of Toronto Press 1987). He is currently studying aspects of Ontario history in the nineteenth century.

**Mariana Valverde** is a member of the sociology department at York University. Her most recent book is *The Age of Light, Soap, and Water: Moral Reform in English Canada, 1880s–1920s* (McClelland and Stewart 1991).

**Graeme Wynn**, the author of *Timber Colony* (University of Toronto Press 1981) and several other essays on the Canadian Maritime provinces, is a historical geographer and associate dean of arts at the University of British Columbia. Most recently he edited *People, Places, Patterns, Processes: Geographical Perspectives on the Canadian Past* (Copp Clark Pitman 1990).

**Brian Young** is professor of history at McGill University. Among the works he has authored is *In Its Corporate Capacity: The Seminary of Montreal as a Business Institution, 1816–76* (McGill-Queen's University Press 1986).

# Colonial Leviathan

# Introduction

ALLAN GREER and IAN RADFORTH

Canadian historians have long been interested in the middle decades of the nineteenth century.[1] This, after all, was a time when the country took shape as a political entity. The republican challenge of 1837–8 was decisively beaten; responsible government emerged as a constitutional practice implying colonial autonomy within the British Empire, as well as a moderate degree of electoral control over government; and then Confederation laid the foundations between 1867 and 1871 of a transcontinental nation. Meanwhile, a basic *modus vivendi* was established between English and French after the defeat of the last serious attempt to anglicize the French Canadians. In the all-important area of relations with the United States, there were significant and lasting shifts: the temptations of annexationism were overcome even as commercial realignment bound the economies of the two countries more closely than ever before.

Through the greater part of the present century, these were the themes that preoccupied historians. Deeply entrenched assumptions about the nature of politics led them to direct their attention primarily to prominent statesmen and to the national visions they enunciated, the politico-constitutional doctrines they propounded, and the parliamentary strategies they pursued. The history of the mid-nineteenth century was the story of William Lyon Mackenzie, Louis-Joseph Papineau, and Joseph Howe, of the theories of Lord Durham, and of the partnership of Robert Baldwin and Louis-Hippolyte LaFontaine; it featured the national vision of John A. Macdonald (or was it George Brown?) and the adroit manoeuvring of George-Étienne Cartier. Of

course 'traditional political history' was never as resolutely biographical or as narrowly 'political' as it is sometimes portrayed. Trade,
bureaucracy, railroads, and labour all receive attention in the works
of Donald Creighton, J.M.S. Careless, and their contemporaries. Yet
these are largely secondary matters, the objects of government policy,
problems to be dealt with, or indicators of political success or failure.
The basic historical process unfolds in Parliament and in the fairly
limited public forum revealed by newspapers and by the correspondence of a narrow group of *hommes d'état*. 'Politics' is the competition
for power and high office within this restricted circle of actors representing different sectoral interests and enunciating conflicting political philosophies. Ironically, though politics was everything in this
approach to history, the state – that is, the object of political conflict
and the prize of political success – was nothing. With their noses
pressed up so close to the windows of politics, historians seemed unable to perceive the edifice of the state itself. The state was assumed
rather than studied.

Admittedly there was an awareness of a certain 'expansion of government' during the Union period, and valuable work was done in
charting the growth and rationalization of a government bureaucracy
before Confederation.[2] New departments were created, functionaries
became more numerous and more professional, budgets grew. At the
same time, colonial governments took over new responsibilities, most
notably in the area of education. A whole new level of government
was instituted in the Canadas when, beginning in the 1830s, municipal
institutions were belatedly set up for the cities and towns. Meanwhile,
colonial legislatures were also widening their purview by authorizing,
chartering, and subsidizing various companies, professional bodies,
clinics, clubs, and charitable organizations. To a generation of historians still imbued with a certain residual whiggishness, these developments seemed incremental and, on the whole, positive. An
essentially machine-like thing – the state – was becoming bigger and
more powerful; it was attending to matters that 'obviously' required
its attention; and it was being run by a new crew.

Beginning in the 1960s, a new generation of scholars arose whose
interests revolved around social, economic, and cultural developments.[3] These practitioners were even less interested in the state than
their predecessors. 'Institutions' and 'legal frameworks' occasionally
appeared in their works, but they were mysterious, rather arbitrary
entities that sometimes affected social phenomena but remained external and peripheral to the concerns of the social historian. Where

the mid-nineteenth century was concerned, responsible government and Confederation and other venerable topics held no allure for these younger researchers. Their inquiries seldom entered entirely unexplored territory, but they did adopt as their primary focus topics once regarded as little more than the 'background' to serious policy debates. The new approach was characterized also by an unwillingness to take the testimony of contemporary observers at face value. New sources and methods were therefore introduced to gain new and more direct evidence of phenomena such as population growth, standard of living, and social mobility.

Thanks to the efforts of social-history researchers in recent decades, we now know that the 1830–70 period saw a number of important transformations outside the political realm. They might be summarized briefly, and excessively schematically, as follows. There was first of all rapid population growth, as well as substantial immigration and emigration. The first wave of massive immigration, almost entirely from the British Isles, flowed into the colonies in the 1830s and 1840s. Even before it had subsided, however, large numbers of Canadians and Maritimers began moving south to the United States. In the predominantly agrarian group of societies that made up British North America, wilderness land suitable for agricultural colonization was fast disappearing south and east of the Canadian Shield. Land shortage was becoming a problem in many parts of the Lower-Canadian countryside before 1830 and, by the 1850s, even the more recently settled Upper Canada was experiencing difficulty.[4] The liquidation of seigneurial tenure in Lower Canada and of the clergy reserves in Upper Canada did little to alleviate the pressure, although it did encourage the commercialization of agriculture.

A spate of construction – canals in the 1840s, railroads in the following decade – provided jobs for many immigrant men. Railroads were indeed among the first enterprises to require a waged labour force permanently and on a substantial scale.[5] The transportation infrastructure, together with the expanded domestic market, had by mid-century fostered the beginnings of large-scale industry. Clearly the 'transition to capitalism' was well under way. Ownership and labour were tending to go their separate ways as it became less unusual to work for a boss. In the forest industry of New Brunswick, to take one enterprise that has been thoroughly examined, the independent, family-run operation was giving way around this time to the mechanized and company-owned sawmill.[6] Elsewhere in British North America, a working-class movement began to emerge in response to the novel situation.[7] Important as these shifts were, it is essential to recall that they still represented little more than a first step on the road to a capitalist social order. Even at the time of Confederation, most Canadians made a living as part of an economically 'independent' household engaged in fishing, farming, or small-scale craft work.[8]

Even though capitalist relations were not yet the exclusive, or even the predominant, form of socio-economic organization, various elements of a colonial bourgeoisie were nonetheless taking an active and influential role in reshaping societies. The learned professions – notably medicine – organized themselves into corporate bodies and fought for and acquired a legal basis for exclusive privileges. Dozens of 'voluntary associations' also made their appearance, and middle-class town-dwellers were at the centre of this process. There were trade associations and literary and scientific societies and religious groups, but the most significant were the philanthropic/social-reform organizations. People joined together to succour the poor and infirm, to establish hospitals and clinics, to press for more humane and effective treatment of criminals, and to urge drinkers to shun the bottle.[9] These initiatives, noble and generous though they seemed in conception, almost invariably implied an extension of supervision and regulation; the rich and privileged were finding new ways to meddle in the lives of the poor and dependent, all in the interests of social peace and security. Governments were sometimes involved to greater or lesser degrees, granting official charters in some cases, providing financial subsidies in others. In French Lower Canada, the Catholic Church played an active part, through lay and clerical bodies, in such social-reform work.[10] Protestant reformers also tended to be religiously inspired, but their organizations were less likely to be directly connected to a church.

Much of this work of social and moral reform was undertaken by women. Feminist scholarship, though still primarily focused on later periods of Canadian history, is beginning to explore the important phenomenon of gender formation in the pre-Confederation era. (See the contribution to this volume by de la Cour, Morgan, and Valverde.) If the concept of 'separate spheres' has any validity (and this proposition is of course increasingly coming under critical attack),[11] then the early to mid-nineteenth century seems to be the moment at which the ideal of feminine domesticity became firmly entrenched in this country. The public sphere in general and politics in particular were, more emphatically than in the past, to be reserved for men. Radical and 'democratic' figures were indeed in the forefront of this movement, as they attacked colonial dependency and other traditional forms of power and privilege, insisted on legal equality for all men, and left sex as the major remaining determinant of political power, dividing those who ought to exercise sovereignty from those rightly subjected to it. Thus it was Louis-Joseph Papineau and the *patriotes* who took the initiative in depriving women of the vote in Lower Canada.[12] Conservatives, though opposed to any notion that all men deserved an active role in the affairs of government simply by virtue of their sex, would certainly have agreed that the proper place for women was in the home, caring for their families and gently subjecting husbands and children to their superior moral and spiritual influence. This particular ideology of sexual difference tended to channel the energies of middle-class women away from the political realm and into charitable organizations and churches where their contribution was valued and where they could to some degree escape the confined existence prescribed by the notion of woman's domestic calling. 'Separate spheres,' then, implied both a masculinization of politics and a feminization of religion and social reform that had profound and lasting effects on public life in nineteenth-century Canada.

It was in the field of education that some of the most dramatic mid-century innovations occurred. The 1840s and 1850s saw the passage of a series of school laws, all of them based on the novel belief that governments ought to take over the instruction and socialization of children. The history of the emergent public school system, particularly as it developed in mid-nineteenth-century Ontario, has been the focus of much recent research.[13] Themes stressed in this diverse and high-quality literature include the growth of increasingly centralized bureaucratic control over all aspects of schooling, the professionalization of teaching and the expanding female presence in the profession, the use of the schools to inculcate social, political, and moral lessons in pupils, the separation of children by age, class, and sex, and the implicit program of forming docile personalities habituated to authority. Where historians of education once perceived nothing more sinister than a general advance of enlightenment and humanity, current work in the field, revolving as it does around the question of power, tends to be less sunny in its assessments.

Nothing illustrates the ongoing historiographic shift better than the changing views of responsible government and its implications. The doctrine of responsible government, pressed for by colonial Reformers and granted by the British in the late 1840s, specified that the Executive Council in each colony should be chosen from the majority party in the Assembly. The practical authority of the governor was severely restricted and a system of cabinet rule instituted. All this implied a loosening of the imperial rule and an enhancement of the power of voters' representatives; accordingly, the advent of responsible government has generally been hailed as an advance for democracy and for Canadian autonomy. Quite apart from any reservations that might be expressed about the use of the term 'democratic' in connection with a franchise that excluded all women, all native Indians, and all poor men, historians are beginning to question the notion that responsible government subjected the executive to the control of the voters. Of Lord Durham and his *Report*, Phillip Buckner observes:

> In part, it is true, he recommended responsible government as a device for giving to the colonists control over their own internal affairs. But he was equally concerned with strengthening the executive so that it could perform effectively its responsibility to govern. It is too easily overlooked that while under Durham's system the Assembly would be able to control the composition and policies of the executive, the executive in turn would be able to give greater direction to the activities of the Assembly.[14]

Responsible government, in other words, implied a tremendous strengthening of executive powers. Accordingly, the government, though answerable to 'the people' in a theoretical and rather indirect way, was in fact much better equipped to make its influence widely felt. Through the medium of party discipline (admittedly, this was a force that did not develop instantly), cabinets were able to gain unprecedented control over the legislative process. Moreover, their ability to regulate civil society was greatly enhanced, not only by the ramifying agencies and institutions at their disposal, but also by the aura of legitimacy surrounding their actions thanks to the doctrine of responsible government. Bruce Curtis has suggested that the contemporaneous granting of responsible government and the establishment of a public school system with a mandate to train up children into governable subjects was by no means accidental. Properly socialized in Ryerson's schools, citizens would use their electoral powers 'responsibly' (that is, in ways unthreatening to the established order).[15] Moreover, the system of cabinet responsibility did not necessarily imply a loosening of the bonds of empire; one imperial historian portrays it instead as, 'a device for retaining Imperial control over the colonies, a means of securing the collaboration of the colonial elites in the perpetuation of Imperial rule.'[16] Considerations of this sort make it impossible to regard responsible government as liberating in any simple sense. Canadian voters (that is, the minority of colonial residents who met the requirements of age, sex, property, and race) did indeed win a measure of control over the affairs of government; at the same time, however, the state gained unprecedented powers that affected individual lives and shaped civil society.

Power is indeed coming to be a central preoccupation of historians* of Canada more generally. This tendency can be seen as a reaction against a version of social history that views social structures, cultural norms, and the routines of everyday life as if they existed in a peaceful realm separate from struggles for control. And yet this can hardly be called a 'return to political history' in any simple sense. After all the socio-historical analysis of the last decades, no one could assume that the study of politics equals the study of politicians. In his recent examination of the politics of mid-nineteenth-century Canadian tariff making, for example, Ben Forster stresses the changing social context – the rise of organized interest groups, the growing ascendancy of class-conscious industrialists, and so forth – in setting the terms of the parliamentary debate.[17] Clearly, then, social history and political history are engaged in a process of interpenetration, as neat distinctions between 'the social' and 'the political' begin to break down.

This volume is, in one sense, the product of these historiographic trends; on the other hand, it also represents a program for extending them while moving towards an enhanced understanding of one portion of the Canadian past. The contributors to this book represent a variety of points of view. Some, though not all, see the state and the state-formation process as phenomena of central importance that offer an integrating focus for scholars concerned with power in a modern society. All agree that state formation requires closer scrutiny.

What do we mean by 'state' and 'state formation'? Well, to begin on a negative note, we do not mean 'government' and 'the growth of government.' Rather we have in mind a broader conception of

---

* Please note that, although we use the term 'historians' as a shorthand expression meaning scholars interested in the human past, in this case nineteenth-century Canada, we have no desire to indulge in disciplinary chauvinism. Some of the most important contributions in the field have been made by sociologists, geographers, and economists. Indeed this book represents an effort at interdisciplinary collaboration.

political power than that implied by these terms, one that seeks to give due recognition not only to the most prominent elements in the executive and the legislature, but also to the constellation of agencies and officers sharing in the sovereign authority. Defining the term 'state' in more precise terms is by no means an easy task; indeed it is one that has bedevilled theorists who have given long and serious thought to the problem. 'A set of administrative, policing, and military organizations headed, and more or less well coordinated by, an executive authority,' according to Theda Skocpol, the state specializes in administration and coercion.[18] Enumerating some of the more important elements of the modern state, Ralph Miliband mentions the government, the civil service, the police and military, the judiciary, municipal and provincial governments, and parliamentary assemblies. Since these institutions are not fully integrated, Miliband adds, it is misleading to speak of the state as a thing: 'What "the state" stands for is a number of particular institutions which, together, constitute its reality, and which interact as parts of what may be called the state system.'[19] Though not an entirely unified and coherent entity in Miliband's view, the state is still an amalgam of tangible institutions.

Another school of thought, one owing much to the sociologist Émile Durkheim as well as to Karl Marx, objects to such 'reification' and prefers a cultural approach according to which the state is essentially an agency of 'moral regulation.'[20] The prime function of the state (and, according to this view, the state cannot really be distinguished from society) is one of legitimation, a matter of justifying class rule through mystification. However perplexing this position may be for anyone attempting to attach a clear meaning to the term 'state,' it does lend itself nicely to the study of state formation, a *process* rather than a *thing*.

State formation might then be seen, following the Durkheimian/ Marxist approach, as a cultural phenomenon (a 'cultural revolution' in Philip Corrigan's words) by which authority became progressively pervasive and efficacious in society. The rule of a minority was made to seem normal and proper through the efforts of agencies that shaped personalities and forestalled alternative visions. The accent in this account is on the developments that contributed to a general discipline in society, whether or not these were actually sponsored by the government. On the other hand, state formation might well be conceived of from Theda Skocpol's perspective. In this view, the focus is on

actual institutions and the process by which they became more effective agencies of coercion and administration, taking fuller control of
civil society and penetrating into previously neglected corners of the
social formation. It is not our intention to make a case here for one
or the other of these conceptions of state formation. Both are represented, along with other theoretical perspectives, in the articles that
follow.

The first three chapters of this book examine reconstruction in the
Canadas after the defeat of the insurrections of 1837–8. It was a
critical moment in colonial state formation. The republican threat
had alerted authorities to the urgent need to enhance state power,
while the annihilation of the radical alternative had cleared the way
for proponents of capitalist transformation. Allan Greer deals with
the colonial authorities' most pressing problem once the gunsmoke
had cleared in Lower Canada: how to intimidate and pacify a defiant
populace. The response involved the establishment of North America's first large, centrally controlled, and professional police forces.
Urban constables pursued a program of moral and social reform,
while mounted policemen tried to maintain political surveillance in
country districts where the state had until then scarcely been seen.
Police reform was largely initiated by the Special Council that governed Lower Canada after the suspension of representative government at the time of the insurrection. Brian Young surveys the Special
Council's many bold initiatives and argues that they amounted to the
enactment of 'a regime of positive law.' In undermining seigneurial
tenure, in establishing land-registry offices, and in altering family
property law, the Special Council's ordinances helped lay the foundations of a capitalist order. Ian Radforth tackles the same reform
process, but focuses on the role of the imperial representative, Governor Charles Poulett Thomson (Lord Sydenham). Thomson treated
the Canadas as a laboratory for reform, an opportunity to demonstrate the effectiveness of his Utilitarian approach. Ideology, Radforth
suggests, played a crucial role in the revolution in colonial government.

Two contributors develop sophisticated theoretical arguments about
colonial state formation. Bruce Curtis follows up on the theme of
administrative reform in the 1840s by taking a close look at the emergence in Canada West of new bureaucratic structures and procedures
in the field of education. New state officials – the school inspectors
– gained authority to define appropriate behaviour and thinking and

to insist upon (though not always to achieve) compliance. Curtis argues that the development of these 'bureaucratically organized cadres' was an important aspect of an ongoing cultural revolution and that the essence of state formation lies in this very process of cultural change. Jean-Marie Fecteau's focus is the changing legal framework defining and regulating associations in nineteenth-century Quebec. Fecteau notes that governments at the beginning of this period were highly suspicious of private corporate bodies, granting them legal recognition only reluctantly and only insofar as they pursued aims approved by the state. As the paradoxically individualistic collectivism of bourgeois liberalism gained power over the course of the century, legislation became increasingly permissive. Corporations, clubs, and unions, by the score and then by the thousands, came to be recognized entities before the law. With these developments as its point of departure, Fecteau's essay takes up a number of fundamental issues, such as the nature of the law, the distinction between 'public' and 'private,' and the problematic concept of liberal 'individualism.'

The implications for gender of mid-century state initiatives are explored in a pioneering essay by Lykke de la Cour, Cecilia Morgan, and Mariana Valverde. This topic has been almost entirely neglected by scholars of the colonial state and by historians of women's experience. The authors force us to look afresh at some familiar topics and point towards new avenues for research. They maintain that the growth of the reforming liberal state made a significant contribution to the ongoing process of gender formation, helping to define sexual difference and consolidate masculine power. Furthermore, they argue, mid-century state regulation tended to sharpen distinctions among women along class and racial lines.

The following three chapters examine the role of the state in the realm of economic and financial affairs. Douglas McCalla draws on his meticulous empirical research on the pre-Confederation Ontario economy to assess the economic impact of the railways and to question the familiar assertion that within the North American context Canadian governments were especially committed to fostering railway construction. In his study of the mid-century revolution in transportation, Peter Baskerville reaches back to the canal-building era and forward to the operating phase of Canadian railway history. Baskerville argues that the activist state in Upper Canada emerged in a ragged fashion in response to changes both within the sphere of imperial relations and on the local scene. Moreover, in the case of the railways – and in contrast to the educational sector – colonial politicians proved reluctant to transfer authority to professionals and a bureaucratic inspectorate. In the next chapter, Michael Piva studies the business affairs of the government itself. He demonstrates how, in response to a series of devastating financial and economic crises, Canadian governments devised various methods for gaining a clearer understanding of the overall financial status of the government, reducing departmental autonomy in spending, and enhancing accountability.

The final chapter is like a refreshing breath of sea air. In Graeme Wynn's essay, the focus shifts from central Canada to the distinctive patterns of development in the Maritime colonies. His presentation also differs from the rest insofar as he sketches a series of 'vignettes' that together convey a sense of the variety and complexity of experience in the region. Moreover, he concludes by prescribing a healthy dose of scepticism. Wynn agrees that, from the perspective of the administrative centres of the Maritime colonies, the state grew more interventionist during the mid-century period. But he questions whether the outport fisherman or back-country farm woman was much affected by the new state initiatives of the era.

This collection of essays is intended to open a discussion, not to close it. The contributors offer no final answers, nor do they pretend to any sort of complete coverage of the subject of mid-nineteenth-century state formation. Many topics of obvious importance have been slighted. Native peoples and the state is one example; the confederation of the British North American provinces, a subject yet to be examined in a theoretically informed manner, is another; the annexation of the West, a third. Those aspects of state and society that are dealt with here have been examined from the standpoint of several academic disciplines and from a wide range of theoretical perspectives. At a substantive level, the articles offer, for all their diversity, a common challenge to what might be called the liberal myth of the liberal state. As against those who take at face value the nineteenth-century rhetoric of 'limited government' and *laissez-faire*, our contributors point to the unprecedented expansion of state institutions and the increasing attempts at government supervision of civic life. Where others have dwelt on legal and constitutional developments that theoretically subjected government to the control of citizens, we insist on the need to study the actual practices by which citizens came under the control of the state.

## NOTES

1 Among the classic works on the period, we might mention Donald
  Creighton, *The Commercial Empire of the St. Lawrence, 1760–1850* (Toronto:
  Ryerson Press 1937); J.M.S. Careless, *Brown of the Globe* 2 vols (Toron-
  to: Macmillan 1959–63); J.M.S. Careless, *The Union of the Canadas: The
  Growth of Canadian Institutions, 1841–1857* (Toronto: McClelland and Stew-
  art 1967); W.L. Morton, *The Critical Years: The Union of British North
  America, 1857–1873* (Toronto: McClelland and Stewart 1965).

2 The most important work in this regard is J.E. Hodgetts, *Pioneer Public
  Service: An Administrative History of the United Canadas* (Toronto: University of Toronto Press 1955).

3 An outstanding example of the social-history approach is Michael
  Katz's influential book *The People of Hamilton, Canada West: Family and
  Class in a Mid-Nineteenth-Century City* (Cambridge, Mass.: Harvard Uni-
  versity Press 1975). It is important to note that Katz has shown much
  more interest in the state in recent years. See Michael Katz, Michael J.
  Doucet, and Mark J. Stern, *The Social Organization of Early Industrial
  Capitalism* (Cambridge, Mass.: Harvard University Press 1982).

4 Fernand Ouellet, *Economic and Social History of Quebec, 1760–1850:
  Structures and Conjunctures* (Ottawa: Gage/Carleton Library 1980);
  David Gagan, 'Land, Population and Social Change: The "Critical
  Years" in Rural Canada West,' *Canadian Historical Review* 59 (1978),
  293–318

5 Paul Craven and Tom Traves, 'Dimensions of Paternalism: Discipline
  and Culture in Canadian Railway Operations in the 1850s,' in Craig
  Heron and Robert Storey, eds, *On the Job: Confronting the Labour Process
  in Canada* (Montreal: McGill-Queen's University Press 1986). See also
  H. Clare Pentland, *Labour and Capital in Canada, 1650–1860* (Toronto:
  Lorimer 1981) and Ruth Bleasdale, 'Class Conflict on the Canals of
  Upper Canada in the 1840s,' *Labour / Le travail* 77 (1981), 9–39.

6 Graeme Wynn, *Timber Colony: A Historical Geography of Early Nineteenth
  Century New Brunswick* (Toronto: University of Toronto Press 1981)

7 Stephen Langdon, *The Emergence of the Canadian Working-Class Movement* (Toronto: New Hogtown Press 1975); Bryan D. Palmer, *Working-
  Class Experience: The Rise and Reconstitution of Canadian Labour, 1800–1980*
  (Toronto: Butterworths 1983), ch. 2; Craig Heron, *The Canadian Labour Movement: A History* (Toronto: Butterworths 1989), ch. 1

8 Allan Greer, 'Wage Labour and the Transition to Capitalism: A Critique of Pentland,' *Labour / Le travail* 15 (1985) 7–24

9 Judith Fingard, 'The Winter's Tale: The Seasonal Contours of Pre-Industrial Poverty in British North America,' *Canadian Historical Association, Historical Papers* 1974, 65–94; Judith Fingard, 'The Relief of the
  Unemployed Poor in Saint John, Halifax, and Saint John's,
  1815–1860,' *Acadiensis* 5 (1975), 32–53; George Hart, 'The Halifax Ex-

periment,' *Canadian Historical Review* 34 (1953), 109–23; Brereton Greenhous, 'Paupers and Poorhouses: The Development of Poor Relief in Early New Brunswick,' *Histoire sociale / Social History* 1 (1968), 103–26; Rainer Baehre, 'Paupers and Poor Relief in Upper Canada,' Canadian Historical Association, *Historical Papers* 1981, 57–80; Huguette Lapointe-Roy, *Charité bien ordonnée: le premier réseau de lutte contre la pauvreté à Montréal au XIXᵉ siècle* (Montréal: Boréal 1987); J.J. Belomo, 'Upper Canadian Attitudes toward Crime and Punishment,' *Ontario History* 64 (1972), 11–26; J.M. Beattie, *Attitudes towards Crime and Punishment in Upper Canada, 1830–1850: A Documentary Study* (Toronto: Centre for Criminology, University of Toronto 1977); Rainer Baehre, 'Origins of the Penitentiary System in Upper Canada,' *Ontario History* 69 (1977), 185–207; Jean-Marie Fecteau, *Un nouvel ordre des choses: la pauvreté, le crime, l'État au Québec, de la fin du XVIIIᵉ siècle à 1840* (Montréal: VLP Éditeur 1989)

10 René Hardy, 'L'activité sociale du curé de Notre Dame de Québec: aperçu de l'influence du clergé au milieu du XIXᵉ siècle,' *Histoire sociale / Social History* 6 (1970), 7–24; Nadia Eid, *Le clergé et le pouvoir politique au Québec: une analyse de l'idéologie ultramontaine au milieu du XIXᵉ siècle* (Montréal: Hurtubise 1978); Brian Young, *In Its Corporate Capacity: The Seminary of Montreal as a Business Institution, 1816–1876* (Montreal: McGill-Queen's University Press 1986), 150–67

11 Linda K. Kerber, 'Separate Spheres, Female Worlds, Woman's Place: The Rhetoric of Women's History,' *Journal of American History* 75 (1988), 9–39

12 Collectif Clio, *Quebec Women: A History*, trans. Roger Gannon and Rosalind Gill (Toronto: Women's Press 1987), 122

13 Among the more important works recently published on this topic, see R.D. Gidney and W.P.J. Millar, 'From Voluntarism to State Schooling: The Creation of the Public School System in Ontario,' *Canadian Historical Review* 66 (1985), 443–73; Bruce Curtis, *Building the Educational State: Canada West, 1836–1871* (London, Ont.: Althouse 1988); Susan Houston and Alison Prentice, *Schooling and Scholars in Nineteenth-Century Ontario* (Toronto: University of Toronto Press 1988).

14 Phillip A. Buckner, *The Transition to Responsible Government: British Policy in British North America, 1815–1850* (Westport, Conn.: Greenwood Press 1985), 335

15 Curtis, *Building the Educational State*, 106

16 Buckner, *Transition to Responsible Government*, 6

17 Ben Forster, *A Conjunction of Interests: Business, Politics, and Tariffs, 1825–1879* (Toronto: University of Toronto Press 1986)

18 Theda Skocpol, *States and Social Revolutions: A Comparative Analysis of France, Russia, and China* (Cambridge: Cambridge University Press 1979), 29

19 Ralph Miliband, *The State in Capitalist Society* (New York: Weidenfeld and Nicolson 1969), 49
20 Philip Corrigan and Derek Sayer, *The Great Arch: English State Formation as Cultural Revolution* (Oxford and New York: Blackwell 1985), 1–13; Philip Abrams, 'Notes on the Difficulty of Studying the State,' *Journal of Historical Sociology* 1 (1988), 58–89

# 1

# The Birth of the Police in Canada

ALLAN GREER

Professional police forces would seem to be an essential arm of the modern state, and yet their appearance in Canada is comparatively recent. It was only around the middle of the nineteenth century that agencies resembling contemporary police departments began to emerge in the towns and cities of British North America. This innovation mirrored similar developments occurring at roughly the same time in other countries in the European cultural sphere, and surely it deserves attention as a major element of the larger process of state formation. Victorian police forces were very much the creatures of government – municipal and, to some extent, provincial – and their personnel were entirely servants of the state. In the salaried, uniformed, disciplined, and professional policeman, the state found an instrument that expanded enormously its practical reach, its ability to observe and to regulate aspects of life and sectors of society once largely beyond its ken.

According to recent studies in Britain, Canada, and the United States, the newly formed police forces of the nineteenth century made their mark mainly by combating 'vice' and by struggling to wrest control of city streets from the unruly 'dangerous classes.'[1] As he travelled his beat, directing traffic, accosting vagrants, and arresting drunks, the policeman brought the power of the state to bear on all citizens, particularly the poor. Not only was the tone of urban life altered as a result, the visage of the state itself was transformed as people were increasingly confronted with a visible human embodiment of the sovereign power.

It had not always been so. Up until the late 1830s in some places (much later in others), city and colonial governments were largely destitute of the means of exercising direct and constant control over 'civil society.'[2] Of course, this does not mean that anarchy prevailed before the advent of the modern police. On the contrary: it appears that communities were, to an important extent, self-regulating. In the French-Canadian countryside (and perhaps in other regions as well) conflicts were often resolved and personal disputes settled by means of informal arbitration.[3] Elsewhere, charivari and other punitive rituals could be deployed against those who breached the rules of proper conduct.[4] Such manifestations of 'popular law,' though not particularly sanctioned by the state, usually upheld norms that were basically the same as those defended by the officially recognized law of the land.

The colonial state and the incorporated cities in this early period did have their own agents charged with enforcing the law and keeping the peace, but these were not entirely divorced from the civil-society milieu of the popular law; neither were they fully controlled by government.[5] Justices of the peace were the central figures in most localities. Assembled in quarter sessions, JPs conducted criminal trials, passed legislation covering routine local matters, and provided for law enforcement. At other times of the year, these magistrates possessed certain judicial authority that they could exercise singly or in pairs. In Saint John, New Brunswick, one of the few cities in British North America that was incorporated before the 1830s, JPs were elected by the freemen of the various wards.[6] In most other places, rural and urban, magistrates were appointed by the colonial government from among the local notables deemed qualified.[7] They were given no salary – though they were permitted to exact fees and to keep a portion of any fines levied – and almost all of them exercised some non-judicial calling that they interrupted as required to swear out a deposition, draw up a bill of indictment, or attend a meeting of the quarter sessions. Free from any sort of routine supervision or administrative control, JPs could not be considered as simply agents of the state, even if they did derive their authority from the king's commission.

In the early nineteenth century, most towns had constables to arrest law-breakers, serve warrants, and attend in court. These officers, too, were elected in the wards of Saint John, whereas in Montreal and Quebec they were named by a government-appointed high constable. Lacking training, uniforms, and salaries, constables were notorious for pursuing the various fees and perquisites of office. 'The constable was in no sense a "peace" officer,' writes T.W. Acheson, 'Essentially he was an officer of the court acting only after the commission of a felony or a misdemeanor in response to a court order.'[8] Additional measures were required to protect the property of the burghers of Lower Canada and New Brunswick after dark. In the second decade of the nineteenth century the magistrates of the three towns organized a salaried night-watch to light torches, look for fires, and pursue any burglars foolish enough to make their presence known. Constables and watchmen might capture the odd thief and make life difficult for vagrants and unlicensed tavern-keepers, but they were not equipped, nor were they numerous enough, truly to master the streets. Moreover, even these rudimentary police forces were strictly urban entities. In the countryside, where the majority of the population lived, there were no constables, although the rural parishes of Lower Canada did have their militia captains, authorized, as under the French regime, to arrest and detain law-breakers.

Institutions and procedures varied to some extent in the different British North American provinces, but there were some common characteristics. Until the 1830s at least, the apparatus for enforcing the law and coercing deviants was quite limited in scope and effectiveness. Far from being manned by 'professional' servants of government, the machinery of repression was in the hands of somewhat negligent magistrates and officers who exercised their powers on occasion rather than continuously. Justices of the peace and constables – elected in some localities, more commonly appointed – were very much members of their respective communities, as were the militia captains of Lower Canada. Indeed, the whole ramshackle affair was deeply embedded in the ambient civil society. Consequently, it could not function as the instrument of an external and superior state power to anything like the degree that modern police forces later would.

On the other hand, there were the British troops that garrisoned most of the major centres of British North America. Certainly they constituted a potent and efficient coercive force, fully at the service of government. The trouble with the military was that it was a singularly blunt instrument, really useful only for dealing with full-scale insurrection. Soldiers were occasionally deployed to deal with urban unrest.[9] However, since there was not much soldiers could do with rioters other than shoot them (as they did during the Montreal election riot of 1832), officers were understandably reluctant to come to the aid of the 'civil power.' Nevertheless, the military presence in the colonies must surely have had a deterrent effect on anyone contemplating anti-government action. In fact, it probably goes a long way to explain why early Canada, without being a very well-policed society, was nevertheless relatively free of the most acute forms of social conflict.

In the middle decades of the nineteenth century, this situation changed drastically as novel institutions of policing took root. Robert Peel's Metropolitan Police, established in London in 1829, provided a model and an inspiration for the colonies, as it did, for that matter, among administrators in other countries in America and Europe. The 'bobby,' lightly armed and dressed in a non-military uniform, was intended to give as little offence as possible to notions of 'English liberty' while subjecting Londoners to unprecedented supervision. He was not to wait for trouble, but to take an active role, walking a beat and delving into the affairs of his district and its residents the better to suppress crime, vice, and disorder. This sort of interference was widely resented. On the whole, and until well into the second half of the nineteenth century, 'the police were seen as unmanly, unnecessary, unconstitutional and unBritish.'[10] Workers in particular opposed the Peel system, but so did members of the traditional ruling classes; consequently, the new police spread only very gradually into the provinces of England. The threat of Chartism did help to overcome the opposition of city fathers and parliamentarians to the new system, but even as late as 1853, half the counties in England lacked modern police forces.[11]

Little wonder, then, that the Peel approach to police was not adopted overnight in British North America. Quite apart from purely economic objections to the costs of police reform, there was a good deal of resistance on the part of colonial élites to any proposal to erect a 'new engine of power and authority' that might undermine the role of traditional institutions. Still, in town after town, the new system was introduced, if only on a limited scale at first. Some excellent local studies give us an opportunity to follow this process of innovation as it unfolded in Saint John and Toronto. After several years of Orange-Green rioting, Saint John took the plunge in 1848–9 and converted its night-watch into a twenty-one-man police force, outfitted with uniforms, armed with pistols, and organized for round-the-clock service.[12] The initiative for this step came from the city itself, and the force was financed by the common council; but the Saint John police was formally the creation of the New Brunswick legislature, and the provincial government appointed a 'stipendiary magistrate' to supervise it.[13] Toronto began its life as an incorporated city with only five constables in 1834, but gradually, over the course of the 1840s and 1850s, this tiny and rather traditional corps grew into a more substantial police force organized along English lines. For a time, the Toronto police, strictly under the control of the Tory town council, were notoriously partisan in their treatment of Reformers and Catholics. Efforts were made, however, to cultivate a more impartial reputation for the force by toning down blatant expressions of Orangeism and by insulating it from the vagaries of civic politics. Naturally, this required a certain measure of provincial supervision of the municipal police, principally through the appointment (1849) of a stipendiary police magistrate to take over some of the judicial powers previously exercised by the elected city council and to play an influential role on the police commission.[14]

Little is known about early police reform in other parts of English Canada. A study focusing on the commercial centre of Hamilton up to 1851 suggests that there were various short-lived experiments with professional policing in the 1840s.[15] Presumably, small towns like Hamilton followed the examples of Saint John and Toronto after some delay. Further research will no doubt clarify matters, but for the moment it appears that the installation of modern police forces and police magistrates was an incremental process that took place in most parts of Canada between the 1840s and the 1870s.

Modern police establishments were instituted earlier and much more rapidly in Lower Canada than in other parts of British North America. In the immediate wake of the Rebellion of 1837–8 the colonial authorities set up an urban police force in Quebec City (1837) and Montreal (1838), as well as a special mounted police acting under the orders of stipendiary magistrates for the rural districts of the western part of the province (1839–42).[16] Since historical research on the nineteenth-century police has so far been exclusively local in scope, no one seems to have noticed the pioneering role of Lower Canada, not only within the British North American context, but in the continent as a whole.[17] Even by the standards of later decades, the post-Rebellion police of Lower Canada were unusually large and well-funded forces, and – as a result of the suspension of municipal institutions at the time – they were fully controlled by the central government of the province.

They were set up under the peculiar circumstances of a revolutionary crisis; accordingly, political surveillance and pacification formed a central part of their mandate. It is important to note, however, the degree to which these precocious police forces (and particularly the urban ones) pursued 'non-political' objectives identical to those pursued in later years by the police of Toronto and Saint John. Ruling circles in Lower Canada favoured the installation of Peel-style police for the same reasons that their counterparts in other provinces desired it, but the suspension of electoral politics and civil liberties surrounding the defeat of the Patriots allowed them to proceed much more rapidly. There is no reason to believe that Lower Canadians were any more willing than English people to entrust additional coercive power to the government (far from it!); the administrators of that colony were nevertheless able to push through the police reforms that suited them in 1838–9 simply because, under the circumstances, no one else's views mattered. This path-breaking police reform must be seen as a response, then, not only to the challenge of revolution, but also to the opportunities afforded by counter-revolution.

On the very day that the redcoats annihilated the rebels at the Battle of St Eustache (14 December 1837), Quebec became the first city in Canada to boast a professional police force. Since the constitution had, to all intents and purposes, been suspended by then (it was revoked by act of Parliament in January 1838), this major innovation occurred without the normal formalities.[18] The new system was extended to Montreal in July 1838. The forces of the two major cities seem to have been organized along lines suggested by the example of the London police. Uniformed constables, abandoning the sentry-boxes of the night-watch, walked their beats, arresting criminals, reporting fires, supervising traffic, and getting to know all the neighbourhood residents. They were on duty round the clock, working six hours on and six hours off in the summer and alternating three-hour shifts in the winter. For small cities, Quebec and Montreal began with remarkably large police forces: 102 officers and men at Quebec and 122 at Montreal. This implies a police-to-population ratio of 274 and 314 respectively. No wonder the newly arrived Governor Sydenham believed the forces were 'unnecessarily large'![19] The men were drawn from both national communities and included army veterans as well as members of the old constabulary and night-watch; in Division A, Montreal, 22 out of 40 men, including the two highest-ranking officers, were French Canadians, a proportion slightly higher than the francophone element in the city's population.[20]

Heading the urban police were two superintendents, Thomas Ainslie Young at Quebec and Pierre-Edouard Leclère at Montreal, both extreme anti-Patriots. Leclère was editor of a conservative newspaper and had previously served the government as head of political espionage and chief interrogator of political prisoners.[21] They were appropriate candidates to lead the new force for, in its first year of operation, when the revolutionary conspiracy of the Hunters' Lodges gathered strength, political surveillance was a major police responsibility. Young at Quebec seems to have been particularly energetic in this regard, sending spies out into the countryside, raiding homes in the city in a search for arms, confiscating the presses of proscribed newspapers, as well as interrogating every 'stranger' his men brought in and imprisoning those who could not give a satisfactory account of themselves.[22]

Hunting out revolutionary subversion was by no means the only occupation of the urban police and, after the spring of 1839, it tended to fade into the background. Instead, constables directed most of their attention to the sailors, labourers, beggars, prostitutes, and destitute immigrants who, more and more over the past decade, had been filling the streets of the province's cities. These itinerant workers and lumpenproletarians had, for the most part, little to do with the Patriot movement, which drew its strength mainly from the most stable elements of the population. Nevertheless, they were regarded – and with some justification – as a serious threat to civic peace and bourgeois property. Even in October 1837 when radical agitation was at its height, the business-oriented *Montreal Transcript* worried about problems of a different order.

> The position of Montreal as one of the large cities of the continent and situated upon one of the great thoroughfares from the ocean, naturally attracts towards, and retains in its neighbourhood, in addition to the unfortunate poor, an immense number of idlers, vagrants and disorderly people, with neither character nor occupation; who, indifferent to every thing beyond the wants of the day, are indifferent to the means by which these wants are satisfied, whether it be by a little labour, by begging, or by pilfering.[23]

Accordingly, the text of the Special Council ordinance that provided a statutory basis for the police of Quebec and Montreal dwelt extensively – almost exclusively – on the duty to apprehend 'idle and disorderly persons' and empowered magistrates to condemn those convicted to up to two months at hard labour. An 1841 police manual defines 'disorderly persons' as: 'all persons, who, being able to work, refuse and neglect to do so – persons exposing themselves indecently

– persons maliciously and wilfully obstructing passengers, by standing across foot-paths, obstructing a thoroughfare, using insulting language, causing disturbance, by screaming, swearing, singing in the streets, tearing down or defacing signs, breaking windows, doors, or door plates, or the walls of houses, yards or gardens; destroying fences, being drunk, and impeding or incommoding peaceable passengers; all common prostitutes – all persons in the habit of frequenting houses of ill-fame.'[24] The fact that such diverse 'offences' as singing, destroying property, prostitution, and unemployment should all be lumped together speaks volumes about the outlook of the framers of this act and shows clearly that they aimed, not at any specific sort of behaviour, but at a particular social class.

The 'disorderly persons' provision of the city police ordinance was no dead letter; the only arrest statistics available (see Table 1:1) indicate that 71 per cent of the 396 arrests made by the Montreal force in the month of September 1838 were for offences that came under that heading.[25] The bare records do not provide a complete picture of police activities by any means, but they do offer valuable clues. Apparently 'drunkenness' was the most common offence, accounting for almost half the arrests in Montreal. Many people were also taken into custody for assault. Robbery and other crimes against property, on the other hand, were relatively infrequent.

Prostitutes seem to have been a particular focus of police attention; in fact the Lower Canada police ordinance of 1839 was, according to Constance Backhouse, 'the first Canadian statute to mention prostitutes specifically.'[26] The Montreal arrest records have to be sorted out by sex to see how this aspect of the law was enforced, for no one was charged with prostitution *per se*. The majority of individuals accused of being 'loose, idle and disorderly persons' were female, and almost all the arrests for vagrancy, loitering in the streets, and indecent conduct concerned women. It is not altogether clear what distinguished these different 'offences' – they may well have been synonyms chosen according to the whim of the recording officer – but they seem to have been reserved mainly for prostitutes. One man was charged in September 1838 with 'keeping a disorderly house,' and some of the males arrested as 'loose, idle and disorderly' may well have been prostitutes' clients; still the figures suggest that the police tended to regulate illicit sex by targeting the women involved.[27] This whole topic deserves much fuller investigation; suffice it to say, for the present, that the new urban police had a moral-reform thrust and a pronounced class and gender bias.

TABLE 1:1
Arrests by Montreal Police, September 1838

| Offence | Males | Females | Total |
|---------|-------|---------|-------|
| Drunkenness | 151 | 35 | 186 |
| Vagrancy | 4 | 14 | 18 |
| Loitering in the street | 2 | 21 | 23 |
| Loose, idle, disorderly | 9 | 10 | 19 |
| Indecent conduct | 0 | 3 | 3 |
| Assault and battery, etc. | 52 | 8 | 60 |
| Assaulting, obstructing or threatening police | 8 | 0 | 8 |
| Larceny | 25 | 9 | 34 |
| Disturbing the peace | 14 | 8 | 22 |
| Other | 20 | 2 | 22 |
| Total | 285 | 110 | 395 |

Not surprisingly, the largely unprecedented interventions on the part of the police provoked considerable resistance. Not long after the establishment of the new system, a Montreal newspaper reported widespread popular opposition.

Depuis quelque temps, il paraît que l'idée de résistance à la police se multiplie d'une manière condamnable, dans différentes parties de la ville; des rixes sérieuses s'élèvent à la moindre apparition d'un exempt de police, et des obstacles sont mis à l'accomplissement de leurs devoirs. Il peut arriver que quelques-uns des hommes attachés à ce corps outrepassent leurs missions et fassent trop sentir aux citoyens l'action de leur présence; mais nous croyons que ce n'est pas une raison suffisante pour se porter à des représailles qui ne peuvent avoir que des suites funestes.[28]

The more prosperous citizens of Montreal, on the other hand, seem to have been well pleased with the blue-coated guardians of order. An 1840 petition from 'Magistrates, merchants and others' praising the new police force and opposing planned reductions in its strength was signed by hundreds of residents, most of them with English names and all of them comfortable enough with a pen to suggest education and non-manual employment.[29]

In the busy port of Quebec City, one particular variety of 'disorderly persons' – sailors – was of special concern to the police.[30] Since most of the town's merchants had fled to the upper city in the wake of the cholera epidemic of 1832, Lower Town was taken over every summer by a rowdy wharfside subculture of naval and merchant seamen, as well as the innkeepers, crimps, and prostitutes who associated with them. One of the city's two police station-houses was located here, and its officers and men prepared for the annual shipping season as for a barbarian invasion. Men suddenly released from the stern discipline of the long transatlantic voyage were inclined to head straight for the neighbourhood's countless taverns where they slaked their gargantuan thirsts. Soon brawls erupted, windows were broken, and passers-by were insulted and intimidated. The police struggled to regain control of the streets, provoking the seamen to riot in the process, and achieving only limited success. It was only with the greatest trepidation that they ventured into Champlain Street where, 'three fourths of the houses ... are common tippling houses and the police are set at defiance.'[31]

It was not only in their attempts to suppress violence and assert control over the streets that the Lower Town police came into contact with the transient maritime community. They were also called upon to assist ships' captains in controlling and disciplining their men. The 'river guard,' a special unit equipped with boats for the purpose, boarded ships and carried off to jail violent or insubordinate sailors. But it was deserters who constituted the main targets of the quayside police.

Quebec, as Judith Fingard has shown in her fascinating study *Jack in Port*, was notorious in the Victorian era for its high rates of desertion.[32] Many factors could induce a seaman to leave his employer, including brutal treatment at the hands of officers and unsafe conditions, but the high wage rates offered on ships outward bound from the colonial port tended to make desertion especially prevalent in Canada's premier seaport. Because the shipping season was short and seasoned hands few in number, sailors who had signed on in Britain for a return voyage to Canada could make much more money by jumping ship at Quebec and hiring on with another captain. To make matters worse from the masters' point of view, a network of boarding-house operators and tavern-keepers assisted the deserting mariners and, for a fee, placed them safely on another returning vessel. Some of these 'crimps' were quite ruthless labour-market *padrones* who did not hesitate to kidnap seamen from one ship in order to sell them to the captain of another. Nevertheless, though they were victimized to some extent in the process, common sailors on the whole benefited from the widespread practice of desertion; their bargaining power was enhanced and their subjection to tyranny and low wages consequently mitigated.

Of course as far as maritime capital was concerned, all this meant delayed sailings, inflated expenses, and lax discipline. With the establishment of the new police at Quebec, however, captains discovered at last a line of defence, legal and to some degree effective, against rampant desertion. When men went missing, application could be made to a magistrate who would issue a warrant for their arrest; and, if all went well, the police might succeed in capturing the fugitives so that they could be punished and/or returned to their ship. It was not at all easy to apprehend deserters, especially in the midst of a hostile population that actively sympathized with the sailors. Yet this would seem to be the task to which the Lower Town police bent the greatest part of their efforts, if the activities described in an unusually detailed report dated 28 May 1840 are at all representative.

At a quarter to twelve o'clock AM the Assistant sergeant major and Sergeant Brady in the police waggon were ordered to pass through Louis Gate and examine barns, sheds and outhouses as far as Sillery Cove, for seamen, deserters from HM ships and merchant service. Searched two barns on the Saint Louis Road and an empty house on the hill above Mr Pemberton's Sillery Cove – There was every appearance of persons having been there – Returned through the coves and Champlain Street – Arrested one man who was drunk and creating a disturbance on the street – At half past one o'clock PM the chief constable, with five of the Lower town Guard, proceeded to Hunt's Wharf and arrested four men who were fighting in a boat – Got them on shore – The Captain of the Independent gave eight of his men (whom he found on the wharf) in charge, for deserting their ship, Sent them to the police office – They were convicted of desertion and committed to gaol – At half past one o'clock PM sergeant Henderson and four men, in a police boat, went on board the ship (at Wolfe's Cove) called the Margret [sic] to arrest a seaman who was creating a disturbance on board ... At two o'clock PM Sergeant Fitzpatrick and six men proceeded through Champlain Street for the purpose of removing ladders that have been put up against the rock leading up to the fortifications, The ladders are placed there by tavernkeepers and others who harbour sailors for the purpose of escape when followed by the police ... Returned over the Plains and brought in with them four seamen, three of them deserters, the other was taken for being drunk and creating a disturbance on the street – The patrols for the night

were marched off at eight o'clock PM – The assistant sergeant major
and eight men to pass through Louis Gate and clear the barns and
plains of all idle, loose and disorderly persons – Arrested two girls of
ill fame, and two men who were in company with them near Bishop
Mountain's in a field and shortly after two men who were much in-
toxicated and unable to walk ... Sergeant Henderson and four men to
patrol Lower town, They brought in four men to the station house
whom they found drunk and fighting on the wharf – The chief constable accompanied the superintendent of police, with three sergeants,
two corporals and ten men, through Lower town to Champlain Street
and the coves – Put two sailors on board their ship Charlotte – Searched
eight taverns and six regular crimp houses for sailors, deserters – Sent
in seven sailors – Met the captain of the ship Jane who stated that his
boy could point out a house near Munn's Cove where two of his men
were concealed – The superintendent of police, the chief constable and
four men returned with him and searched the house, did not find
his men – Searched two other crimp houses at his request without success – Arrested two men who were drunk and creating a disturbance
on the street – Returned to Lower town a few minutes before midnight ...33

The police did not catch every deserter in Quebec that day but certainly they tried! And they did in fact manage to arrest at least eleven
sailors for desertion. Of course we know nothing about what exactly
transpired between the captain of the *Independent* and his eight men,
and we cannot find out what the 'disturbance' aboard the *Margaret*
was about; indeed, the policemen do not seem to have been very
interested in such questions. It was the captains who laid the complaints and provided the police with the information they thought
relevant. There can be no question as to whose interests the police
were protecting in their very considerable interventions in the maritime labour market of Quebec City.

In 1843, after political stability had returned to Lower Canada and
municipal government had been restored, the province transferred
control of the urban police to the town corporations. Now required
to pay for this expensive establishment out of civic coffers, the two
city councils immediately reduced their police forces to a fraction of
their former strength.34 Given this devolution, in conjunction with
the progressive police reform that was beginning to take shape in
other colonial cities, the Quebec and Montreal forces gradually ceased
to be unique in British North America. They had nevertheless led

the way, prevailing over popular resistance and entrenched privilege, thanks to the authoritarian climate that followed the defeat of rebellion.

The urban police had been operating for more than a year before modern policing was extended into the Lower-Canadian countryside. A mounted force, the Rural Police, began patrolling the farmlands of the District of Montreal only in the early months of 1839, after all the fighting in the 1837–8 crisis had come to an end. This delay might seem strange to anyone familiar with the history of the Lower-Canadian Rebellion; after all, the Patriots were always strongest, not in the cities, but in the agrarian regions surrounding Montreal, and it was here that most of the serious conflict took place during the revolutionary episode.[35] Why then did the government establish police first in the cities, where its authority was never seriously challenged, rather than in the rural parishes where insurrection boiled? The answer lies partly in an aversion, widespread in this era, to any professional policing in rural areas. A rural police force was expensive and difficult to supervise, for the men had to be dispersed and provided with horses. Moreover, it was difficult to justify such a costly undertaking in the terms used to defend English-style police reform. The crime, vice, and disorder that policemen were supposed to remedy were regarded as essentially urban problems; certainly before 1837 no one thought these were serious problems in the countryside of Lower Canada. The purposes of a rural police force were almost by definition political; the image of mounted *gendarmes* patrolling the countryside tended to be associated with the authoritarian monarchies of Europe or with oppressed lands such as Ireland. Accordingly, it took a serious threat to the security of the state to overcome the misgivings that even colonial administrators must have felt about such an un-British innovation.

Rural police appeared rather late in the day also because they were not well suited for service against armed revolt on a significant scale. As long as the Patriots remained a serious military threat, the government naturally relied on soldiers rather than constables. From the fall of 1837, therefore, troops from Montreal and Quebec, as well as from outside Lower Canada, poured into the western countryside, first to do battle with the insurgents and then to remain as an occupying force. (It was the movement of troops from the capital to the troubled Montreal District, incidentally, that explains why Quebec City had the very first police force; it was here that the garrison was most depleted and most in need of a supplementary force to maintain order.) After defeating the rebels on the field of battle in November-December 1837 and again in November 1838, the British regulars and the Tory Volunteers played an important part in chastising the pro-Patriot population. They arrested thousands of men, burned hundreds of buildings, and plundered and pillaged many more farms. Certainly this punishment was far less ferocious than that visited upon defeated insurgents in many parts of the world. Nevertheless, the military occupation of 1838 was effectively intimidating; and, to that extent, it made a contribution towards the pacification of rural Lower Canada.

Yet military punishment and military occupation could never, by themselves, provide a basis for stable rule; as Bismarck once observed, you can do all sorts of things with bayonets, but not sit on them. When the colonial state was reduced to what radicals had always insisted was its violent and coercive essence, people could be expected to fear the government but hardly to accept it as a legitimate, much less a benign, power. To make matters worse, it was impossible, in spite of the best efforts of the authorities, to wield the unsheathed sword of military intervention with surgical precision. Often, rebel leaders went free while individuals marginally involved in the risings languished in jail. 'Abuses' were bound to occur and they did: soldiers of the 71st regiment gang-raped a woman at L'Acadie; an unarmed and unresisting prisoner was stabbed repeatedly by a drunken Volunteer in the arresting party; a dragoon sergeant entered a habitant's house and, 'without any manner of provocation he discharged a pistol at the owner and subsequently laid the man's cheek open with a blow of that weapon.'[36] All these incidents occurred, it should be noted, in 1839, long after the heat of battle had subsided. They are certainly extreme cases, but they point towards the general truth that direct rule by armed forces is bound to be arbitrary. 'Martial law,' as the Duke of Wellington observed, 'is no law at all,'[37] and martial law was exactly the nature of the government regime in the District of Montreal. Effective as it may have been at humiliating rebels and snuffing out organized resistance, it could lay no credible claim to regularity, equity, and justice. It was thus a very poor vehicle for securing the 'voluntary submission' that, according to Max Weber, is the response that distinguishes true authority.[38]

What seemed to be needed after the November 1838 rising had been fully suppressed was a more delicate instrument of surveillance and coercion, such as the recently formed Irish Constabulary (later dignified with the title 'Royal').[39] Like the Irish Constabulary, the Rural Police of Lower Canada was designed to permit the central government to bypass traditional local institutions and assert direct control over agrarian communities. However, it did not have to fight pitched battles with large peasant bands, as the Irish force did, and so it could make do with a comparatively small number of men who could operate in groups of three or four rather than travelling in large bodies. Established in the early months of 1839, the Lower-Canadian Rural Police was initially composed of between 200 and 300 constables of various ranks (the sources are rather ambiguous as to the strength of the force),[40] distributed among more than thirty stations, almost all of them in the troubled parishes of the District of Montreal.

The new force was largely the creation of its first commissioner, Augustus Gugy, a fluently bilingual Lower Canadian of Swiss Protestant ancestry. Gugy had achieved notoriety in the pre-Rebellion House of Assembly as a fiercely anti-Patriot orator and, when insurrection broke out, he rushed to enlist on the government side and played a prominent part in the battles of St Charles and St Eustache.[41] These services, and the patronage of the stern General John Colborne who was left in charge of the province after the departure of Lord Durham, had earned Gugy the command of the rural police.

While Commissioner Gugy had overall command of the rural police, day-to-day supervision was entrusted to fourteen 'stipendiary magistrates' established at various points across the countryside. The office of stipendiary magistrate (renamed 'police magistrate' in 1840) was as much a novelty in Lower Canada as that of rural constable. The first stipendiary magistrates had appeared in London in 1792; at a time when JPs in the metropolis tended to be corrupt and difficult to locate, stipendiary magistrates were paid a salary to provide cheap justice to all comers at any time of the day.[42] In Canada, stipendiary magistrates were not appointed to deal with any explosion of thefts and murders (ordinary crime remained comparatively rare in rural French Canada), but rather to play a vital role, complementing that of the police, in the government's program of pacification. The salaried judge had a crucial role to play, not only in directing the efforts of the less-educated constables in their political surveillance and other duties, but also in ensuring that the laws were enforced in an effective and even-handed manner.

The first duty of the rural police/stipendiary magistrate system was to suppress subversion, as the civil secretary of Lower Canada stated quite clearly. 'The immediate object of its institution was to prevent the recurrence of those combinations of the people which in the two preceeding years had led to such disastrous results, and to supply the Government with a means of intelligence in those localities where discontent and disaffection appeared to have taken deepest root.'[43] Optimists such as Augustus Gugy hoped that the new agency's role would not be entirely negative; they saw the police as a means by which the government might 'worm itself into the interests of the people': 'The presence of the soldiery, to say the least of it, is not calculated to do more than ensure obedience to the law. The police are instructed, and I believe disposed and qualified, to make the great mass of the people respect and revere it. Indeed I propose to myself nothing less than to convert into adherents the former enemies of government.'[44] Stipendiary magistrates in particular were supposed to present a face of wisdom and benevolence to the community and thus win for themselves the position of local leadership previously occupied by the radical notaries and doctors of the Patriot party. General instructions addressed to the new magistrates had little to say about the suppression of felonies and misdemeanours; instead they stressed this political role: 'The attention of the Stipendiary Magistrates will be directed to the advantages which may be derived from their assiduous labours, in giving advice to the *habitants* and to the Magistrates in their vicinity; in attending promptly to every species of complaint; in obtaining the confidence of the people, and in destroying the pernicious influence which produced the disturbances of 1837 and 1838.'[45] The punitive state was giving way to the didactic state.

Or was it? The rural police were not, in fact, a substitute for the colonial military garrison, but rather a complement to it. Indeed, British troop strength in Canada rose steadily during the brief life of the rural police (1839–42), reaching an all-time peak (periods of war excluded) of 12,029 in 1842.[46] The soldiers kept more to the background than they had in 1838 – the undisciplined Volunteer Corps were disbanded and the redcoats stayed close to their forts and barracks – but no Canadian could have been unaware that they were close at hand and ready to intervene if needed. It was surely this potent military backing that allowed the rural police to patrol the lately rebellious districts, lightly armed and in small parties, but without fear of attack. Though they benefited in this way from the army's presence, and from its prior chastisement of the insurgent countryside, the stipendiaries and police were nevertheless at pains to distance themselves from the redcoats. The government's pacification strategy depended on a separation of the two visages of authority – the one violent and punitive in the face of defiance, the other firm but equitable and paternalistic – with different roles assigned to the army and the police. This was an intelligent approach, one that made use of the principle lying behind the modern 'good cop/bad cop' technique of interrogation that attempts to make a prisoner regard the less frightening of his adversaries as an ally and confidant. No doubt this psychological mechanism was at work in the Patriot communities that had so recently suffered the rigours of military occupation and, for some, it probably had the effect of making the police seem not simply a lesser evil but even a legitimate authority.

Yet the police never gained the acceptance Gugy had hoped they would. Undermining his efforts to present the police as a neutral agency of law enforcement was the fact that initially some 80 per cent of the men were English speaking, and many of them appear to have been British army veterans. To make matters worse, the commissioner was well known for his Tory convictions. Moreover, he and several of the stipendiary magistrates had taken an active role in the suppression of the rebellions. There was little chance then that the connection between violent repression and paternalistic pacification could be disguised. Evidently, considerations of public duty were no match for Gugy's and Colborne's determination to secure jobs for their friends and fellow countrymen! On the other hand, the partisan complexion of the new organization was not simply the result of personal failings. The governor and the commissioner might well object that, under the circumstances, no one but their friends could be trusted with coercive powers. Moreover, Gugy insisted that the linguistic imbalance in the rural police stemmed from the fact that francophones simply would not join it.[47] In 1839 the colonial state was still widely regarded – particularly in the French-Canadian countryside – as a tyrannical regime; it is therefore highly unlikely that any police force established by the government – regardless of the reputation of its commissioner and the language of its personnel – would be seen as anything but an enemy. Nothing could make the fundamental polarization prevailing in the District of Montreal disappear overnight, but, over the years, Gugy did manage to recruit more French Canadians as part of his effort to make the rural police appear less like an alien and repressive imposition and more like a public service.

The commissioner hoped that the police and stipendiary magistrates would eventually gain respect and acceptance 'because in the impartial administration of equal justice they will repress or punish all breaches of the peace and violence.'[48] Accordingly, his men devoted considerable attention to the suppression of common-or-garden-variety crime of the sort that rural justices of the peace were supposed to deal with. Arrest figures from the monthly returns of three randomly selected stations (Table 1:2) show that drunkenness, disturbing the peace, assault, and minor theft were the most common offences.[49] Several cases of insulting, resisting, or assaulting a constable indicate that the police were far from being universally accepted. Charges connected to the 'sleigh ordinance' are another symptom of the struggle for local control, as we shall see below. They figure prominently only in the Ste Martine data, the only ones in Table 2 that give full coverage to the winter of 1840–1 when the law came into effect. What is perhaps most significant about the rural arrest statistics is the very small total number of offenders. The returns for Chambly and Ste Scholastique suggest an average of only one arrest every five days (arrests actually tended to come in bunches; often weeks or months would elapse with no arrests), and in Ste Martine there were, on the average, fourteen days between arrests. This accords with the observations of visitors who found the Lower-Canadian countryside, with its 'honest peasantry,' remarkably crime-free. Moreover, the offences were mostly of a fairly minor nature; the returns from the three stations list no arrests for murder, attempted murder, or aggravated assault, though one person was charged with rape and another with arson.[50]

Of course the main purpose of the rural police was not the suppression of crime but the prevention of subversion, and the fruits of that activity seldom showed up in arrest statistics. The political intelligence methods of the Lower-Canadian police were laughably ineffective by the standards of a modern internal security system. Uniformed constables, many of them with an imperfect command of French, could hardly secure much in the way of secret information. 'Permit me to remark,' a testy stipendiary magistrate wrote to his superior, 'that even the sight of a police man in this part of the country renders everybody of the Canadian population from the child of 7 years upwards perfectly dumb.'[51] Mail was intercepted and undercover spies were employed in an effort to detect conspiracies like the failed *coup d'état* launched by the Hunters' Lodges; but, since no such conspiracies existed after November 1838, it is difficult to determine how efficient the espionage was.[52]

Much more important than any such cloak-and-dagger work, how-

TABLE 1:2
Arrests by Rural Police

| Offences | Chambly Oct./39–May/40 | Ste Scholastique June/40–Dec./40 | Ste Martine June/40–July/42 |
|---|---|---|---|
| Theft | 13 | 3 | 1 |
| Assault, etc. | 7 | 8 | 4 |
| Drunk (and disorderly) | 8 | 6 | 12 |
| Breach of peace | 1 | 3 | 10 |
| Desertion | 7 | 0 | 0 |
| Resisting police | 1 | 7 | 5 |
| Liquor licence | 3 | 0 | 1 |
| Sleigh ordinance | 0 | 3 | 12 |
| Other | 7 | 9 | 4 |
| Total | 47 | 39 | 49 |

ever, was the straightforward business of observing open political activity and intervening when necessary. Apart from anything else, stipendiaries proved useful simply in reporting on the general mood in their localities, something on which the colonial government might not otherwise have had reliable information. They also indicated which newspapers 'the ill disposed' in the villages were reading so that the urban authorities could close down their presses.[53] Above all, the magistrates and their policeman saw to it that public speeches against the government ceased. In 1837 and earlier, church-porch oratory by Patriot leaders after Sunday mass had been central to the forging of an anti-government movement; it did not take very sophisticated methods to prevent the recurrence of that phenomenon. Augustus Gugy was inordinately proud of the role of his police in thus ending 'the desecration of the sabbath for political purposes,' and he invoked the threat of radical demagoguery when warning against any idea of reducing the size of the force: 'The first consequence of that measure would be to ensure impunity to certain popular orators and apostles of sedition who are now restrained by the police.'[54]

The police did have to relent somewhat in their campaign against the public expression of proscribed opinions when electoral politics of a sort were restored in Lower Canada during the election campaign of 1840. Yet we still find a stipendiary magistrate attempting to intimidate participants at an opposition rally at Rivière-du-Loup. After assuring himself that the anti-government candidate was unlikely to win, he decided not to institute legal measures. The magistrate did, however, promise to 'continue to watch the movements of all who are opposed to Lord Sydenham's present plans.'[55] His approach was a very British one: without clamping down on all dissident views, the police and stipendiaries tried to contain political discourse within acceptable limits. This strategy was really remarkably successful, and the proof is in the fact that the very unpopular union of Upper and Lower Canada was indeed pushed through without serious incident. Obviously, a variety of circumstances conspired to further 'Lord Sydenham's plans,' but the efforts of the rural police to suppress open republican agitation must be recognized as a major contribution, not only to the implementation of the Union bill, but also, more generally, to the political pacification of French Canada.

The stipendiary magistrates and policemen were perceptive enough to realize that there was more to the Patriot movement than middle-class oratory. As well, the community life and popular culture of the habitants had sustained the revolutionary challenge to colonial rule. Accordingly, the police tended to be suspicious not just of overtly political meetings but of gatherings of almost any sort. At La Prairie, the stipendiary magistrate banned the annual festival of the parish's patron saint, while the vigilant Sergeant Brown flushed out equally dangerous activities late one night at St Césaire. 'I found in the residence of Bats. Bellere,' he reported, 'a large assembly of people of the worst description who had a drum, triangle, and two fidelles playing ...' Acting with the approval of the local stipendiary who believed that noisy parties of this sort were often a screen for subversive plotting, the policeman used force to break it up.[56] In most rural parishes, Sunday was a particularly busy day for the police, since that was the day habitants came in from their scattered farmsteads and gathered for church services, shopping, and socializing. It was this last activity that taxed the vigilance of the new authorities. The *curé* of Yamaska approved entirely of the efforts of the police in this regard: 'Previous to their coming the people collected in large numbers, before, and after church, the public houses filled on Sundays, which has not occurred since.'[57] Taverns were not supposed to sell liquor on Sundays except in small quantities to non-resident travellers. The police began enforcing regulations that had long been ignored in the countryside.

Taverns – those 'hotbeds of disaffection,' as Augustus Gugy called them – were a major preoccupation for the rural police. Concern stemmed partly from a moral and religious conception of political disaffection. The Protestant Gugy, in particular, seems to have subscribed to views associated with the nascent temperance movement;

for him, drunkenness and idleness were vices that naturally led to opposition to constituted authority. Suspect from a moral point of view, taverns were also dangerous simply because they were gathering places. The stipendiary magistrate of Ste Marie-de-Monnoir justified his crackdown on liquor-licence offences in just these terms.

> It is almost unnecessary to advert to the intimate relation which exists between these places of public resort and the tranquility of the country parts. The plans of the late revolt were generally concerted in taverns. Taverns have been among the most conspicuous rebel strongholds. Tavern keepers have been prominent rebel leaders and the insurgents themselves have rarely made head except under the immediate influence of spirituous liquors.
>
> Even now these houses unless strictly regulated and closely looked after become the hotbeds of idleness, immorality and disaffection. Here are retailed the absurd and exaggerated reports which impose so easily upon the credulous and susceptible Habitant ...
>
> Independent of the dissipation engendered by this practice, Sunday, from the occupations of the habitants, is the only day upon which they can meet in any numbers, and their meeting under such circumstances, cannot but be productive of evil.[58]

Taverns were additionally of significance in that they were licensed by government and therefore a source of patronage and political leverage. In practice, licensing was traditionally under the control of a committee of local dignitaries – JPs, churchwardens, and militia officers – who issued the certificates the government required of all applicants. 'The grant of these certificates is considered valuable patronage, as indeed it is to persons who have local interests, or personal objects to effect,' the stipendiaries complained, and the result was that licences often fell into the wrong hands and taverns proliferated.[59] For the same reason, justices of the peace were unwilling to make themselves unpopular by revoking the licences of innkeepers who openly violated the regulations. The salaried magistrates accordingly made every effort to wrest control of the mechanisms of awarding licences from the overly lenient local authorities. They were intent on reducing the number of taverns, while ensuring that only loyal subjects benefited from the state's licensing powers. The stipendiary magistrates may not have been entirely successful in this struggle, but the thrust of their efforts is clear. Their offensive was aimed at reforming the morals of the populace and undermining a threatening popular culture. At the same time, and not accidentally, it tended to enhance central administrative control at the expense of local autonomy.

The stipendiaries had been instructed to endeavour to gain influence, not only over the peasantry, but also over 'the Magistrates in their vicinity.' Local justices of the peace – at least the 'loyal' ones who had survived the political purges – retained their traditional powers under the new system. Yet even conservative magistrates found little favour under the new system.[60] Most were village merchants or professional men, deeply embroiled in the factional feuds of parish life. They were therefore all too prone to laxity or flagrant partisanship in exercising their powers over such matters as the awarding of tavern licences. Stipendiary magistrates were accordingly expected to dominate their unpaid colleagues or simply ignore them, all in the interests of a more regular, impersonal, and equitable enforcement of the law. With their policemen, their legal training, and their lack of distracting business commitments, the salaried magistrates generally secured the upper hand in their localities, though not always without provoking sharp conflict with the ordinary JPs. In Vaudreuil, for example, the police ran into trouble when they attempted to execute a search warrant on the property of a man suspected of possessing stolen timber. The man was a friend of J.A. Mathison, a local justice of the peace, and so he naturally took umbrage at the intrusion and violently resisted the constables. Mathison, who had been at the forefront of the struggle against Vaudreuil's Patriots in 1837, had come to resent the police and their stipendiary master. He consequently tried to prosecute for riot the men his friend had driven off, and, when that approach did not work, he fined them for trespass![61] Friction of this sort was inevitable, for the pacification of Lower Canada required that power be transferred from local notables – Tory as well as radical – to salaried agents of the colonial government.

In the seemingly mundane matter of the famous 'sleigh ordinances,' police efforts to enforce the law had a similar thrust. The aim of these three pieces of legislation passed between 1839 and 1841 was to improve winter roads in the colony. Convinced that faulty design of the traditional French-Canadian *calèche* was to blame for the formation of bone-jarring mounds of snow along the highways, the Special Council laid down rules regulating such things as the length of a sleigh's runners, the height of the carriage, and the type of hitch. The new measures, well-intentioned though they may have been, were bitterly resented throughout French Lower Canada. Habitants must have found compliance difficult and expensive, if not impossible, for every year revised standards required different modifications to their vehicles. However, the sleigh ordinances provoked a reaction that seems out of proportion to these inconveniences. Stephen Kenny has pointed out that the legislation served as a lightning-rod for widespread disaffection.[62] Here was Governor Sydenham, fresh off the boat from England and convinced he knew more about snow than native-born Canadians, employing authoritarian measures to set things right. His vexatious winter-road regulations must have appeared to many habitants as the archetype of the 'reform' measures carried out by an urban and metropolitan élite over the dead body of the defeated democratic opposition. The fact that the unpopular rural police bore the main responsibility for enforcing the ordinances would not have made the latter more palatable. Monthly returns from the various stations indicate that, in the winters of 1840–1 and 1841–2, the police laid many charges against individuals caught driving prohibited *calèches* (see Table 1:2). Those convicted faced fines of ten shillings plus costs, or even jail terms.[63] Infractions clearly stemmed from resistance and not simply negligence. At St Pierre-les-Becquets the windows of the police station were broken because a model demonstrating the approved sleigh design was on display there. 'I was very freely told by Mr Rousseau and others,' wrote the local stipendiary magistrate, 'that the habitants were determined not to comply with the ordinance regulating winter sleighs.' The magistrate was equally determined to win this 'trial of strength' and force the habitants to 'yield to the law.'[64] Obviously, for all parties concerned, much more was at stake than the design of sleigh runners; it was a contest to see who was to rule in the Lower-Canadian countryside.

As an experiment in centrally directed social and political engineering, the rural police/stipendiary magistrate system proved to be short-lived. Once the revolutionary crisis was over and parliamentary government had returned, there seemed no further need to maintain such a costly apparatus. Canadian legislators, faced in 1842 with the prospect of paying for the rural police out of colonial revenues, quickly voted to disband such a 'useless and unnecessary' body.[65] Yet the mounted force of constables commanded by a salaried magistrate had established itself as a model and, when trouble reared its head outside the cities, the government wasted no time in resurrecting it, though on only a temporary and local scale. Rural police were sent to deal with unruly navvies on the Lachine and Beauharnois canals in 1843; in 1850, constables and stipendiary magistrates were dispatched to the 'guerre des éteignoirs' in the District of Trois-Rivières where habitants were resorting to riot and arson in combating the new school laws.[66]

To some degree, the Rural Police was a victim of its own success in carrying out its mandate to pacify the rebellious districts. 'As to the Lower Province,' a satisfied British officer wrote in the fall of 1839, 'we have now the French Canadians in complete subjection. We have a regular police with stipendiary magistrates, who if they do their duty cannot fail to prevent conspiracy ...'[67] By the early 1840s, radical republicanism was no longer a force to be reckoned with in the Lower-Canadian countryside. Yet clearly this outcome cannot be attributed entirely to the efforts of the police and the stipendiaries. The latter did indeed contribute greatly to the destruction of the radical political culture of rural parishes. On the other hand, they did not manage to secure, as Gugy had hoped they would, 'the confidence of the people,' never a realistic ambition. Sensible stipendiary magistrates realized that they were feared but not loved.

> I cannot however report that the tranquility which exists is the result of any alteration of the political opinions of the People. On the contrary, I believe that, in addition to the existence of the feeling which has shown itself in open rebellion, they are now labouring under a sense of sullen disappointment and of disgrace at the failure of their illegal proceedings which would again break into open resistance to the Government if a favourable opportunity offered.
>
> ... I attribute the present tranquility of the district entirely to the presence of the Rural Police; to the fact that no illegal meeting can be held without their knowledge ... and to the immediate assistance of a military force if required ...[68]

Still, the police did 'show the flag' of colonial sovereignty in corners of the province where its influence had not been felt on a regular basis, and surely this too was a crucial element in the process of pacification. Directly answerable to government, regular and predictable in their demands, the police could plausibly present themselves as agents of the state and its law in a way that militia captains, JPs, and occupying troops could not. To habitants and villagers who had known 'the Crown' as a remote, mysterious, and occasionally vengeful entity, they represented a state that was immediate, active, and comparatively familiar. The colonial state had been 'no where felt or seen' during the crisis of 1837, Commissioner Gugy observed, but two years later, 'the first consequence of the establishment of the force has been to make the government visible to the most ignorant.'[69]

The Rural Police episode was not the last occasion on which a Canadian government instituted a new police force in order to meet a revolutionary challenge. The Royal Canadian Mounted Police was formed in 1919 by the amalgamation of the Dominion Police and the Royal North-West Mounted Police and in response to the labour strife of that year. 'It is no exaggeration,' concludes S.W. Horrall, 'to say that the Royal Canadian Mounted Police is but one more offspring of the Winnipeg General Strike.'[70] The political origins of the Rural Police and the RCMP point to one of the major aspects of policing in this country, the prevention of revolt and subversion. This mission, currently assigned to the 'civilian' Canadian Security and Intelligence Service, is essentially defensive. Even though rough and aggressive – not to mention illegal – tactics have frequently been employed, in this century and the last one, the fundamental goal is to protect the security of the state and thus preserve the basic political status quo.

The thrust of urban police reform in mid-nineteenth-century British North America was rather different. The path-breaking police establishments of Montreal and Quebec, like the municipal forces established later in Upper Canada and the Maritimes, were not founded with overtly political purposes in mind. Of course, one might well make the case that the focus on 'disorderly persons' and 'dangerous classes' signalled essentially 'political' concerns, in the broadest sense of the word. Yet it is clear that sailors, prostitutes, and drunks did not constitute a serious threat to the security of the state, even in the midst of the Lower-Canadian Rebellion. Instead these unruly elements in society were regarded as a menace to the property and safety of their more well-heeled neighbours. More generally, they constituted an affront to middle-class standards of propriety, as well as a sad waste of potentially useful labour power. The primary role of the police, accordingly, was to respond to this social problem by bringing order and safety to the streets of urban Canada and by introducing discipline into the lives of those living on the margins of the law and of the labour marketplace.

This second aspect of policing should be seen as an ambitious measure of social reform, partaking of the general mid-century movement to remake society through institutional innovation. About the time police forces were first introduced, novel approaches in a variety of fields were aiming to place the poor, the deviant, and the unassimilated under the tutelage of professional agencies, usually under government auspices. Criminals were placed in penitentiaries, children in public schools, paupers in poorhouses, and lunatics in asylums. The spirit animating these measures was not an essentially conservative one; this was not a matter of 'social control' in the sense in which that phrase is often used to suggest an attempt to preserve an immutable social hierarchy by placing subaltern classes under the thumb of authority. After all, school children and mental patients were even less threatening to the social order than were the vagrants and rowdies with whom the police dealt. What was proposed in the area of policing, as in the other fields, was genuine social reform, that is, the reshaping of society. In attempting to modify the outlook and behaviour of major sectors of the population – those specifically where thrift, quiet, and sober, regular effort were not strongly represented – social engineers from Augustus Gugy to Egerton Ryerson were contributing to the wholesale transformation of Canadian society. Results seldom measured up to the wildly optimistic expectations of the reformers, and Canada was never turned into the peaceful and industrious bourgeois Utopia they envisaged, but the schools, the police, the hospitals, and the penitentiaries surely did collectively help to facilitate the orderly transition to a capitalist social order.

The significance of the Rebellion of 1837–8 in this context is that it (or rather the resounding defeat of revolution) paved the way for the expanded social role of the state of neutralizing opposing forces. This is not to say that there would have been no police without the annihilation of the Patriot party. Indeed the Patriots themselves favoured measures to supervise and reform the urban poor. Yet they were highly suspicious of any agency that might threaten the independence of the small-proprietor-male-head-of-household. They always fought for decentralization and democratic control of coercive institutions, and so their continued presence on the provincial political scene would certainly have slowed the pace and diverted the thrust of police reforms. As it was, the government had a free hand in this and in other aspects of social reform. This is not to say that violent counter-revolution was everywhere the necessary prerequisite of statist social engineering. We know that most Canadian measures along these lines had their counterparts in the Maritime provinces, where nothing resembling the Rebellion occurred. But then, there was never a potent political force in the Maritimes that shared the Patriots' fundamental hostility to enhanced government power. Only in Lower

Canada, and to a lesser extent Upper Canada, did popular republicanism offer a significant obstacle to the reconstitution of society.

What has all this to do with state formation? I have argued that the Lower-Canadian Rural Police acted mainly to secure the state by pacifying a rebellious populace, whereas the urban police forces, in Lower Canada and throughout British North America, fit into more aggressive programs of social transformation. A common feature of these two aspects of pre-Confederation policing is their tendency to extend the reach of state control over civil society. To prevent renewed rural insurrection, Gugy's police and the stipendiary magistrates sought to contain popular culture and undermine the autonomy of local JPs. At the same time, the policemen of Montreal and Quebec, and later Toronto and Saint John, were gathering information and combating vice in the dark streets, the crimp-houses, and the rough taverns where agents of the law had seldom been seen before. No one would suggest that these early police forces gained anything faintly resembling complete control, but the thrust of their presence is clear enough. By their agency, the state – provincial and municipal – appropriated unto itself a measure of the power and authority previously possessed by civil society.

## NOTES

My thanks to Ed Montigny, who contributed to this paper as a research assistant, and to Mariana Valverde, Jim Winter, and Brian Young, who offered helpful comments.

1 For an excellent synthesis of the international literature on the subject, see Clive Emsley, *Policing and Its Context 1750–1870* (London: Macmillan 1983).

2 This statement applies properly to only the post-Conquest period. The situation under the French regime might be considered at least a partial exception. See below, n5.

3 Jean-Marie Fecteau, 'La pauvreté, le crime, l'État: essai sur l'économie politique du contrôle sociale au Québec, 1791–1840' (thèse de doctorat, Université de Paris 1983), 139; Jean-François Leclerc, 'Un aspect des relations sociales en Nouvelle-France: les voies de fait dans la juridiction de Montréal, 1700–1760' (MA thesis, Université de Montréal 1985), 18

4 Bryan D. Palmer, 'Discordant Music: Charivaris and White-capping in Nineteenth-Century North America,' *Labour / Le travail* 3 (1978), 5–62

5 This was not the case in an earlier period when Canada was controlled by a power then generally recognized as the world leader in the field of policing. The French colonial regime disposed of a small Maréchaussée of between six and fifteen men to pursue felons and guard prisoners. Ordinances governing such matters as weights and measures, chimney sweeping, and liquor sales were enforced by court officials (bailiffs, primarily) who undertook occasional 'tournées de police' through the streets of Quebec and Montreal. Colonial administrators also disposed of large numbers of soldiers and used them to guard government property and to deal with riots and demonstrations in the cities. André Lachance, *Crimes et criminels en Nouvelle-France* (Montreal: Boréal 1984), 18–19; André Lachance, 'La régulation des conduites dans la ville canadienne au XVIIIe siècle (1700–1760): essai,' in F. Lebrun and N. Séguin, eds, *Sociétés villageoises et rapports ville-campagnes au Québec et dans la France de l'ouest XVIIe–XXe siècles* (Trois-Rivières: Université du Québec à Trois-Rivières 1987), 327–36; John Dickinson, 'Réflexions sur la police en Nouvelle-France,' *McGill Law Journal* 32 (1986–7), 496–522; Christopher Moore, *Louisbourg Portraits: Life in an Eighteenth-Century Town* (Toronto: Macmillan 1982), 1–54

6 T.W. Acheson, *Saint John: The Making of a Colonial Urban Community* (Toronto: University of Toronto Press 1985), 214–16

7 David T. Ruddel, 'Quebec City, 1765–1831: The Evolution of a Colonial Town' (PH D diss., Université Laval 1981), 435–537

8 Acheson, *Saint John*, 215. For information on the constables and watchmen of other cities, see Fecteau, *La pauvreté, la crime, l'État*, 176–81, 283–7, 391–5; William Kelly and Nora Kelly, *Policing in Canada* (Toronto: Macmillan 1976), 3–9; C.K. Talbot, C.H.S. Jayewardene, and T.J. Juliani, *Canada's Constables: The Historical Development of Policing in Canada* (Ottawa: Crimcare Inc. 1985), 17–46.

9 Elinor Kyte Senior, 'The Influence of the British Garrison on the Development of the Montreal Police, 1832 to 1853,' *Military Affairs* 43 (Apr. 1979), 63–8; Elinor Kyte Senior, *British Regulars in Montreal: An Imperial Garrison, 1832–1854* (Montreal: McGill-Queen's University Press 1981), 11–23

10 John Field, 'Police, Power and Community in a Provincial English Town: Portsmouth 1815–1875,' in Victor Bailey, ed., *Policing and Punishment in Nineteenth-Century Britain* (London: Croom Helm 1981), 47

11 J.J. Tobias, *Crime and Police in England 1700–1900* (Dublin: Gill and Macmillan 1979), 98; David Phillips, ' "A New Engine of Power and Authority": The Institutionalization of Law-Enforcement in England 1780–1830,' in his *Crime and the Law: The Social History of Crime in Western Europe since 1500* (London: Europa 1980), 189; Philip Corrigan and

Derek Sayer, *The Great Arch: English State Formation as Cultural Revolution* (Oxford: Blackwell 1985), 158

12 Acheson, *Saint John*, 226–8

13 Greg Marquis, ' "A Machine of Oppression under the Guise of the Law": The Saint John Police Establishment, 1860–1890,' *Acadiensis* 16 (Autumn 1986), 59

14 Nicholas Rogers, 'Serving Toronto the Good: The Development of the City Police Force 1834–84,' in Victor Russell, ed., *Forging a Consensus: Historical Essays on Toronto* (Toronto: University of Toronto Press 1984), 116–40; Paul Craven, 'Law and Ideology: The Toronto Police Court 1850–80,' in David Flaherty, ed., *Essays in the History of Canadian Law*, vol. 2 (Toronto: Osgoode Society, University of Toronto Press 1982), 248–65

15 John Weaver, 'Crime, Public Order, and Repression: The Gore District in Upheaval, 1832–1851,' *Ontario History* 78 (Sept. 1986), 188. See also, Michael B. Katz, Michael J. Doucet, and Mark J. Stern, *The Social Organization of Early Industrial Capitalism* (Cambridge, Mass: Harvard University Press 1982), 201–41.

16 See Elinor Senior's important study *British Regulars in Montreal*, which forms the starting point for what follows.

17 Thus T.W. Acheson asserts that, 'The first North American police force was created in Boston in 1838 ...' (*Saint John*, 302), whereas, in fact, Quebec City had a much more substantial force half a year before the city fathers of Boston hired their first contingent of six men. See Roger Lane, *Policing the City: Boston, 1822–85* (Cambridge, Mass.: Harvard University Press 1967), 37.

18 National Archives of Canada (NA), Young Papers, W. Rowan to T.A. Young, 26 Apr. 1838. Six months later, the Tory-controlled Special Council provided a statutory basis for the Quebec and Montreal police forces. Lower Canada, *Ordinances of the Special Council, 1838–1841*, 2 Vic., cap. 2, 28 June 1838

19 Archives nationales du Québec, événements de 1837–1838 (ANQ 1837), no. 3352, Young to Murdoch, 20 Oct. 1839. Figures on police strength are from Senior, *British Regulars*, 26; NA, Lower Canada (LC) Police Records, vol. 2, Murdoch to Daly, 6 Mar. 1840; Newton Bosworth, *Hochelaga Depicta; Or the History and Present State of the Island and City of Montreal* (Montreal: William Greig 1839), 180–1. The police-population ratios were calculated on the basis of 1839 populations of 27,920 for Quebec and 38,348 for Montreal. These estimates were calculated by interpolating figures from the 1831 and 1844 censuses.

20 NA, LC Police Records, vol. 1, Report of Division A, Montreal Police, 1 Oct. 1839

21 Senior, *British Regulars*, 25–6

22 NA, Young Papers, vol. 8–9, and LC Police Records, passim. On the de-

tention of 'strangers,' see ANQ 1837, no. 3367, Young to Murdoch, 15 Nov. 1839.

23 *Montreal Transcript*, 3 Oct. 1837, as quoted in Jean-Claude Robert, 'Montréal 1821–1871: aspects de l'urbanisation' (thèse de doctorat, École des hautes études en sciences sociales, Paris 1977), 312

24 Lower Canada, *Ordinances of the Special Council, 1838–1841,* 2 Vic., cap. 2; *Regulations for the Governance of the Police Force, Rural and City, Province of Canada* (Montreal: J. Starke 1841), 34

25 ANQ 1837, no. 3390, 'List of Persons arrested by the Montreal New Police between the 1st and 30th September 1838 both days inclusive.' Note that English police forces of this period were also primarily concerned to deal with the 'idle and disorderly.' See Victor Bailey, 'Introduction,' in Bailey, ed., *Policing and Punishment*, 15.

26 Constance B. Backhouse, 'Nineteenth-Century Canadian Prostitution Law: Reflection of a Discriminatory Society,' *Histoire sociale / Social History* 18 (Nov. 1985), 389

27 In this, the police were only acting in harmony with the anti-female thrust of Canadian legislation affecting prostitution in the nineteenth century, as described in ibid.

28 *Le Populaire* as quoted in *Le Canadien*, 7 Sept. 1838

29 NA, LC Police Records, vol. 2, petition to Lord Sydenham, 13 Apr. 1840

30 Between 22 July and 20 Oct. 1839, 477 seamen were taken into custody and charged either with desertion or with being drunk and disorderly. ANQ 1837, no. 3352, Young to Murdoch, 20 Oct. 1839

31 ANQ 1837, no. 3345, Young to Goldie, 6 Aug. 1839. See also, ibid., no. 3324–6.

32 Judith Fingard, *Jack in Port: Sailortowns of Eastern Canada* (Toronto: University of Toronto Press 1982)

33 NA, LC Police Records, vol. 3, unsigned memo, 28 May 1840. This is the only such detailed account of activities in the collection.

34 Jean Turmel, 'Premières structures et évolution de la police de Montréal (1796–1909)' (Montreal: Service de police de la ville de Montréal nd), 54; Antonio Drolet, *La ville de Québec: histoire municipale*, 3 vols, vol. 3, *De l'incorporation à la Confédération (1833–1867)* (Quebec: Société historique de Québec 1967), 41

35 Allan Greer, 'La dimension ville-campagne de l'insurrection de 1837,' in Lebrun and Séguin, eds, *Sociétés villageoises*, 231–8

36 NA, LC Stipendiary Magistrates, vol. 2, Quesnel to Goldie, 1 Jan. 1839; ibid., Gugy to Coffin, 17 Jan. 1839; ibid., Gugy to Goldie, 25 Mar. 1839

37 Quoted in Jean-Marie Fecteau, 'Mesures d'exception et règle de droit: les conditions d'application de la loi martiale au Québec lors des rébellions de 1837–1838,' *McGill Law Journal* 32 (July 1987), 471

38 Talcott Parsons, ed., *Max Weber: The Theory of Social and Economic Organization* (New York: Oxford University Press 1947), 324

39 Galen Broeker, *Rural Disorder and Police Reform in Ireland, 1812–36* (Toronto: University of Toronto Press 1970), 223

40 The number of constables and stations changed frequently, and there are no complete figures for either in the early years. A return dated Sept. 1839 lists 192 constables and twenty-nine station-houses, but it does not include men posted in the District of Trois-Rivières. About the time that list was drawn up, Gugy referred to the police as 'a civil force not exceeding three hundred men.' In 1841, when the threat of revolution had faded, a reduced force of 98 men was spread among forty-one stations. NA, LC Stipendiary Magistrates, vol. 3, 'Return of the Rural Police in the District of Montreal, 30th September 1839'; ibid., Gugy to Murdoch, 4 Nov. 1839; *Journals of the Legislative Assembly of the United Province of Canada*, vol. 1 (1841), App. z

41 Senior, *British Regulars*, 27; Jacques Monet, 'Bartholomew Conrad Augustus Gugy,' *Dictionary of Canadian Biography*, vol. 10 (Toronto: University of Toronto Press 1972), 320–2

42 Tobias, *Crime and Police*, 45

43 NA, LC Police Records, vol. 2, Civil Secretary to Cathcart et al., 27 Apr. 1840

44 NA, LC Stipendiary Magistrates, vol. 3, Gugy to Murdoch, 4 Nov. 1839; NA, Colborne Papers, vol. 28: 8238, anonymous and undated memorandum

45 *Rules for the Government of the Rural Police: Circular Memorandum for the Information and Guidance of the Inspecting Stipendiary Magistrates ... in the Montreal District* (Montreal: James Starke 1839), 5. Not surprisingly, the emphasis in another police manual published two years later had shifted to ordinary non-political crime, see *Regulations for the Governance of the Police Force*.

46 Carol Whitfield, *Tommy Atkins: The British Soldier in Canada, 1759–1870* (Ottawa: Parks Canada 1981), 143

47 NA, LC Stipendiary Magistrates, vol. 3, Gugy to Murdoch, 4 Nov. 1839

48 ANQ 1837, no. 3614, Gugy to Coffin, 23 Feb. 1839

49 NA, LC Police Records, vols 13 and 67. The figures in Table 1:2 make use of only a small portion of the hundreds of monthly station returns preserved in this collection. Chambly, Ste Scholastique, and Ste Martine were selected simply because their files were fairly complete (two months are missing for Ste Martine) over an extended period.

50 I am well aware of the risks involved in any attempt to infer crime rates from arrest figures. However, without wishing to claim any statistical precision, I do feel convinced that the incidence of serious crime was truly quite low in the areas covered by the rural police, for the

extensive correspondence of the stipendiary magistrates gives no hint that murderers and rapists were eluding the police in large numbers.

51 NA, LC Police Records, vol. 4, McCord to Coffin, 12 July 1840

52 Ibid., vol. 11, Leclère to Coffin, 14 Oct. 1841; NA, LC Stipendiary Magistrates, vol. 5, Bowie to Goldie, 16 Apr. 1839

53 Archives nationales du Québec, dépôt de Montréal (ANQM), affaires criminelles, vol. 50, Chaffers to Coffin, 20 Mar. 1839

54 NA, LC Stipendiary Magistrates, vol. 3, Gugy to Murdoch, 4 Nov. 1839. The commissioner's religious language is highly appropriate, for, though he was himself a Protestant, he earned the gratitude of the Catholic clergy, which had not much appreciated the Sunday-afternoon oratory – anti-clerical as well as anti-government – of the Patriots. The rural police then played their part in securing the triumph of the Catholic Church, as well as the colonial state, in the recalcitrant French-Canadian countryside.

55 NA, LC Police Records, vol. 5, Hanson to Coffin, 19 Oct. 1840

56 ANQ 1837, no. 3725, Weatherall to Goldie, 10 Sept. 1839; ANQM, affaires criminelles, vol. 50, Brown to Chaffers, 22 May 1839

57 ANQM, affaires criminelles, Hanson to Coffin, 19 Mar. 1839

58 ANQ 1837, no. 3575, Coffin to Goldie, 23 Aug. 1839. See also, ibid., no. 3726, Weatherall to Goldie, 23 Aug. 1839; ibid., no. 3737, Weatherall to Goldie, 18 Mar. 1840; NA, LC Stipendiary Magistrates, Gugy to Murdoch, 4 Nov. 1839.

59 ANQ 1837, no. 3737, Weatherall to Goldie, 18 Mar. 1840

60 Lord Durham, a good administrative rationalizer, was highly critical of the JP system in the Canadas and advocated the establishment of 'a small stipendiary magistracy.' Charles Lucas, ed., *Lord Durham's Report on the Affairs of British North America*, 3 vols (Oxford: Clarendon Press 1912), 2: 130–1

61 NA, LC Police Records, vol. 3, Bayley to Coffin, 30 June 1840

62 Stephen Kenny, ' "Cahots" and Catcalls: An Episode of Popular Resistance in Lower Canada at the Outset of the Union,' *Canadian Historical Review* 65 (June 1984), 184–209

63 NA, LC Police Records, vol. 13, 65, 67, passim. See also Table 1:1.

64 Ibid., vol. 5, Hanson to Coffin, 23 Oct. 1840. Cf, Kenny, ' "Cahots" and Catcalls,' 202–3.

65 Elizabeth Nish, ed., *Debates of the Legislative Assembly of United Canada* (Montreal: Centre d'Etude du Québec 1970), 2: 191

66 H. Clare Pentland, *Labour and Capital in Canada 1650–1860* (Toronto: Lorimer 1981), 191–2; NA, RG4, C1, vol. 286, no. 2187, Johnson and Delisle to Leslie, 29 Sept. 1850

67 George Cathcart to Lord Cathcart, 13 Oct. 1839, quoted in Michael Mann, *A Particular Duty: The Canadian Rebellions 1837–1839* (Salisbury, Eng.: Michael Russell 1986), 155

68 ANQ 1837, no. 3731, Weatherall to Civil Secretary, 14 Nov. 1839. Cf ibid., no. 3554, Coleman to Assistant Civil Secretary, 21 Mar. 1839.

69 NA, LC Stipendiary Magistrates, vol. 3, Gugy to Murdoch, 4 Nov. 1839. One might suggest that the experiment in rural policing helped pave the way for later, and more lasting, extensions of state power into the countryside. In this connection it seems noteworthy that the rather centralized system of elementary education introduced in the late 1840s met with little resistance in the District of Montreal where the police had been concentrated, while in the neighbouring Trois-Rivières region the *guerre des éteignoirs* raged for several years. See Wendie Nelson, 'The "Guerre des éteignoirs": Popular Resistance to School Reform in Lower Canada during the 1840s' (MA thesis, Simon Fraser University 1989).

70 S.W. Horrall, 'The Royal North-West Mounted Police and Labour Unrest in Western Canada, 1919,' *Canadian Historical Review* 61 (1980), 169–90. One might also mention the case of the pre-Confederation Secret Police, set up by John A. Macdonald to seal off the borders of Canada West to Fenian infiltrators. Similarly, the North-West Mounted Police itself, though not a response to insurrection, was nevertheless a political instrument designed to assert Canadian sovereignty over the dominion's vast new western domain. (The force was conceived in 1869 before news of the Red River Resistance reached Ottawa, and it was not actually established until years after Manitoba had been incorporated into Canada.) As far as I can tell, Macdonald and his colleagues were unaware when they set up the NWMP of the Lower-Canadian precedent; their model was in fact the Royal Irish Constabulary, which had also set the pattern for the Rural Police of 1839–42. Jeff Keshan, 'Cloak and Dagger: Canada West's Secret Police, 1864–1867,' *Ontario History* 79 (Dec. 1987), 353–81; S.W. Horrall, 'Sir John A. Macdonald and the Mounted Police Force for the Northwest Territories,' *Canadian Historical Review* 53 (June 1972), 179–200

# 2

# Positive Law, Positive State: Class Realignment and the Transformation of Lower Canada, 1815–1866

BRIAN YOUNG

Attention to the theme of 'social change and state formation' encourages reflection on the meaning of the early and mid-nineteenth century – the post-Napoleonic period, the Rebellions of 1837–8, the process of institutionalization, changing social relations in the 1840s, and their relationship to the process of the transition of Lower-Canadian society to industrial capitalism. It stimulates a reconsideration of periodization in Quebec history, of class realignment, of the emerging ideology of free contract, of the process of institutionalization, and of the role of positive law. For me, this essay represents a way-station between earlier work on the Quebec bourgeoisie, the church, and the seigneurial system and an 'in-progress' study of Lower-Canadian private law in the post-rebellion period.

The essential argument of this essay is that the Special Council, which ruled Lower Canada from 1839 to 1841, played a central role in shaping state and institutional structures that were receptive to and supportive of capitalist relations; this work was solidified and legitimized by the indigenous bourgeoisie that assumed power in the 1840s under responsible government. The particular result was a mixture: alongside new social, educational, workplace, and political structures, there was a persistence of the merchant, legal, and religious élites. Pre-industrial relations and ideology – the church, seigneurial tenure, and traditional paternal, class, and master-servant relations – were not swept away but were blended into a new social contract.

Periodization is a central element in historical explanation, and the editors of this collection perhaps erred in taking 1830 as their beginning year. I would prefer to stretch this period of class realignment and institutional change back to the first years of the century. Here we can witness the Napoleonic Code, the Concordat with Rome, and the re-enhanced authority of the state. The first two decades of the century saw the establishment of Canada's first banks, the appearance of steamships on the St Lawrence, the construction of the Lachine Canal, the rapid expansion of the francophone professional bourgeoisie, and mounting attacks on pre-industrial institutions. It was a period marked by changing world-views: science, law, and education were profoundly influenced by a rationalism that expressed itself in a willingness to collect, codify, and inventory and to build new systems.[1] Taking this frame, the rebellions, the subsequent period of authoritarian rule, and the pre-Confederation decades of neophyte bourgeois democracy form the centrepiece in which class relationships and the state took forms in Quebec that lasted until our own lifetimes.

From this perspective, the transformation of Lower Canada's class and institutional structures sketched below represents less a breathtaking rupture with the past than the *mise en place* of ideological and institutional currents that pre-dated the rebellions by several decades; similar processes occurred in France, Britain, the United States, and Upper Canada.[2] The collapse of the rebellions served to clear the political marketplace and facilitated the establishment of a society in which capitalist relations would dominate.

Since at least the beginning of the century, feudal institutions in the colony faced a variety of attacks. Seigneurialism, Lower Canada's predominant landholding system, was in a schizophrenic state. On the one hand, some seigneurs moved into industrial production and many capitalists bought seigneuries, using them to expropriate wealth in both town and countryside.[3] At the same time, seigneurialism was buffeted by fundamental and dangerous attacks – witness the Canada Tenures Act (1825), the 92 Resolutions (1834), and the Assembly report of 1836.[4] The non-payment of seigneurial dues in Montreal extended from small farmers to such normally discreet citizens as the sons of John Molson, the colony's first great industrial capitalist.

Another feudal institution, the Roman Catholic Church, showed its insecurity at regular intervals. Priests of the Seminary of Montreal, for example, lived in a permanent state of fear of the francophone bourgeoisie and the popular classes. Law was another sore point and, since at least 1814, jurists and legal commentators had been publishing tracts, codes, and law reports aimed at bringing order, uniformity, and modernity to the province's civil-law system.[5] Although we know precious little about the participants in the rebellions, their social class and goals, the crisis was particularly acute in the Montreal region where capitalist relations, urbanization, and industrial production were the most advanced.[6]

## Special Council

Canada's tradition of parliamentary democracy was still fragile in the early nineteenth century, and both Murray Greenwood and Jean-Marie Fecteau have detailed the savaging of British civil liberties in post-rebellion Lower Canada; both draw thick lines connecting 1837–8 and the use of the War Measures Act in our lifetimes.[7] Suspending the Assembly and the Legislative Council, British authorities replaced them with a Special Council in which the suspension of habeas corpus and the formation of new police forces were only the opening rounds. The council responded with alacrity to class concerns expressed so strongly in the pre-rebellion period: fear of popular resistance; the protection of landed property, of capital invested therein, and of mortgages based thereon; promotion of a bourgeois-dominated society based on equality and individual rights but in which other élite elements such as the upper clergy and seigneurs would have important privileges and responsibilities; and the establishment of a centralized, bureaucratic state that would support transportation projects and industrial production.[8]

To this end, the Special Council implemented law that initiated a universal land-registry system, that redefined seigneurial tenure on the island of Montreal, that established civil authority in the countryside, and that set in motion the organization of modernized institutions from asylums to municipalities, and a system of education for the popular classes. Lawmakers on the Special Council aimed high, creating Benthamite systems that emphasized centralization, uniformity, and inspection. For example, an ideological whole was inherent in solicitor general Charles Dewey Day's Common School Bill (1841), in which he described his projected school network as part of a 'great general system of national education,' which would 'extend to the whole Province and embrace the whole population.'[9]

In short, the Special Council's work subjected a whole envelope of social relations – the family, childhood, marriage, community, work, and region – to a regime of positive law and an expanding role for the state. Granted that its legislation was only temporary, was often hastily conceived, and was unlikely to receive popular support; the Special Council's crucial contribution was the structuring of an institutional framework that would be legitimized later by Lower Canada's indigenous political class under the rubric of responsible government.

Westminster empowered the governor to appoint members to the Special Council, which had the power of a legislature to 'make' laws. Ordinances were to be approved in the presence of at least five members of the council and would remain in effect until November 1842. Drafts of ordinances, such as that dealing with the commutation of seigneurial lands on the island of Montreal, were worked out privately and were then submitted by the governor to meetings normally presided over by the chief justice. In June 1840 the council's members included former *patriotes* John Neilson and Frédéric-Auguste Quesnel, industrial producer John Molson, notary and mill operator Joseph-Edouard Faribault, merchants Peter McGill, George Moffatt, and Samuel Gerrard, and William Walker, Joseph Dionne, Amable Dionne, Edward Hale of Sherbrooke, Robert Unwin Harwood, and Paul Holland Knowlton.[10]

In its first ordinances the Special Council moved quickly to neutralize juries as well as judges like Joseph-Rémi Vallières de Saint Réal who were favourable to *patriote* pleas or to the application of British civil rights.[11] In April 1838 the council empowered officials to hold without bail persons in prison for treasonous activities; judges and justices of the peace were forbidden to grant bail without approval from the governor. Another ordinance declared that the right of habeas corpus passed in the reign of Charles the Second 'is not, nor has ever been in force in this province.'[12] This ordinance specifically freed the jail-keeper in Quebec City, an officer in the Foot Guards, and the superintendent of police in Quebec City from contempt charges brought against them by local justices for not respecting writs of habeas corpus. Other ordinances made it lawful to transport prisoners to Bermuda, provided for a common jail in Montreal, and permitted the transfer of trials, and the transfer of prisoners charged with treason to other jails, 'any Law, Usage or Statute to the contrary thereof in anywise notwithstanding.'[13]

The Special Council's legislation surprises by its broad scope. While popular resistance was defused by important police, militia, judiciary, social-control, and education measures, registry, municipal, and seigneurial (at least in the Montreal area) legislation gave new and absolute guarantees to landed property, its improvement, and mortgages.

The state interfered much more positively than it had previously in questions of land and the enforcement of property rights. At the same time, dozens of schools, Catholic colleges, literary societies, and institutions for indigents, orphans, widows, foundlings, and the elderly or sick were established (and often subsidized). The council responded to local demands for transportation improvement by chartering railways and subsidizing bridges, roads, and the Chambly Canal.

The registry ordinance required all conveyances, mortgages, and land transactions to be registered.[14] It ended the pre-industrial secret hypothecary system and put aside the Custom of Paris privileges of special-interest groups – seigneurs, women, minor children, heirs – in favour of simple priority by order of registration. Even more important for holders of capital, it restricted the traditional practice whereby every notarial deed bore a tacit general hypothec. It also ended the traditional priority given to customary dower rights; to be valid under the new regime, dower rights had to be registered by the husband. Contemporary observers had no doubts as to the significance of registry:

> Though its prime object was merely to establish Registry Offices, it sweeps, in fact, over the whole field of the Law of Real Property ... To the Lawyer, to the Notary, to the Merchant, to the Landholder, to the Capitalist, to every one who may be placed in the position of borrower or lender ... a thorough knowledge of its provisions would seem indispensable. ... On the rules it establishes depends the scanty pittance of the widow: the ignorance of a single clause or paragraph may snatch from the orphan the means which parental foresight and affection had laid up for his maintenance.[15]

In short, registry – like freehold tenure, which was lurking in the wings – gave assurance of absolute title and increased the security of capital by ensuring to mortgage creditors the immovable property of their debtors.

Seigneurialism and the social relations inherent in it were, as we have noted, beneficial to those who possessed seigneuries, while they were increasingly offensive to urban capitalists, rural land speculators, and industrial producers, who objected to the system's milling privileges, the mutation levies on land improvements, and seigneurial control over waterways and power sites. The critical ordinance concerning the transformation of land in the Montreal area in freehold tenure was passed by the Special Council in June 1840 permitting what it called the 'gradual extinction' of seigneurialism on the lands of the Seminary of Montreal. It allowed the *censitaire* to capitalize his or her seigneurial dues, thus converting the land to freehold land; this permitted its alienation and incorporation into the free market. Commutation was voluntary and, by its very definition, was limited to individuals with access to capital. Over 3,000 commutations of land – most of it within urban Montreal – occurred in the four decades after the ordinance, with the largest number occurring in the years from 1841 to 1845.[16]

## Bourgeois Democracy

When Louis-Joseph Papineau returned to Montreal from Paris in 1845, he found the world on its head. His beloved seigneurialism was taking a dive from which it would never recover, and the social relations inherent in the pre-industrial society he cherished were being lapped by the ideology of freedom – of market, of contract, and of labour. The Catholic Church, towards which his feelings were so ambiguous and ultimately hostile, was emerging from the rebellion period subordinate to the state but with its hold on its lands and social authority reinforced. Nationalist groups like the Saint Jean Baptiste Society that had helped germinate a democratic tradition in the 1830s had become passive friendly societies subject to church and state. In popular education, the Christian Brothers – who arrived in Montreal in the midst of the rebellions – had 1,550 students in their Montreal schools and 1,600 in Quebec City by 1844; they had succeeded in dividing the sexes in the classroom and were purging the schools of lay teachers.[17] The anglophone bourgeoisie of Montreal, whom Papineau distrusted, were moving into alliance with younger francophones like Louis-Hippolyte LaFontaine and George-Étienne Cartier. Anglophones whom Papineau would undoubtedly have dismissed as 'urban smoothies' – Alexander Galt, Charles Dewey Day, Lewis Drummond, and John Young – were becoming central players in establishing registry offices, responsible government, new legal forms, and industrial and commercial enterprises in a society increasingly affected by urban values. And what of the Young Turks who had come to dominate the francophone political class in Papineau's absence? The period of the rebellions and the Special Council shook down the francophone bourgeoisie. Politicians like LaFontaine and Cartier believed in modernization, ethnic harmony, and alliances with the great landowners and industrial capitalists. Their generation left

behind the *Angst* of Papineau and accepted the subordination of the
pre-industrial élite (particularly the seigneurs and Roman Catholic
clergy) to the imperatives of industrializing Lower Canada. Whatever
Jacques Monet's faith in LaFontaine's respect for British parliamentary democracy and my own grudging respect for Cartier's surviva-
bility, the essential point was the two men's assumption of the political
mantle – not of Papineau but of the Special Council. Of course they
fought hard on language, ethnic, and religious questions, contending
with the vulgarity of the Clear Grits and the rigidity of the Rouges,
and agitating over the implications of 'rep by pop' for French Canada
and the location of the Canadian capital (please not in volatile Montreal, said Montrealer Cartier!). In defence of their central concerns,
they were prepared to relegate popular sovereignty, republicanism,
radical land-reform measures, and new concepts of citizenship to the
scrap heap of Quebec history. Distancing themselves from any hint
of the radical consciousness of 1838, they left just enough wind in
the rebellion sails to ensure their reputations as 'reformers' and retained enough ideological punch to enable Bourassa (Henri, that is)
and Mackenzie King to puff up their radical origins.

Much of the Special Council's work lacked popular legitimacy, and
many of its measures were never enforced. When Jacques Crémazie
was sent out to visit the new registry offices in the Gaspé and Quebec
regions and to report on how the council's new registry law was being
applied, he reported back that the Special Council had 'set about
making laws, pruning and cutting to the quick into all the institutions
of the country.' In his opinion, the 'unpopularity' of the Special Council had ensured that, aside from traders and speculators who hurried
to register their lands, people 'took no trouble to obey it.'[18] Petitions
were received from the inhabitants of Portneuf attacking Special
Council tax, registry, and police legislation as 'dangerous' and 'unconstitutional'; Denis-Benjamin Viger attacked the council's municipal legislation as being 'of such a character as no man could approve
it. It had been passed by a set of men who did not represent the
people. By it a new machinery of government had been established,
for which there was no example in the whole civilized world.'[19]

The francophone politicians, intellectuals, and civil servants like
LaFontaine, Cartier, Jean-Baptiste Meilleur, Étienne Parent, Joseph
Cauchon, and Joseph-Charles Taché had the roots and local authority
to put down both rural and urban resistance, to ally with the church
to establish new institutions of social control, and to institute new
taxation, police, and judicial measures. Within the emerging minis-

tries and bureaucracies, they resolved questions about such things as land titles, mortgages, registry, Crown lands, education, courts, and the police, with all that these implied for social relations, Lower-Canadian regionalism, labour as a commodity, and the particular privileges of women and other family members. Confederation, the National Policy, and the Quebec infrastructure of institutions were the result.

And what of the ideology implied in the Special Council's actions? Did assemblies elected after 1841 reject the thrust of the authoritarian Special Council? On the contrary: in virtually every domain the Assembly reinforced and legitimized the ideology of the council. The result of its school legislation of 1845 and 1846 was to strengthen a universal elementary school system with compulsory taxation. A striking feature of institutionalization by the Special Council had been its specificity to the district of Montreal; this corresponds, of course, to the area of the rebellions and the region in which industrial production and capitalist relations in the countryside were the most advanced. The setting up of the Rural Police in the district of Montreal, the new city charter (and that of Quebec City), and the provision for commutation of seigneurial lands on the island of Montreal are key examples of the importance of the Montreal area. After 1841 the Assembly made these measures universal across the province. Such attempts at uniformity recurred constantly. Cartier, for example, was frustrated by the fact that Lower Canada had two forms of land tenure; he also worked to co-ordinate parish and municipal structures with a view to harmonizing the province's administrative structure.[20]

As for the registry system, deemed so essential to reassure capital invested in land in the form of mortgages, LaFontaine himself published a 116-page text and a 123-page appendix attacking the Special Council's bill as a 'scissors and paste job,' as a hopeless mixture of English and French legal traditions, and as written in language that was unintelligible for the masses. But he did not oppose the principle of registry reform and of abolishing secret mortgages; he simply wanted a better and more coherent law; in 1843 the Assembly clarified and amended the registry act, giving the population more time to conform and making the act more universal in application.[21]

On the crucial question of seigneurialism, the Assembly went much further than the 1840 ordinance for the commutation of seigneurical lands, which applied only to parts of the Montreal region. A comparison of Assembly commissions examining seigneurialism in 1836 and 1843 illustrates graphically the shift across the period in attitudes to freehold tenure.[22] A few years later, LaFontaine clearly stated how seigneurial tenure – a form of land tenure he had 'appreciated' 'up to a period relatively recent' – had 'ceased to be in harmony with the social usages of [society].'[23] By the early 1850s, the process of establishing freehold tenure across Lower Canada had been set in motion.

In the legal sector, the ordinances of 1838–41 were extended with the establishment of courthouses, sheriffs, and other judicial structures in remote areas. Bankruptcy laws were revised and, in the 1850s, the lengthy codification process was begun. To read their comments on registry, seigneurialism, and codification gives a strong sense of the lawmakers' attempts to mix old and new, to adjust pre-industrial institutions and social relations to the reality of an emerging capitalist society; their libraries, speeches, judicial decisions, and commentaries included Justinian, Pothier, and Bentham.

And if compromises were found with the seigneurs, what of that historic enemy, the Catholic Church? The Rebellions of 1837–8 and the suppression of the *patriotes* were a godsend for the church. Despite the revolutionary role of a handful of priests, the church was strongly identified with conservative, hierarchical, anti-revolutionary, and anti-democratic forces. Its weight in the pulpit and with the sacraments, its leadership with important 'swing' groups such as the Irish, and its collaboration with British forces are clear.

After the rebellions the Roman Catholic Church served as the glue holding together Lower Canada's diverse class elements. Powerful religious communities like the Sulpicians were given new legal and economic rights by the Special Council, and these were further strengthened by the francophone bourgeoisie later in the 1840s. At the base of these reinforced privileges was the reality that the church's capital and its ideological influence were to serve the state. The church was to remain an ideological and institutional force in Quebec society until our lifetimes – flexible, socially useful, equally at home in the milieu of the urban proletariat and the small Québécois farmer, usually comfortable with the province's bourgeoisie from George-Étienne Cartier through Lomer Gouin, reinforcing gender norms, and legitimizing industrial realities.

## Some Conclusions

'There are also three prime principles of positive law; whose aim and interest is the profit and utility of man ... the maintenance, flourishing and peace of society, the security of property, and the freedom of commerce.'

James, Viscount of Stair[24]

'Positive Law' and 'Positive State' meant much more than our traditional view that the expansion of the pre-Confederation state served essentially to subsidize railways and distribute patronage. The great Scottish jurist Viscount Stair perceived positive law as something much more fundamental: its goal was 'the profit and utility of man,' and by this he meant civil peace, protection for property, and freedom of commerce. Across the first decades of the nineteenth century, traditional pre-industrial relations of the Lower-Canadian family, of husband and wife, and of seigneur and tenant were subject to a variety of new state regulations through innovations in registry law, changes in land tenure, and the hammering out of the civil code. These penetrated to the very core of civil society. New definitions of delivery, contract, sale, corporation, and bankruptcy served to organize, publicize, and standardize private business relations; other elements of positive law infiltrated across the social spectrum, touching the rights of women in philanthropic societies and the organization of the legal and notarial professions.

And what of social change across the period? Legitimacy for Lower Canada's emerging capitalist structures came from the establishment of bourgeois democracy and the francophone bourgeoisie who assumed political power under it. We can clearly discern dominant elements in the francophone political class distancing themselves from any vestige of radical consciousness or any leadership of the popular classes. Instead, their bedfellows were priests, capitalists, and colonial officials. Nowhere was this symbolized more clearly than in the Confederation-year election in Montreal where Médéric Lanctôt and his Great Association of Workers went nose to nose with George-Étienne Cartier, who was nominated by William Molson and strongly supported by the Catholic hierarchy.

This class stance by the francophone political leadership was an important factor in the great resilience shown by the pre-industrial élite. Emboldened by its supportive role in quelling the rebellions and reinforced in status, legal rights, and institutional responsibilities, the Catholic hierarchy scoured France and Ireland for religious communities that might be of service in industrializing Quebec. Nor did seigneurs roll over and die in industrial society. Many of them were already deeply involved in industrial production, and they conducted an important rearguard action to protect their seigneurial rights and to maximize their return in the settlement of seigneurial claims.[25] For its part, pre-industrial capital – both merchant and seigneurial – accumulated by families and institutions like the McGills and the Seminary of Montreal reproduced itself in the industrial capitalist mode and legitimized itself through legacies to the institutions of modern Quebec.

Perhaps the last word in summarizing these changing class structures and the breakdown of autonomous relations through the vehicle of positive law / positive state should be left to the Special Council. In the rules drawn up in 1839 for rural police in the Montreal district, policemen were ordered not only 'to know, but in their intercourse with the people, to respect their manner and usages' so that authorities could 'obtain the confidence of the people and ... destroy the pernicious influence which produced the disturbances of 1837 and 1838.'[26] It was this harmonizing of authority, class, and ideology that was to retard successful resistance in Quebec.


# APPENDIX

## Important Ordinances of the Special Council, 1838–41


*Social Control*

Ordinance providing for the trial of rebels by court martial (1838)
Ordinance establishing the Montreal Lunatic Asylum (1839)
Ordinance for the better regulation of taverns and tavernkeepers (1840)
Ordinance establishing regulations concerning aliens (1840)
Ordinance for the incorporation of Montreal and Quebec City (1840)
Judicial ordinance for 'civil causes' of 'small pecuniary value' (1840)
Common School Bill (1841)


*Economic Regulation*

Ordinance establishing the British Bankruptcy Law in Lower Canada (1839)
Ordinance for the commutation of seigneurial lands on the seigneuries of the Seminary of Montreal (1840)
Ordinance for the borrowing of money for construction of the Chambly Canal (1840)
Registry Act (1841)

*Civil Authority in the Countryside*
Institutionalization of Rural Police in Montreal area (1839)
Municipal Act (1840)
Ordinance to establish an efficient system of police in Montreal and Quebec City (1840)
Ordinance to regulate the office of sheriff (1841)
Ordinance to establish court houses and gaols in certain districts (1841)

## NOTES

The comments of Allan Greer and Alan Stewart were particularly useful in the reworking of this paper.

1 This ideology is defined effectively in Suzanne Zeller's *Inventing Canada: Early Victorian Science and the Idea of a Transcontinental Nation* (Toronto: University of Toronto Press 1987).

2 This emphasis on continuity is strongly made by Peter Mandler. See his 'The Making of the New Poor Law Redivivus,' *Past and Present* 117 (Nov. 1987), 131. From another perspective, Paul Romney argues that disrespect for the rule of law in Upper Canada long pre-dated the rebellions. 'From the Types Riot to the Rebellion,' *Ontario History* 79:2 (June 1987), 115, 140

3 See, for example, Louise Dechêne, 'La rente du faubourg Saint-Roch à Québec, 1750–1850,' *Revue d'histoire de l'Amérique française* 34 (Mar. 1981), 569–96.

4 See Lower Canada, House of Assembly, 'First Report of the Standing Committee on Lands and Seignioral Rights,' in *Journals of the House of Assembly of the Province of Lower Canada*, App. EEE (1 Mar. 1836).

5 For examples of commentators see J.F. Perrault, *Questions et réponses sur le droit criminel du Bas-Canada dediées aux étudiants en droit* (Québec 1814), his *Code rural à l'usage des habitants tant anciens que nouveaux du Bas-Canada concernant leurs devoirs religieux et civils, d'après les lois en force dans le pays* (Québec 1832), and Henry Des Rivières Beaubien, *Traité sur les lois civiles du Bas-Canada* (Montréal 1832). Also important is Jonathan Sewell's *An Essay on the Juridical History of France, So Far as It Relates to the Law of the Province ...* (Quebec 1824).

6 For the participation of different social groups in the rebellions see George Rudé, *Protest and Punishment: The Story of the Social and Political Protesters Transported to Australia, 1788–1868* (Oxford: Oxford University Press 1978), 42–51, 96–9, and Jean-Paul Bernard, *Les rébellions de 1837–1838* (Montréal: Boréal Express 1983), 284–337. For broader examples of popular unrest in Lower Canada before and after the rebellions see Michael Cross, ' "The Laws Are Like Cobwebs": Popu-

lar Resistance to Authority in Mid-Nineteenth-Century British North America,' in T. Barnes, P. Waite, and S. Oxner, eds *Laws in a Colonial Society: The Nova Scotian Experience* (Toronto: Carswell 1984), 103-24, and Stephen Kenny, ' "Cahots" and Catcalls: An Episode of Popular Resistance in Lower Canada at the Outset of the Union,' *Canadian Historical Review* 65:2 (June 1984), 184–209.

7 For Greenwood see 'The Chartrand Murder Trial: Rebellion and Repression in Lower Canada, 1837–1839,' *Criminal Justice History* 5 (1984), 129–59, and his more recent 'The General Court Martial of 1838–39 in Lower Canada: An Abuse of Justice,' *Papers Presented at the 1987 Canadian Law in History Conference* (Carleton University, 8–10 June 1987), 307–56. Fecteau draws the parallel between 1837-8 and the use of the War Measures Act in 'Mesures d'exception et règle de droit: les conditions d'application de la loi martiale au Québec lors des rébellions de 1837–1838,' *McGill Law Journal* 32:3 (July 1987), 495.

8 This interpretation should be compared, for example, to the ethnic emphasis given by André Cellard and Dominique Nadon, 'Ordre et désordre: le Montreal Lunatic Asylum et la naissance de l'asile au Québec,' *Revue d'histoire de l'Amérique française* 3 (Winter 1986), 345–68.

9 For the bill's ideological implications see Bruce Curtis, *Building the Educational State: Canada West, 1836–1871* (London, Ont.: Althouse 1988), 52–4.

10 Charles Grey, Durham's brother-in-law, sat on earlier sessions of the Special Council. For membership, votes, and motions, see *Journals of the Special Council of Lower Canada* (Quebec: Desbarats 1840); for the ordinances, see *Ordinances Made and Passed by the Excellency the Governor General and Special Council*, 6 vols (Quebec: Fisher and Kemble 1841).

11 *Judicial Decisions on the Writ of Habeas Corpus Ad Subjiciendum and on the Provincial Ordinance 2 Vic Cap 4 Whereby the Habeas Corpus Ordinance of 1784 Has Been Suspended* (Three Rivers 1839)

12 Lower Canada, *Ordinances of the Special Council* 1 Vic., cap. 2; 2 Vic., Cap. 15

13 Ibid., 2 Vic., cap. 11, 12

14 Ibid., 4 Vic., cap. 30 (1841)

15 John Bonner, *An Essay on the Registry Laws of Lower Canada* (Quebec: Lovell 1852), 5

16 Young, *In Its Corporate Capacity: The Seminary of Montreal as a Business Institution, 1816–1876* (Kingston and Montreal: McGill-Queen's University Press 1986), 95

17 Nive Voisine, *Les frères des écoles chrétiennes au Canada* (Sainte-Foy: Editions Anne Sigier 1987), 54

18 Jacques Crémazie, *Report of J. Crémazie, Esquire: Appointed by Virtue of the Act of the Fourth Victoria ...* (Montréal 1846)

19 Elizabeth Nish, ed., *Debates of the Legislative Assembly of United Canada*, 3 Aug. 1841 (Montreal: Centre d'Étude du Québec 1970), 105, 494

20 See, for example, the Lower Canada Municipality and Road Act, 18 Vic., cap. 100.

21 L-H. LaFontaine, *Analyse de l'ordonnance du Conseil Spécial sur les bureaux d'hypothèques* (Montréal: Louis Perreault 1842); *Statutes of Canada*, 7 Vic., cap. 21 (1843)

22 Tom Johnson, 'In a Manner of Speaking: Towards a Reconstitution of Property in Mid-Nineteenth-Century Quebec,' *McGill Law Journal* 32:3 (July 1987), 636–72

23 Lower Canada Reports, *Decisions des tribunaux du Bas-Canada: Seignioral Questions* (Québec and Montréal: Coté and Duvernay 1856), vol. 4

24 James, Viscount of Stair, *The Institutions of the Law of Scotland* (Edinburgh: Bell and Bradfute [1684] 1832) 1:14

25 For Papineau, a seigneur engaged in industrial production, see R. Cole Harris, 'Of Poverty and Helplessness in Petite Nation,' in Jack Bumsted, ed., *Canadian History before Confederation* (Georgetown, Ont.: Irwin Dorsey 1979); for Joliette see Jean-Claude Robert, 'Un seigneur entrepreneur, Barthélemy Joliette, et la fondation du village d'Industrie (Joliette), 1822–50,' *Revue d'histoire de l'Amérique française* 26 (Dec. 1972), 375–95. See also David Schulze, 'Rural Manufacture in Lower Canada: Understanding Seigneurial Privileges and the Transition in the Countryside,' *Alternate Routes* 7 (1984), 134–67.

26 *Rules for the Government of the Rural Police: Circular Memorandum for the Information and Guidance of the Inspecting Stipendiary Magistrate ... in the Montreal District* (Montreal: James Starke 1839), 2

# 3

# Sydenham and Utilitarian Reform

IAN RADFORTH

For many years now, historians of Britain have been exploring the process of state formation, debating the causes of the nineteenth-century 'revolution in government.' Much of the debate has centred on the role of ideas – evangelicalism, humanitarianism, and especially Utilitarianism – in shaping the pace and direction of government growth. At one extreme, Oliver MacDonagh dismissed the influence of ideas. During the 1950s he studied closely the increase in state intervention under the nineteenth-century Passenger Acts, and largely on the basis of his case study he developed a model for understanding state formation in nineteenth-century Britain. According to the MacDonagh model, state intervention grew naturally, as officials responded in practical ways to intolerable social problems and as an internal dynamism compelled experts within government departments to seek increased powers.[1]

MacDonagh's model gained wide but by no means total acceptance. In the 1960s, Jennifer Hart, for one, attacked MacDonagh's 'Tory interpretation,' which sought to explain change by reference to 'blind forces.' Hart pointed to the key role Utilitarians played in establishing both a standard for assessing intolerability – the principle of least pain and greatest happiness – and specific models for reforms. Without such standards and models, conditions might have been regarded as tolerable for much longer and the process of reform thus have been delayed.[2] Other historians have pointed to the contributions of individual Utilitarians who served as the agents of growth in specific departments of government. Compelling evidence of the profound impact of reformers armed with ideas apparently persuaded even MacDonagh himself to revise his argument. In his 1977 survey, *Early Victorian Government*, the influence of ideas receives considerable weight.[3]

Research into the process of state formation in mid-nineteenth-century British North America has been far less extensive; the role of Utilitarianism has scarcely even been considered.[4] Yet, as individuals in the colonies grappled with similar questions of authority, discipline, and motivation associated with capitalist transformation, they drew heavily on transatlantic intellectual currents – currents such as Utilitarianism.[5] Moreover, the imperial connection facilitated the transfer of ideas from Britain to the colonies. While there is considerable scope for research on the sharing of ideas within the North Atlantic triangle, this paper will focus on the direct transfer of Utilitarianism via the imperial tie. By following the career of one highly influential Utilitarian – Governor General Charles Poulett Thomson (later Lord Sydenham) – the analysis presented here will transcend the limitations of the blind-forces approach and demonstrate how one human agent influenced the process of colonial state formation.[6]

Throughout his two-year tenure, beginning in September 1839, Governor Sydenham poured his enormous energies into reforming government structures for the Canadas and establishing new ones. In doing so, he worked within a Utilitarian framework. This did not mean that he followed a blueprint set down before his arrival at Quebec. Rather, he approached issues with Utilitarian concepts in mind and worked out his reforms by taking into account political realities in the colonies and at the imperial centre. In negotiating with members of the colonial élites the Governor encountered some opposition that forced him to revise certain plans and abandon others. Yet, to a great extent Sydenham got his way. In part, his achievements resulted from the unprecedented authority he enjoyed as governor at a counter-revolutionary moment in the colonies' history. In part, it derived from his own political finesse. But it also stemmed from the colonial situation, where a consensus had emerged among key officials and politicians in favour of administrative reforms and Utilitarian solutions. The triumph of counter-revolution in the wake of the rebellions had eliminated democratic and republican alternatives, while the rebellions themselves had alerted conservatives to the need for administrative and other reforms that would strengthen their hold and permit economic improvement along capitalist lines. Sydenham provided various proposals and the means for advancing reforms.

This paper, in short, will argue that the process of state formation in the Canadas was indeed affected by Utilitarianism. It mattered that the governor who engineered the union of the Canadas and set the new province on its way was a Utilitarian.

Before pursuing Thomson's career, it is important to make clear what British historians have meant by Utilitarianism. At the heart of the current was Jeremy Bentham. As many political philosophers have emphasized, Bentham wrote a great deal during his long life, and his ideas and those of his circle (known variously as Utilitarians, Benthamites, and Philosophic Radicals) evolved over time.[7] For our purposes, it is enough to understand that Utilitarianism emerged in England along with the Industrial Revolution itself. The Benthamites shared much with the outlook of the rising industrialists whose preoccupations were efficiency, simplicity, and organization. They applied the methods of the counting-house and factory to matters of law and government.

First and foremost the Utilitarians insisted on applying the test of utility to law and policy making. As early Victorian men of property saw it, that test could lead in the direction of either less government or more. On the one hand they sought to simplify, to strip away the messy inheritance of the past, the protections and privileges of the parasitical. In matters of trade especially, Utilitarians could go along with the rhetoric of *laissez-faire* and hope that with greater freedom a rational order would prevail. On the other hand, however, the Utilitarians came up against vested interests that could not be easily swept aside, and they discovered irrational behaviour everywhere. For the tiny group of Philosophic Radicals who sat in Parliament, democratic reforms provided one solution to the problem. But Bentham himself equivocated on the question of democracy. For most Utilitarians, advances could best be made by the state's taking on a tutelary role. At least for the present, the state would intervene to set matters right, to provide a framework of rules and regulations, to inspect the behaviour of citizens. 'The function of the legislator,' writes one student of Utilitarianism, was 'to produce institutions which [would] induce individuals in pursuing their own particular interests to contribute to the general good of the whole community.'[8] More often than not, the Benthamites advocated the introduction of powerful, centralized state structures designed to promote uniformity and efficiency. In part Utilitarianism amounted to a strategy for shoring up state power, one advanced by a group of intellectuals given influence by an emergent fraction of the ruling class of industrializing Britain.[9]

By the 1830s the general notions associated with Utilitarianism had entered into the mainstream of the dominant culture of the English-speaking world. Bentham's contribution had become inseparable from the emerging consensus that favoured reforms intended to promote individualism, efficiency, and order. By contrast, the Utilitarians – those followers of Bentham who had a deeper appreciation of his proposals and ideas – remained few in number. But their influence was great. As S.E. Finer shows, the Utilitarians enjoyed enormous influence because of their much-sought expertise, their effective networks, and the positions they held in the civil service, on commissions of inquiry, and in Parliament.[10] One man who brilliantly reflects their influence is Charles Poulett Thomson.

### Thomson's British Career

Charles Edward Poulett Thomson (1799–1841) came from a prosperous mercantile family that had engaged in the Baltic and Russian trade for several generations. Charles's father, John Poulett Thomson, was senior partner in J. Thomson, T. Bonar and Co., which had establishments at St Petersburg and London. At the age of sixteen, after completing a private education, Charles was sent to St Petersburg to begin learning the family business under the direction of an elder brother. For nearly a decade Charles worked intermittently between bouts of illness and long tours through Europe, where he gained fluency in several languages and a taste for high society. In 1824 the young *bon vivant* settled in London where he speculated in business ventures that nearly ended in disaster, became a partner in the family business, and began taking an interest in liberal political issues and in Utilitarianism.[11]

It might seem natural that in the mid-1820s a young man with family and commercial ties to the Baltic timber trade would oppose Britain's colonial timber preferences and urge freer trade. But we are told by his brother and biographer, George Poulett Scrope (Thomson), that Charles's 'strong opinions of a liberal character' were 'entirely self-formed,' and that 'those of his family, of his father certainly, were rather of the opposite character.' Whatever the reasons for his independence of thought, Charles made friends with like-minded people, including such Benthamite notables as John Bowring, Henry War-

burton, Joseph Hume, and James Mill. Scrope says that by 1825 Charles
had even been 'occasionally admitted to the hermitage of the eccentric
and amiable Bentham.' About the same time, Charles was elected to
the Political Economy Club and began making a name for himself as
an outspoken free-trader and follower of the Ricardian economist
J.R. McCulloch.[12]

By the age of twenty-six, Thomson had already demonstrated a
driving ambition and a hunger for power. Political life attracted him
because it offered both the opportunity to move beyond the constraints of being a third son in a family business and the chance to
seek the company of the titled and powerful. In the summer of 1825
Thomson began negotiations with liberals at Dover with a view to
becoming a candidate in the next parliamentary elections. In this, his
Utilitarian friends played a crucial part, and they canvassed for him
in the 1826 campaign. Even Jeremy Bentham himself, Scrope main-
tains, 'broke through all the habits of his hermitage existence, [and]
actually took up his residence at Dover, canvassed daily for him, opened
his home, and allowed himself to be accessible to all Mr. Thomson's
friends.'[13] The great man's influence – and more than £3,000 – contributed to Thomson's victory. He took his seat in the Commons on
18 November 1826.

Thomson's performance in the House, though lacklustre, gained
him the admiration of the rising industrialists and some of their aris-
tocratic Whig allies. He consistently supported liberal causes, such as
the secret ballot, Roman Catholic liberties, and reduced appropriations for the military. But he rejected the call of the parliamentary
Philosophic Radicals for democratic reforms. Even more to the point
were his pro-business positions on class-charged issues relating to the
Passenger Acts and the Factory Acts, and his unremitting calls for
freer trade. Thomson's Ricardian pronouncements drew the ire of
some who, for instance, referred to 'the ostentation of *doctrine* in his
reasoning' or dubbed him 'the greatest of purists and political economists.'[14] Nevertheless, with the help of Viscount Althorp, chancellor
of the exchequer in Lord Grey's ministry, Thomson was made vice-
president of the Board of Trade in 1830. During the first election
after the Reform Act, the industrialists of Manchester saw to his election in their constituency, even though Thomson himself had campaigned only at Dover. Elected in both ridings, Thomson opted to
become the representative of the great Manchester mill owners. In
1834 he entered Lord Melbourne's Whig cabinet, becoming president
of the Board of Trade, a post he held until his appointment to Canada

in 1839. It was his work at the board that earned him his reputation as an outstanding Utilitarian.

When Thomson joined the Board of Trade in 1830, it was a small department of government whose main function was to advise the lords of the Treasury and the Foreign Office on matters of trade. From the time of his arrival, Thomson dominated the board and worked to expand its size and influence. In terms of his own career, Thomson saw the board as a springboard from which he might leap to a loftier height as chancellor of the Exchequer. In terms of his wider agenda, the board could become a potent force for reform along Utilitarian and Ricardian lines. At the board Thomson created several openings to which he appointed energetic free-traders and Benthamites, including John Bowring, George Villiers, and G.R. Porter. As his private secretary, Thomson chose Arthur Symonds, author of *Mechanics of Lawmaking* and a protégé of Edwin Chadwick. The process whereby Thomson served as the agent for the infiltration of Utilitarians at the board has been examined in detail by Lucy Brown and cited by S.E. Finer as a prime example of 'the transmission of Benthamite ideas.'[15] Thomson and his men collected information and prepared arguments to advance Utilitarian and free-trade causes. Their research was presented to Parliament by Thomson and Althorp. As expert witnesses the Board of Trade Utilitarians appeared before countless select committees where they urged reform of the Corn Laws, the Factory Acts, the Poor Laws, the public health system, municipal government, and more.

As an illustration of the way in which Thomson sought to extend the influence of the board, there is none better than the creation of the Statistical Department. It had been suggested by a select committee in 1832 that such a department might collect on a wide front information 'of great public Utility.'[16] For Thomson, a statistical department would have a political utility as well; it could provide him with research materials to counter his opponents' arguments in the House. And for a Utilitarian, there was an obvious appeal in the establishment of a central office for codifying and collecting runs of data provided by local agents. Moreover, as Lucy Brown explains, Thomson himself was 'moving along in the full stream of a contemporary intellectual current': the flourishing statistical movement. Thomson played an instrumental part of founding, for instance, the Manchester Statistical Society (1833) and the London Statistical Society (1834), which brought together amateurs eager to collect and classify 'the facts.'[17] Such organizations might build a popular base for Benthamism and at the same time provide the Statistical Department with local information on the cheap. Through shrewd means such as this, Thomson drew attention to his abilities. Political promotion appeared inevitable.

## The Canadian Assignment

Thomson's decision in August 1839 to assume Her Majesty's commission as governor general of British North America represented a radical departure in his career. He had never visited North America, and in the Canadas he was known only as a bitter enemy of colonial preferences. Thomson had no experience of managing colonial affairs, and only recently had he begun to take an interest in Canadian problems. Free trade, Westminster politics, and the business of the Board of Trade had been his all-consuming interests. As Thomson noted in his journal soon after his departure for distant Quebec, his 'greatest ambition' had been the chancellorship of the Exchequer, a position at last offered to him that August.[18] Yet he had turned down the opportunity in preference for the Canadian appointment.

Thomson provided his own explanations for a decision he called 'strange.' At the Exchequer all he could do would be 'to get through some BAD tax.' There was 'no chance of carrying the House with ... any great commercial reform, timber, corn, sugar, etc; party and private interest [would] prevent it.' By contrast, the Canadas offered '*a great field*.' In his journal, Thomson explained in a high-minded and Benthamite phrase the appeal of Canada: 'Lord A[lthorp] said he thought Canada "the finest field of exertion for any one, as affording the greatest power of doing the greatest good to one's fellow-creatures." I agree with him.'[19] Thomson believed that in Canada he might enhance his personal reputation, and that of the government, by gaining the Canadians' consent for the Whigs' major Canadian policy initiative, the union of the Canadas. And he would have plenty of scope for devising the best form of political union, the terms of the new constitution, and the administrative structures of the United Province. As if extricating the Whigs from the Canadian crisis would not be reward enough, Thomson had struck a deal: success in the Canadas would bring him a peerage. The House of Lords would answer his need for relief from the pressures of the Commons and satisfy his craving for status.

Moreover, success in Canada appeared within his grasp. Thomson could count on support at the Colonial Office from his friend and mentor, Lord John Russell, the strongest of the Whig ministers. They shared a faith in executive power as the implement of reform and a contempt for democratic excess. Thomson enjoyed, as well, the co-operation of Lord Durham, who coached him on Canadian affairs. It was critically important that, in the wake of the rebellions, representative government had been suspended in Lower Canada since February 1838. Thus, initially Thomson would have the powers of a dictator, an enormous advantage in pushing through his reform objectives. And, as always, Thomson possessed great self-confidence. 'I have a better chance of settling things in Canada than anyone they could have found to go,' he wrote.[20] Thomson's brother and biographer agreed, listing his sibling's exceptional qualifications: Parliamentary experience that had prepared Thomson for the challenge of manoeuvring among colonial politicians, a knowledge of government finances and economics that would permit him to deal effectively with the mess in Upper Canada, and administrative expertise that could help in setting up the proposed United Province of Canada.[21] As it turned out, Thomson himself came to see his Canadian mission in terms of reform in these three spheres: politics, finances and economic development, and administration.

## Politics and the Constitution

Perhaps Thomson's greatest challenge lay in the political realm. The chief goals were to restore representative government in Lower Canada and to establish a harmonious, working relationship between colonial politicians and the imperial centre. Whig politicians believed that in order to keep the Canadas within the Empire, it was imperative to find an alternative to the current, and inevitably disruptive, policies of arbitrary rule and coercion. Furthermore, the absolutism of Lower Canada's Special Council was not only an embarrassment to Whig politicians at home but also an affront to the loyal citizens of the colony. Edward Ellice expressed the viewpoint of the former: 'an English Ministry governing by means of an English Parliament can never propose the permanent establishment of arbitrary government.' Thomson reported soon after his arrival in Lower Canada that the loyal colonists 'look[ed] with impatience to the continuance of despotism, and regret the loss, through no fault of their own, of what they consider as their birth right.' At a later date Thomson's organ in the province, the *Monthly Review*, stressed the fundamental principles of the Whigs' Canadian policy:

First, That Canada is to remain a part of the British Empire.
Second, That the connexion between them is not to be maintained by
military power, but by means of that mixed form of government which
is embodied in the British constitution.
Thirdly, That as the connexion to be enduring must be mutually beneficial, so the administration of government must be in general agreement with the interests of the people.[22]

The central questions, as Thomson saw them, amounted to the
following: Could French Canadians be entrusted with a mixed form
of government? And were Canadians on the whole willing to support
the British connection and establish a mutually beneficial relationship?
After discussions held in Quebec, Montreal, and Toronto, Thomson
answered yes to both questions, though there were qualifications.
Confirming the main thrust of Russell's policy, Thomson proposed
for the Canadas a legislative union with a legislature in which the
English would be slightly over-represented. Thus, representative government could be restored, but the French would be prevented from
numerically dominating the Assembly.[23] In the matter of the English
Canadians' support for the British connection, as Russell and the
Whigs had anticipated, Thomson found they would remain true, but
only if certain reforms were made. The ultra-loyal but impossibly
rigid Compact politicians who resisted Whig overtures had to be pushed
to the margins. Moderate, wavering Upper Canadians needed to be
bribed with a 1.5-million imperial loan to complete the scheme of
public works. And 'harmony' had to be established.[24]

Harmony became the watchword of Thomson's Canadian administration. It was Russell's and Thomson's response to the thorny and
hotly debated question of responsible government. When Durham
discussed the matter with Thomson before the latter's departure for
Quebec, presumably he had urged modest concessions in the direction
of responsible government as part of his broad strategy of smoothing
imperial relations and curtailing the movement for colonial independence. 'Finality Jack' (Russell's nickname in England where he
opposed further concessions beyond those of the Great Reform Act
of 1832) rejected responsible government outright because he believed that colonial ministers responsible to a colonial assembly could
not also be responsible to the imperial government; acceptance of the
principle would inevitably mean the breakup of the empire. What
Russell proposed instead was another mode of operation: 'maintaining
the utmost possible harmony between the policy of the legislature

and of the executive government.' It was left to Thomson as the chief executive officer and representative of the imperial government to promote that harmony, to develop a following in the colonial legislature.[25]

Russell provided assistance to Thomson in his other famous dispatch of October 1839. He made it perfectly clear, if it was not already so, that executive councillors were to serve only at the governor's pleasure and that they might be removed for political reasons. The governor henceforth was to have complete freedom to choose men whom he judged willing and able to carry out the main lines of imperial policy in the colony. At the same time, Thomson devised ways to ensure that at least most of his councillors, as individuals, had the confidence of a majority in the Assembly. Coalitions were to be sought; one-party governments avoided. Although later the policy was correctly perceived as a major step towards colonial self-government, neither Russell nor Thomson intended it as such. To be sure, they recognized the need to allow the colonists a free hand in matters that were of no consequence to Britain, but otherwise the aim was to strengthen the British connection and ensure that imperial interests were protected.[26]

To that end, Thomson set about remaking the Executive Council into something approaching a cabinet. First in Upper Canada, and later in the United Province, Thomson assigned each councillor the responsibility for a department of government, which the minister managed at the governor's pleasure. Most of Thomson's councillors had to find seats in the Assembly. Here was an important step in the direction of responsible government. But Thomson's ministers were individually, not collectively, responsible for their actions. Moreover, while each councillor needed the support of a majority in the Assembly, ultimately he derived his power from Thomson, who had no hesitation in exercising the governor's prerogative to appoint and dismiss. Because Thomson could be sure of his authority, he could with confidence grant his councillors the power both to administer their departments with a free hand (at least in routine matters) and to participate in policy making along with the governor.

The executive branch gained yet more authority because councillors were given responsibility for introducing money bills in the Assembly. By following the practice of the House of Commons, Thomson hoped to provide strong executive direction and thus eliminate the chaos he perceived in the Upper-Canadian Assembly. With characteristic hyperbole, Thomson privately described past practices of the

Upper-Canadian executive: 'It has never taken the slightest lead in the introduction of measures of legislation, or attempted to guide the proceedings of Parliament; the result is that the Assembly has usurped many of the rights of the Crown, that the most disgusting jobbery has prevailed, the finances have been ruined, and not a single measure really beneficial to the province generally carried through.'[27] The profound implication of the introduction of the money-bill principle is noted by Janet Ajzenstat in her discussion of Durham's proposals: 'The executive would thus initiate the major legislative program, and the assembly be confined to review of government budgets and spending.'[28]

Under the new arrangement the Crown, i.e., the governor and his council, would develop policy and manage the business of the Assembly. The governor himself would play a highly active and interventionist role in matters of importance. Thomson described to Russell how he passed his days during the legislative session of 1841: 'lecturing Members every morning & schooling my Cabinet.' Though he complained about the burden of being '*Leader* myself,' he insisted that such intervention was essential in order to achieve the goal of harmony.[29]

Similarly, Sydenham actively campaigned in the election of 1841. He saw no need to apologize for his blatant interference on the hustings. As his *Monthly Review* delicately put it: 'His Excellency presents his servants before you, to say, in effect, "These men have my confidence; I present them to you to ascertain if they have your's in order that we may work harmoniously together." '[30] What is more, Sydenham maintained that firm leadership from the governor's office was exactly what the colonists themselves wanted. After his political tour of Canada West, he wrote: 'The fact is, that the truth of my original notion of the people and of this country is now confirmed. The *mass* only wanted the vigorous interference of a well-intentioned Government.' It didn't hurt that Sydenham had prepared for the election by resorting to a sweeping gerrymander and intimidation at the polls on a scale that far outstripped even the standards of that era.[31]

Sydenham hoped that his own gubernatorial interventionism would become the model for future governors. When it came time to step down, he urged Russell to send 'as my successor someone with House of Commons and ministerial habits – a person who will not shirk from work, and who will govern, as I do myself, *himself*.' T.W.C. Murdoch, Sydenham's private secretary in Canada and the chronicler of his

Canadian administration, insisted that 'a colony is only to be preserved
and rendered a real source of strength, power, and wealth to the
mother country,' when the governor is a statesmen 'who, without
trenching on the freedom of representative matters, knows how to
maintain the supremacy of the Imperial authority.'[32]

In pursuing his political strategy, Thomson had answered only
some of the demands of the Reformers in the colonies. To be sure,
Compact Tories had been shunted aside, and the Legislative Council
no longer had great weight. But he had avoided granting responsible
government in the sense of collective ministerial responsibility to the
Assembly and its corollaries – one-party rule and colonial self-government in important matters. Most significantly, the demands of the
Reformers for a devolution of power to the elected Assembly had
been utterly rejected. Power now lay even more firmly in the hands
of the executive, and especially those of the governor.

Throughout Thomson's discussions of constitutional reform there
are no allusions either to God's will or to natural rights. In this,
Thomson was true to the spirit of the Utilitarians. 'According to the
principle of utility,' explains a student of the Benthamites, 'the ex-
pediency of any act of government must be judged solely by its consequences and not regarded as ruled out in advance by some
metaphysical system of rights.'[33] Thomson's emphasis was on practical
measures that would both promote improvement and distract the
people from intractable constitutional issues. Hence, he expressed his
exasperation with the French in Lower Canada where 'not a man
cares for a single practical measure – the only end of a better form
of government.'[34] And he outlined his general strategy in this way:
'If I can only fasten the attention of the members to practical improvements *as I shall do*, and I think I can, for whatever they may
say, I know that the *People* of Upper Canada are determined upon
them to the exclusion of theoretical discussions upon limits of Gov't.'[35]
In a characteristically self-congratulatory phrase, he later reported
that 'the People of Montreal ... I am happy to say, are now chiming
in with their Upper Canadian neighbours – they are slow to learn,
but they have yielded to the practical conviction of better roads, better
streets, Quays.'[36] There is in fact some evidence to suggest that practical improvements were popular.[37] In any event, Thomson insisted
that it was well worth pursuing measures that had a practical utility
and went down well with the public. In his estimation, Utilitarianism
had a genuinely popular appeal.

## Finances and Economic Development

From the start, a prime purpose of Thomson's mission involved rearranging the finances of the colonies, particularly those of Upper Canada, and thus setting the Canadas once again on a path toward economic development. Lord Howick, a Whig cabinet minister, saw the links among several matters of concern to his government: the restoration of Upper Canada's finances, colonial property values, the maintenance of the British connection, and the political well-being of the Whigs. On 13 August 1839 he wrote privately:

> If we cannot relieve the financial embarrassments of that province and render property there at least as valuable as worse land in the adjoining States, we shall soon find ourselves abandoned even by our own party and be left with scarcely an adherent, and if it once becomes the general opinion there that it will be for the interest of the colony to be independent of us we shall not be able to coerce them into obedience like the poor French in the Lower Province.

To help settle matters, Howick believed that Thomson – 'much the best person to be sent to Canada' – should be authorized by cabinet 'to offer a good large loan upon favourable terms to relieve them from the pressure of the high interest rate they are now paying on their debt and to enable them to complete the great works they have in progress to improve the navigation.'[38] One week later, Melbourne's government approved the proposal. And so Thomson sailed for Canada armed with the authority to offer £1.5 million if the Canadians proved amenable to 'a final and satisfactory settlement.'[39]

Upon his arrival in Toronto, Thomson found conditions 'far worse than ... expected': 'The deficit of £75,000 a year; more than equal to the income ... All Public works suspended – & emigration going on fast *from* the Province – Every man's property worth only half what it was.'[40] It was not long before Thomson concluded that to promote prosperity and economic development, and thus further his goal of harmony, he would have to rearrange Upper Canada's finances and make reforms in the field of emigration and land policies.

Thomson was quick to make use of the promise of an imperial loan. As a politician he knew full well that it amounted to a powerful inducement to colonial politicians who might otherwise hesitate to support the union proposal. Thomson believed that public opinion in English Canada called for the resumption of such improvements:

'the Country are wild for it.'[41] Indeed, prominent colonial officials backed him all the way. As Michael Piva has shown, Upper-Canadian officials well versed in the province's troubled financial affairs had concluded that there was no choice but to accept the loan offer and to reform provincial finances along the lines Thomson was suggesting. Thus, when it came time to negotiate the details of the loan arrangement in 1841, in Canada West at least there were no objections raised regarding Thomson's specific proposals.[42]

While the immediate purpose of the loan was to relieve the colony of its burden of debt, ultimately the objectives were canal building and economic improvement. As Thomson explained in his dispatches to Russell,[43] Upper Canada had borrowed heavily to finance public-works projects to improve navigation along the Great Lakes – St Lawrence transportation route. A bankruptcy in 1837 had pushed the province to the breaking point. As things stood in 1839, work on the canal improvements had stopped, the credit of the province was exhausted, and the debt load had become unbearable. Because of the unfinished state of the canals, revenue from tolls remained low and the prosperity promised by the improvements had not materialized. If Britain failed to render assistance the canals would fall into an even worse state of disrepair, and thus the entire expenditure would have been an enormous waste. On the other hand, by loaning the funds at a modest rate of interest the imperial government at one stroke would delight the English Canadians, turn a financial drain into a profitable investment, and provide a great stimulus to economic development in the colonies.

In justifying the loan, Thomson completely accepted the point of view long advanced by development enthusiasts within the colonies. For twenty years canal building on a massive scale had been supported by prominent Upper-Canadian businessmen and Tory gentlemen who insisted that such initiatives would link the garden that was western Upper Canada to British markets and thus give a huge boost to provincial prosperity.[44] Meantime, Laurentian commercial interests (particularly in Montreal) had looked to canals as a means to ward off competition from Americans in the struggle for the trade of the Great Lakes basin.[45] Like development-minded Canadians, Thomson envisioned a great empire of the St Lawrence. Also like them, he downplayed the natural impediments to navigation along the Laurentian route, as well as the costs of overcoming them, and waxed eloquent about the benefits to be gained from canal improvements. The colonists would capture a greater share of the trade of the Midwest;

accessible markets would make Upper-Canadian agriculture profitable; property would increase in value at last; capital would be attracted to the colony; and enormously increased canal traffic would cause provincial revenues to soar. Thomson never questioned whether the state should play a substantial part in canal building. The enormous development potential and the political rewards made it imperative for the state to step in where private enterprise would not dare to tread.

Closely connected to Thomson's vision of Canadian development through state-funded canal building were his hopes for effective emigration and land policies. 'In immediate connection with the outlay of capital upon public works,' he declared in his Speech from the Throne opening the first session of the Assembly of the United Province, 'is the subject of Emigration, and the disposal of private land. There exist within the Province no means so certain of producing a healthy form of Immigration from the Mother Country, and of ultimately establishing the Immigrant as a settler and proprietor within the colony, as the power of affording a sure employment for his labour on his first arrival.'[46]

In making his case for a policy aimed at increasing settlement, Thomson once again presented the colonial perspective. He rarely mentioned the stock arguments of enthusiasts in Britain for colonial emigration: relief from the burden of a redundant population or the creation of markets for British manufactured goods. Neither is there in Thomson's writings a Durhamite emphasis on swamping the French Canadians with British arrivals, though he accepted that as one of the benefits of large-scale emigration to Canada. Instead, he stressed that an influx of emigrants would mean prosperity and growth in the colony. Like articulate members of the colonial élite, Thomson looked to the skills, capital, and labour that emigrants would bring to Canada.[47]

For the Governor, there were two types of suitable emigrants: 'hardy, well-disposed labouring men, with or without families, possessed of sufficient means ... to reach the interior of the province,' and 'industrious families possessed of moderate capital and accustomed to farming pursuits.' These he hoped to encourage. By the same token, Thomson actively discouraged men of means seeking an easier life, and he condemned emigration schemes that threw 'starving and diseased paupers under the rock at Quebec,' a crime that 'ought to be punishable as *murder*.'[48] Thomson added one other caveat: Americans should not be actively recruited. Although he admired 'their energy and intelligence,' and felt compelled to admit that 'as pioneers of civilization, they [were] superior to every other people,' he maintained that the 'spirit of propagandism among American citizens ... [made] it necessary to observe great caution.'[49] His views, then, coincided with the broad outline of post-1815 British immigration policy in the Canadas.[50] What he hoped to do was to push ahead with actual recruitment.

In adopting means to advance his emigration and land policies, Thomson rejected the arguments of Edward Gibbon Wakefield. In England, 'systematic colonization' had had an appeal for Thomson the Utilitarian. But after Thomson assessed the Canadian situation at first hand, the neatness of Wakefield's scheme and its apparent logic no longer held. In letters to Russell, Thomson dismissed Wakefield as a 'scamp' and the central tenet of his scheme, the creation of a large labouring class in the colonies, as 'utterly impractical.' Farmers, though they wanted labourers, could not afford to pay them. Furthermore, Canada suffered not from 'the acquisition of land by *poor* men, but the speculation of the rich.' The remedy certainly was not an increase in land prices, for no one would pay the higher price when opportunities were better in the neighbouring States. And furthermore, massive state assistance for emigration paid for out of revenues from land sales was simply out of the question given the current low levels of sales and revenues. Indeed, in the matter of land and emigration policy, Thomson found it 'impossible to frame any great plan such as people seem to look for, and which has been hinted at but never *explained* in Lord Durham's report.'[51]

Rather than attempting to impose a plan of systematic colonization on the Canadas, Thomson made pragmatic administrative reforms, and he took some policy initiatives. To stimulate interest in emigration and in assisting emigrants, Thomson hired Dr Thomas Rolph, a well-known proponent of emigration and settlement who himself had recently settled at Ancaster. Thomson had been impressed by Rolph's success in both Britain and Upper Canada at establishing emigration societies that raised interest in settlement and provided assistance to individuals departing the British Isles and arriving in Upper Canada. With a £500 grant arranged by Thomson, Rolph toured Britain, explaining the promising prospects the Canadas offered to hard-working people with at least some means. He also described Thomson's energetic efforts to establish a system of emigrant sheds along the frontier, to create jobs for emigrants on public works, and to establish a network of agencies that would assist newcomers in reaching 'those parts of Upper Canada where labour was in very great demand.'[52] While Thomson rejected massive state financial aid to emigrants, he arranged for imperial funds, and for the reimposition of a five-shilling head-tax on emigrants, in order to help pay for the assistance. He justified these measures as an attempt to deter arrivals at Quebec from heading immediately for the United States. Ultimately, the point of providing public-works jobs was not to create a capitalistic labour market *per se*, but rather to assist settlement on the land. As Thomson saw it, people who took such jobs 'save money, become accustomed to the country, climate and hardships of *bush life*, and eventually provide for themselves as settlers.'[53]

Thomson gave considerable attention to proposals for reforming land policies, because for him colonial development depended first and foremost on the settlement of yeoman farmers. In taking this position, Thomson was standing alongside most members of the Upper-Canadian élite who also rejected Wakefieldian notions about creating a landless proletariat and who associated immigration and settlement with the sale of their speculative land holdings at good prices. The Governor supported the initiatives of the Canada Emigration Association formed at Toronto in 1840 to co-ordinate and stimulate private land sales. Nevertheless, Thomson vigorously attacked land speculation both by land companies and individuals. After discovering that the British American Land Company had reneged on its agreement with the government, Thomson negotiated a deal that saw the return to the Crown of 500,000 acres.[54] To combat speculation on a broad front, Thomson first proposed a general land tax, but then found a more politically acceptable approach: in the local-government measures he devised, Sydenham granted the District Councils the power to tax landholders. Blame for the tax would thus be diverted to the local level, while the objective was reached all the same.[55] His other major initiative lay in the provision of free lands for settlers who lacked sufficient capital to make purchases at the going prices. In fact, a similar plan had been carried out from the late 1820s until authorities insisted on a cash-only policy a decade later. Under the system worked out by Thomson, with Lieutenant-Governor Arthur's assistance, poor emigrants might qualify for a fifty-acre free grant in certain strategic locations where public-works employment could provide the cash they needed to survive the early pioneer phase. Road building and British settlement in such areas would simultaneously fulfil imperial political or military objectives.[56]

All land policies would be administered by a newly created Department of Crown Lands.[57]

What needs to be emphasized is that Thomson had advanced a coherent development policy for the Canadas. The imperial loan would permit Canadians to complete their great transportation system and thus restore the competitiveness of the Laurentian commercial route while linking the farmers of the western peninsula to much-needed markets. With a few administrative reforms, improved publicity, and some government assistance, tens of thousands of emigrants might be induced to enter the province. Jobs on transportation construction projects would halt the exodus of newcomers to the United States. By curbing speculation and providing needy settlers with free grants, land policies could assist in turning the emigrants into successful settlers. The trinity of transportation improvements, immigration, and land policies amounted to a development strategy that would prove irresistible to imperial and Canadian policy makers in subsequent decades. As Michael Piva has shown, Thomson's basic policy, as pursued by Francis Hincks, carried Canada through the crisis years later in the 1840s when Britain turned to free trade.[58] Moreover, despite Thomson's adherence to *laissez-faire* economics while at home, in the colony he assumed that the state would provide a very visible hand. In his *Report* Durham had sought to legitimize such a role for the state by likening state involvement in colonial transportation to European state commitments to defence: 'The defence of an important fortress, or the maintenance of a sufficient army or navy in exposed spots, is not more a matter of common concern to the European, than is the construction of the great communications to the American settler; and the State, *very naturally*, takes on itself the making of the works, which are a matter of concern to all alike.'[59] Throughout Thomson's Canadian administration he, too, accepted as a given the *natural* role of the imperial state in matters so crucial to the well-being of the colony and hence to the British connection and Whig policy itself.

## Administrative Reform

Governor Thomson poured tremendous energy into administrative reform. As he saw it, this work was absolutely essential for the maintenance of effective imperial rule in the Canadas and for the smooth functioning of government. It became an obsession: 'I actually breathe, eat, drink, and sleep on nothing but government and politics.'[60] In overhauling the departments of government, Thomson created new structures, reassigned tasks to more appropriate offices, and gave authority to several hand-picked administrators, most of whom became executive councillors. While Thomson was the one who got things done, much of the groundwork had been prepared by Durham's investigators and those inquiries undertaken with Lieutenant-Governor Arthur's blessing in Upper Canada.[61] Thomson was also assisted by the consensus in favour of the administrative reform that had developed among English Canadians. Even the most conservative in Upper Canada insisted on reforms because they saw administrative improvement as a way of avoiding concessions in the direction of democracy or responsible government.[62] Furthermore, the financial troubles of Upper Canada necessitated the creation of new administrative structures 'capable of exerting influence over the course of events.'[63]

Thomson tackled an enormous range of matters: police and judicial reform, the incorporation of the cities of Montreal and Quebec, the abolition of seigneurial tenure on the Island of Montreal, government finances, registry law, emigration services, district government, public works, banking reform, etc. What will be examined here are only those topics about which the Governor wrote most extensively in his letters home and in his official dispatches.

In his own assessment, the single most important administrative reform Thomson introduced was a system of local government beyond the handful of incorporated municipalities. By the late 1830s, English Radicals and Whigs had come to see local, representative forms of government as crucial to improvement and stability in the colonies, as vital 'political structures which would incorporate men from the class of small capitalists and from the petty bourgeoisie.'[64] The Whig ministers had assumed that such a system was essential to the success of the union of the Canadas. In the Union bill that Thomson drafted for Parliament and sent to England in January 1840, he made provisions for district councils as units of local government. But Russell had dropped the relevant clauses for reasons related to parliamentary politics.[65] Thomson received the news about their omission 'with the deepest mortification,' and he responded with a long dispatch making explicit his views on the purposes of local government.[66]

In the first place, Thomson had hoped that the creation of district councils would mean that purely local matters could be relegated to the districts, thus freeing the Assembly from time-consuming discussions of matters upon which members were ill-equipped to make sound judgments. The introduction of a system of local government was in part, then, a Utilitarian bid for greater efficiency, a rational allocation of powers and resources. At the same time, with the introduction of district councils, a great amount of political jobbing over local grants and offices might be removed from the floor of the Assembly, with one result being that the governor's job of managing the Assembly would become far easier. The old abuses of the legislative process might thus be made to vanish. Moreover, a new danger had arisen. With the Act of Union, all money votes were to originate with the government; in the absence of local governments, the executive would 'be called upon to propose every grant of 5£. or 10£. for a road or bridge 600 or 700 miles from the seat of government.' Because the executive was unprepared to assess such proposals, the population would condemn it for its inaction or wrong moves. As things stood, then, the criticism of the executive was likely to become even more widespread. If harmony were to prevail, local governments were needed to deflect criticisms from the Crown and to permit informed decisions on strictly local matters.

A second purpose of district councils was to provide a training ground in representative government and an outlet 'for the gratification of ambition in a narrow circle.' In the absence of local government, wrote Sydenham, 'the people acquire no habits of self-dependence for the attainment of their own local objects.' Instead, they avoided taxation and looked to the centre, making the 'specious and popular' argument that it was 'the *duty* of the Government to find money for all their wants.' While Sydenham readily accepted the idea that the state must support colonial economic development, the central government was to concern itself with matters of 'general utility.' For local improvements, the people must look to themselves. In doing so they might nevertheless advance Crown policies. Local taxes on wild lands might curb speculation and hasten settlement; local improvements funded by local taxation would create jobs for newly arrived emigrants. Bruce Curtis has stressed how this tutelary purpose of local government had profound implications; new forms of local, representative government

were not intended 'to bring government to the people,' or at least not in the common interpretation of freeing and empowering. Rather, representative governmental institutions were to stand between 'the people' and the 'Government,' disciplining the former, habituating them to the limitation of their political power, to the containment of their 'talents' in 'a narrow circle,' situating the source of their potential complaints in their own activity.[67]

For Sydenham, a third and equally important purpose of local government was the provision of means for more effectively carrying out the policies of the governor and his council. Without local councils, 'the Government ... has neither any officer in its own confidence in the different parts of these extended provinces from whom it can seek information, nor is there any recognized body enjoying the public confidence with whom it can communicate, either to determine what are the real wants and wishes of the locality, or through whom it may afford explanation.' Especially in Lower Canada, he maintained, the 'hand of Government' was 'entirely unknown and unfelt.' The governor had no means for communicating with the outlying districts of Lower Canada, except through the rural police, 'called into existence by the rebellion, and for whose permanency there is no security whatever.'[68] Sydenham had made his plans for reforming the judicial and correctional systems on the assumption that the Act of Union would contain his local-government clauses. Without them, he wrote privately, 'all those measures which I have passed in that [Lower] Province for District Courts, Stipendiary Magistrates, Police, Prisons etc. would fall through.'[69]

The centralist aspects of Sydenham's local-government plans became even clearer in his actual proposals for laws and regulations. In the Union bill that Sydenham sent home in January 1840, he gave the governor the power to disallow all local by-laws, dissolve district councils, and appoint the most important local officers. After the district-government clauses were dropped by Russell, Sydenham believed it would prove impossible to persuade the assemblymen to agree to delegate authority (especially over patronage) to the local level. Therefore, he used his despotic powers to push through the Special Council in Lower Canada an ordinance requiring the establishment of district councils on his model. Once the union had come into effect, his ministers could argue that Canada West needed the same institutions.[70] And that is exactly what transpired. The Governor's District Councils bill of 1841 was very nearly defeated, but to all the protests of opposition members, Sydenham's ministers pressed the case for putting the two halves of the province on an equal footing.[71] The bill became law, despite the strong opposition, which

Sydenham described privately as follows: 'one party hated the measure because it was to give power to the people; another because it placed that power under the wholesome control of the Crown; a third because it deprived the members of all their past power of jobbing.'[72]

The District Councils Act, 1841 (4–5 Vict. cap. 10) created councils of locally elected men of property, each of which was overseen by a warden appointed by the governor. Subject to the governor's approval, the warden appointed important district officers, such as the district surveyor responsible for superintending local public works in consultation with the central Board of Works. The governor himself appointed the district treasurers and district clerks from lists of names submitted by the councils. The governor had the sole power to dissolve a council, disallow any by-law within thirty days, and call extraordinary meetings of the councils. Thus, the district councils had their representative elements, but the people's power was indeed 'under the wholesome control of the Crown.'

In his discussion of the District Councils Act, J.E. Aitchison stresses its highly centralist features, attributing them to Tory pressure that forced Sydenham's hand. (The Tories insisted that local democratic powers be firmly checked both as a matter of principle and in order to restrict the district councils' freedom to tax wild lands, in which the Tories and their supporters speculated heavily.) Aitchison underestimates Sydenham's own strong commitment to centralism and to maximizing the governor's means for exercising authority. This commitment becomes all the clearer when other of Sydenham's reforms are examined.[73]

Thomson's single most important administrative reform in the field of economic development was the creation in August 1841 of the provincial Board of Works. One purpose of the board was to coordinate the hundreds of public-works projects either under way or proposed. In the estimation of Thomson, as well as others, political jobbing had been behind past projects rather than any rational plan for improvement. This offended Thomson the Utilitarian. Moreover, the lack of a uniform structure jeopardized the success of his major economic initiative: the completion of the canals. As things currently stood, there was every reason to believe that even the great £1.5-million loan might be squandered for lack of an administrative structure to oversee how it was spent. Thus, on 20 August 1841, Thomson had announced the plan for a new Board of Works:

It has appeared to the Governor General of great importance that

Parliament as well as the Executive should have distinctly brought before them in one general plan, the whole of the different works which
are demanded by the public voice, and tend likely to the increase of
trade and to the advantage of the country. Such works as the Legislature shall decide upon adopted, may thus be conducted upon one
uniform system, having reference as well to each particular work as
the whole, and a great advantage will result as to their execution and
in making provision for the funds necessary for their undertaking.[74]

Co-ordination and a uniform system, then, were key objectives in
creating the board.

The actual structure of the board and its procedures also reflect
Thomson's influence. In order to get the canals built with all possible
speed, the board had a highly centralized structure with authority
concentrated in one man, Hamilton Killaly. Soon after Thomson had
made it known that the imperial government was prepared to offer
the loan, Killaly had written to the governor's office offering his
services as a civil engineer. The applicant explained that he had spent
several years superintending large works for the Irish government
before taking his current position as chief engineer of the Welland
Canal Company.[75] Thomson promptly gave Killaly the job of inspecting the public works of Upper Canada 'with a view to what
needed to be done immediately to prevent deterioration.'[76] The Governor apparently was impressed by Killaly's reports and, after extensive discussions, commissioned Killaly to inspect the entire navigation
system and works of both Canadas and to recommend how to proceed
with the major campaign of improvements. The idea was to establish
a list of priorities and make cost estimates so that actual construction
could proceed at the earliest possible time. The Governor urged Killaly to rush. As the engineer later explained, to have completed detailed surveys and accurate estimates 'would have occupied all the
professional assistance then in the Province, at least three years and
at the moderate rate of five per cent, would have cost £100,000.'
What Killaly did instead, with the Governor's approval, was to make
approximate estimates, 'arrived at from calculations founded on previous experience and on the general cost of such works.'[77] Killaly's
rapidly produced reports gave the Governor something definite to
work with, and they soon became the basis for the appropriations
that saw canal building begin on a major scale under the direction of
Killaly and the Board of Works.

The board itself was structured so as to maximize the power of

Thomson's right-hand man, Hamilton Killaly. Under the Board of Works Act (4–5 Vict. cap. 38), the governor was given the power to appoint five board members who sat at the governor's pleasure. Only two were salaried: the chairman and the secretary. On paper the chairman was given considerable authority; for instance, only the chairman's signature was required for the board to enter into contracts or to buy and sell property. Nevertheless, the act did provide at least the illusion of some checks on the chairman's power. The secretary could serve as internal auditor; money could be spent only if it had been appropriated for the purpose by the legislature; the non-salaried board members might challenge or shape board policies; and the chief engineer had important responsibilities separate from those of the chairman.

As an 1846 inquiry and Doug Owram have shown, however, these checks amounted to very little.[78] The first secretary refused to accept responsibility for the accounts. Legislative appropriations were routinely overrun. The board itself met rarely and then mainly to rubber-stamp decisions already made by the chairman. And for the first few years Killaly served in the dual capacity of chairman and chief engineer. In other words, Killaly ran the show pretty much as he pleased, subject to the Thomson's approval.

After Sydenham's death, subsequent governors took a less active interest in public-works projects, with the result that Killaly had a completely free hand until his methods became a political issue in the mid-1840s. Persistent cost overruns alarmed assemblymen, and land-holders and other interests complained when they were harmed by Killaly's deviations from plans. Killaly was politically vulnerable, and in September 1845 the government appointed a Commission of Inquiry into the affairs of the board. The reports of the commissioners revealed a financial and administrative tangle. They found fault with both the structures and the procedures of the board: 'Armed with immense power, – and acting as though irresponsible in its operation, – it plunged into heavy engagements with contractors ... without any regards to the wholesome checks imposed by legislative enactment, and with no preparation to meet the results which were sure to follow so total a disregard of every rule laid down for its guidance.'[79]

Administrative histories of the board repeat similar charges and imply that the lack of effective checks on the chairman had been an oversight in the 1841 act.[80] This was not the case. Sydenham had wanted to concentrate power at the top. By choosing his chairman astutely, and by having the chairman answer directly to himself,

Sydenham believed he had devised the best means to ensure that the canals got built. Past abuses – jobbery and a lack of co-ordination – could be minimized under the new system, and imperial funds could be used for their intended purpose: to improve transportation and stimulate the economy. Checks and balances within the board itself, and between the legislature and the board, would only mean conflicts and delays. At only one point in the final report of the Commission of Inquiry did the commissioner hint that, despite all the failures of due process, the results might have been worth it: 'taking into consideration the immense advantage to the province of having the Public Works completed at this important crisis of our Commercial history it is questionable in the minds whether it may not more than counterbalance the evil that has resulted from the illegality of proceeding without due authority.'[81] Certainly this is the way Sydenham and his chief engineer would have seen it. The end did justify the means.

Soon after Thomson had won colonial approval for the Union, in the spring of 1840 he turned to reforming postal services. For many years colonists had grumbled about the poor but expensive services provided by the Post Office, a branch of the General Post Office of Great Britain and administered by two independent deputy postmasters general, one at Quebec, one at Halifax. Thomson perceived that certain reforms might be highly popular and eliminate a source of friction between imperial authorities and the colonists. As a Utilitarian he could not resist tackling the inefficiencies and residue of abuses at the Post Office in an effort to bring order, efficiency, and uniformity to the system. Furthermore, improved services might advance his development schemes, strengthen the British connection, and permit yet another opportunity to enhance the power of the governor.

At the time that Thomson became governor, colonial grievances about postal services were not only long-standing but acute. For many years Reform politicians in Upper Canada had criticized the quality of service and the uneven allocation of resources – some densely settled places lacked services entirely, while sparsely populated ones had frequent service. In legislative committees and the press, Upper-Canadian Reformers had also complained vociferously about the high rates, especially when sending letters to Britain from the western part of the province. The public expressed their views equally forcefully. It was estimated that private, illegal operators and the U.S. Mail handled at least one-third, and in many areas a far larger proportion, of the Upper-Canadians' transatlantic correspondence. Newspaper publishers, too, found mailing charges excessive and devised ways to avoid paying the full amounts. To add insult to injury, the deputy post-master at Quebec, Thomas Allen Stayner, made a staggering income that had averaged £3,185 per year in the period 1831–4. A substantial part of the revenue that did not end up in this imperial official's pocket was sent to Britain rather than being spent on improvements in the colonies. Such imperial gouging was occurring at the very time Britain itself was moving towards the highly popular penny post.[82]

Governor Thomson was determined to intervene in Post Office affairs. Breaking with the pattern of past governors, he treated Stay-ner as a subordinate, calling him to account. Thomson demanded Stayner's presence at Montreal for countless meetings at which Stay-ner was required to disclose the affairs of his domain, co-operate in developing new procedures, and even draft a bill for the overhaul of the colonial postal service according to Thomson's own 'outlines or principles.' Stayner's letters to the postmaster general in England bristle with resentment, and he goes to some lengths to emphasize that all his proposals are in fact those of the governor: 'His Excellency directs me ...'; 'His Excellency desires ...'; 'The Governor General is exceedingly anxious to have ...'[83] Perhaps sensing that his innovations might be stonewalled by the postmaster general and lords of the Treasury, Thomson arranged that his own mentor in cabinet, Lord John Russell, would order a full inquiry into the affairs of the colonial postal service. A Commission of Inquiry was thus established in July 1840 'to ascertain whether any and what alterations can be made to promote the efficiency of the Post-office establishment, and to ad-vance the convenience of the public.'[84] Before the commission had reported, however, Thomson had his own program of reforms un-derway.

Thomson's first concern was to reduce the postal charges for col-onists. Action was imperative, not only to make the Post Office more attractive and ward off competitors, but also because, coincidental with Thomson's arrival, Stayner had misinterpreted instructions from England and announced a postage-rate reduction in excess of what had been intended. Rather than attempting to withdraw the popular measure, Thomson persuaded authorities to approve a rate of one shilling and two pence for a letter travelling between any destination in Britain and any in British North America. Naturally this reduced and fixed rate was welcomed by the colonists.[85] Thomson also vig-orously opposed an imperial policy change that would have denied colonists the privilege enjoyed by people at home – the option of having the recipient rather than the sender pay the postage. In making his case to the Colonial Office, and hence to cabinet, the Governor argued that the imperial tie and the policy of colonial emigration would both be strengthened by permitting colonists to charge their letters to those at home. In newly settled districts where cash was in short supply and barter prevailed, 'the inconvenience of prepayment would be excessive': 'But it is peculiarly in such Districts that the most Effects of a facility of Communication is most advantageously felt; It is there that the recent Emigrants are located – Those whose Attachment to the Mother Country is still fresh and whose representations would be most calculated to induce their friends to join them.'[86] The cabinet concurred. Thomson had eliminated another colonial grievance. And, at least in his own mind, he had helped to strengthen the British connection and encourage emigration to the Canadas.

The Governor's second concern in postal matters was to improve at the colonial end the handling of transatlantic mail. In September 1838 imperial authorities had asked for tenders to carry the mail by steam packets running twice a month between Liverpool and Halifax, and between Pictou and Quebec; the Cunard Company, the successful bidder, began its service in July 1840. This gave Thomson the opening he needed to insist upon innovations. Using his unique powers in Lower Canada, he had the Special Council allot funds for improvements to the portion of the intercolonial winter road running between the New Brunswick border and Quebec. And by working through Lieutenant-Governor John Harvey, he succeeded in getting the New Brunswick legislature to pay for road upgrading in that province.[87] Along the same lines, at the Governor's request Stayner recommended that two clerks be put aboard the Cunard steamer plying between Pictou and Quebec to sort mail from Britain so that when the steamer arrived at Quebec there would be 'no material delay.'[88] Thomson tried to strike a bargain with steam-vessel owners on the St Lawrence and the Great Lakes in order to establish frequent and regular mail runs there, but he failed. Undaunted, he proposed that the excess Post Office revenues routinely sent to England be used to construct lake steamers for carrying mail. Where private enterprise failed, imperial objectives might be met through state ownership.[89]

By measures such as these, then, the Post Office would become so attractive that it could 'put a stop to the illicit traffic now carried on throughout the whole length of the Country, upon a scale that weakens the Post Office revenue most materially.'[90] The state monopoly in mail services might thus be made more than merely a legal fiction.

As it turned out, this goal proved more elusive than Sydenham had expected.

Permanent changes in the administrative structure of the Post Office came in the wake of the Report of the Commission of Inquiry into the Post Office. Although he did not live to see the formal presentation of the report penned by his carefully coached commissioners, Sydenham's influence on them is easy to discern. After compiling and assessing an enormous mass of statistical and other information, the report recommended a host of practical and popular reforms: lower rates, more post offices at convenient locations, longer and more regular hours of service to the public, the strict enforcement of mail contracts, the establishment of salary schedules for postmasters, and so forth. Even more obvious is Sydenham's influence on the central assessments and recommendations. The report pointed especially to 'the want of uniformity within the system, and the uncontrolled power of representatives of the postmaster general in the colonies.'[91] The following correctives to these defects were recommended: the dual system (a deputy at Halifax and an independent deputy at Quebec) would be replaced by a single, uniform system under the direction of one deputy postmaster stationed at the seat of the Canadian government. In addition to following the instructions of the lords of the Treasury and the postmaster general in England, the deputy in Canada would 'be required to obey the lawful orders of the Governor General.' This, the report argued, 'would subject the officer to a real, because no longer a distant responsibility.'[92]

Just as Sydenham had urged in other spheres, here too the issue of accountability or responsibility was to be resolved by placing authority in one officer and making him accountable to the governor general. The governor's power would thus be enhanced, in his case at the expense of another (and prior to Sydenham) independent imperial authority. After Sydenham's death, the wings of Deputy Postmaster Stayner were not clipped to the extent Sydenham and the report advised. Nevertheless, in some matters Stayner was formally placed under the authority of the governor general. Steps were also taken to co-ordinate, though not to unite, the postal services provided in the several colonies.[93] In this sphere, too, the Sydenham legacy lived on.

Another matter to which Thomson directed some attention was education. In his instructions from Russell, Thomson had been told that in relation to Lower Canada he was to pay attention to 'the promotion of education among all classes of people.' For details, Rus-

sell referred the Governor to the Durham Report.[94] Lord Durham
had found that schooling was inadequate almost everywhere in the
Canadas, and he had urged that the state provide for a general, non-
sectarian educational system throughout a united province. Durham's
main preoccupation, however, had been the shortcomings of education in Lower Canada. There, according to the report, not only
the Catholic church but the Protestant churches too had jealously
guarded their control of schooling at the expense of the state and at
the risk of promoting sectarianism and allowing ignorance to prevail.
Imperial neglect of education had contributed to the Canadian crisis
by leaving the French without a system of institutions that could have
'assimilated their character and habits, in the easiest way, to those of
the Empire.' The masses had been led astray by a tiny group of
educated men who had gained 'extraordinary influence' over the
'uninstructed population.' The people, in short, had been rendered
'ungovernable.' A state system of public instruction was thus urgently
needed for political reasons: to undercut the influence of the radicals,
restore public tranquility, and remake the masses into governable
subjects.[95]

In his Speech from the Throne opening the new legislature of the
United Province, Sydenham introduced the topic of education, expressing his hope that progress would be made towards the 'establishment of an efficient system.' He observed: 'A due provision for
Education of the People is one of the first duties of the State; and,
in this Province, especially, the want of it is grievously felt.' Sydenham
anticipated controversy. 'If it should be found impossible ... to reconcile conflicting opinions,' he stated, 'I trust that, at least, steps may
be taken by which an advance to a more perfect system may be made.'[96]

On 20 July 1841, an educational bill prepared by Sydenham's sol-
icitor-general east, Charles Day, was introduced in the legislature.[97]
It may well be that Sydenham viewed the Day bill as his ideal, a first
offer that he expected would be cut down and revised. Certainly the
provisions of the bill bear the Sydenham imprint. A single uniform
system was to provide for education throughout the United Province.
Management was to be highly centralized in the person of the chief
superintendent of education, an individual appointed by the governor
and who held office at the governor's pleasure. Authority would flow
down from the top through layers of administration. The appointive,
rather than the elective, principle was to prevail. In the towns and
cities, for instance, the governor was to appoint the members of the
boards of examiners responsible for the course of study, textbooks,

rules and regulations, and licensing of teachers. In rural districts the chief superintendent, the governor's appointee, had the authority to appoint district boards of examiners.

As Sydenham had anticipated, opposition to the Day bill forced amendments. In committee, Reformers, with their localist traditions and suspicions of imperial intervention, insisted that the centralist and appointive features of the bill be watered down. The Common School Act of 1841 (4–5 Vict. cap. 18) nevertheless retained some principles of the original Day bill. A single superintendent of education for the United Province, appointed by the governor, was to administer the school system and enjoy sweeping powers. Although district boards of examiners were eliminated, important financial and other powers were invested in the district councils, which acted as boards of education. (It will be recalled that the appointive principle was prominent at the district council level.) Management of local schools, however, rested with elected township commissioners of common schools. As Sydenham lay dying, he composed a final address that referred to the Education Act as 'a measure of great value,' and expressed his 'peculiar satisfaction in reporting to the Queen the assent I have been enabled to give.'

Historians of education since John George Hodgins have roundly condemned the 1841 act, labelling it unworkable. In part the difficulties derived from those who bungled its implementation. But the act itself had serious shortcomings. As Bruce Curtis explains: 'The ambiguities produced by the Act can be traced to the political situation out of which it emerged. The centralized organization proposed in the draft bill was subverted by Reformers in committee, but no articulated plan for local autonomy took its place.'[98] Sydenham's own preference, the Day bill, at least had the virtue of coherence. It is unlikely, however, that any governor or superintendent of education could have succeeded in imposing uniformity on the two halves of the United Province or on its two cultures. For all the act's weaknesses, it has been widely acknowledged as marking a major step towards what Susan Houston and Alison Prentice refer to as 'a government school system.' Curtis calls it 'a serious but confused attempt to discipline the colonial market through the construction of public administrative structures.'[99]

One final instance of Sydenham's interest in administrative reform merits consideration – his plans for banking and currency reforms. Sydenham hoped to introduce in the Canadas what he called a Government Bank of Issue with sole authority for issuing all notes in the province. It would do so only to the extent that there was bullion or coin to back up the paper. 'As an advocate of the Currency School of Banking,' explains Peter Baskerville, Sydenham 'believed that guaranteed convertibility of notes into coin was the *sine qua non* of an effective financial system.'[100] Some politicians had argued that the colony's independent banks had tended to over-issue paper, with adverse implications for a sound economy. Sydenham thought that his reforms would strengthen banking and finances in the colony; furthermore, the United Province would gain an additional, and potentially lucrative, source of revenue. Such revenues might be used for public works or the liquidation of the provincial debt.[101]

Sydenham knew that substantial obstacles lay in the way of legislative approval for his banking reforms. Certain business interests, including local banks, would object. And because the matter involved what he called 'private and *class* interests,'[102] Sydenham could not be sure of his majority in the Assembly. As it turned out, he failed to win the Assembly's approval. Nevertheless, his banking plans are significant because they reveal once again Sydenham's commitment to expanding the role of the state, his faith in centralization and uniformity (a sole bank of issue), and his determination to develop a coherent cluster of policies (banking reforms meant financial stability and revenues for public works). Moreover, these plans represent the clearest example of Sydenham's perception of the colonies as a laboratory for Utilitarian experimentation. As governor, he believed he had the chance to test a policy he had long advocated: 'There never was such an opportunity for the trial.' A successful experiment would further the cause of fellow members of the Currency School back home. As Sydenham saw it, the measure would 'not only be good for this country, but will set an example to England, by which she may profit in a year or two when the Bank Charter is to be reviewed.' In fact, he explained to Russell that he himself planned 'to take advantage' of the experiment upon his return to England.[103] But colonial bankers and his horse rode roughshod over his plans.

In the dog days of 1841, as his administration was drawing to a close, Sydenham reflected upon his brilliant accomplishments and expressed his utter confidence that his Canadian contribution would endure: 'Nothing ... can now prevent or mar the most complete success and Canada must henceforth go on well, except [if] it is most terribly managed.' An Upper-Canadian Tory politician had an altogether different sense of the Governor's measures; John Macaulay referred to the Sydenham system as 'a house of cards' dependent on the temporary presence of 'the great magician ... working upon the hopes of one man, the fears of another, the ambition of some, & the cupidity of others.'[104] Historians have tended to accept the latter view, stressing the fragility of Sydenham's arrangements. In colonial politics, the Sydenham coalition collapsed upon his death in September 1841. His successors at Government House could not resist the rise of political parties, and 'mismanagement' alone does not account for their failure to make the Sydenham system work. Very soon, too, responsible government was an established fact in the triple sense of party rule, cabinet government, and colonial autonomy. Furthermore, the uniformity Sydenham had sought to impose on the Canadas by way of constitutional and administrative reforms quickly gave way to the forces of duality (French versus English; Lower versus Upper Canada) and to the 'emergence of the federal concept.'

Certainly the Province of Canada in 1849 did not conform with Sydenham's ideal, but his legacy was more enduring than the conventional wisdom would have it. In terms of politics and the constitution, Sydenham had sought to concentrate power with the Crown, with the governor and his advisers. Developments of the late 1840s would see a significant transfer of authority within the executive from the governor to the council or 'cabinet.' Nevertheless, the Canadian Reformers' strategy of the 1830s that aimed at transferring power to the Assembly had been subverted. Power remained with the executive, at the top, where Sydenham had wanted it. The innovations of Sydenham's administration – British-style budgeting and departmental management by executive councillors – made that executive power far more potent. In terms of the economy, Sydenham had proposed a three-pronged development strategy that entailed state-aided transportation improvements, large-scale immigration, and efficient land policies. Future colonial leaders would take up this essential strategy, even as new technologies (railways), changing policies (Britain's turn to free trade), and rising interests (manufacturers' demands for protection) necessitated adaptation. In terms of administration, where Sydenham's Utilitarianism ran freest, he laid important foundations in a host of areas, including local government, public works, the postal service, and education. The state had expanded into new areas, and more centralized structures had been introduced to make state power more effective. Naturally, in the years ahead further initiatives and endless tinkering would enhance the reach and grasp of the state apparatus. But Sydenham's reforms amounted to a leap in that direction.

In the course of examining the Sydenham reforms, this paper has attempted to demonstrate that one man, armed with ideas, could indeed have a profound effect on the process of state formation. To be sure, his initiatives were restricted in some spheres, such as in banking, where opposing interests prevailed. And he drew on the knowledge, experience, and political influence of men in the Canadas. Nevertheless, as the governor of colonies recently racked by insurrection, Sydenham was in a position to do a great deal. And as a leading English Utilitarian, he had a potent set of ideas for enhancing state power. Sydenham shouted the last hurrah of the old, highly interventionist governors, giving to the executive branch more effective powers than his predecessors had known. Inavertently, he prepared the way for a new era when the colonial executive itself would attempt to call the shots.

## NOTES

1 Oliver MacDonagh, 'The Nineteenth-Century Revolution in Government: A Reappraisal,' *Historical Journal* 1 (1958), 52–67; Oliver MacDonagh, *A Pattern of Government Growth, 1800–1860: The Passenger Acts and Their Enforcement* (London: MacGibbon and Kee 1961)

2 Jennifer Hart, 'Nineteenth-Century Social Reform: A Tory Interpretation of History,' *Past and Present* 31 (1965), 30–61. For an extensive bibliography and a survey of the literature, see Roy MacLeod, ed., *Government and Expertise: Specialists, Administrators and Professionals, 1860–1919* (Cambridge: Cambridge University Press 1988).

3 Gillian Sutherland, *Studies in the Growth of Nineteenth-Century Government* (London: Routledge and Kegan Paul 1972). See also Paul Richards, 'State Formation and Class Struggle, 1832–48,' in Philip Corrigan, ed., *Capitalism, State Formation and Marxist Theory: Historical Investigations* (London: Quartet 1980), and Oliver MacDonagh, *Early Victorian Government, 1830–1870* (London: Weidenfeld and Nicolson 1977).

4 The pre-eminent study remains J.E. Hodgetts, *Pioneer Public Service: An Administrative History of the United Canadas, 1841–1867* (Toronto: University of Toronto Press 1955).

5 The relationship between industrial capitalism and the revolution in government is stressed in Philip Corrigan and Derek Sayer, *The Great*

Arch: *English State Formation as Cultural Revolution* (Oxford: Blackwell 1985), ch. 6. Explorations in transatlantic intellectual history include Robert Kelley, *The Transatlantic Persuasion: The Liberal-Democratic Mind in the Age of Gladstone* (New York: Knopf 1969); David A. Wilson, *Paine and Cobbett: The Transatlantic Connection* (Kingston and Montreal: McGill-Queen's University Press 1988). On the wider imperial scene, see John Eddy, 'The Technique of Government: Governing Mid-Victorian Australia,' in MacLeod, ed., *Government and Expertise*, 166–84; Eric Stokes, *The English Utilitarians and India* (Oxford: Clarendon 1959); R.V. Jackson, *Jeremy Bentham and the New South Wales Penal Settlement* (Adelaide: Australian Historical Association 1986).

6 For a superb example of the biographical approach to issues of imperial administration, see D.M. Schreuder, 'Ireland and the Expertise of Imperial Administration: Hercules Robinson, the "Irish Fairs and Markets Commission" (1853), and the Making of a Victorian Proconsul,' in MacLeod, ed., *Government and Expertise*, 145–81.

7 Key works include Mary Peter Mack, ed., *A Bentham Reader* (New York: Pegasus 1969); H.L.A. Hart, *Essays on Bentham: Studies in Jurisprudence and Political Theory* (Oxford: Oxford University Press 1982); S.E. Finer, *The Life and Times of Sir Edwin Chadwick* (New York: Barnes and Noble 1952), ch. 2; Elie Halévy, *The Growth of Philosophic Radicalism* (London: Faber and Faber 1950); L.J. Hume, *Bentham and Bureaucracy* (Cambridge: Cambridge University Press 1981).

8 Frank H. Underhill, 'Bentham and Benthamism,' *Queen's Quarterly* (1932), 659. The relationship between Utilitarianism and *laissez-faire* is discussed in Arthur John Taylor, *Laissez-Faire and State Interventionism in Nineteenth-Century Britain* (London: Macmillan 1972); Henry Walter Parris, *Constitutional Bureaucracy: The Development of British Central Administration since the Eighteenth Century* (London: Allen and Unwin 1969).

9 On the class position of the Utilitarians, see Richards, 'State Formation and Class Struggle,' 57–9.

10 S.E. Finer, 'The Transmission of Benthamite Ideas, 1820–50,' in Sutherland, *Studies*, 11–32

11 George Poulett Scrope, *Memoir of the Life of the Right Honourable Charles, Lord Sydenham*, G.C.B., 2nd ed. (London: John Murray 1844); Adam Shortt, *Lord Sydenham* (Toronto: Morang 1908); Phillip Buckner, 'Thomson, Charles Edward Poulett, 1st Baron Sydenham,' *Dictionary of Canadian Biography*, vol. 7 (Toronto: University of Toronto Press 1988), 925–34; Jacques Monet, SJ, 'The Personal and Living Bond, 1839–1849,' in W.L. Morton, ed., *The Shield of Achilles: Aspects of Canada in the Victorian Age* (Toronto: McClelland and Stewart 1968), 6–93

12 Scrope, *Memoir*, 14

13 Ibid., 16

14 E.T. Littleton (Lord Hatherton), cited in Lucy Brown, *The Board of Trade and the Free-Trade Movement, 1830–4* (Oxford: Clarendon 1958), 17

15 Brown, *Board of Trade,* 15–22; Roger W. Prouty, *The Transformation of the Board of Trade, 1830–1855: A Study of Administrative Reorganization in the Heyday of Laissez-Faire* (London: Heineman *c.* 1957); S.E. Finer, 'Transmission of Benthamite Ideas,' 11–32

16 Public Records Office, Board of Trade Records, Thomas Lack to the Treasury, 31 Mar. 1832, cited in Brown, *Board of Trade,* 76

17 Brown, *Board of Trade,* 80; see also M.J. Cullen, *The Statistical Movement in Early Victorian Britain: The Foundations of Empirical Social Research* (Hassocks, Eng.: Harvester 1975).

18 Thomson's journal entry, 1 Sept. 1839, cited in Scrope, *Memoir,* 102

19 Ibid., 101–2

20 Ibid.

21 Ibid., 102–4

22 National Library of Scotland, Ellice Papers, F.85, Ellice to S. Gerrard, 4 July 1838, cited in Phillip A. Buckner, *The Transition to Responsible Government: British Policy in British North America 1815–1850* (Westport, Conn.: Greenwood 1985), 51; Thomson to ?, 8 Dec. 1839, cited in Scrope, *Memoir,* 149; *Monthly Review* (Toronto), 1 Jan. 1841

23 Buckner, *Transition,* 56

24 Thomson to ?, 20 Nov. and 8 Dec. 1839, cited in Scrope, *Memoir,* 148

25 Durham's views on responsible government are discussed in Janet Ajzenstat, *The Political Thought of Lord Durham* (Kingston and Montreal: McGill-Queen's University Press 1988), 43–72.

26 Russell's key dispatches are reprinted in W.P.M. Kennedy, *Statutes, Treaties and Documents of the Canadian Constitution, 1713–1929* (Toronto: Macmillan 1930); on Thomson and constitutional matters, see also Buckner, *Transition,* 259–60; William G. Ormsby, *The Emergence of the Federal Concept* (Toronto: University of Toronto Press *c.* 1969); J.M.S. Careless, *The Union of the Canadas: The Growth of Canadian Institutions, 1841–1857* (Toronto: McClelland and Stewart 1967), 38.

27 Thomson to Lord Melborne, 1 Dec. 1839, cited in Lloyd C. Sanders, ed., *Lord Melbourne's Papers* (London: Longmans Green 1889), 446

28 Ajzenstat, *Political Thought,* 59

29 Sydenham to Russell, 7 June 1841, cited in Paul Knaplund, ed., *Letters from Lord Sydenham Governor General of Canada, 1839–1841 to Lord John Russell* (London: Allen and Unwin 1931), 146–7

30 *Monthly Review,* 1 Jan. 1841

31 Thomson to ?, 18 Sept. 1840, cited in Scrope, *Memoir,* 190; I.M. Abella, 'The "Sydenham Election" of 1841,' *Canadian Historical Review* 47 (1966), 36–43. See also, Carol Wilton-Siegel, 'Transformation of Upper Canadian Politics in the 1840s' (PH D diss., University of Toronto 1984).

32 Thomson to Russell, 7 June 1841, in Knaplund, ed., *Letters*, 147; T.W.C. Murdoch, 'Administration of Lord Sydenham in Canada,' in Scrope, *Memoir*, 288

33 Lionel Robbins, *The Theory of Economic Policy in English Classical Political Economy* (London: Macmillan 1961), 40–1, cited in Hart, 'Nineteenth Century Social Reform,' 47

34 Thomson to Russell, 13 Jan. 1840, in Knaplund, ed., *Letters*, 40

35 Sydenham to Russell, 7 Sept. 1840, in Knaplund, ed., *Letters*, 93

36 National Archives of Canada (NA), MG24, A2, Ellice Family Papers, 5525-8, Sydenham to Ellice, 9 May 1841

37 'Reply to the Speech from the Throne,' in Elizabeth Nish, ed., *Debates of the Legislative Assembly of United Canada*, 15 June 1841 (Montreal: Centre d'Etude du Québec 1970) 1:14–16; NA, RG5, Records of the Civil and Provincial Secretaries, B3, Petitions and Addresses, vols 12–13, see for example, 'Address of the Township of Mosa, London District to the Governor, 1840,' 142–3.

38 NA, MG24, A2, Ellice Family Papers, 4706, Lord Howick to Ellice, 13 Aug. 1839

39 Russell dispatch to Thomson, 7 Sept. 1839, *British Parliamentary Papers*, Colonies/Canada (*BPP* Col./Can.) (Shannon: Irish University Press 1968–72), vol. 13, 10

40 Thomson to Russell, 5 Nov. 1839, in Knaplund, ed., *Letters*, 36–7

41 Sydenham to Russell, 8 Aug. 1841, in ibid., 163

42 Michael J. Piva, 'Financing the Union: The Upper Canadian Debt and Financial Administration in the Canadas, 1837–1845,' *Journal of Canadian Studies* (forthcoming)

43 Sydenham dispatch to Russell, *BPP* Col./Can., vol. 16, 38–44

44 Robert L. Fraser, 'Like Eden in Her Summer Dress: Gentry, Economy, and Society: Upper Canada, 1812–1840' (PH D diss., University of Toronto 1979)

45 Donald Creighton, *The Empire of the St. Lawrence* (Toronto: Macmillan 1956); Gerald J.J. Tulchinsky, *The River Barons: Montreal Businessmen and the Growth of Industry and Transportation, 1837–53* (Toronto: University of Toronto Press 1977)

46 'Speech from the Throne,' in Nish, ed., *Debates*, 15 June 1841, 1:15

47 Sydenham dispatch to Russell, 26 Jan. 1841, in *BPP* Col. Can., vol. 15, 73

48 Thomson to ? cited in Scrope, *Memoir*, 308

49 Sydenham dispatch to Russell, 1 Oct. 1840, in *BPP* Col./Can., vol. 15, 36

50 Helen I. Cowan, *British Emigration to British North America: The First Hundred Years* (Toronto: University of Toronto Press 1961)

51 Ibid., 183; Sydenham dispatch to Russell, 1 Oct. 1840, *BPP* Col./Can., vol. 15, 35

52 'First Report from the Select Committee on Emigration, Scotland'
   (1841), Evidence of Dr Thomas Rolph, in *BPP* Emigration Series, vol. 3,
   132–6; Thomson to Russell, 3 Dec. 1840, enclosing Rolph's correspondence with Sydenham and Murdoch in *BPP* Col./Can., vol. 15,
   50–4; Russell dispatch to Sydenham, 9 Mar. 1841, in ibid., 54. See also
   Cowan, *British Emigration*, 123–5.

53 Sydenham to ?, 3 Nov. 1840, cited in Scrope, *Memoir*, 200

54 J.K. Johnson, 'Land Policy of the Upper Canadian Elite Reconsidered:
   The Canada Emigration Association, 1840–1841,' in David Keane and
   Colin Read, eds, *Old Ontario: Essays in Honour of J.M.S., Careless* (To-
   ronto: Dundurn 1990); Cowan, *British Emigration*, 138

55 Sydenham to ?, *c.* Dec. 1840, cited in Scrope, *Memoir*, 202

56 Sydenham dispatch to Russell (and enclosures), 14 Jan. 1841, in *BPP*
   Col./Can., vol. 15, 61–3. For subsequent developments, see Sir Charles
   Bagot dispatch to Stanley, 11 Apr. 1841, in *BPP* Col./Can., vol. 16, 396.

57 Hodgetts, *Pioneer Public Service*, ch. 8

58 Michael J. Piva, 'Continuity and Crisis: Francis Hincks and Canadian
   Economic Policy,' *Canadian Historical Review* 66 (1985), 185–211

59 Lord Durham, *Report on the Affairs of British North America*, cited by
   H.G.J. Aitken, 'Defensive Expansionism: The State and Economic
   Growth in Canada,' in W.T. Easterbrook and M.H. Watkins, eds, *Ap-
   proaches to Canadian Economic History: A Selection of Essays* (Toronto:
   McClelland and Stewart 1967), 183

60 Thomson to his brother, 8 Aug. 1841, cited in Scrope, *Memoir*, 43

61 Barbara C. Murison, ' "Enlightened Government": Sir George Arthur
   and the Upper Canadian Administration,' *Journal of Imperial and Com-
   monwealth History* 8 (1980), 161–80; Phillip Buckner, 'Arthur, Sir
   George,' *Dictionary of Canadian Biography*, vol. 8 (Toronto: University
   of Toronto Press 1985), 26–31

62 Carol Wilton-Siegel, 'Administration Reform: A Conservative Alternative to Responsible Government,' *Ontario History* 78 (1986), 105–5

63 Piva, 'Financing the Union'

64 Bruce Curtis, 'Representation and State Formation in the Canadas,
   1790–1850,' *Studies in Political Economy* 8 (1989), 70

65 Buckner, *Transition*, 56–7

66 Thomson dispatch to Russell, 16 Sept. 1940, in *BPP* Col./Can., vol. 14,
   496–9

67 Curtis, 'Representation and State Formation,' 72–3

68 Sydenham dispatch to Russell, 16 Sept. 1840, in *BPP* Col./Can., vol. 14,
   497

69 Sydenham to Russell, 16 Sept. 1840, in Knaplund, ed., *Letters*, 88

70 Ibid.

71 James Herneston Aitchison, 'The Development of Local Government

in Upper Canada, 1783–1850' (PH D diss., University of Toronto 1953), 150–2

72 Sydenham to his brother, 8 Aug. 1841, cited in Scrope, *Memoir*, 242

73 Aitchison, 'Development of Local Government,' 149. For a Tory's fears of the increased taxation and 'draughts of exhilarating democratic gas,' see John Macaulay to Sir George Arthur, 9 Aug. 1841, in C.R. Sanderson, ed., *The Arthur Papers*, vol. 3 (Toronto: University of Toronto Press 1959), 44.

74 'Message from Governor Sydenham to the Legislative Assembly of the Province of Canada,' 20 Aug. 1841, BPP Col./Can., vol. 16, 230

75 NA, RG5, Records of the Civil and Provincial Secretaries, 5A1, Upper Canada Sundries, vol. 34, Hamilton H. Killaly to T.W.C. Murdoch, 5 Dec. 1839

76 NA, RG7, G17A, Governor General's Office Letterbooks, vol. 1, Thomson to Arthur, 20 May 1840

77 NA, RG11, Records of the Department of Public Works, 1D1, Board of Works, vol. 141, Commission of Enquiry on the Management of the Board of Works, Evidence of H.H. Killaly

78 NA, RG11, 'First Report of the Commission of Enquiry into the Board of Works,' 1D1, vol. 141, 28 Mar. 1846; Doug Owram, ' "Management by Enthusiasm": The First Board of Works of the Province of Canada, 1841–1846,' *Ontario History* 70 (1978), 171–88

79 NA, RG11, 'First Report,' 9

80 Owram, ' "Management by Enthusiasm" '; Hodgetts, *Pioneer Public Service*, 190–1

81 NA, RG11, 'Final Report of the Commission of Enquiry into the Management of the Board of Works,' 1D1, vol. 141, 1 Sept. 1846

82 William Smith, *The History of the Post Office in British North America, 1639–1870* (Cambridge: Cambridge University Press 1920), 122–57; 'Report of the Commission of Inquiry into the State of the Canadian Post Office,' in BPP Col./Can., vol. 16, 953–5

83 NA, MG40 L, U.K. General Post Office, Canadian Records, vol. 9, see Thomson–T.A. Stayner correspondence, Apr.–July 1840.

84 T.W.C. Murdoch (Chief Secretary) to the Commissioners, 6 Oct. 1840, cited in 'Report ... into the ... Post Office,' 907

85 Smith, *History of the Post Office*, 227; NA, MG40 L, vol. 10, Treasury Minute, 6, July 1840

86 NA, MG40 L, vol. 10, Sydenham to Lt-Col. Maberly (Deputy Post Master General), 11 Dec. 1840

87 Ibid., Sydenham to Sir John Harvey (Lt-Gov. of New Brunswick), Feb. 1841; Stayner to Maberly, 6 Mar. 1841

88 Ibid., vol. 9, Stayner to Maberly, 17 June 1840

89 Ibid., Stayner [citing Thomson] to Maberly, 17 June 1840

90  Ibid., Stayner to Maberly, 9 Oct. 1840
91  'Report ... into the ... Post Office,' 947
92  Ibid., 951
93  Smith, *History of the Post Office*, 40
94  Russell dispatch to Thomson, 7 Sept. 1839, *BPP* Col./Can., vol. 13, 10
95  Gerald M. Craig, ed., *Lord Durham's Report* (Toronto: McClelland and Stewart 1963), 28–34, 71–2, 101
96  'Speech from the Throne,' in Nish, ed., *Debates*, 15 June 1841, 1:16
97  'Original Common School Bill of 1841,' cited in J. George Hodgins, *Documentary History of Education in Upper Canada* 28 vols (Toronto: Department of Education 1897), 4:41–3
98  Bruce Curtis, *Building the Educational State: Canada West, 1836–71* (London, Ont.: Althouse 1988)
99  Susan E. Houston and Alison Prentice, *Schooling and Scholars in Nineteenth-Century Ontario* (Toronto: University of Toronto Press 1988), ch. 4; Curtis, *Building the Educational State*
100  Peter Baskerville, ed., *The Bank of Upper Canada: A Collection of Documents* (Toronto: Champlain Society 1987), lxxxix
101  'Memorandum on the Paper Currency Suggested for Canada, by Lord Sydenham,' in Scrope, *Memoir*, App. 2, 314–19
102  Sydenham to ?, 11 July 1841, cited in Scrope, *Memoir*, 236
103  Sydenham to Russell, 1 July 1841, in Knaplund, ed., *Letters*, 150
104  John Macaulay to Sir George Arthur, 9 Aug. 1841, in Sanderson, ed., *Arthur Papers*, 3, 442

# 4

# Class Culture and Administration: Educational Inspection in Canada West

BRUCE CURTIS

Much of the historiography of the central-Canadian state in the 1830s and 1840s has been preoccupied with the coming of 'responsible government,' with the conditions leading to colonial parliamentary autonomy and cabinet authority. Less attention has been directed to the coincident development, beyond the walls of the legislature, of new routines and rituals of rule and new instruments of governance. Responsible government and self-government are often treated as if they were matters of the power of the colonial parliament relative to the imperial state. The translation of parliamentary policy into effective practices had been largely ignored, and shifts in the composition and relative weight of sections of the colonial élite have not attracted much interest.[1]

Many contributors have been content to ignore the questions of *who actually ruled* in the colony and *how* the internal organization of rule was altered in the decade of the 1840s. The unseating of the colonial oligarchy in the parliament of the United Province and the organization of local government do attract passing attention in the standard accounts. But the class position of the rising ruling groups has been little studied, and the passing of local government acts has often been seen simplistically as an 'improvement.' The scope of research in political power has been restricted primarily to directly legislative questions, and the historical problematic has become one of parliamentary politics. Yet political governance is not simply a matter of the relative powers of colonial and imperial parliaments. To be effective, a regime must engage those who are ruled in particular kinds of routines and rituals, activities and beliefs.

Participants in the literature have shown far less awareness of the import of changing forms of political governance than did contemporary Canadian and English writers, largely because they have tended to ignore rule as a class, gender, and ethnic question and, especially, as a practical question.[2] Colonial and imperial politicians themselves were not entirely preoccupied by constitutional issues. Many of those active in Canadian politics were as much concerned with ways of making a particular kind of rule real and effective as they were with the question of 'responsibility.' Indeed, in its administrative sense, 'responsibility' tended to refer to a system of regularized and at least tendentially bureaucratic authority, in which central policy initiatives would in fact be executed effectively in all localities. Responsible government was as much a particular kind of social administration as it was cabinet government.[3]

This appears clearly in contemporary political analysis. Charles Buller, for instance, argued that the main problem with irresponsible government was its inefficiency and the incompetence of administrative cadres. Measures were judged by the affiliation of their sponsors, and obviously incompetent people were kept in office. On the whole, Buller remarked, 'the public officers, to whom the civil administration of affairs in the Canadas has been usually entrusted, have been second-rate lawyers ...'; and he repeated the observation that a common reason for revolution was the absence of local governmental institutions to provide mobility channels for the middle class and to absorb political energies at the local level.[4] These sentiments were echoed by many other writers, from J.S. Mill to Charles Poulett Thomson: indeed, in England by the end of the 1830s they were commonplaces derived from the struggles for the Reform Act in which many of those shaping imperial policy in the Canadas had been active.

## The 'Revolution' in Government

The prevailing preoccupation with parliamentary responsibility in the Canadian literature flies in the face of a well-established English debate over the 'nineteenth-century revolution in government.'[5] English writers have long been concerned to notice that the period between about 1830 and 1870 especially witnessed a remarkable transformation in the scope and nature of governmental activity. New, centralized agencies came to regulate factories, emigrant ships, mines, prisons, schools, the public health, and other aspects of economic and social policy. Bureaucratized procedures – the regular collection of standardized knowledge, formal record keeping, rationalized financial management, the development of 'expertise,' etc. – gained an increasingly solid hold over newly constituted public activities. This 'revolution' in the organization and operation of the state system went forward through the agency of a generation of energetic and largely middle-class (i.e., bourgeois) intellectuals. Strategically located intellectuals and state servants agitated for and organized the placement of new state agencies and the elaboration of new kinds of state activity.

The transformation of the English state took place in a context shaped by the generalization of capitalist relations of production and abstract forms of property. These relations, as Corrigan and Sayer so forcefully remind us, are inseparable from definite forms of character, comportment, and consciousness. The generalization of new forms of political activity involved the generalization of new forms of intellectual and moral regulation.[6]

Such a view makes it difficult to treat the 'coming of responsible government' in the Canadas simply in terms of political 'progress.' True, during the decade of the 1840s the power of representative government increased. But representation collapsed the political will of society into the will of a very small number of propertied 'British' men and their allies. Non-representative forms of governance were in decline – those on which the dominance of the 'Family Compact' were based, as well as the forms of non-representative democracy that existed in the interstices of the Family Compact system of governance.

Representative government was (and remains) a process of domination and subordination, and we must be careful not to identify representation with the rule of 'the people.' Rather, representation was a way – and was conceived by political liberals quite explicitly as a way – of limiting and containing 'the people.' New forms of 'public' administration created new mechanisms and institutional bases for respectable men of property to conduct a process of rule, to form and to inform 'the people.' Changes in the selection mechanisms for those men of property who were to rule did entail a limited 'democratization' of governance. Men formerly excluded were admitted to the exercise of governmental office, at the same time as governmental activity was reorganized and a major centralization of authority was undertaken. These processes, or their extension beyond certain limits, generated opposition and struggle.[7] But rule remained the rule of one class, one gender, and, largely, one ethnic group.

## The State as a Process of Rule

How can we better apprehend the political development of the Canadas? In his instructive 'Notes on the Difficulty of Studying the State,' Philip Abrams presents a perceptive critique of much work on the state. Distinguishing between the state system – a palpable set of institutions, prisons, bodies of armed men, and so on – and the state project as the legitimation of the illegitimate, Abrams recalls Marx's insistence that 'the' state is overwhelmingly an ideological phenomenon. The state, Abrams argues, is better understood as a collective misrepresentation, as a process of what he calls 'politically organized subjection.' Abrams urges our attention upon the practical organization and maintenance of political subjection – of political governance as *process*. This process contains regulatory and disciplinary elements whose efficacy resides in their influence upon consciousness and self-identity.[8]

Such a view makes accessible to analysis the political character of culture, modes of knowing, and forms of experience. It has the potential to open to scrutiny some of the ramifications of changing structures of rule that are commonly left opaque in political history and sociology. It allows one to draw connections between such phenomena as the growing cultural popularity of quantitative calculation and the growth of nineteenth-century bureaucratic governmental structures. At the same time, as Valverde and Weir point out, such an approach challenges us not to assimilate all forms of regulation to state forms.[9]

The resonances of the approach suggested by Abrams are loud in a variety of works of social theory. From Max Weber, for instance, we hear that, 'Like the political institutions historically preceding it, the state is a relation of men dominating men, a relation supported by means of legitimate (i.e. considered to be legitimate) violence. If the state is to exist, the dominated must obey the authority claimed by the powers that be. When and why do men obey? Upon what inner justifications and upon what external means does this domination rest?'[10] In the passage cited, Weber poses the question of rule as a twofold process, involving both administrative means of governance backed ultimately by physical violence, and the elaboration of justifications amongst the governed that lend legitimacy to these. Elsewhere, Weber and writers who follow him also stress the economic basis of rule organized through taxation.[11]

Again, Antonio Gramsci argues that an understanding of the processes of governance is furthered by an analysis of 'two major super-structural "levels": the one that can be called "civil society," that is the ensemble of organisms commonly called "private," and that of "political society" or "the State." These two levels correspond on the one hand to the function of "hegemony" which the dominant group exercises throughout society and on the other hand to that of "direct domination" or command exercised through the State and "juridical government." The functions in question are precisely organisational and connective.' Gramsci continues this passage, which stresses the importance of 'intellectuals' in processes of rule, with a further elaboration of the distinction between 'social hegemony and political government.'

> These comprise:
> 1. The 'spontaneous' [i.e., organized] consent given by the great masses of the population to the general direction imposed on social life by the dominant fundamental group; this consent is 'historically' caused by the prestige (and consequent confidence) which the dominant group enjoys because of its position and function in the world of production.
> 2. The apparatus of state coercive power which 'legally' enforces discipline on those groups who do not 'consent' either actively or passively. This apparatus is, however, constituted for the whole of society in anticipation of moments of crisis of command and direction when spontaneous consent has failed.[12]

Gramsci is himself uneasy about the distinction of state and civil society as 'levels,' given efforts by state agencies to regulate 'private' life. But that intellectuals bearing an 'organic' connection to a dominant class work to give direction to culture in the broadest sense in support of class domination is a fundamental insight.[13]

A more satisfactory approach to the Canadian state than the earlier focus on cabinet responsibility should involve an analysis of the formation of at least the three dimensions of rule indicated above: finance and taxation, administrative means backed (ultimately) by violence, and the organization of the consent of the governed by ideological means. Did the nature of the administrative means change in the Canadas in the 1840s? Did the personnel implicated in the engineering of consent change? Were new ideological initiatives undertaken aimed at legitimating the (changed) conditions of rule? What was the financial basis of rule? These are questions one might fruitfully attempt to answer.

## The Imperial Relation

The organization of administration and the construction of 'consensus' were concerns of state servants in both England and the colonies.

In *How Is Ireland to Be Governed?* (1834; 1836) G. Poulett Scrope stressed that successful rule over people in that colony demanded 'removing their just causes of complaint.' Poulett Scrope insisted upon the organization of a Board of Works to set the poor to work. This would be cheap, would be attended by moral improvement, and would eventually lead to the creation of a class of Irish yeomen. Further coercion was regarded as sure to be unsuccessful.[14]

Poulett Scrope did not estimate his brother Charles Poulett Thomson's (Lord Sydenham's) career in terms of his contribution to the coming or impeding of cabinet government in the Canadas. Poulett Thomson accomplished five things in the Canadas, according to Poulett Scrope: 'the establishment of a board of works with ample powers; the admission of aliens; a new system of county courts; the regulation of the public lands ... and lastly, this District Council Bill.'[15]

This was not one brother simply attributing to the other a love for his own political panaceas. Poulett Scrope was repeating a dominant English view of what needed to be done to make the Canadas governable. These measures, as Ian Radforth details at length in this volume, involved the extension of governmental activity through the formation of new agencies and practices. They were measures for economic development, for the smooth administration of justice, and, centrally as well, for the moral regulation of the population. Both Charles Buller and John Stuart Mill, for instance, repeatedly emphasized that local electoral government was a form of moral training – a great 'normal school' for the people, to use Mill's phrase.

Poulett Thomson himself was a man eminently experienced in the substitution of 'rational' bureaucratic procedure for the patterns of governance known in England as 'Old Corruption.' Working already in the timber trade in St Petersburg at the age of sixteen, Thomson joined the Political Economy Club in London in the 1820s and studied with J.R. McCulloch.[16] His close associates were James Mill, Joseph Hume, and Henry Warburton. His election to the seat for Dover in 1826 was aided by Jeremy Bentham, who personally conducted the canvass. Thomson took the posts of treasurer of the navy and vice-president of the Board of Trade in 1830. In the following year he revived the office of inspector general of imports and exports, and attempted to transform the Board of Trade into the main statistical branch of the English state. He introduced the practice of double-entry accounting for the keeping of public accounts in 1831 and altered the manner in which trade bills were presented to the house. Thomson was heavily involved in both the Bank Charter and the Factory Acts of 1833. The factory inspectors were supervised by the Board of Trade, of which Thomson became president in 1834. Thomson also instituted a School of Design at Somerset House in 1837, and in the summer of that year spent two months touring Ireland in anticipation of the Irish Poor Law.[17]

Thomson's brother, it should be noted, remarks on Thomson's intimate relations with Durham. They were on 'confidential terms' in 1831 and were involved in commercial treaty negotiations with France. Thomson was primed for his Canadian tour by discussions with Durham and Buller.[18]

What Thomson attempted to do was to reorganize the conditions of Canadian governance to bring them broadly into line with administrative and ideological initiatives undertaken in England itself.[19] The reforms he put in place were in large measure those sought by most English Whigs and by the Radicals associated with Durham. These reforms were extended and consolidated in the 1840s, even in the midst of debates over ministerial responsibility. I do not mean to suggest that Canadian state formation in the period following immediately upon the Union is to be read simply as the unfolding either of Thomson's or of imperial political interests. Tory opposition in England prevented a local-government clause in the Act of Union. Reform opposition in the Canadas impeded Thomson's educational plans; many other instances undoubtedly existed. But it is important to notice the colonial parallels to the English governmental 'revolution,' and that the decade of the 1840s in the Canadas witnessed the disposition of both administrative and ideological agencies and practices. At issue are both the development of administrative bureaucracy and ideological initiatives aimed at political hegemony and consensus.

### Education

The case of education, with which I will be more particularly concerned below, is instructive in this regard. Through the early months of 1839, the Whig ministry worked to extend some version of the educational system in place in Ireland from 1831 to England and Scotland. Lord John Russell presented a scheme modelled on the Irish system to the Commons in February and, while opposition from Tories in both houses led to its substantial modification, later that year a Committee of Council on education was organized and undertook to inspect grant-aided schools.[20] While there is no direct evidence of Thomson's participation in these schemes, he was undoubtedly aware of them. Thomson represented Manchester in the 1830s where he knew Dr James Kay, later Sir James P. Kay-Shuttleworth, first secretary to the Committee on Education. Leonard Horner, the factory inspector and translator of Victor Cousin's influential report on education in Holland, was a fellow member of the Political Economy Club. Thomson was also closely connected to other advocates of public educational institutions – Sarah and John Austin, for instance. Kay was particularly vocal on the need for educational and sanitary reform and demonstrated the efficacy of Scottish and Irish methods in his own Normal School at Battersea. And all these people saw the education of the working class as central to the maintenance of their version of Christian morality, paternal authority, and private property.

## The School Acts in Canada West

Debates over the practical political potency of 'educating the people' were well established in colonial political circles, and educational policy had been an important subject of contention between elective and appointive branches of the colonial assemblies. Prussian, Scottish, Irish, and American educational models were proposed by members of different political parties, for adaptation to Canadian circumstances.

One of the first bills introduced by the Sydenham ministry in the United Province was an education bill, largely modelled by Sydenham on Arthur Buller's plan for Lower Canada, and also closely resembling the Irish system adapted to work under Canadian elective local government. The bill was substantially modified by Reformers in committee, but in the decade of the 1840s educational organization, in Canada West especially, came to approximate the Buller plan and the Irish model.

Under the Baldwin-LaFontaine ministry, a second education act – the School Act of 1843, drafted by Francis Hincks – was articulated and received assent after the resignation of the ministry. There remained a broad terrain of agreement among the governing classes about some dimensions of social policy, even at the height of the struggles over ministerial responsibility. While the clamour for political responsibility surrounded parliamentary practice, the School Act passed by the Reformers extended the supervision of popular education by respectable men of property.

## Inspection

Of particular interest are, on the one hand, the social background and activities of educational inspectors appointed under this act and its successor, the act of 1846, and, on the other, the appearance in the developing education office itself of an increasingly bureaucratic practice. There was a dynamic relation involved here. Standardization was in part a process that involved the institutionalization of ways of doing things pioneered by respectable men of property. Bureaucratic procedure made educational governance by a certain class of men ordinary. Of course, the education office did not begin to function in a vacuum: bureaucratic practice was established in other jurisdictions and was accessible to educational activists as a model.[21] Inspection as an instrument of governance appeared in England in the 1830s for factories and Poor Law unions. Irish school inspectors worked for the National Board from 1831, and there were continental precedents, as well.

Regularized inspection of the public domain began in the Canadas with the School Act of 1843 in Canada West. And, for a considerable period of time, educational inspectors enjoyed a wide latitude for the making of determinations about the social value of educational practices and practitioners. At the same time, inspection as a practice involved the centralization and standardization of knowledge.

Canada West's School Act of 1843 made the education office directed by the assistant superintendent of education the centre of educational information gathering. The assistant superintendent distributed the state school fund to district councils on the basis of population and on condition that the councils raise matching grants by taxation and make annual reports. The act of 1843 was designed to complement the Municipal Bill of 1843, which aimed at county municipalities, but which failed. The School Act created township superintendents of common schools to be appointed by township councils and to inspect township schools, to certify teachers, to collect and transmit to higher authority reports from each school, and to distribute township school monies. Township superintendents were to be supervised by county superintendents of common schools, who would collect township school reports, inspect all county schools, certify teachers (or annul certificates granted by township superintendents), hold and distribute county school monies, and report annually to the assistant superintendent. County superintendents were to be appointed, instructed, and paid by county councils, which would also function as boards of education.

With the failure of the Municipal Bill, the School Act was altered by order in council to conform to the District Councils Act. District councils were to function as boards of education (except in the towns, where Sydenham's plan continued), district superintendents exercised the functions of county superintendents, and township superintendents were lamed. The act gave no positive authority to the central authority over curriculum, pedagogy, or school management.

This act was substantially altered by the School Act of 1846, authored by Egerton Ryerson. Under the act of 1846, township superintendents were abolished, and district superintendents were made explicitly responsible for carrying out such instructions as the now chief superintendent of education for Canada West might deliver. A central Board of Education was created with the power to specify curriculum and school rules, and the chief superintendent could also specify school rules and regulations and resolve all local educational disputes on appeal. Still, district superintendents remained the appointees and employees of district councils, and amendments to the District Councils Act in 1846 allowed these bodies greater autonomy in the selection of their own officers. Several councils passed by-laws specifying the duties of the superintendents of schools in 1847. A key dimension of the reconstruction of colonial governance in the 1840s, indeed, was the creation of local state bodies, with a consequent development of conflict and contest between centre and locality. This conflict certainly shaped colonial governance as well, but it is beyond the scope of this essay at the moment.

Especially by the mid-1840s, if not before, key state servants insisted upon the importance of inspection as a powerful instrument of governance. Egerton Ryerson advised the superintendent general of Indian affairs in 1847 on the best means of organizing schools.

The interference or control of the Government should be confined to that which the Government can do with most effect and the least trouble – namely, to the right of inspecting the Schools from time to time by an agent or agents of its own – to the right of having detailed reports of the Schools as often as it shall think proper to require them, at least once or twice a year; and the right of continuing or withholding the grant made in aid of these Schools. It is in this power over the grant, the exercise of which will be determined by the inspections made and the reports given, that the paramount authority of the Government in respect to these Schools will be secured; while the endless difficulties arising from fruitless attempts to manage the Schools in detail will be avoided.[22]

Again, in a letter outlining the power of his office to William Millar, newly appointed Eastern district superintendent, Ryerson stressed that Millar's 'powers – though not extending to anything which properly belongs to the people themselves or their representatives, unless they appeal to you – extend to what is essential to the improvement of the Schools: – the object contemplated by the Legislative Grant.'[23] Of course 'the improvement of the Schools' was not a technical term whose meaning was either morally or politically neutral. 'Improvement' was at the heart of the hegemonic project of men of property.[24]

As Ryerson himself pointed out, finance and inspection were the key elements of educational governmental power. I will deal with each in turn.

### Rationalized and Non-Rationalized Rule

It is useful to bear in mind in what follows a distinction between 'rationalized' (legal) and 'non-rationalized' (moral/ideological) elements of governance. The former term refers to those elements at least tendentially bureaucratic in nature – practices and procedures relatively indifferent to the personae of practitioners. The latter term refers to elements whose thrust is particularly towards moral regulation; elements whose efficacy lies in whole or in part in the power of social classes and groups to define the moral, the culturally worthy, the proper, and the appropriate in the realms of behaviour and consciousness, and to endow these partial definitions with a general prestige.[25]

While mid-nineteenth-century governance in the Canadas involved an extension and intensification of rationalized state forms, these forms owed a considerable amount to the institutionalization of specific non-rationalized ways of ruling. And rationalized state forms continued to co-exist and depend upon non-rationalized forms of rule.

The operation of educational inspection is a case in point. Inspectors, for instance, gathered specific items of information in an increasingly standardized manner for a central authority. Their access to local sites of provision, however, was at least facilitated by their own individual characteristics – manner of dress, self-presentation, and other things marking them as a particular 'kind of person.'

Bureaucratic development, both classic and contemporary accounts frequently suggest, is a response to increases in the scale and complexity of social institutions. Even if this were true – and I would argue that political struggle propels such development – one would then be left to regard bureaucracy simply as a means. But bureaucratic administrative systems also have substance. This substance, in the Canadas and in large part, was constituted by the moral, cultural, and political interests of the rising middle classes.[26]

### Finance

The legal structure of the School Acts created a financial framework within which educational 'improvement' was organized. The acts presented a regulated space for educational initiatives, and provided central and district state servants with particular kinds of leverage over educational practice. The administration of the school grant was obviously of central importance.

'All states,' Weber reminds us, 'may be classified according to whether they rest on the principle that the staff of men themselves *own* the administrative means, or whether the staff is "separated" from these means of administration.'[27] One dimension of educational administration in the 1840s in Canada West was the development of pressure for rationalized management.

This is evident in a variety of instances that worked to standardize procedures and to make them relatively indifferent to the personae of office-holders. These ranged from the organization of an education office with its own architectural identity (in place of Egerton Ryerson's house, where the General Board of Education met during much of 1847), to matters of correspondence. 'Act as you think the circumstances of the case render proper,' wrote Dominique Daly to Robert Murray in 1844, 'but in all cases, let the drafts, or steps to be taken, be suggested by you, in the same manner as the business connected with the other Departments, are done by the Assistant Secretaries.'[28] Murray's successor was chastised for deviating from acceptable procedure by including several requests of the government in the same communication.[29] The documents generated by the exercise of educational inspection were not to be the personal property of inspectors.[30]

Pressure for rational management is also evident with respect to the school monies. Nowhere in Canadian financial administration did agencies or bodies tax to spending estimates. Monies were expended, or services performed, and tax revenues were raised only after the fact. This applied to all educational offices as well. Teachers, for instance, were paid yearly, in August at the earliest, after their year's labour. The school grant was placed at the disposal of the district superintendents, usually (but not always) after the school taxes were placed on the collector's roll, but often before the tax was collected.

Two 'irrational' consequences ensued. First, although only licensed teachers could draw the school grant, throughout the 1840s and despite the agitations of the education office, teachers continued to teach and to present themselves for certification when they came to collect their pay. Some superintendents found themselves engaged in bitter disputes when they refused to pay unqualified teachers who nonetheless had kept school in the expectation of payment.[31]

Second, superintendents held the entire school monies until these were paid to teachers.[32] There is no evidence to suggest that separate accounts for school monies were kept – the opposite seems to have been the general practice. And although the education office held the expectation that district councils would pay the salaries of district and township superintendents out of general funds, in fact these officers were commonly paid (as were most public officials) a percentage of the monies passing through their hands. Alexander McNab, Ryerson's deputy while the latter was in Europe, was alarmed to discover in the autumn of 1845 that most superintendents were paid out of the school monies. This was true not only of district superintendents but also of township superintendents, in addition to township collectors and, in some cases, district clerks. The fund actually reaching teachers or devoted to educational 'improvement' was substantially diminished for this reason.[33]

The education office attempted to end the practice, writing to district councils that superintendents' salaries were to be paid out of district funds, and that school monies were intended solely for the payment of teachers. Despite the opposition of the education office, some superintendents continued to draw their own salaries from the school monies in their possession until the educational reforms of 1850.[34]

Despite concern about the diminution of the school fund in this way, the education office worked on the assumption – was constrained to work on the assumption – that charge of these monies could be entrusted to the respectable men chosen as district superintendents.

Public and personal finance were little separated. But the practical experience of this method of management led to changed principles in the School Act of 1850.

Already in mid-1845 the education office had had reason for unease. Acting Assistant Superintendent McNab had received an anonymous letter accusing Elias Burnham, Colborne district superintendent, of a range of offences, including losing his barrister's gown, being convicted of perjury, and 'living in open concubinage.' Burnham was also said to have loaned the school monies 'to Mr Percy of Cobourg to purchase wheat at an exorbitant rate of interest for a few months say 10 per cent.' This led McNab to consult Attorney General Draper with respect to his powers to demand an accounting from Burnham. When Draper responded that the assistant superintendent of education could demand an accounting from any district superintendent in detail and at any time, McNab demanded from Burnham a detailed accounting of the school monies of 1843–4, including 'where you keep unexpended School Moneys, whether you employ them in any way for *your own* benefit, or otherwise, and if employed, how, on what conditions and when to be repaid.' The apportionment for 1845 was withheld until Burnham replied, which he did to McNab's satisfaction.[35] Complaints that Dr McLean, the Kingston superintendent, did not divide money fairly led to a similar demand for an accounting in 1847.[36]

Again, late in 1845 John Steele, the warden and district superintendent for the Newcastle District, a trustee of Queen's College, and a man extremely active in support of public improvement, was removed by Order in Council from the wardenship. In a letter to the press, Steele copied his denial of the colonial secretary's claim that he was in 'difficulties ... in matters connected with public moneys,' but some time within the next six months he had ceased to be district superintendent of schools. Steele's financial difficulties likely concerned the district school monies.[37]

The limitations of allowing selected individuals to manage personally the district school monies was demonstrated to the education office by the activities of John Bignall, Huron district superintendent. From his first appointment, Bignall was extremely lax in his accounting and reporting procedures. It is not clear that he presented any systematic report, as required by law, in 1844 or 1845. He responded to Assistant Superintendent Murray's demands for a report in the former year with the statement that he hadn't completed it, as he was 'living eight miles from the village, and [was] busily employed just now in getting in [his] crops.'[38] His report for 1847 was lacking in detail, but he did assure the education office that he had managed to make council appropriate £100 for the purchase of Irish schoolbooks.[39] However, little if any school money was actually reaching teachers. Public attacks on Bignall's non-performance by the Reform editor of the *Huron Signal* were followed by public meetings of school trustees in Goderich in March 1848 'for the purpose of taking into consideration the reason of the District moneys not having been paid to the school teachers for the last year.' After a resolution of a second meeting, at which Bignall's non-performance was complained of loudly, memoranda were addressed to both the district council and the district superintendent himself, and a letter was sent to the education office.

Bignall responded to this with the claim that he was 'prepared and anxious to answer any attack that has been made upon me, as a public servant,' and Ryerson himself intervened to chastise Bignall's critics and to express his entire confidence in Bignall's financial management. But at the May meetings of the Huron council questions were again raised about Bignall's activities. One councillor wondered if Bignall had in fact reported to the education office in 1844 and 1845. If he had not, why had he not been fined by the superintendent of education? And if he had, why had the district received so little school money? When Bignall did not respond, council moved at its October sessions in 1848 to require him to appear, and to produce all his correspondence with Egerton Ryerson between 1846 and 1848. Bignall ignored this summons, and a motion passed council on 7 October 1848 requiring him to appear in February with all his papers, or his office would be considered vacant. An information was laid against him on 9 October for embezzlement after it was discovered that Bignall had fled with the school monies. Council had failed to receive adequate sureties, and the taxpayers were constrained to make good the loss.[40]

At the other end of the colony the following summer, the Eastern district superintendent absconded with £500,[41] and in July 1849, Ryerson had watched as the Colborne District Council fired Benjamin Hayter as superintendent of schools after Hayter refused to pay surplus school monies into the district treasury – though for Hayter to do so would have violated the School Act.[42]

These instances of peculation led to the placing of the management of school monies in the hands of county treasurers under the School Act of 1850. 'Under this system,' Ryerson noted, 'local Superintendents will be under no temptation, at any time, from considerations of personal convenience, to withhold or delay the payment of school moneys ...'[43]

## The Inspectoral Corps

In contrast to these cases, which point to some of the dangers of personal management of public finance, many of the educational superintendents active in Canada West in the 1840s subsidized the office out of their own revenues. Samuel Ardagh spent £44 on postage, stationery, and travel in 1844, but received only £25 from the Simcoe District Council.[44] Newton Bosworth was eventually awarded £50 from the Brock District Council for his efforts in 1844 and again in 1846, an amount commonly regarded as insufficient to cover his correspondence costs.[45] William Fraser complained that the educational superintendency of the Eastern District cost him £7 of his own money in 1849, a sum he could ill afford.[46] Some superintendents responded to the low pay offered them by district councils by performing only clerical functions; but those named above and several others were particularly active in educational inspection and propaganda – 'the good cause,' as William Hutton called it.[47]

In fact, then, the office of district superintendent was a transitional one in the development of bureaucratic public administration. These were public officials, but many of them lived 'for' rather than 'off' public administration.[48] Their personal commitment was an important element in their inspectoral activities. They were situated midway between administration by notables and administration by professional bureaucratic cadres.

In terms of class position, the superintendency drew primarily upon members of the rising middle classes. A few large capitalists and farmers with pretensions to gentility and a few superior private-venture schoolmasters joined clerics, lawyers, and judges to compose the inspectorate. The presence of one small master craftsman (a 'mechanic,' in contemporary parlance) among these men was a matter of parliamentary debate. There were no poor farmers, workers, women, or people of colour. These men were joined in a common project of 'improvement,' in which rational religion, useful knowledge, and personal self-discipline were seen as keys to both social order and individual advancement. This was the 'good cause,' and the superintendency gave to them a social space and a set of social instruments – administrative and ideological – to pursue this cause. They were positioned to be able to make and enforce (more or less) *determinations* about the quality of teaching and learning, about the condition of education, and about what needed to be done.

Financially, their room to manoeuvre was sustained by clauses allowing for the discretionary expenditure of surplus school monies. Initially, superintendents were granted wide latitude. For instance, despite the fact that the School Act of 1843 recognized only *one* state school in any school district, John Strachan of the Midland District was allowed to subsidize two to promote 'harmony' in one district. Ryerson wrote, 'In cases in which we have any discretion we should administer and apply the law ... in such a way as will contribute most to the harmony & wishes of the community.'[49] McNab permitted Ardagh to distribute surplus monies in 1845 in any way he and the local superintendents could agree upon.[50] The same practice continued under the act of 1846. Ryerson encouraged George Hendry to distribute surplus monies to needy schools[51] and commented on the discretionary-monies clause to Charles Fletcher; 'I have found this clause of the Act extremely useful in many instances – enabling District Superintendents to maintain the law on the one hand, and yet on the other meet various special cases which clearly form exceptions to the general rule.'[52]

Particularly notorious in the 1840s was educational administration in the Dalhousie District, a region of the colony settled largely by former army officers who styled themselves a class of gentry. No educational tax was levied in this district in the 1840s, but the education office continued to distribute the school grant to the superintendent and warden, Hamnett Pinhey, until 1848. Pinhey distributed this money in ways that *he* determined to be just, and until the accession of the Reform ministry and the publication of Dalhousie council's opposition to the School Act, the education office offered tacit support.

### The Terrain of Inspection

While they were employed by district councils and, after 1846, legally bound to follow the instructions of the chief superintendent, district inspectors exerted a considerable influence over the conduct of local educational development. The powers they exerted went far beyond those specified by statute. Many of the things they did were not demanded of them by the School Act, and one assumes that they were able to do many things by virtue of the prestige that their social positions more generally conferred upon them.

Gramsci reminds us that the dominant class in any society must not only dominate but also lead if it is to remain in power,[53] and, as we have seen above, he argues that the maintenance of social hegemony is facilitated by the prestige that the representations of the dominant class can command. This power is real, but is quite distinct from that exercised by what Gramsci denotes the coercive state apparatuses. The district school inspectors occupied a terrain that allowed them to engage in wide-ranging initiatives aimed at 'improvement.' While these initiatives did not always succeed, they were significant in establishing particular conceptions of 'what needed to be done' in education.[54] The transition to new forms of bureaucratic management was undoubtedly facilitated by the continuities in the transitional period in the identity of office-holders. I do not mean this teleologically – that capitalists, substantial landowners, clerics, and respectable intellectuals were appointed as district superintendents *in order* to facilitate this transition. Still, the right of access to and intelligence-gathering in what had formerly been community institutions was probably more readily granted to familiar members of the dominant classes than it would have been to anonymous functionaries. As well, the capacity of school superintendents to engage in activities beyond the compass of the School Act was at least partly due to their same privileged position (although general ignorance of the act's provisions undoubtedly also played its part).

Hamnett Pinhey persuaded Dalhousie council – of which he was warden – to appropriate funds for a district Model School. He hired a teacher from the Irish Kildare Place Society and summoned all the teachers in the district to be examined in the Model School.[55]

Several other inspectors actively pursued teacher-training plans. Alexander Mann ran a training school in his house. Richey Waugh engaged Johnston Neilson, another Irish-trained teacher, to conduct a Johnstown Model School, and John Strachan was active in securing funds for the Newburgh Academy. Strachan also sent promising young teachers to board in the house of a teacher he regarded as particularly competent. Patrick Thornton organized and served as first president of the Dumfries Teachers' Association, conducted normal training, and convinced the teachers to allow none but those examined by him to teach in the district. Thornton also wrote and published a series of school-books with his brother, R.H. Thornton of Whitby. Newton

Bosworth secured a supply of school-books from the British and Foreign School Society for the Brock District.

In the Niagara District, Jacob Keefer – whose father was president of the Welland Canal Company, and who was himself later the largest miller in the colony – conducted an investigation into the political loyalties and national origins of teachers, to lay to rest the continuing fears of conservatives about republican teachers in the schools. In one school district, Keefer assembled those involved in a dispute over a school site in an effort to promote peace.[56] John Steele called together all the school trustees and township superintendents of the Newcastle District in a convention to consider the progress of the School Acts.

The superintendents were active in agitating for educational improvement. Many of them urged the adoption of the Irish National school-books before these were made the official texts in 1847. They urged revisions to the curriculum in areas in which they found it weak – Canadian history and geography, for instance. They pushed for improved schoolhouses – buildings with cross-ventilation, privies, wells, and woodsheds, and often devices for separating the sexes. They tried to establish new schools and sometimes offered to subsidize them out of their own pockets.[57] They counselled teachers to use gentle methods and to dispense with corporal punishment. Many – although clearly not all – of these men were motivated by a sincere desire to make what they considered a better world; and, in contemporary terms, several of them were politically progressive.

In some cases, the superintendents were quite prepared to oppose their own conceptions of educational improvement to those of the education office. Richey Waugh, for instance, routinely sanctioned the use of banned American books in an effort to overcome perceived shortcomings in the official curriculum after 1846. Thomas Donnelly attempted to license only those teachers who met the minimum standard specified by the education office in 1847, but found that this led to vacant schools and extra work for school visitors. Prince Edward council explicitly sustained him in his violation of the School Act in this regard. And Patrick Thornton was embroiled in a very bitter dispute with Ryerson in 1849 over his refusal to recognize the certificate granted to the widowed Mrs Merry by a school visitor. Ryerson earned the rebuke of the governor in council in this matter for exceeding his authority, although Thornton was finally instructed by Gore District Council to pay the woman.[58] But these were not forms of opposition intended to call into question the more general educational project – that respectable men of property should regulate the educational development of society.

The educational leadership of these men cannot be separated from their social leadership more generally considered. For many of the clerical superintendents, educational and religious circuits over-lapped. Superintendents were active in mechanics' institutes, county agricultural societies, fire and mutual assurance companies, road companies, Bible and missionary societies, the temperance movement, and ethnic associations.

## Intelligence

MacDonagh has stressed the centrality of the generation of public perceptions of social 'problems' by strategically situated intellectuals in processes of state formation.[59] The educational superintendents were involved in the production of the intelligence on which 'scientific' views of educational progress were formulated. Their views – which were by no means their *individuals* views – provided the basis for informed debate about educational organization and development. Information gathering by superintendents was indispensable to the operation of the act. There was no reliable census in the colony, and the state grant was distributed to councils according to population. Superintendents drew up censuses.[60]

From the outset, district superintendents were left to devise their own standards for evaluating educational questions. Many of them sought standardized forms of reporting and assessing when they initially took office, but until 1847 such forms were not in existence. The criteria by which teachers and schools were evaluated and the organization of the information reported were left to individual superintendents entirely until 1847, and only general guidelines were specified thereafter. In 1845, for instance, Charles Eliot classified schools in the Western District using terms like 'good' and 'not good'; Thomas Donnelly described schools as 'middling,' 'very bad,' and 'bad.'[61] Even when the education office printed report forms that demanded the classification of schools in terms of quality, no criteria for making these determinations were provided, and remarkably little discussion occurred.

John Flood's remarks in 1849 were an exception. 'I am not aware of any established definitions,' he wrote, 'by which to distinguish first class Schools from others but I have arranged in this column all that I considered the best in the District and which always have English grammar ...' A well-ventilated school for Flood had a window on each of its sides.[62]

With respect to the evaluation of teachers, the official forms after 1847 claimed that 'Common School Teachers may be naturally divided into three classes,' but added that 'the line of demarcation between these three classes of certificates must, at present, be left to the judgment of each District Superintendent. Further consultation and preparation are desirable before making the legal classification of Teachers as contemplated in the 41st section of the Act.'[63]

The significance of these kinds of categorizations lies in their *meaningfulness* to both superintendents and those in the education office. They believed that the conceptualization of the world simply reflected the categories of nature. Their examinations of teachers, even by the standards of a half-century later, seem perfunctory in the extreme, precisely because they believed they could recognize at a glance a qualified teacher.

Superintendents transformed select bodies of information about the organization and progress of education by applying their 'best knowledge' or 'local information.' From the outset, local superintendents' reports and those of school trustees were described as imperfect, and this fact was recognized by the education office. Still, district superintendents' annual reports were returned to them for correction and revision when incomplete. Elias Burnham of Peterborough had this experience repeatedly. 'I have received none anything like as defective as yours,' Ryerson wrote to him about his report in 1849, and again in 1850 told him 'in its present state your report was comparatively worthless.' Burnham confessed that the task of filling out the report so daunted him (there were five sheets, and when assembled the form was six feet long and three feet wide) that he had hired the clerk of the peace to complete it, whereupon Ryerson instructed him in detail as to its assembly.[64]

'Knowing how necessary it is in all statistical reports that every column should be attended to,' W.H. Landon remarked in 1849, 'I have supplied these according to the best of my judgment ... in many of the particulars the truth is only approximated.'[65] 'I have been under the necessity to guess a great deal in trivial matters,' William Fraser remarked, and John Flood echoed, 'I have been obliged to fill up this report in many places from my own knowledge of the schools.'[66] While inspecting schools, John Strachan at least kept a 'Memorandum Book' that allowed him to supplement the information reported to him by trustees, but most superintendents acted from memory.[67]

My point is not that these reports were inadequate or suspect because they guessed at some set of natural facts that more adequate procedures would have revealed more completely. These reports *were* the facts: Ryerson delivered them to the legislature as the official view of educational organization in Canada West. He used them to defend centralized educational administration against the attacks of the left of the Reform party in 1849.[68] They formed the basis of demands for educational improvement. When the Reform ministry split over the direction of reform in 1849, district superintendents were invited to collect and transmit the views of the most 'intelligent' trustees and teachers in their jurisdictions on alterations to the School Acts.[69] In short, the estimates, guesses, and perceptions of educational superintendents formed a corpus of hegemonic knowledge. Oppositional voices did not make it into the official record.[70]

### Collapsing Space

The district educational superintendency was in existence rather briefly – for about five years – before it was dismantled. A conclusive account of the causes for its demise would be premature, but it is possible to sketch some of the limitations of this mode of educational supervision.

We have seen that, from the viewpoint of the education office, the superintendency presented problems of financial management, but there were others. The level of activity of some inspectors was increasingly seen to be unsatisfactory. While people like Patrick Thornton, John Strachan, William Elliot, and William Clarke visited all schools in their districts, other superintendents were unable or unwilling to do so. There were more than 300 schools in the Home District superintended by Hamilton Hunter, but Hunter spent almost all his time in his office in Toronto distributing the school monies and examining teachers. William Hutton conducted one annual educational tour of inspection, which normally lasted about six weeks. There were 113 schools in his district, and it is highly improbable that he managed to see them all. Hutton was certainly not the least active inspector. In any case, schools moved around and were hard to find in a period when reliable maps did not exist and roads were often of dubious quality. For one man to find, let alone investigate, all the schools in two counties was a formidable task.

The level of inspectoral activity was less than the education office found necessary for its purpose. A lively debate surrounded just what kind of inspectoral organization was best, and the system of township and county inspection agreed upon under the act of 1850 was shaped by non-administrative questions, but the education office was interested in some decentralization of inspection. Perhaps the experience of the Irish National Board was also relevant here, for that body had moved from a national to a regional inspectoral system in 1837.

Again, despite the efforts of the education office to bind district superintendents to official instructions under the School Act of 1846, the conduct of inspection came to figure in conflicts between central and local states, a trend that seriously limited the power of the centre. Both Alexander Mann in 1847 and Benjamin Hayter in 1849 were dismissed by district councils for acting in keeping with the School Act but against the expressed interests of the councils.

The demands of district councils for increased jurisdiction in educational matters were themselves made less credible, however, by the failure of the provisions for district model schools under the direction of district superintendents. And the efforts of the left of the Reform party to replace the 'Prussian' system of centralized educational authority with regional educational autonomy were casualties in larger political struggles over the nature of political 'responsibility.' The Reform ministry had already been acting to reduce the exercise of 'discretion' in educational finance. The room for manoeuvre of superintendents was shrinking.

Late in 1849, Francis Hincks, the inspector general (finance minister), and Ryerson resolved on a revised School Act that eliminated the district superintendency. They canvassed the superintendents themselves for their opinions, and most of them gave their support, either at once or when they were told of the policy the ministry had decided to follow. The School Act of 1850 reduced the autonomy and localized the authority of school inspectors while increasing the leverage the central office could exert over them. Educational inspection was more thoroughly bureaucratized.

## Conclusion

The decade of the 1840s witnessed a series of major transformations in the organization of colonial governance. In this remarkable period, there was a clear tendency to replace government by notables with government by bureaucratically organized cadres. This tendency has been largely neglected in a literature concerned with the parliamentary powers of the representatives of propertied white men, and attention to it seems imperative. It can be argued that one important dimension of the transition was the creation of political spaces that allowed respectable men of property to organize rule through new instruments and mechanisms. The standardization and normalization of some of the views and practices of these men were important sources for bureaucratic procedure. Such procedure both grew up in and was sustained by non-rationalized forms of governance.

Attention should also be given, however, to more elusive cultural transformations that were implicated in the state formation of the 1840s. People came to see themselves and others differently and to understand the nature of the public voice in new ways. They did so with reason, both because the public voice became louder and because its pitch and tenor became more exclusively those of the propertied male.

We hear this voice being exercised in new ways: in efforts to modulate developing popular literacy, for instance, from the organization of mechanics' institutes to the institutionalization of particular reading methods.[71] Many educational officials had related experiences in other areas of their lives. Newton Bosworth resigned as pastor of the Woodstock Baptist communion over his refusal to allow women to 'speak their gifts' in church. William H. Landon, also from Woodstock, also attempted to guide the 'popular' voice when people spoke their gifts.

> In some of the Baptist churches in the western part of the province one week day in each month was set aside as an occasion for confessing orally to the Articles of Faith which were read aloud by the church clerk. After a sermon the individual members were expected to 'improve their gifts' by addressing the meeting. Elder W.H. Landon, of Oxford, has left the comment that the people had to be taught cautiously that the Holy Spirit had not conferred the same gifts upon all men and women. It took many years to have this comprehended.[72]

In the same decade, the Methodist Egerton Ryerson – not an insignificant participant in developing processes of governance – found himself unable to support the Methodist Conference's established practice of requiring public declarations of faith. Ryerson felt this incompatible with the private nature of religious belief. And while he undoubtedly justified his opposition by reference to religious principles, the practical result of such decisions was towards the privatization of the religious voice.[73]

These anecdotes do not 'prove' a cultural transformation, of course, but they do indicate another important dimension of the 'coming of responsible government.' The forms of representation put in place in the Canadas after the Rebellions of 1837–8 allowed adult male property-holders to speak for society generally, while 'democratizing' the manner in which representatives of this class of men were selected. In the same period, forms of collective democracy that allowed other kinds of voices to be heard were modulated, muted, or silenced. This very dark side of the history of representative democracy also calls for our attention.

## NOTES

1 The main exception is in the domain of educational policy in Canada West. A particularly important contribution with respect to questions of procedure is Alison Prentice's pathbreaking 'The Public Instructor: Ryerson and the Role of the Public School Administrator,' in N. Mc-Donald and Alf Chaiton, eds, *Egerton Ryerson and His Times* (Toronto: Macmillan 1978), 129–59. Also, Susan Houston and Alison Prentice, *Schooling and Scholars in Nineteenth-Century Ontario* (Toronto: University of Toronto Press 1988). My argument in this chapter is extended and detailed in my *True Government by Choice Men? Inspection, Education, and State Formation in Canada West* (Toronto: University of Toronto Press 1992).

2 John Manning Ward, for instance, in his *Colonial Self-Government: The British Experience, 1759–1856*, notices in passing that Durham perceived self-government at the local level as political discipline. But Manning himself more commonly elides rule by the representatives of natural-ized adult white male property-holders into the interests of the 'peo-ple.' For example, in writing of the success of the Tories in Upper Canada in 1836, Ward states: 'The election of 1836 cannot be ex-plained wholly in constitutional terms. Most electors were probably not interested in the principles of government disputed between Head and the reformers. Electors were colonists, intent on economic growth and its necessary condition, political stability. On such matters the Family Compact, for all its oligarchic tendencies, was nearer to the mass of the people than were the reformers ...' And so, electors – naturalized adult white men of property – become 'the people.' This instance is symptomatic of a larger tendency on the part of some writers to accept political governance as primarily a parliamentary phenomenon; to es-chew the kind of analysis of social class and political practice necessary to see the extension of governance beyond the walls of parliaments. The practical operation of rule and its structure are left unexamined in such views.

3 I elaborate this argument in 'Representation and State Formation in the Canadas, 1790–1850,' *Studies in Political Economy* 28 (1989), 59–87.

4 Charles Buller, *Responsible Government for Colonies* (London: James Ridgway 1840), 40–3. An identical analysis was made by his brother, Arthur Buller, in his discussion of educational conditions in the Durham report. See Sir Charles Lucas, ed., *Lord Durham's Report on the Affairs of British North America* (Oxford: Clarendon Press 1912).

5 Oliver MacDonagh, 'The Nineteenth-Century Revolution in Government: A Reappraisal,' *Historical Journal* 1 (1958), 52–67. MacDonagh makes the point *inter alia* that the colonies were particularly important in the transformation of English governance in that they provided opportunities for experimenting in social policy. For Peel's Irish experiments with police, see Galen Broeker, *Rural Disorder and Police Reform in Ireland, 1812–36* (Toronto: University of Toronto Press 1970). The volume of literature in the English debate is far too vast to summarize here, but see a more recent contribution by MacDonagh, *The Inspector General: Sir Jeremiah Fitzpatrick and Social Reform, 1783–1802* (London: Croom Helm 1981).

6 See P. Corrigan and D. Sayer, *The Great Arch: English State Formation as Cultural Revolution* (Oxford: Blackwell 1985). I have presented the English literature as if it were not internally differentiated, while in fact there have been three major cleavages at least: among 'Tory,' 'Fabian,' and several kinds of Marxist analysis. For more on this point, see Peter Gowan, 'The Origins of the Administrative Elite,' *New Left Review* 162 (Mar.-Apr. 1987), 4–34.

7 In Canada East in particular, systematic and frequently violent opposition to representative local government by seigneurs, some large landed proprietors, and habitants operated as a serious brake on the centralization of authority, certainly until the abolition of the seigneurial system.

8 Philip Abrams, 'Notes on the Difficulty of Studying the State,' *Journal of Historical Sociology* 1:1 (1988), 58–89

9 Marianna Valverde and Lorna Weir, 'The Struggles of the Immoral: Preliminary Remarks on Moral Regulation,' *Resources for Feminist Research* 17:3 (1988), 31–4. See also Patricia Cline Cohen, *A Calculating People* (Chicago: University of Chicago Press 1982) for some fascinating instances of the psycho-cultural dimensions of quantification.

10 Max Weber, 'Politics as a Vocation,' in his *Essays in Sociology*, ed. H.H. Gerth and C.W. Mills (Oxford: Oxford University Press 1958), 78

11 This is particularly the case, for instance, with Norbert Elias, *The Civilizing Process* (New York: Pantheon 1978–80).

12 Antonio Gramsci, *Selections from the Prison Notebooks* (New York: International Publishers 1971), 12

13 A similar line, although glossed differently, is found throughout much of Durkheim's work on the state, e.g., *Professional Ethics and Civic Morals* (Glencoe: Free Press 1958); and later as well in that of Pierre Bordieu, e.g., *Outline of a Theory of Practice* (New York: Cambridge 1977).

14 G. Poulett Scrope, *How Is Ireland to Be Governed?* (London: Ridgway 1846), 4, 33–54

15 G. Poulett Scrope, *Memoir of the Life of the Right Honourable Charles, Lord Sydenham* (London: John Murray 1843), 254

16 The importance of the Political Economy Club for the permeation of the state system with Benthamite figures and the importance of Thomson in this regard are detailed in S.E. Finer's remarkable essay 'The Transmission of Benthamite ideas, 1820–50,' in Gillian Sutherland, ed., *Studies in the Growth of Nineteenth-Century Government* (London: Routledge and Kegan Paul 1972), 11–32; see also A. Tyrrell, 'Political Economy, Whiggism and the Education of Working-Class Adults in Scotland, 1817–1840,' *Scottish Historical Review* 48 (1969), 151–65.

17 Poulett Scrope, 'Thomson, Charles Edward Poulett,' *Dictionary of National Biography* passim

18 Scrope, *Memoir*, 46, 100. I think Ged Martin, *The Durham Report and British Policy* (Cambridge: Cambridge University Press 1972), leads us astray in his attempts to discount the influence of Durham's report on colonial policy. On education, local government, land tenure, public works, and other measures he had the entire support of a broad cross-section of the English ruling class. The question is surely less one of whether these were Durham's personal ideas than of their currency.

19 With exactly what success remains a matter of debate. Whatever the level of success, it should be noted that this was a class project.

20 Nancy Ball, *Her Majesty's Inspectorate, 1839–1849* (Edinburgh: Oliver and Boyd 1963), ch. 2

21 Archives of Ontario (AO), RG2, C6C, Keefer to Murray, 6 Mar. 1844; Keefer suggests that since the School Act of 1843 was modelled largely on the one in place in New York, the instructions to inspectors by the superintendent in that state could be adopted in Canada West. AO, RG2, C1C, Ryerson to Daly, 27 Mar. 1846. In this letter, which accompanied his *Report on a System of Public Elementary Instruction for Upper Canada*, Ryerson quoted Victor Cousin on the value of 'learning from abroad.' In AO, MU1375, Hodgins Papers, Ryerson to Draper, 30 Mar. 1846, Ryerson revealed that he was preparing to translate some of the books of instructions for inspectors in use in France.

22 AO, RG2, C1C, Ryerson to George Vardon, Superintendent General, Indian Affairs, Montreal, 26 May 1847

23 AO, RG2, C1C, Ryerson to Millar, 18 Mar. 1847

24 A point I argue at length in *Building the Educational State: Canada West,*

*1836–1871* (London, Ont.: Althouse; Sussex: Falmer 1988) and that Corrigan and Sayer make repeatedly.

25 This distinction is taken from Corrigan and Sayer, *The Great Arch*, where it is a central insight. See also P. Corrigan, 'On Moral Regulation: Some Preliminary Remarks,' *Sociological Review* 29:2 (1981), 313–37. In Weber's essay on bureaucracy in *Essays in Sociology* the distinction is already present, and Weber stresses that bureaucracies can only work on the basis of such irrational forces as the loyalty of bureaucratic cadres.

26 This addresses old theoretical debates in sociology. Compare Weber's account of the rise of bureaucracy in *Essays in Sociology*, with Durkheim's criticism of a social science claiming to speak only to the validity of means in his *The Rules of the Sociological Method*, ed. Steven Lukes (Glencoe: Free Press 1982). For some further remarks on this debate in educational history, see my 'Policing Pedagogical Space: "Voluntary" School Reform and Moral Regulation,' *Canadian Journal of Sociology* 13:3 (1988), 283–304.

27 Weber, *Essays in Sociology*, 81

28 AO, RG2, C6C, Daly to Murray, 17 Apr. 1844

29 AO, RG2, C6C, Daly to Education Office, 9 Sept. 1845

30 AO, RG2, C1D, Ryerson to Colin Gregor, Guelph, 10 Dec. 1847

31 AO, RG2, C1D, Ryerson to Hamilton Hunter, 19 Aug. 1847

32 Very large sums of money, in contemporary terms, were at issue. For instance, William F. Clarke, according to the Talbot District Auditors (AO, RG2, C6C, Feb. 1849), held as much as £1,486.14.4 during 1849, and had large balances in hand at the end of the year as well. This in a period where the Congregational churches were paying ministers like Clarke in principle about £75 per annum (although payment was usually late and often in kind).

33 See AO, RG2, C6C, 28 July 1845, for example: Samuel Hart, Eastern District superintendent, revealed in response to a circular letter from McNab that his salary '(totally inadequate as it is) was fixed by the Distr. Council at a percentage of 4 per cent to be deducted from the Government monies passing thro his hands ...'

34 G.E. Boyce, *Hutton of Hastings* (Belleville, Ont.: Hastings County Council 1972), shows that William Hutton was attacked in council after 1850 for taking his salary out of the school funds.

35 AO, RG2, C6C, bundle including McNab to Hopkirk, 25 Aug. 1845, with Draper's opinion on the outside, and Hopkirk to McNab; also McNab to Elias Burnham, Peterboro', 30 Aug. 1845

36 AO, RG2, C1C, Ryerson to Dr McLean, 5 May 1847; 27 May 1847; 7 May 1847

37 Cobourg *Star*, 10 Dec. 1845

38 AO, RG2, C6C, John Bignall, Goderich, 25 May 1844

39 AO, RG2, F3A, Huron District Report, 1847
40 In November the following advertisement ran in the Goderich paper:

$400 REWARD

Whereas John Bignall, Superintendent of Common Schools of the Huron District, has absconded with a large sum of Public Money, the above Reward will be paid to any one apprehending the said John Bignall and recovering the amount stolen; or the reward will be paid in proportion to the amount recovered. The money, *Three hundred and forty eight pounds*, was in $10 notes of the Bank of Montreal. The above John Bignall is a remarkably large man, with coarse features, about six feet three inches in height; very round in his shoulders, haughty in his address, and about 50 years of age, hair straight inclined to grey, whiskers white.

The *Huron Signal* provides a complete account and post mortem. See especially the issues for 17 and 31 Mar., 14 Apr., 12 May, 27 Oct., 3 and 17 Nov. and 15 Dec. 1848; 19 Jan. 1849.

41 AO, RG2, C6C, William Fraser, Lochiel, to Ryerson, 11 July 1849: 'Mr. Millar ... is a defaulter in a sum not less than £500 & according to all appearance has left the country.' Again, F3A, Eastern District Report, 1849, William Fraser: 'my predecessor William Millar who absconded & brought with him a little more than £500 of the publick money.' No Cornwall paper from the period survives to provide a fuller account.

42 AO, RG2, C6C, Oct. 1849; a large bundle of documents concerns the Hayter case.

43 'Circular from the Chief Superintendent to the Wardens of Counties and Unions of Counties ...' in *Journal of Education for Upper Canada* 3:8 (1850), 114

44 AO, RG2, C6C, 3 May 1845; Ardagh had offered to serve as superintendent gratuitously, if the district council would cover his expenses. 'These including Clerk – Office – Stationery – Postage & Travelling' for 1844 'amounted to about £44.' But the district council 'refused to allow more than £25.'

45 McMaster University Archives, Newton Bosworth Diary, 1843–7, 16 Feb. 1844

46 AO, RG2, C6C, William Fraser, Aug. 1849

47 AO, RG2, C6C, William Hutton, Belleville, 25 Dec. 1845

48 To use Weber's distinction, in *Essays in Sociology* (84), 'Either one lives "for" politics or one lives "off" politics.'

49 AO, RG2, C6C, John Strachan, Ernest Town, 21 Oct. 1844; C1B, Ryerson to Strachan, 26 Oct. 1844

50 AO, RG2, C1B, McNab to S.B. Ardagh, 3 Mar. 1845

51 AO, RG2, C1D, Ryerson to George Hendry, 23 Aug. 1847

52 AO, RG2, C1F, Ryerson to Charles Fletcher, 6 Aug. 1849

53 Gramsci, *Prison Notebooks*, 57–8

54 I like to think of this as a kind of ideological 'softening up' exercise, unlike some educational historians who dismiss these activities as 'formal' and hence as not really about power. See my critique in 'Policing Pedagogical Space.'

55 AO, RG2, C6C, Hamnett Pinhey, 20 Sept. 1845

56 AO, RG2, C6C, Jacob Keefer, 30 Sept. 1845

57 E.g., AO, RG2, C6C, Elias Burnham, 24 June 1845

58 See AO, RG2, C6C, Leslie to Ryerson, 5 July 1849, for the official rebuke.

59 MacDonagh, 'Nineteenth-Century Revolution in Government.' In my opinion, however, he tends to ignore the class-bound nature of 'expert' views, and also to neglect the struggles through which these views in many cases triumphed.

60 Cf AO, RG2, C1B, McNab to Daly, 16 and 23 May 1845.

61 AO, RG2, F3A, Western District Report, Prince Edward District Report, 1845. But these reports are strikingly similar in their categorization and forming of knowledge. These are also often remarkable physical documents, some of them enormously large and presented on numerous sheets sewn together. The domestic context of this knowledge production demands an attention I cannot give it here.

62 AO, RG2, F3A, Dalhousie District Report, 1849

63 *Forms, Regulations and Instructions for the Better Organization and Government of Common Schools in Upper Canada* (Toronto: J.H. Lawrence 1847), 7

64 AO, RG2, C1D, Ryerson to Burnham, 5 Apr. 1848 and 4 Apr. 1849; C6C, Burnham to Ryerson, 12 Apr. 1849; C1F, Ryerson to Burnham, 13 Mar. 1850

65 AO, RG2, F3A, Brock District Report, 1849

66 AO, RG2, F3A, Eastern District Report, Dalhousie District Report, 1849

67 AO, RG2, C6C, John Strachan, Ernest Town, 15 Mar. 1849

68 See AO, RG2, C1D, Ryerson to Leslie, 12 May 1849; the reports were used in his defence despite Ryerson's earlier cautions about their utility: e.g., C1D, Ryerson to Governor General, 28 June 1847; Ryerson to Daly, 29 June 1847.

69 The responses to a circular from Francis Hincks are collected in J.G. Hodgins, *Documentary History of Education in Upper Canada*, 28 vols (Toronto 1894–1910), 9:54–70.

70 See, for instance, AO, RG2, C6C, Thomas Moyle, Adelaide, 25 Feb. 1845: 'there are too many Superintendents with an unlimited power to raise their Salary's to whatever they please and of no service whatever to the Children attending School If the Parents or Guardians of children combined with the Trustees and School Master, who are always on the spot, do not look to their Interests, it cannot be done by a Su-

perintendent residing at a distance, occasionally paying them the complement [*sic*] of a Dollar and a half's visit ...'

71 See, for instance, my 'The Speller Expelled: Disciplining the Common Reader in Canada West,' *Canadian Review of Sociology and Anthropology* 22:3 (1985), and ' "Littery Merrit," "Useful Knowledge," and the Organization of Township Libraries in Canada West, 1840–1860,' *Ontario History* 77 (1986), 283–312.

72 Fred Landon, *Western Ontario and the American Frontier* (Toronto: McClelland and Stewart 1967), 100

73 C.B. Sissons, *Egerton Ryerson, His Life and Letters*, 2 vols (Toronto: Clarke, Irwin 1947), 2:285–326; also, William Westfall, *Two Worlds: The Protestant Culture of Nineteenth-Century Ontario* (Montreal: McGill-Queen's University Press 1989)

# 5

# État et associationnisme
# au XIXᵉ siècle québécois :
# éléments pour une problématique
# des rapports État / société
# dans la transition au capitalisme

JEAN-MARIE FECTEAU

Au premier abord, rien ne semble plus éloigné d'une réflexion sur l'État qu'une étude sur le phénomène associatif. En effet, l'association n'est-elle pas un phénomène propre à la société civile ? Forme d'agglomération des volontés individuelles, elle semble issue bien davantage du dynamisme des initiatives privées que des contraintes propres au politique. Cette approche « civile » de l'association semble d'ailleurs accréditée par les recherches que les différentes sciences sociales ont consacrées à ce phénomène : la psychologie et la sociologie ont ainsi interrogé les formes de communication et les modes d'organisation sous-jacents aux divers groupements sociaux. La dynamique des rapports interindividuels au sein des associations, de même que l'efficace propre de celles-ci sur l'ensemble social, forment donc les balises d'un questionnement scientifique où l'association apparaît comme un phénomène social à disséquer. La science politique, elle-même, n'a pas peu contribué à confiner l'association à une forme spécifique de manifestation de la société civile entretenant des rapports plus ou moins particuliers avec l'instance politique. L'association devient, dans cette optique, un « groupe de pression » dont les rapports avec l'État restent à mesurer et à évaluer. Ainsi est implicitement posé le postulat d'une *extériorité* du phénomène associatif par rapport au politique.

De son côté, l'historiographie s'est trop souvent contentée d'appréhender le phénomène associatif comme incident à l'étude d'une thématique particulière (l'histoire économique, par exemple). Les analyses historiques de type « biographiques », s'attachant à faire l'histoire d'une association particulière, forment une variante de cette approche, dans la mesure où ces monographies ponctuelles sont rattachées au champ d'étude intéressé par l'association sous analyse [1].

Qu'elle soit étudiée en elle-même ou dans ses rapports multiples avec l'ensemble social, l'association est donc la plupart du temps perçue comme une réalité polymorphe dont les conditions d'apparition sont avant tout assignables à l'infinie variété des rapports sociaux. En ce sens, le phénomène associatif est partie constitutive du « social », cette nébuleuse de rapports où l'existence individuelle se fond dans les exigences du collectif, où la gestion des grands nombres interpelle les égoïsmes particuliers, aux marges du politique proprement dit.

Disons-le tout de go : depuis un demi-siècle au moins, la problématique de l'association a soigneusement exclu de son questionnement la dimension fondamentalement *politique* du phénomène. L'avatar corporatiste et l'avènement de l'État-providence ont paradoxalement contribué à désamorcer le problème politique posé par l'existence même de groupements associatifs dans l'ensemble social. Ce processus d'occultation s'est accompli de deux façons : en délégitimant, dans la foulée de l'échec des théories corporatistes, l'autonomie des groupes constitués, et en dévaluant cette autonomie dans le cadre du pouvoir régulateur grandissant attribué à l'État.

Le présent essai a pour objectif de replacer le phénomène associatif dans sa problématique politique. Pour ce faire, on devra étudier les rapports complexes qui s'instituent entre l'État et l'association au XIX<sup>e</sup> siècle. Ce texte s'attachera surtout à mettre en lumière les problèmes théoriques et méthodologiques qui se posent à ce champ d'étude, tout en évaluant son apport à l'analyse du rôle de l'État dans la transition au capitalisme.

## 1. L'association comme forme socio-politique

L'avenir, on peut l'espérer du moins, appartiendra à l'association. Seule elle saura apporter un remède efficace aux vices de la culture morcelée, à l'éparpillement des forces sociales, aux chocs quotidiens dans lesquels elles s'annulent et s'absorbent, aux sacrifices que conseille une concurrence déréglée. Elle aura seule la puissance de terminer une longue querelle qui se perpétue entre le principe de la liberté et le principe de l'autorité. Dans le monde des passions, dans le monde de l'intelligence, dans le monde des intérêts, l'harmonie ne se fondera que par l'association. Rien n'est encore prêt pour son avènement ; gouvernement et peuple, personne n'est mûr, tout résiste et pourtant un besoin d'union, de concert, se fait sentir de mille côtés. Partout où l'association a offert quelque sécurité, quelque garantie, on est allé vers elle sans effort, avec abandon. La dette publique, les banques, les grandes entre-prises commerciales et industrielles, sont les produits de cet instinct, de ce besoin. Sur une échelle plus réduite, le principe règne dans le domaine des affaires. Les capitaux se cherchent et se groupent, les intérêts se combinent et se coalisent. L'association a aussi pénétré dans les sphères morales et pour des fins toutes de sentiment. En haut se forment des sociétés de charité et de philanthropie ; en bas des sociétés de secours mutuels. Les symptômes sont donc consolants, et si notre cœur ne nous trompe, l'avenir sera beau ... Les abus de l'autorité ont dû conduire à la liberté, c'est-à-dire à l'expression la plus élevée de la force individuelle ; les abus de la liberté individuelle conduiront à l'as-sociation qui doit être la manifestation la plus complète de la force collective [2].

Il fut un temps où l'association, comme mode d'ébullition du social, se situait au cœur du débat politique. Certes, sa définition commune [3] n'évoque qu'un réflexe social plus ou moins transitoire, et à finalité ponctuelle. Mais c'est oublier que l'association, *comme phénomène glo-bal*, est un mode historiquement spécifié de constitution du social. Beaucoup plus qu'un type de sociabilité, plus qu'une pulsion com-municationnelle inscrite au cœur de l'animal social qu'est l'individu, l'association est un phénomène de coagulation du social dont le dé-veloppement est un des aspects les plus fascinants et à la fois les plus méconnus de la transition au capitalisme. Interroger l'historicité de ce phénomène permet de pénétrer au fondement même de l'ordre politique [4] qui s'instaure au cours de cette transition. En d'autres termes, dans la mesure où la transition au capitalisme implique un bouleversement fondamental du mode de régulation des sociétés occidentales [5], le développement du phénomène associatif doit être saisi comme un mode original d'auto-institution du social, comme réorganisation en profondeur des modes d'intervention sur le destin collectif des hommes et des femmes. Association et démocratie sont donc des dimensions constitutives et complémentaires d'une redéfi-nition du politique qui se situe au cœur de la transition [6].

### A. *Une vision dichotomique du social : le libéralisme*

Dans sa lutte séculaire contre le féodalisme, l'idéologie libérale a mis en place une série de couplages dont la logique binaire est encore au fondement de la représentation du monde dans nos sociétés, et qui sous-tend par le fait même les problématiques dominantes d'interprétation de l'histoire. Deux de ces couples fondamentaux distribuent l'ensemble social selon des paramètres distinguant le privé et le public, l'individu et la société [7].

Le privé et le public sont un couple d'opposition supposant le découpage du social en sphères à la fois autonomes et complémentaires. Le privé est ce qui s'attache à l'individu et aux rapports interindividuels. La production et la survie de cette cellule sociale qu'est l'individualité sont pensées dans une logique d'harmonisation spontanée des comportements individuels, postulat et a priori fondamental de la vision libérale du monde et de l'histoire. Dans ce contexte, la sphère publique se présente comme un « espace [8] » d'intervention où s'agglomèrent les besoins et les enjeux collectifs, c'est-à-dire ce lieu de l'existence humaine qui tout à la fois permet et limite la dynamique des rapports privés. Le privé et le public sont donc deux *dimensions*, potentiellement contradictoires, de l'existence en société [9]. Dans cette logique de démarcation du social, le privé est premier, dans la mesure où ce n'est que lorsque sont épuisées ses potentialités qu'il est permis d'en appeler au public, comme forme dernière et nécessaire de l'existence en société.

Le couple individu/société est également caractéristique de la configuration théorique à l'œuvre dans l'interprétation libérale du monde, et impose également une lecture particulière de l'ensemble social. Ici encore, cette lecture du social a comme prémisse fondamentale que l'unique est la source du collectif, que le social, la « société » est un *construit* concevable uniquement à partir de l'agrégation des individus. Individu et société apparaissent donc comme les deux termes indépassables de la problématique sociétale qui devient hégémonique au XIX<sup>e</sup> siècle.

Tout le débat sur le social à l'époque en viendra à s'articuler autour de l'importance respective à accorder à ces éléments du binôme social. Cette lecture dichotomique de l'existence en société imprègnera, au XIX<sup>e</sup> siècle, tout le débat sur le destin des collectivités humaines.

### B. *L'association comme contradiction*

La société qui s'organise autour de cette vision du monde ne laisse virtuellement aucun espace entre les pôles d'interprétation du social que sont le privé et le public, l'individu et la société, binômes qui semblent épuiser toute la richesse de la vie en société. Entre le privé et le public, entre l'individu et la société, il n'y a rien, si ce n'est

quelques brèves manifestations du social que l'on s'empresse de ra-
battre sur un des termes de l'équation à deux inconnues qu'est de-
venue la société.

Dans ce contexte, on comprend la difficulté de concevoir le statut
de l'association, cette forme hybride de regroupement qui, d'une part,
tient de la volonté individuelle et de l'initiative privée et, d'autre part,
comporte toutes les caractéristiques de l'existence collective et occupe
une place remarquée dans l'espace public. Dans la logique dichotomique au fondement du libéralisme classique, l'association sera
d'abord une présence obsédante que l'on s'efforcera d'évacuer. Ainsi,
Adam Smith la conçoit avant tout sous la forme des multiples corps
et monopoles formés ou supportés par la monarchie. C'est à lutter
contre toutes ces formes de regroupement, des corporations artisanes
aux compagnies à charte, que Smith s'emploiera dans son œuvre
principale [10]. Cependant, c'est à Jean-Jacques Rousseau que revient
l'honneur d'avoir dégagé avec le plus de clarté les implications de la
dichotomisation individu/société pour l'association. Ce remarquable
passage vaut d'être cité au long :

> Il y a souvent bien de la différence entre la volonté de tous et la volonté
> générale : celle-ci ne regarde qu'à l'intérêt commun, l'autre regarde à
> l'intérêt privé, et n'est qu'une somme de volontés particulières : mais
> ôtez de ces mêmes volontés les plus et les moins qui s'entre-détruisent,
> reste pour somme des différences la volonté générale.
>
> Si, quand le peuple suffisamment informé délibère, les citoyens
> n'avaient aucune communication entre eux, du grand nombre de pe-
> tites différences résulterait toujours la volonté générale, et la déli-
> bération serait toujours bonne. Mais quand il se fait des brigues, des
> associations partielles aux dépens de la grande, la volonté de chacune
> de ces associations devient générale par rapport à ses membres, et
> particulière par rapport à l'État ; on peut dire alors qu'il n'y a plus
> autant de votants que d'hommes, mais seulement autant que d'asso-
> ciations. Les différences deviennent moins nombreuses et donnent un
> résultat moins général. Enfin, quand une de ces associations est si grande
> qu'elle l'emporte sur toutes les autres, vous n'avez plus pour résultat
> une somme de petites différences, mais une différence unique ; alors
> il n'y a plus de volonté générale, et l'avis qui l'emporte n'est qu'un avis
> particulier.
>
> Il importe donc pour avoir bien l'énoncé de la volonté générale qu'il
> n'y ait pas de société partielle dans l'État et que chaque citoyen n'opine
> que d'après lui. Telle fut l'unique et sublime institution du grand

Lycurgue. Que s'il y a des sociétés partielles, il en faut multiplier le nombre et en prévenir l'inégalité, comme firent Solon, Numa, Servius. Ces précautions sont les seules bonnes pour que la volonté générale soit toujours éclairée, et que le peuple ne se trompe point [11].

Forme dégénérée de coagulation du social, l'association restreint la libre circulation des idées et des marchandises, constituant par là-même un obstacle à l'harmonisation spontanée des volontés assurée par le libre marché. L'association, comme contrat particulier, est donc l'ennemi du contrat social, et doit être prohibée. Si cette maladie sociale ne peut être extirpée, on peut tout au moins limiter ses effets nocifs en la banalisant et en la réduisant à une poussière de petites associations que leur faiblesse rend égales.

Loin d'être moyen de promotion du privé, l'association apparaît donc pour les philosophes et économistes libéraux du XVIIIe siècle comme une menace, une forme de détournement des volontés individuelles aux dépens du salut public. Comment s'étonner alors de la méfiance envers l'association dont témoignent les révolutionnaires français de 1789 [12] ? Loin d'être conçu comme l'un des droits fondamentaux attachés à l'intégrité, la sûreté et la promotion de la personne, le droit d'association est une conquête difficile dont on retrouve les traces tout au long du XIXe siècle [13].

C'est que l'association est un phénomène qui, dans le contexte de l'avènement de la démocratie, pose une série de problèmes fort épineux. L'association peut être considérée comme un processus de cristallisation du tissu social dont le développement mine, potentiellement tout au moins, la double souveraineté dont l'idéologie libérale revêt l'individu et l'État. On vient de voir que devant le danger, la réaction spontanée des autorités révolutionnaires a été de faire obstacle à la croissance du phénomène. Cependant, le développement fulgurant d'une multitude de formes associatives au XIXe siècle rend illusoire cette option. Il ne peut s'agir que de contrôler la progression de cette tendance en la balisant juridiquement.

C'est ici que l'on retrouve la dimension fondamentalement politique de l'association. On est en présence d'une forme sociale contradictoire dans l'ordre libéral, et ceci à trois titres principaux :

1. D'abord, l'association est un *collectif* se déployant dans un espace qui n'est ni strictement privé, puisqu'il implique une capacité d'agir qui transcende la volonté individuelle, ni complètement public, car il ne doit son existence qu'à une série d'initiatives circonstantielles d'ordre privé, fondées sur cette même volonté individuelle.

2. Ensuite, ce collectif a une *durée* propre, indépendante de ses membres particuliers, et qui échappe par là même au contrôle de l'individu isolé.

3. Enfin, ce même collectif est doté d'une *organisation* spécifique, c'est-à-dire d'une capacité d'agir qui lui assure une présence autonome dans l'espace social.

Ces caractéristiques structurelles attachées à la forme associative s'imposent de plus en plus comme une contrainte incontournable dans le monde éthéré de la marchandise et de la concurrence [14], comme une négation obsédante de la toute-puissance de l'individu et un défi au monopole du pouvoir collectif conféré à l'État. Cette question fera, à l'époque, l'objet d'un long débat sur lequel il nous faut nous attarder quelque peu.

## C. La peur du vide : le débat sur l'association au XIXᵉ siècle

On l'a dit, démocratie et association sont deux dimensions essentielles du débat qui sous-tend le bouleversement des rapports politiques au XIXᵉ siècle. Au-delà du discours rousseauiste, cependant, c'est bien dans l'acte de se réunir et de s'associer pour débattre de la chose publique que philosophes et penseurs radicaux du XVIIIᵉ siècle ont permis la définition d'un *espace public* dont les contours diffèrent fondamentalement du pouvoir féodal. Le discours des Lumières, négateur de l'association, instaure paradoxalement une dynamique où la *pratique* du politique passe par l'association. Paradoxe de la Révolution qui abolit toutes les formes connues de regroupement au même moment où se multiplient de façon fulgurante les clubs et sociétés politiques. L'écart entre une théorie de l'individu souverain et une pratique de dissémination des volontés individuelles dans l'activité associative va entraîner une mutation du débat sur l'association, mutation perceptible surtout à partir de la seconde décennie du XIXᵉ siècle.

Auparavant élément perturbateur de la souveraineté collective, l'association va de plus en plus être perçue comme un moyen valide d'unification des volontés, et plus encore, comme un *mode d'exister* propre au siècle nouveau. N'est-il pas en effet naturel de voir l'époque qui a vu s'instaurer la démocratie moderne inventer de nouvelles formes de regroupement, à la mesure de l'homme nouveau qui se profile à l'horizon ? Au fond, une fois que l'on a détruit les corps et les monopoles féodaux, l'association ne répond-elle pas à un besoin de l'individu ? Les associations « volontaires » [15] ne sont-elles pas une forme particulièrement sophistiquée de manifestation de l'individuel dans le social ? Naguère vestige des temps féodaux, l'association est désormais promue au rang de modalité collective et polyvalente d'intervention qui décuple les capacités d'agir des individus.

La période qui va de 1840 à 1870 environ voit se développer une véritable mystique de l'association. Déjà, à la fin des années 1830, Tocqueville avait insisté sur le lien essentiel entre la forme associative et la démocratie [16]. On voit dorénavant dans l'association un mode d'organisation idéal, permettant de compenser la faiblesse individuelle par la force collective, et ce sans devoir en appeler au pouvoir impersonnel de l'État :

> La puissance de l'association a été fortement sentie de nos jours par les esprits d'élite, par des hommes jeunes, sincères, enthousiastes. Dans un temps où la hardiesse de la pensée, l'esprit d'innovation, et l'amour de l'humanité agitaient si profondément les âmes, dans un temps où la chute des vieilles institutions avait brisé la plupart des liens qui rattachaient les unes aux autres les diverses classes de la société, et n'avait laissé, entre les individus, que les rapport affaiblis de la famille, ou les rapports, importants sans doute, mais un peu abstraits, de la politique, l'association se présentait naturellement aux esprits, comme le principe qui devait, à la fin, régénérer et organiser les sociétés nouvelles. Cette pensée ne manquait pas de vérité. On l'a dit mille fois, dans les sociétés modernes, l'individu est trop isolé, trop concentré en lui-même ; cette même fierté, qui l'isole, l'affaiblit, et cette même indépendance personnelle, qui l'élève, devient une cause de retardement et de faiblesse pour tous. Le correctif, c'est l'association volontaire ; le progrès social ne peut consister à dissoudre toute association, mais à substituer aux associations forcées, oppressives des temps passés, des associations volontaires et équitables [17].

Le groupement plus ou moins contingent d'individualités diverses, unies dans un but commun, se présente donc comme une forme particulièrement pertinente d'organisation de la société civile, que ni la famille, ni l'État ne peuvent remplacer. De l'individu au collectif suprême qu'est l'État, la société se donne comme une gradation de collectifs divers impulsés par la dynamique complexe des échanges entre les hommes et les femmes [18].

Dans cette harmonie retrouvée de la société avec elle-même, dans cette fête de la sociabilité qui a le marché pour animateur, la vieille dichotomie libérale entre l'individu et la société s'estompe quelque peu et fait place à un discours de l'unité. Même chose en ce qui concerne le couple privé/public : l'association n'est-elle pas un moyen de faire l'économie du public en « socialisant le privé » [19] ? En somme, le libéralisme triomphant du milieu du XIXᵉ siècle a cru conjurer la menace potentielle que représentait, pour l'intégrité de l'individu, l'agrégation, même ponctuelle, des volontés individuelles lui-même : ne suffisait-il pas, comme l'avait déjà mentionné Rousseau, de « multiplier le nombre » de ces « sociétés partielles » et de « prévenir l'inégalité » entre elles ?

À ce titre, les vertus de l'association vont vite apparaître particulièrement attrayantes dans les « pays neufs » comme le Québec. Aux lendemains de la défaite cuisante de 1837–1838, ne pouvait-on pas trouver dans l'association une nouvelle forme d'unité, une panacée sociale apte à guider une société désorientée ?

> Si en Europe, dans tous les États civilisés, on a senti depuis quelques années, combien les associations ont produit et sont susceptibles de produire de bons, de puissants effets, pour augmenter le nombre de biens dont les progrès du siècle vous ont doté ; si les sommités des sociétés, les hommes d'élite, ont découvert ce nouveau pouvoir, cette nouvelle puissance que donne la réunion des individualités, le concours des hommes agissant collectivement vers un même but, nous, peuple du continent américain, nous qui voulons marcher sur leurs traces, nous devons également sentir combien il est important pour nous, sé-parés sur un territoire étendu, immense, composé de tant de matières hétérogènes, nous, chez qui les institutions gouvernementales et cons-titutionnelles sont encore à l'état d'enfance et de théories, nous devons comprendre, disons-nous, combien les associations seraient pour nous d'un grand secours, d'abord dans un but d'intérêt politique ; la Société Canadienne n'a pas de centre commun ; elle est éparse, disséminée sur une surface de terre d'une immense étendue ; elle s'agite sans force et sans chaleur, sans cette rigueur que donne le concours collectif d'une masse forte d'hommes et de principes, forts par le nombre et par les idées [20].

Instrument de progrès dans tous les secteurs de l'activité humaine, l'association verra son importance reconnue et encadrée par une série de lois qui mettent en place un véritable droit des associations au XIXᵉ siècle. Nous y reviendrons. Ce qu'il est, pour l'instant, important de signaler, est le caractère profondément ambigu de cette euphorie associative. Ambiguïté d'une propagande qui ne voit dans ces grou-pements plus ou moins fortuits qu'une contribution décisive au progrès des individus. Ambiguïté aussi d'une vision du monde où les collectifs humains ainsi créés s'insèrent sans heurt dans une harmonie communautaire sanctionnée par la loi objective du marché.

Le désenchantement viendra vite, lorsque la coalition bénigne des volontés en vue du progrès fera place à l'union des efforts en vue de la lutte collective. Alors, la contradiction pénètre au cœur de l'association. D'instrument de progrès, elle se fait instrument de défense. Toute une dimension du phénomène associatif, plus ou moins occultée au milieu du XIX^e siècle, se dévoile de plus en plus clairement à mesure que s'aggravent les contradictions du capitalisme. Se manifeste ainsi l'immense équivoque d'un discours de l'unité qui peut aussi bien revêtir les traits d'un consensualisme de bon aloi que ceux de la lutte de classe. Déjà, le discours rassembleur des promoteurs de l'association poussait parfois l'appel à l'unité dans les régions troubles où l'égalité menace de devenir nivellement [21]. Mais lorsque l'égalité de droit aura débouché sur l'inégalité des conditions de vie, un champ nouveau sera ouvert à l'association : nouvelle dimension de l'activité collective dont, très tôt, Lamennais rendra bien l'esprit :

> Lorsque l'homme est seul, le vent de la puissance le courbe vers la terre, et l'ardeur de la convoitise des grands de ce monde absorbe la sève qui le nourrit. Ne soyez donc point comme la plante et comme l'arbre qui sont seuls : mais unissez-vous les uns aux autres, et appuyez-vous, et abritez-vous mutuellement ...
>
> Entre les hommes, quelques-uns ont plus de force ou de corps, ou d'esprit, ou de volonté, et ce sont ceux-là qui cherchent à s'assujettir les autres lorsque l'orgueil ou la convoitise étouffe en eux l'amour de leurs frères. Et Dieu savait qu'il en serait ainsi, et c'est pourquoi il a commandé aux hommes de s'aimer, afin qu'ils fussent unis, et que les faibles ne tombassent point sous l'oppression des forts [22].

Se profile ainsi une philosophie associative qui fait de l'union des individus non plus un prolongement de l'activité individuelle, mais un substitut à ses carences. L'association devient alternative : devant l'aggravation des inégalités et l'approfondissement des contradictions de la régulation par le marché, on verra dans le regroupement des efforts à la fois un mode de *promotion* et de *défense* :
– un mode de promotion : la recherche d'une économie associative basée sur l'entraide plutôt que sur la compétition débouche sur la croissance de l'organisation coopérative et sur le développement d'une

idéologie mutualiste [23], tendance remarquable à partir des années 1860 surtout [24] ;
– un mode de défense : en parallèle, le développement des sociétés de secours mutuels vient compenser partiellement le manque de protection accordée aux victimes du système économique dominant, de même que les syndicats agissent comme sauvegarde des intérêts ouvriers dans le monde de la production.

Dans le dernier tiers du XIXe siècle et au début du XXe, la problématique de l'association a donc pris une ampleur nouvelle, au long des crises du capitalisme. D'une part, le processus de regroupement en associations volontaires a donné lieu à la mise en place, dans le domaine économique, d'énormes entreprises cherchant à monopoliser le marché. La réalité associative occupe maintenant dans l'espace social une telle place qu'elle semble repousser au second plan toute interprétation individualiste de l'ordre social. Le progrès de l'association débouche sur la crise des monopoles. D'autre part, la systématisation des regroupements de défense de la classe ouvrière – et leur reconnaissance tardive par l'État – apparaît à l'époque comme une autre force profondément perturbatrice.

Par ailleurs, l'émergence des pouvoirs régulateurs de l'État, en réponse à la crise profonde qui traverse l'ordre libéral, contribue à réinsérer encore plus fortement la problématique de l'association dans sa dimension *politique*. En effet, la puissance nouvelle de l'État, sa propension de plus en plus nette à intervenir dans la régulation des rapports sociaux, met encore davantage en lumière l'impuissance de l'individu isolé dans le monde qui se construit. L'émergence du « social », cette nébuleuse d'exigences collectives qui impose à l'époque ses incontournables contraintes aux nations occidentales, accélère l'obsolescence déjà marquée de la dichotomie individu/société [25]. L'association, dans ce contexte de crise, apparaît comme une forme d'organisation collective qui, systématisée, pourrait être susceptible de faire contrepoids à l'État, sinon le remplacer [26]. L'idée qu'entre l'individu et l'État puissent exister des groupements humains authentiques, transcendant la volonté individuelle et échappant à l'emprise de l'État, a donné lieu à une polémique virulente à l'époque [27], polémique qui s'est vite reflétée dans le débat sur la portée de la personnalité juridique qui fait rage au début du XXe siècle [28].

Cette tentative de « naturalisation » de l'association sape les fondements même de la philosophie politique libérale. Elle réduit l'État à n'être au fond que la plus grande et la plus compréhensive des formes communautaires d'agglomération des individus. Se dégage ainsi, de la crise du libéralisme, un des grands ensembles idéologiques du XXᵉ siècle : le corporatisme. À partir de ce moment, l'enjeu principal du débat sur le social consistera à déterminer le rôle potentiel de l'État – et de la démocratie – dans un ensemble social où l'association se présente comme alternative sociale et politique. Le keynésianisme et l'État-providence résoudront la question de la façon que l'on sait.

## 2. L'État et le phénomène associatif au XIXᵉ siècle : de la défiance à l'encadrement

Mode d'auto-institution du social inscrit au cœur de la transition au capitalisme, l'association ne pouvait qu'entretenir des rapports ambigus et contradictoires avec l'instance suprême du pouvoir social : l'État. Le développement du phénomène associatif impliquait en effet la prise en compte par l'État de l'existence de collectifs agissant dans le champ de la société civile. Dès l'abord, deux problèmes concomitants se posent :

1. Quel sera le *statut* de ces associations dans un monde d'échanges privés où le droit est axé avant tout sur la défense et la promotion de l'individu ?

2. Quels seront les pouvoirs conférés à ces institutions de la société civile, sachant qu'au-delà des droits de la personne, tout pouvoir est assignable en dernière instance à la souveraineté du peuple ?

La résolution de ces problèmes complexes doit de plus être replacée dans le contexte mouvant de transition que connaît l'économie du pouvoir au XIXᵉ siècle. On verra donc se refléter, dans les rapports entre État et associations, la mutation des critères d'exercice des pouvoirs publics en cette matière.

### A. Les nouveaux modes d'action collective et la défiance de l'État jusqu'au milieu du XIXᵉ siècle

À la fin du XVIIIᵉ siècle, la géographie institutionnelle des pays occidentaux consacre à la fois la puissance et la fragilité de l'État féodal et monarchique. Puissance d'un État qui assure son hégémonie sur ce qui reste des anciennes communautés associatives de l'ordre féodal : jurandes et maîtrises, couvents et monastères, confréries et hôpitaux, compagnies à charte et communes n'exercent leur juridiction que dans le cadre d'une réglementation assurant aux officiers du roi, dans bien des cas, un droit de regard. Mais faiblesse aussi de cet État qui reste empêtré dans le fin réseau des juridictions assumées de façon immémoriale par une infinité de corps semi-politiques attachés à leurs privilèges [29].

À ce stade de l'histoire des associations, les divers groupements existants sont essentiellement des institutions coutumières, encadrant étroitement l'activité communautaire. Mais à partir du XVIIIe siècle se développent de nouvelles entités collectives en Occident. Associations d'affaires [30], académies et clubs divers, cabinets de lecture et associations charitables, écoles de charité, hôpitaux privés et sociétés de secours mutuels constituent des formes radicalement nouvelles, se posant plus ou moins explicitement comme réactions critiques aux institutions féodales traditionnelles. Ces types d'association remettent brutalement en question la logique ancienne de regroupement, et ce à plusieurs titres :

– elles revendiquent une autonomie farouche par rapport à la hiérarchie féodale ou à toute autre forme de pouvoir politique ;

– leur mise en place relève d'un processus d'adhésion volontaire, exempt des multiples dépendances de l'ordre féodal et de la distinction des statuts ;

– leur organisation et leur contrôle renvoient au principe de la délégation libre de pouvoir et à la souveraineté de l'assemblée des membres ;

– elles assument une fonction spécifique, scrupuleusement délimitée dans l'espace social, et n'encadrent que partiellement, sous un angle précis et restreint, la vie des membres qui la constituent ;

– elles sont dotées d'une existence abstraite distincte des membres qui la composent, et soigneusement adaptée au but spécifique poursuivi ;

– leur durée et leur transformation éventuelle dépend essentiellement de la volonté décisionnelle de leurs membres, selon les circonstances changeantes de leur évolution ;

– elles mettent en place une structure institutionnelle souple et éminemment adaptable aux multiples enjeux et aux divers problèmes propres au développement des rapports sociaux ;

– leur hiérarchie interne est moins une résultante de la tradition qu'une décision explicite et contingente émanant des membres, décision conforme au but poursuivi.

On verra ces formes d'organisation de type démocratique se mouvoir, à l'époque, dans un flou juridique qui trahit l'embarras du pouvoir. L'attitude des autorités envers ces divers types de regroupement ira de la répression brutale à la reconnaissance hésitante, de la surveillance méfiante à la tolérance tatillonne. Le statut légal de ce type d'association est aussi assez peu clair. En France, on peut les considérer comme illégales, puisque la doctrine semble attribuer au souverain le pouvoir de sanctionner tous les corps constitués [31]. En Angleterre, même si le droit de réunion et d'association peut être considéré comme inhérent aux « libertés anglaises », le *Common Law* ne reconnaît pas comme entité légale les associations non incorporées [32].

Exemplaire à ce titre est l'aventure des premières sociétés de secours mutuel au Bas-Canada. Fondée en 1789, la « Société bienveillante de Québec » demande l'incorporation légale dans une pétition adressée en 1795 à l'Assemblée législative du Bas-Canada [33]. L'association invoque, dans sa requête, l'exemple de l'Angleterre, qui a adopté deux ans auparavant l'Acte pour l'encouragement et le soulagement des sociétés amicales [34]. Malgré l'appui accordé par un comité de la Chambre à cette pétition [35], il faudra attendre jusqu'en 1807 pour qu'une loi d'incorporation particulière vienne confirmer l'existence légale de cette association. La loi finalement adoptée prévoit d'ailleurs des procédures strictes de contrôle de l'institution : les règlements doivent être approuvés par la cour du Banc du Roi, et le gouverneur peut, de façon discrétionnaire, dissoudre la société [36].

La « Société bienveillante des artisans de Québec », fondée en 1810, se heurtera à une résistance encore plus systématique. La société demande l'incorporation en 1812, en se fondant cette fois sur le précédent constitué par la loi de 1807 dont il vient d'être question. Le projet de loi présenté échoue cependant devant la volonté du Conseil législatif d'insérer dans la loi d'incorporation une clause donnant pouvoir aux juges de paix de disperser les assemblées de la société [37]. Une loi d'incorporation est finalement adoptée en 1817 [38]. Cependant, par un incident probablement unique dans nos annales parlementaires, le roi a laissé s'écouler le délai maximal de deux ans accordé par l'acte de 1791 avant de sanctionner cette loi, la rendant nulle par le fait même !

Ces tribulations n'ont rien de fortuit : elles trahissent l'embarras et les hésitations des autorités face à ces « corps intermédiaires » qui, non contents de proliférer à la surface de la société civile, demandent en plus une sanction légale qui puisse leur assurer la permanence. La réticence des milieux traditonnels face à cette prétention est fort bien rendue dans les raisons données, en 1821, par le Conseil législatif pour justifier son insistance à conférer au gouverneur un pouvoir de dissolution en cas d'incorporation :

Parce que des Institutions, sous quelque nom qu'elles puissent être établies, soit comme Corps politiques ou comme Sociétés, par lesquelles une nombreuse assemblée de personnes peut être réunie, ne devraient pas être rendues permanentes, en première instance, dans un pays où les effets qu'elles peuvent produire n'ont pas encore été démontrés par l'expérience.

Parce qu'il est expédient et sage, dans toutes telles institutions, soit de les assujettir à une existence limitée ou d'y insérer une clause donnant le pouvoir de les dissoudre, et l'exercice de tel pouvoir ne peut point être plus sûrement confié qu'au pouvoir exécutif de la Province [39].

Il est clair qu'au début du XIXᵉ siècle, l'incorporation est encore une mesure exceptionnelle : la parcimonie avec laquelle elle est utilisée témoigne de la méfiance de l'État devant les mouvements de la société civile : les attitudes de l'ancien régime social et politique sont encore prévalentes.

Est-il étonnant, dans ces conditions, que la très grande majorité des incorporations concédées touchent des domaines où l'utilité publique est avérée : construction de ponts, de canaux et de chemins à péage, gestion des communes de village, services d'aqueducs ou d'incendie, assurance contre le feu, banque, etc. ? La politique étatique est ici en pleine continuité avec les critères d'incorporation suivis au XVIIIᵉ siècle en Angleterre, critères qui font de l'incorporation un instrument permettant de valider les institutions assurant des services collectifs dont le besoin se fait de plus en plus sentir. Sous cet angle, on peut considérer l'octroi d'une charte d'incorporation comme un *privilège* trouvant sa justification dans l'intérêt public [40].

Jusqu'au milieu du XIXᵉ siècle, le rapport entre État et institutions oscille donc entre une tolérance plus ou moins ouverte d'associations au statut légal flou et l'octroi parcimonieux de la personnalité corporative à certaines d'entre ces mêmes associations. L'accélération du processus de formation des associations, à partir des années 1830 surtout [41], va venir bouleverser cet équilibre précaire.

### B. Le problème du cadre juridique

Le développement du mouvement associatif au XIXᵉ siècle pose un problème juridique d'envergure. En effet, deux questions centrales se posent : quel est le mode d'existence juridique d'un *collectif* de personnes doté d'une organisation propre, et dans quel cadre légal peut-on concevoir la capacité d'agir de ce collectif ?

## 1. La question de la personnalité juridique

La reconnaissance d'une personnalité juridique aux associations est au cœur de toute la problématique des rapports entre État et associations au XIX<sup>e</sup> siècle. Dans le modèle féodal de régulation, ce problème trouvait une solution relativement simple : au-delà des formes coutumières d'organisation communautaire, seul le souverain semblait avoir la prérogative de créer des corps nouveaux [42]. Bien sûr, toutes les formes d'organisation ne jouissaient pas de tels privilèges. Les systèmes juridiques français et anglais ont ainsi vu se développer de multiples modes de regroupements ayant reçu une certaine forme de reconnaissance juridique.

En droit français, les divers types de sociétés reconnues [43] constituent en fait des agglomérations d'intérêts ne jouissant pas de la personnalité civile : des règles juridiques strictes répartissent plutôt entre les associés les responsabilités et les devoirs. Il s'agit donc moins d'un collectif formel que de la réunion circonstantielle des intérêts de certains individus en vue d'un but précis. Par ailleurs, les corps constitués, reconnus par le souverain, forment le seul autre type d'association possible en droit français.

Le droit anglais, pour sa part, a permis le développement d'une plus grande diversité de formes associatives [44]. Chacun des trois grands segments du droit anglais a contribué à cette relative profusion. Le *Common Law* a développé le concept de *corporation sole*, personnalité juridique conférée à l'unique occupant d'une fonction déterminée – notamment le curé, l'évêque, le souverain – et qui s'étend au-delà de la vie des individus particuliers qui assument successivement cette dernière. De même, le *partnership*, équivalent de la société commerciale française, issu du droit commercial féodal, fut intégré au *Common Law* à partir du XVII<sup>e</sup> siècle. À la même époque sont apparues les sociétés par actions (*joint-stock companies*), associations qui ont utilisé les règles de *Common Law* touchant le mandat (*agency*) pour répartir les responsabilités entre les actionnaires et la direction. Ces deux dernières formes d'association ne jouissaient pas de la personnalité juridique. De son côté, la juridiction en *Equity* a permis la mise au point de cette relation fiduciaire originale qu'est le trust. Cette forme inédite de dévolution en matière de responsabilités de gestion, hautement adaptable, a longtemps permis aux compagnies anglaises non incorporées de contourner les restrictions draconiennes mises à l'incorporation par le *Bubble Act* [45]. Finalement, le souverain, par l'émission de lettres patentes, ou le Parlement, par l'adoption d'une loi d'incorporation, pouvaient conférer la personnalité juridique à tout type de regroupement. Cet acte, émané du pouvoir souverain, pouvait permettre d'adapter les privilèges légaux conférés aux besoins spécifiques de l'association et à la volonté de contrôle de l'exécutif ou du Parlement. Si le *Common Law* et l'*Equity* mettaient surtout en place des *procédures* permettant une certaine formalisation des rapports entre associés et avec autrui, la charte apparaissait de son côté comme un mode de délégation du pouvoir souverain ajusté à chaque cas particulier [46].

### 2. La capacité d'agir des collectifs : l'incorporation

On voit donc que la concession d'une personnalité juridique à certains collectifs n'est qu'*une* des formes de reconnaissance de l'association par le droit. Cependant, cette procédure revêt une importance particulière, dans la mesure où l'attribution de cette personnalité fictive donne à l'association la faculté d'étendre sa sphère d'action. L'*incorporation* sera donc le véhicule majeur d'attribution aux collectifs de pouvoirs spécifiques [47]. L'énoncé des principaux pouvoirs ordinairement dévolus par l'incorporation permet de prendre la mesure de l'importance de cette procédure :
– capacité de détenir des biens *en commun*, y compris, dans certains cas, des pouvoirs d'aliénation et d'emprunt ;
– faculté de l'association de pouvoir poursuivre et être poursuivie indépendamment des membres qui la composent ;
– succession perpétuelle et continuation de l'existence corporative au-delà des personnes qui constituent à un moment donné le regroupement ;
– aptitude à exercer les pouvoirs nécessaires à l'atteinte des fins de l'association (pouvoirs incidents) ;
– pouvoir de la corporation de réglementer son activité interne et de contraindre légalement les membres à respecter ces règlements ;
– jouissance, le cas échéant, de certains avantages spécifiques : entrent dans cette vaste catégorie la limitation de la responsabilité des associés, l'exemption de taxes ou d'impôts ou le monopole d'exécution de certaines opérations.

La puissance potentielle de regroupements dotés de tels pouvoirs légaux est donc au cœur de la question de l'incorporation au XIXe siècle. On retrouve ici, sous sa forme juridique, le grand débat du siècle dernier sur l'association. En somme, les moyens légaux existent, permettant de faire de l'association une des formes suprêmes de la société civile et le support des volontés coalisées. Bientôt d'ailleurs, le recours de plus en plus fréquent à l'incorporation particulière de la part des associations contribuera à banaliser cette forme légale. Au Bas-Canada, ce mouvement est surtout perceptible à partir des années 1830. Au milieu du XIX<sup>e</sup> siècle, malgré la popularité persistante des formes légales traditionnelles de regroupement (*trusts* et *partnerships* notamment), l'incorporation apparaît clairement comme la forme la plus riche d'avenir. Mais ceci étant reconnu, comment faire pour que le droit non seulement appuie, mais stimule ces regroupements qui surgissent de toute part ?

### C. L'encadrement légal de l'association : les lois générales

L'octroi, par voie parlementaire ou par lettres patentes, de chartes d'incorporation particulières impliquait que le développement de cette forme légale demeure sous le contrôle étroit de l'État. Dans cette logique, la croissance des institutions pouvait être subordonnée à l'intérêt public, chaque charte octroyée apparaissant ou bien comme un moyen d'assurer certains services essentiels, ou bien comme une concession de privilèges justifiée par l'utilité sociale particulière d'une association. Dans un cas comme dans l'autre, l'État se réservait le droit de jauger la validité de la demande d'incorporation à l'aune de sa politique générale.

À partir du milieu de XIX<sup>e</sup> siècle cependant, une importante mutation de la politique d'incorporation s'amorce. Le développement fulgurant du nombre des associations à l'époque a contribué, on l'a vu, à infléchir la perception du phénomène associatif. Instrument de progrès et moyen de mise en œuvre des énergies individuelles, l'association avait cessé d'apparaître comme un danger, ou comme un écart exceptionnel à l'individualisme ambiant. Dès lors se pose la question de l'*accessibilité* de cette forme de socialisation des efforts particuliers. La protection légale, jusqu'ici accordée plus ou moins parcimonieusement, ne devrait-elle pas être étendue au plus grand nombre possible d'associations, afin que le dynamisme de la société civile puisse s'exprimer librement et prendre son essor ? Pourquoi les avantages conférés par l'incorporation seraient-ils réservés à un petit nombre de regroupements privilégiés dont l'État s'arrogerait la sélection ?

S'enclenche à partir de ce moment un processus d'expansion sans précédent de la forme corporative. En parallèle à l'accroissement des incorporations particulières, les États occidentaux adoptent une série de *lois-cadres* mettant en place des procédures *générales et uniformes* d'incorporation selon les différents types d'association. Ce moment est crucial dans l'histoire des rapports entre associations et État : celui-ci renonce, de fait, à exercer sa discrétion dans l'octroi des avantages corporatifs. Il se contente d'établir des règles générales qui serviront de paramètre au libre développement de la forme associative. Dorénavant, la reconnaissance des divers collectifs organisés se banalise en procédure administrative d'enregistrement. À mesure que l'on s'avance dans le siècle, la crise de l'économie de marché ne fait que rendre plus nécessaire cette reconnaissance systématique, et fait apparaître comme de plus en plus arbitraire la discrimination qui touche les associations syndicales [48].

À cet égard, le cas du Québec est exemplaire. À quelques exceptions près, ce n'est vraiment qu'à partir de 1850 qu'apparaissent les grandes lois générales permettant d'encadrer la formation de compagnies par actions, de sociétés de secours mutuels, d'associations charitables et ouvrières, etc. Les temporalités diverses d'apparition de ces lois restent évidemment à étudier plus à fond ; elles correspondent d'ailleurs à l'évolution perceptible en France et surtout en Angleterre.

Reste que le schéma de développement est clair : par strates successives, la plupart des types d'association pourront trouver dans la législation une protection légale minimale. Pour sa part, l'incorporation par loi particulière demeure un recours accessible dans les cas spéciaux [49]. L'association a désormais définitivement conquis sa légitimité face à l'État. Le paysage du libéralisme en sera bouleversé à jamais.

## Conclusion

« Nous considérons, qu'après le privilège qui appartient à chaque individu d'agir pour lui-même, d'après les bases mêmes de la société, celui de joindre toute son énergie à celle de ses concitoyens dans tous les projets qui ont pour but la défense ou l'intérêt mutuel, et par conséquent le droit d'association, est un droit aussi sacré et aussi aliénable que celui de la liberté personnelle [50]. »

Aux sources de l'association ... la démocratie. À l'heure où les hommes et les femmes découvrent les contraintes et les possibilités attachées à un destin collectif dont ils et elles auraient le contrôle, au moment même où le pouvoir apprend à se légitimer par la volonté collective, le fait de *s'unir* prend un sens tout à fait particulier. La coalition des volontés se présente alors comme transcendance de l'individu dans un social à construire. L'individu se sublime, et semble par l'association se renvoyer l'image multipliée de lui-même.

Mais l'association est aussi contradiction, ambiguïté, saut périlleux où, dans le passage de l'individuel au collectif, quelque chose se perd qui est l'unique en chacun de nous. Car l'union est *aussi* cette dissolution de l'unicité, cette création de la volonté collective comme *moyenne*, cette résolution des aspirations particulières en objectif commun. Au fond, ne pourrait-on pas avancer que c'est par le fait de ces associations fragiles, éphémères, éclatées, toujours recommencées et jamais épuisées, que les femmes et les hommes du XIX<sup>e</sup> siècle ont fait l'apprentissage de la démocratie comme *pratique* ?

L'ensemble social est certes un construit, mais un construit abstrait et global, où l'exercice du pouvoir, comme la soumission, se réfracte et se formalise dans la puissance de l'État. Alors que l'association est ce lieu concret et immédiat où l'individu apprend à confronter son unicité avec celle des autres, et voit naître de cet échange une action commune. Pratique subversive, réfractaire au formalisme bureaucratique comme à l'égoïsme particulier, mais en même temps toujours susceptible de se figer dans l'un ou de s'épuiser dans l'autre.

L'association, lieu privilégié d'apprentissage du social comme *collectif*, est donc une forme sociale ouverte à la multiplicité des rapports sociaux. En elle se fond l'infinie variété des entreprises collectives d'une société qui apprend à s'instituer elle-même. De l'association charitable à la compagnie, de la société de secours mutuel à la banque, des clubs sportifs aux syndicats, le collectif s'impose comme forme indépassable de l'existence en société. Déjà, au XIX<sup>e</sup> siècle, la prolifération des regroupements de toutes espèces trahit la fonction ultime de l'association moderne : faire de la démocratie, plus qu'une forme de pouvoir, une pratique quotidienne.

## NOTES

Cet essai est la résultante d'un projet de recherche en cours sur « le droit d'association au Québec au XIX<sup>e</sup> siècle ». Nous remercions le Conseil de recherche en sciences humaines du Canada et le Fonds pour la Formation des chercheurs et l'aide à la recherche du Québec pour le support financier accordé à cette recherche.

1 Les travaux de M. Agulhon sont en ce sens une exception rarissime,

dans la mesure où Agulhon étudie l'association comme un phénomène *global*, au-delà des thématiques particulières sous lesquelles on peut subsumer chaque type d'association. Ceci dit, l'approche d'Agulhon est essentiellement d'ordre sociologique : il conçoit l'association avant tout comme une forme de *sociabilité*, donc comme émanation de la société civile. Voir M. Agulhon, *Le cercle dans la France bourgeoise, 1810–1848* (Paris : A. Colin 1977) ; M. Agulhon et M. Bodiguel, *Les associations au village* (Le Paradour, Actes Sud 1981).

2 M. Reybaud, *Études sur les réformateurs ou socialistes modernes* (Paris 1841) 296

3 « Groupement de personnes qui s'unissent en vue d'un but déterminé » (*Petit Robert*)

4 On aura compris qu'il n'est pas question, dans ce texte, de confiner le politique à cette sphère d'activité centrée autour de l'État et du pouvoir. Le politique est aussi, et surtout peut-être, *une procédure de mise en forme de l'espace social.* « Que quelque chose comme la politique en soit venu à se circonscrire à une époque, dans la vie sociale, a précisément une signification politique, une signification qui n'est pas particulière, mais générale. C'est la constitution de l'espace social, c'est la forme de la société, c'est l'essence de ce qu'on nommait autrefois la cité qui est mise en jeu avec cet événement. Le politique se révèle ainsi non pas dans ce qu'on nomme l'activité politique, mais dans ce double mouvement d'apparition et d'occultation du mode d'institution de la société. Apparition, en ce sens qu'émerge à la visibilité le procès par lequel s'ordonne et s'unifie la société, à travers ses divisions ; occultation en ce sens qu'un lieu de la politique (lieu où s'exerce la compétition des partis et où se forme et se renouvelle l'instance générale du pouvoir) se désigne comme particulier, tandis que se trouve dissimulé le principe générateur de la configuration de l'ensemble », C. Lefort, « La question de la démocratie », *Essais sur le politique, 19ᵉ–20ᵉ siècle* (Paris : Seuil 1981), 19–20.

5 Je me suis expliqué sur ce point dans J.-M. Fecteau, *Régulation sociale et transition au capitalisme : jalons théoriques et méthodologiques pour une analyse du XIXᵉ siècle canadien* (Quebec : Projet Accumulation et Régulation au Québec 1986).

6 « Dans les pays démocratiques, la science de l'association est la science mère ; le progrès de toutes les autres dépend des progrès de celle-là. Parmi les lois qui régissent les sociétés humaines, il y en a une qui semble plus précise et plus claire que toutes les autres. Pour que les hommes restent civilisés ou le deviennent, il faut que parmi eux l'art de s'associer se développe et se perfectionne dans le même rapport que l'égalité des conditions s'accroît », A. de Tocqueville, *De la démocratie en Amérique*, 2 vols (Paris : Garnier-Flammarion [1840] 1981), vol. 2, 141.

7 On pourrait parler ici, en suivant Patrick Tort, d'éléments idéologiques dont le lien organique forme un véritable « complexe discursif ». Sur ce dernier concept, voir P. Tort, *La pensée hiérarchique et l'évolution* (Paris : Aubier 1983), 43–58.

8 J. Habermas, *L'espace public* (Paris : Payot 1978)

9 Le caractère *nouveau* de cette dichotomie est bien mis en lumière par Hartog : « We shall have to discard our easy reliance on anachronistic assumptions of the mutual exclusivity of public and private spheres of action. Men and women of the first half of the 18th century did not organize the world into the categories common to our experience and to our legal system. They not only thought different thoughts, they thought those thoughts differently. Where we see a legal universe of repressive and mutually exclusive categories of law against politics, substance against procedure, and public against private, it may be that Americans then saw a universe in which the main institutions of social order were integrated and joined in a complex and unstable pattern of authority and hierarchy », H. Hartog, « Because All the World Was Not New York City : Governance, Property Rights and the State in the Changing Definition of a Corporation, 1730–1860 », *Buffalo Law Review* 28 (1979), 109.

10 « A monopoly granted either to an individual or to a trading company has the same effect as a secret in trade or manufactures. The monopolists, by keeping the market constantly under-stocked, by never fully supplying the effectual demand, sell their commodities much above the natural price, and raise their emoluments, whether they consist in wages or profit, greatly above their natural rate ... The exclusive privileges of corporations, statutes of apprenticeship, and all those laws which restrain, in particular employments, the competition to a smaller number than might otherwise go into them, have the same tendency, though in a less degree. » A. Smith, *An Enquiry into the Nature and Causes of the Wealth of Nations*, 2 vols (Chicago : University of Chicago Press [1784] 1976), vol. 1, 69. Voir aussi vol. 1, 70–6, 132, 160, 489–95 ; vol. 2, 75–87, 146–58 et 244–82. À l'inverse, Hobbes se contente d'énumérer les « corps politiques » existant au sein de l'État : T. Hobbes, *Leviathan* (New York : Collier [1651] 1962), 169–79.

11 J.-J. Rousseau, *Du contrat social* (Paris : Garnier-Flammarion [1762] 1966), 66–7. Voir aussi M.L. Goldschmidt, « Rousseau on Intermediate Associations », J.R. Pennock et J.W. Chapman, eds, *Voluntary Associations* (New York : Atherton Press 1969), 119–37.

12 Loi Le Chapelier abolissant les corporations et les compagnonnages (juin 1791), abolition de l'ordre des avocats (sept. 1790), des académies littéraires (août 1793), des chambres de commerce (sept. 1791), des congrégations religieuses et charitables (août 1792). Le Chapelier, dans l'exposé des principes de la loi de juin 1791, affirmera qu' « il doit sans

doute être permis à tous les citoyens de s'assembler, mais il ne doit pas être permis aux citoyens de certaines professions de s'assembler pour leurs prétendus intérêts communs. Il n'y a plus de corporations dans l'État ; il n'y a plus que l'intérêt particulier de chaque individu et l'intérêt général. Il n'est permis à personne d'inspirer aux citoyens un intérêt intermédiaire, de les séparer de la chose publique par un esprit de corporation ». Cité par P. Nourrisson, *Histoire de la liberté d'association en France depuis 1789*, 2 vols (Paris : Sirey 1920), vol. 1, 119–20

13 En France, inscrit dans l'éphémère constitution de 1848, il ne sera finalement formellement reconnu qu'en 1901. En Angleterre, ce droit s'entoure d'un ensemble de restrictions qui en limitent grandement la portée. Nous reviendrons plus loin sur ce point.

14 On nous permettra une brève remarque à ce point. Il apparaît symptomatique de l'hégémonie de l'approche libérale dans notre historiographie qu'un phénomène de l'envergure de l'association au XIX^e siècle n'ait jamais vraiment été étudié en lui-même. Tout se passe comme si chaque groupement n'était digne d'étude qu'en raison de son importance ponctuelle, ou parce que la fin qu'il poursuit permet de subsumer son analyse sous une thématique d'étude particulière. On a étudié les entreprises, les banques, les syndicats, les associations charitables, les sociétés littéraires, les clubs sportifs, les coopératives, les sociétés de secours mutuel, mais pratiquement jamais *l'association* comme phénomène original de société. Est-il besoin pourtant de souligner qu'une histoire de la transition qui ne reposerait que sur la saga de l'entrepreneur privé ou sur les aléas de l'État libéral serait ridiculement réductrice – comme d'ailleurs la vision qui persiste à faire du XIX^e siècle le siècle de l'individualisme ? La présence massive des associations dans tous les domaines d'activité sociale doit être saisie comme un des phénomènes majeurs de la transition au capitalisme.

15 L'emprise de cette dimension volontariste de l'association est tellement puissante qu'elle déterminera l'orientation d'une grande partie des travaux anglo-américains sur l'association. Voir D.L. Sills, « Voluntary Associations », *International Encyclopaedia of Social Sciences* (Londres : Macmillan 1968), 357–79.

16 « Dans les sociétés aristocratiques, les hommes n'ont plus besoin de s'unir pour agir, parce qu'ils sont retenus fortement ensemble.
Chaque citoyens, riche et puissant ; y forme comme la tête d'une association permanente et forcée qui est composée de tous ceux qu'il tient dans sa dépendance et qu'il fait concourir à l'exécution de ses desseins.
   Chez les peuples démocratiques, au contraire, tous les citoyens sont indépendants et faibles ; ils ne peuvent presque rien par eux-mêmes, et aucun d'entre eux ne saurait obliger ses semblables à lui prêter leur concours. Ils tombent tous dans l'impuissance s'ils n'apprennent à s'aider librement. Si les hommes qui vivent dans les pays

démocratiques n'avaient ni le droit ni le goût de s'unir dans des buts politiques, leur indépendance courrait de grands hasards, mais ils pourraient conserver longtemps leurs richesses et leurs lumières ; tandis que s'ils n'acquéraient point l'usage de s'associer dans la vie ordinaire, la civilisation elle-même serait en péril. Un peuple chez lequel les particuliers perdraient le pouvoir de faire isolément de grandes choses sans acquérir la faculté de les produire en commun retournerait bientôt vers la barbarie ». Tocqueville, *De la démocratie en Amérique*, vol. 2, 138–9

17 *La Minerve*, 5 juin 1843 (tiré de *L'Économiste*). Dans ce contexte, l'association s'harmonise parfaitement avec le pouvoir démocratique : « Dans les pays despotiques, c'est à peine s'il existe une trace quelconque du principe d'association. Voyez au contraire, les pays libres, ceux où l'unité n'est qu'un moyen de puissance et de grandeur pour un gouvernement national. Là, rien ne gêne l'action individuelle, que les lois d'ordre public et de police. Loin d'en redouter le développement, l'autorité le désire et le seconde, et les associations particulières viennent, dans le domaine de la science, du commerce, de l'industrie, se coordonner, dans une puissance harmonie, avec l'association par excellence, la société civile » , ibid.

18 Dynamique de cristallisation des rapports sociaux bien décrite par *L'Avenir* du 30 octobre 1850 : « C'est le commerce qui est ce lieu sacré, qui nous fait comprendre notre impuissance et la nécessité des relations qui est le premier mobile de toute société. Nous nous devons les uns aux autres des services réciproques, c'est ce qui donna naissance au commerce. Jamais donc il n'y eut de société sans commerce : car d'homme à homme il créa les familles, de famille à famille, il forma les sociétés, de société à société, il réunit les empires et d'empires à empires, il rapproche le monde entier. » Cité par Y. Lamonde, « Les associations au Bas-Canada : de nouveaux marchés aux idées (1840–1867) », *Histoire sociale* 8 (1975), 364

19 On voit la dérive possible d'un tel cheminement vers les théories corporatistes. Nous y reviendrons.

20 *Revue canadienne*, 8 févr. 1846. Évidemment, quand il s'agit d'association, la dimension politique de l'enjeu se manifeste très clairement : « Association, éducation, progrès : ces trois mots renferment tout et signifient tout. Instruisez le peuple, fortifiez le peuple, moralisez le peuple, afin que lorsque l'heure de l'indépendance sonnera pour nous, afin que lorsque la démocratie viendra régénérer et grandir notre pays, nous soyons digne de vivre sous un gouvernement libéral, démocratique et républicain. » *Le Pays*, 1ᵉʳ mars 1852

21 « Rallions donc nos faibles ressources, réunissons nos facultés matérielles et nos facultés morales, associons-nous, faibles et forts, car tous individuellement nous sommes faibles, et les plus hautes entreprises seront

à notre portée. La société sera heureuse alors, car tous ses membres seront utiles et toutes ses forces actives, car la concurrence qui ruine les uns pour enrichir les autres aura fait place au concours qui enrichit tout le monde. » *La Minerve*, 5 juin 1843

22 Lamennais, « L'esprit d'association », cité dans *L'Avenir*, 2 août 1849

23 Sur ce type d'association et son statut au Québec au XIXᵉ siècle, voir J.-M. Fecteau (avec la collaboration d'Isabelle Dupuis) *Association et Autonomie populaire. L'émergence de l'idéal coopératif et l'État au Québec, 1850–1914* (Montréal : Cahiers de la Chaire de coopération de l'Université du Québec à Montréal 1989).

24 On verra des ténors du libéralisme, tels J. Stuart Mill, se rallier à cette alternative. Voir J.S. Mill, *Principles of Political Economy* (New York : A.M. Kelley [1848] 1961), 752–94.

25 Voir la remarquable description de ce phénomène chez J. Donzelot, *L'Invention du social* (Paris : Fayard 1984). On pourra consulter aussi sur toute cette question F. Ewald, *L'État providence* (Paris : Grasset 1986).

26 Est-ce un hasard si, après la Commune de 1870, se développent deux théories plus ou moins parallèles du dépérissement de l'État, la théorie marxiste et la théorie corporatiste, cette dernière s'appuyant sur les conceptions organiques du social de Gierke, Durkheim, Hauriou et Tönnies.

27 Voir notamment O. Gierke, *Political Theories of the Middle Ages* (Boston : Beacon Press [1900] 1958) ; Gierke, *Natural Law and the Theories of Society, 1500 to 1800* (Cambridge : Cambridge University Press [1934] 1958) ; E. Durkheim, *De la division du travail social* (Paris : Presses Universitaires de France [1893] 1978) ; M.H. Elbow, *French Corporative Theories, 1789–1948* (New York : Octagon Books 1966) ; R.H. Bowen, *German Theories of the Corporative State, 1870–1919* (New York : McGraw-Hill 1947).

28 La bibliographie est énorme. Qu'il nous suffise de citer : M. Hauriou, « De la personnalité comme élément de la réalité sociale » , *Revue générale du droit, de la législation et de la jurisprudence* 22 (1898), 1–119 ; F.W. Maitland, « Moral Personality and Legal Personality, » *Collected Papers*, 2 vols (Cambridge : Cambridge University Press, 1911) vol. 3, 304–20 ; L. Michoud, *La théorie de la personnalité morale et son application au droit français* (Paris : Librairie Générale de Droit et de Jurisprudence 1924), 2 vols ; P. Saleilles, *De la personnalité juridique* (Paris : Rousseau 1910); Marquis de Vareilles-Sommières, *Les Personnes morales* (Paris : Librairie Générale de Droit et de Jurisprudence 1919).

29 Même si la redécouverte du droit romain tend à renforcer le pouvoir du souverain en cette matière. Sur le statut des différents corps dans le droit romain, voir O. Gierke, *Association and Law : The Classical and Early Christian Stages* (Toronto : University of Toronto Press 1977).

30 Dans ce dernier cas, il s'agit notamment des compagnies par actions britanniques (*Joint-stock companies*), qui se développent malgré les restrictions inscrites dans le Bubble Act de 1720. Voir A. DuBois, *The English Business Company after the Bubble Act, 1720–1800* (Londres, Octagon [1938] 1971). Nous reviendrons sur les formes de regroupements issus de la coutume commerciale féodale, tels la société et le *partnership*.

31 « Nous pouvons dire que tout corps ou collège est un droit de communauté légitime sous la puissance souveraine. Le mot de légitime emporte l'autorité du souverain, sans la permission duquel il n'y a point de collège » : J. Bodin, *La République* (1577). Sur les corporations médiévales et l'État, voir A. Black, *Guilds and Civil Society in European Political Thought from the Twelfth Century to the Present* (Ithaca, NY : Cornell University Press 1984).

32 Sur ce problème, voir plus loin. On pourra aussi consulter F.W. Maitland, « The Unincorporated Body », *Collected Papers*, vol. 3, 271–84 ; A.F. Sheppard, « Some Aspects of the Law of Unincorporated Associations », *University of British Columbia Law Review*, 3:1 (1967–8), 137–60.

33 *Journaux de la Chambre d'Assemblée du Bas-Canada*, 1795, 242–4

34 33 Geo. III (1793), cap. 54. Cette loi vient surtout valider juridiquement l'existence des associations de secours mutuels déjà fondées à l'époque.

35 Le comité va même jusqu'à recommander l'adoption d'une loi *générale* : « Le Comité est d'opinion que d'après l'utilité évidente de sociétés amiables ou bienveillantes, en pourvoyant pour le soutien des membres d'icelles, en vieillesse, maladie et infirmité, et de l'expérience du bien qui en résulte dans la Grande-Bretagne, ce qui leur a procuré le soutien et la protection du Parlement, il est à souhaiter que la demande des pétitionnaires soit accordée, en introduisant un Bill pour être passé en loi, accordant à ces sociétés en général les moyens légaux de pouvoir mettre leur fonds en sûreté pour les effets auxquels il est approprié, et de faire les règlements nécessaires pour leur conduite interne et le gouvernement de leurs intérêts, sur des principes semblables à ceux établis pour les Sociétés amiables dans la Grande-Bretagne par les actes du Parlement britannique, les faisant varier toutefois, suivant que les circonstances locales de la Province pourront le requérir. » *Journaux de la Chambre d'Assemblée du Bas-Canada*, 1795–6, 314

36 47 Geo. II (1807), cap. 17

37 *Journaux de la Chambre d'Assemblée du Bas-Canada* 1812, 557. La Chambre d'Assemblée rejette cette prétention de la Chambre haute, « parce qu'en supposant même que les circonstances rendissent de semblables dispositions nécessaires, elles ne devraient être adoptées que par une loi générale calquée sur l'étendue du mal qu'il serait nécessaire de détruire, ou de prévenir, et ne devrait pas être dirigée seule-

ment contre une classe particulière de citoyens qui n'ont pas encore fourni aucun sujet de plainte ni donné lieu aux craintes que les amendements semblent avoir pour objet » : ibid., 565.

38 57 Geo. III (1817), cap. 39

39 *Journaux de la Chambre d'Assemblée du Bas-Canada* 1820–1, 256. Il s'agit toujours de la même association d'artisans, dorénavant nommée « Société amicale de Québec ». Elle obtiendra finalement l'incorporation tant recherchée... en 1830, soit 18 ans après sa première requête en incorporation. Signe des temps, le gouverneur ne dispose pas, dans la loi finalement sanctionnée, du pouvoir de dissolution de l'association (10–11 Geo. IV [1830], cap. 49).

40 Cette procédure nous met d'ailleurs en garde contre la tentation de distinguer le privé du public dans le modèle ancien de régulation. H. Hartog a fait là-dessus une remarque fort pertinente : « What was the purpose of government ? What was government supposed to do ? In 18th century terms, perhaps the best answer to those questions would have been that government ought to do little, that its role was to ensure that others did as they ought to. One would not separate public from private action since private individuals were characterized by their public obligations. And the function of government was ... to enforce the peace – to maintain the order of society by insisting that private individuals fulfilled their public responsibilities » : H. Hartog, « Because All the World Was Not New York City », 98–9.

41 Les États-Unis semblent ici faire exception par la précocité du mouvement associatif et de l'ajustement juridique impulsé par ce mouvement. Voir H. Hartog, ibid. 91–109 ; E. Dodd, *American Business Corporations until 1860* (Cambridge, Mass. : Harvard University Press 1954 ; J.W. Hurst, *The Legitimacy of the Business Corporation in the Law of the United States, 1780–1970* (Charlottesville, Virginie : University Press of Virginia 1970) ; R.E. Seavoy, « Laws to Encourage Manufacturing : New York Policy and the 1811 General Incorporation Statute, » *Business History Review* 46 (1972), 84–95.

42 « Les communautés sont des assemblées de plusieurs personnes unies en un corps formé par la permission du prince, distingué des autres personnes qui composent un État, et établi pour un bien commun à ceux qui sont de ce corps, et qui ait aussi son rapport au bien public » : Dean Domat, *Lois civiles* Livre I, titre 15, sec. 1, cité par C. de Lorimier et C.A. Vilbon, *La Bibliothèque du Code civil de la province de Québec* (Montréal : La Minerve 1874) 175. Voir aussi plus haut, n31.

43 Le Code civil québécois distingue les sociétés universelles, particulières et commerciales.

44 Sur toute cette question, on pourra se référer au remarquable article de A.J. Jacobson, « The Private Use of Public Authority : Sovereignty and Associations in the Common Law », *Buffalo Law Review* 29

(1980–1), 599–665. Notons que le droit anglo-américain, notamment le *Common Law*, n'a pas de concept global similaire à l' « association » en droit français : « Anglo-American law de-emphasizes the formal definition of "association," except as a technical word to "club" ... "Association" in our legal system, in contrast to those of the Continent, has never been the focus of political or systematic legal dispute ... "Association" unmodified means only a "confederacy or union for particular purposes, good or ill," Allen v. Stevens, 33 AD 485, 507, 54 NYS 8, 23 (1898), and has limited doctrinal significance. When modified, as in "business association," it is typically replaced by a particular technical term, such as "partnership," or "corporation." The "law of associations" commonly refers to the branch of law regarding clubs, fraternal organizations, and the like » : ibid., 603–4.

45 Issu du scandale financier entourant la faillite de la South Sea Company, le *Bubble Act* de 1720, en restreignant la profilération des compagnies par actions, voulait éviter le retour de la fièvre spéculative (« bubble ») qui avait accompagné la crise in 1720. Voir A. DuBois, *English Business Company*.

46 Une précision s'impose ici : les dispositions *légales* qui encadrent l'activité de certains types d'associations – comme les trusts et les partnerships – ou qui président à la formation des corporations n'épuisent pas les possibilités de regroupement prévues par le droit anglais. En effet, on ne retrouve dans le *Common Law* ou dans le droit statutaire britannique aucune *prohibition générale* des associations. Au contraire, les sujets anglais peuvent contracter et s'associer à tout moment, aux seules conditions que l'association ne poursuive pas des fins illicites, et qu'elle évite de porter atteinte à la liberté du commerce ou du travail. Ces dernières réserves se manifestent notamment par les sanctions pénales touchant l'émeute et la conspiration en *Common Law*, règles complétées par les lois du Parlement. Rappelons cependant que de telles associations, si elles sont permises, n'ont aucune existence légale autonome, et ne constituent que des regroupements plus ou moins fortuits de citoyens en regard du *Common Law*.

47 Nous n'aborderons pas ici la question de savoir si l'incorporation ne constitue que la reconnaissance d'un certain type de rapport contractuel, ou implique la dévolution d'une partie de la souveraineté de l'État. Comme le mentionne Jacobson, « the enemies of sovereignty must surrender their notion that private relations can be constructed entirely from spontaneous agreements among persons, without reference to sovereignty. They must reconcile themselves to the proposition that private persons who enter into associations make use of a portion of sovereign power. So too, the friends of sovereignty must allow a portion of sovereignty to be distributed among private persons so that it can in fact be an instrument in the autonomous construction

of private associations » : A.J. Jacobson, « Private Use of Public
Authority », 602. Voir aussi sur ce point les références citées à la n27.

48 La reconnaissance du droit d'association pour les ouvriers est la résultante tardive mais logique de cette tendance.

49 Notre équipe de recherche a entrepris la mise en traitement informa-
tique de toutes les lois d'incorporation, générales et particulières,
adoptées de 1791 à 1914.

50 « Adresse des Fils de la Liberté de Montréal aux jeunes gens des colonies de l'Amérique du Nord » (4 oct. 1837), J. Hare, *Les patriotes,
1830–1839* (Montréal: Éditions Libération 1971) 104

# 6

# Gender Regulation and State Formation in Nineteenth-Century Canada

LYKKE DE LA COUR, CECILIA MORGAN, and
MARIANA VALVERDE

Few people will now dispute that gender is a major axis of social and political power, and that it therefore deserves to be regarded as one important analytical category for the study of state formation. The impact of early Canadian state structures and policies on the organization of both masculinity and femininity ought to be a topic of major interest for pre-Confederation historians, as well as for feminist scholars, because the period provides the opportunity to study the very origins of most Canadian state institutions from the point of view of gender. And yet there is very little published literature on this topic, particularly if one seeks some synthesis and interpretation rather than a monographic description of a single aspect of social life. This article is therefore a modest attempt to formulate some questions that we believe merit further study, with the aid of a review of the existing fragmentary work on gender regulation and the state.

One of the questions that emerges from a study of the available secondary literature concerns what one might call the masculinization of public power in the period of the rebellions.[1] The term 'masculinization' is perhaps misleading: we do not mean to suggest that women were somehow better off under the colonial government of the eighteenth century. What we want to draw attention to, as a potentially fruitful area for further study, is the process by which the centralization and bureaucratization of public power has the effect of consolidating masculine powers that certainly existed before but perhaps in a less organized and airtight form. For example: the 1790s were by no means the golden age of feminism, and yet some women in both Upper and Lower Canada were able to vote (though it appears that only Quebec women actually did so). This 'anomaly' was eliminated in the reorganization of government with the union of the Canadas; from then until well into the twentieth century, women as a group were formally excluded from the suffrage. There was, thus, a rigidification of gender distinctions in the political arena, one that took place, we hasten to add, not through any plot on the part of male legislators but rather as a possibly unintended result of a wider process of political rationalization. This article will stress that the regulation of gender by the state is seldom carried out consciously and directly: rather, it takes place in a helter-skelter manner and through complicated relations to other types of regulation (of race and class, of the economy, of 'moral' problems, and so on).

One of the two themes of this article will be the rigidification of gender distinctions and the institutionalization of a near-monopoly, on the part of men, not only of political power but of other forms of power (such as that of the medical profession) that are sanctioned by the state. The other and equally important theme concerns the divisions among women created at the same time that women as a whole were being formally and informally excluded from many areas of social life. Precisely because gender regulation takes place indirectly, many of the state structures and policies affecting the situation of women do not affect all women equally but rather set up intragender distinctions and even conflicts. Racial distinctions, particularly between Native and white women, hardened in this period, as did distinctions based on social class and on moral respectability. This problem of contradictions among women is being increasingly addressed by feminist historians, in Canada as elsewhere, but it perhaps helps to explain the past lack of interest, among most Canadian feminist scholars, in the period covered by this book.

Canadian feminist historiography has devoted much of its energies to outlining the ways in which some women – educated Anglo-Saxon women in large urban centres – gained some entry into both state and non-state public spheres around the turn of the twentieth century.[2] The decades from the 1880s to the 1930s are admittedly crucial for gender formation, but their over-representation in the literature may have led both non-feminist historians and non-historian feminists to assume that gender became problematic only in the late nineteenth century. The hard-won acquisition of some social power by a relatively small group of women is sometimes regarded as 'the beginning,' and indeed many suffragists, deprived through a masculinist educational system of any knowledge of women's history, thought of their work as precisely that – pioneering beginnings. But the work of the famous pioneers can be reinterpreted as intervening in a prior history of gender rather than as originating such a history, just as the work of white pioneers of both sexes can be reinterpreted as intervening in Native history rather than as beginning Canadian (white) history.

This article also argues that, since a great deal of 'the story' of gender in this period consists not of women's organized resistance against exclusion but of the imposition and consolidation of forms of masculine rule, the method most suitable to the work we believe needs to be done is that of the new 'gender history' rather than that of 'women's history.'[3] Gender history goes far beyond descriptions of 'women's experience': it analyses shifts in the relations between masculinity and femininity, thus examining the whole social formation, not just women, and it consistently analyses the fragmentation of gender along racial and class lines – and other divisions, such as the female moral/sexual roles crucial in the early Victorian period. It therefore attempts to look at history as a whole from the point of view of the shifting relations among race, class, gender, and other forms of social power, rather than taking for granted a unitary category (women) and then proceeding to document its particular history. The complex relations between Canadian state formation and different forms of social power in the pre-Confederation period are, we believe, well suited to the methods of gender historians.

### Gender and the State: A Note on Method

The relation between gender and the state is a difficult and controversial question being debated across disciplines by feminist scholars. Since the present article is a programmatic review rather than a case study, it is appropriate to evaluate some approaches that have already been used by Canadian scholars and to suggest one theorization that we think might prove fruitful, namely that designated by the phrase 'state regulation of gender.'

Although many historians have described the emergence of modern states, and have analysed changes in the relation between state and civil society, the theorization of such changes has been primarily undertaken by Marxist and neo-Marxist historians. Marxist analyses generally begin by envisaging the (bourgeois) state as reproducing capitalist economic and social relations; until recently, such analyses tended to be marred by overly hasty assumptions about the instrumental character of the state *vis-à-vis* the capitalist economy. Recent Marxist theorists, influenced by Gramsci, are critical of instrumentalist and economistic views.[4] Rather than seeing the state as a neutral instrument of economic class, recent work stresses the 'relative autonomy' of state institutions.[5] It also generally puts more emphasis on the state's 'legitimation function' and less on the 'accumulation function,' drawing attention to the cultural and moral dimensions of state activity. These latter dimensions are clearly crucial for any study of gender, although this does not mean that economic factors are not also determining in gender formation.

Marxist economism in state theory has been challenged not only by neo-Gramscian analyses of cultural hegemony but also by Foucault and by the French 'regulation' school. As historical sociologist Jean-Marie Fecteau indicates, the notion of 'social reproduction' used by Marxist political economy (most notably in analyses of the welfare state) tends to suggest that the state's role is to maintain and recreate a social order that, though characterized by rapid changes at the surface of social life, is or should be structurally static.[6] His use of the term 'regulation' rather than 'reproduction' seeks to emphasize the dynamism, and indeed the contradictory movements, of state activity.[7]

We believe that both the neo-Marxist analyses of the state as engaged in reproducing the capitalist mode of production and the French regulation school's concept of 'social regulation' are fruitful for theorizing the activity of the Canadian state in relation to gender in the nineteenth century. The fruitfulness of the first approach can be seen in a study that, though it does not focus on the state, is a landmark in integrating gender into analyses of changes in the mode of production: Majorie Cohen's *Women's Work, Markets, and the Economy in Nineteenth-Century Ontario*.[8] Cohen shows that the staples economy was fundamentally gendered, with women's petty commodity production and domestic labour being essential for the maintenance of farm families through the ups and downs of the staples market.

The political-economy approach is thus one of the necessary tools of Canadian historians of gender formation; but, in the context of examining state activity, this approach can sometimes produce distortions. An example is the functionalist fallacy visible in an otherwise extremely insightful essay by Jane Ursel on the legal regulation of gender in nineteenth- and early twentieth-century Canada.[9] Envisaging 'patriarchy' and/or 'capitalism' as structures generating certain social requirements that are then met by state-dictated measures certainly draws attention to the substantive bias of formally neutral liberal states. The structuralist method, however, tends to oversimplify the actual historical process of state formation: for instance, Ursel explains social reforms in terms of 'the disorganization of production relations occasioned by the lack of fit between the old [familial] patriarchal order and the new economic system.'[10] This obscures the negotiations and struggles involved in the genesis of social reforms. Furthermore, it cannot account for differences between Canada and other countries that experienced similar large-scale shifts in socioeconomic forces but produced different social 'solutions.' It also tends to encourage a rather passive view of gender formation, with gender theorized as the product of structural change and state activity but not as also constituted in gender struggles.

In the attempt to refine and go beyond the important contributions of the political-economy school and other Marxist analyses of the relationship between the state and social categories such as gender, we have found it useful to take up the French regulation school's critique of two key Marxist concepts, 'mode of production' and 'social reproduction.' Canadian Marxist feminists have argued at length that the notion of 'mode of production' is not sufficient for the theorization of gender.[11] The newer concept of 'social reproduction' has not been critically evaluated to the same degree, however, particularly in feminist circles. Writers in the French regulation school (who are not concerned with gender, as far as we know) argue that the very term 'reproduction' tends to underestimate the dimensions of change; they further question the implicit assumption that the means used to reproduce the social order are neutral instruments. A more dynamic approach, one that highlights the constantly emerging contradictions created by the means chosen to reproduce a certain social equilibrium, is that intended by the term 'social regulation' and its corollary, 'mode of regulation.'[12]

From this perspective, any means chosen to reproduce a particular order will always have a certain weight of their own and will create new contradictions that require new solutions. Gender, like class, is thus never merely reproduced: it is always in the process of being actively constituted, maximized, and regulated by state and extra-state activities and practices that, once created, acquire a certain autonomy and generate new regulatory dilemmas. The see-sawing policies for regulating prostitution in the late nineteenth and early twentieth centuries are a notable example of this: the problem of 'streetwalkers' gave rise to attempts to contain 'vice' in a single district;

this in turn prompted moral reformers to campaign to close down the red-light districts, once more scattering prostitutes and threatening the distinction between respectable and vicious femininity that the original regulation had sought to establish.[13] There is little evidence of any structural continuity in this inherently contradictory and constantly shifting mode of regulating women's moral identity.

The concept of regulation can also encourage non-reductionist analyses of the relationships among gender, race, and class, as opposed to (as in some feminist historiography) views of gender as a fixed social structure that can be analysed in isolation. Social regulation is always a multidimensional process, and the gender effects of a particular practice may be consistent or inconsistent with the race and class dimensions of the same regulatory practice. For instance, Constance Backhouse's detailed study of Married Women's Property Acts shows that the legal system was highly reluctant to give married women any autonomy from their husbands, but that such acts became necessary when class relations developed to the point at which creditors needed the legal ability to sue women running small businesses.[14] Backhouse herself remarks only that legal changes were not simply due to either feminist pressure or state benevolence; but one could fruitfully use her research to begin an analysis of the regulatory crisis posed for the bourgeois patriarchal legal order by the de facto operation of small businesses by married women.

We will therefore use the term 'gender regulation' to refer to various state activities that had a clear impact on gender organization. and/or gender relations – without thereby implying that one can clearly separate state regulatory activity affecting gender from the state regulation of other social relations. We will also not assume, as many feminists in the political-economy tradition do, that the regulation of gender takes place in the sphere of reproduction, while class is formed and re-formed in production relations. Rather, class, gender, and race are all created and regulated in both production and reproduction, as well as in the cultural/moral realm.

### The Legal Regulation of Gender

Having established some theoretical guidelines, let us begin by considering one mode of state regulation of gender, namely the legal mode. In this we are hampered by the dearth of studies of gender in legal history, and by the fact that most of the studies that do exist tend to assume the categories of the criminal code and then document changes in the content of these categories (e.g., how rape law or abortion law changed in a certain time period). This perspective certainly sheds light on the history of laws, their enforcement, and their impact on women. It does not lend itself, however, to an analysis of the relations between the legal apparatus and other parts of the state, as well as institutions outside the state. It is thus very difficult to draw any conclusions about state formation at the legal level and gender regulation from the limited number of studies in women's legal history that do exist (most of them produced by the admirable research of Constance Backhouse). We can, however, gain from these studies some sense of patterns in legal and judicial nineteenth-century developments affecting Canadian women.

Two tentative generalizations emerge from a critical review of some of the literature on women's legal history. First, while some nineteenth-century state provisions (e.g., on suffrage qualifications) established a universal distinction based on gender and in this sense institutionalized masculine power as power of men in general over women in general, women were more often regulated indirectly through socio-legal categories that fragmented gender. Some of these were based on race and/or class; some were moral categories, such as 'deserted married women,' 'girls of previously chaste character,' or 'nightwalkers ... not giving a satisfactory account of themselves.'[15] In other words, women are simultaneously divided into mutually exclusive groups and united through their subjection to masculinist ideologies about femininity and virtue. That the divisions created by legislation often used moral categories emphasizes the need for an analysis of the relative autonomy of moral regulation *vis-à-vis* both production and reproduction. Moral distinctions, we must hasten to add, were not merely ideological but were in turn given much of their content through race and class criteria. Thus, the somewhat abstract notion of femininity was concretized in multiple and often antagonistic ways through the interactions among gender regulation and racial, class, and moral regulations. For example, women declared by the federal state to be status Indians had a very different relationship to citizenship than white women, and were also subject to special moral regulations – notably provisions regarding prostitution and procuring – that cast doubt on any generalizations about 'the' relationship of Canadian women to the state.

The second theoretical conclusion regarding the legal regulation of gender is that generalizations about the feminist or anti-feminist character of particular laws are risky indeed. Even the increasing criminalization of abortion in the second half of the century,[16] a process that might appear as an instance of straightforward gender regulation, has to be analysed by reference to shifts in the relation between the state and professional organizations. Professionalization went hand in hand with masculinization, as will be shown below in the case of the physicians' political campaign against midwives. But the question of professionalization is analytically distinct from gender, as became clear much later when women doctors began to exercise power over other women.

Custody law would appear to be one area in which women definitely gained throughout the nineteenth century, since the complete power over (legitimate) children held by fathers by 1800 gradually gave way to the doctrine of 'tender years,' favouring maternal custody. And yet, Backhouse is forced to conclude that the changes in custody law and practice were probably due to changing conceptions of childhood rather than to an affirmation of women's rights; furthermore, mothers' newly acquired rights were rather precarious in the face of an increasingly powerful welfare state.[17] Similarly, although rape law seemed to evolve in gender-progressive fashion, insofar as the offence eventually become one against the woman herself rather than against her father or husband, by the late nineteenth century both legislation and case law concerning rape, seduction, and abduction were, in Backhouse's words, 'paternalistic' rather than feminist. This is not to say that positive changes did not occur. It is, however, to remark that it is extremely hazardous to draw from legal history general conclusions about the status of women, or even about the legal apparatus's social construction of femininity. Patriarchy is not to be measured quantitatively; male domination can take different forms, from outright male property rights over women and children to state 'protectionism,' and it would be futile to attempt to compare the quantity of oppression generated by each form. Furthermore, insofar as the legal system is largely aimed at the protection of private property and the legitimation of the state itself, the gender organization of law cannot be studied in isolation from shifts in class, property, and race relations.

Can any generalizations be made concerning the legal status of women and/or the role of the legal apparatus in organizing gender? The answer is no if by 'generalizations' one means statements about all women and their relation to the law in general. Some legal shifts, especially in family and property law, gave a limited number of new rights to respectable married women, but women engaged in prostitution, women needing an abortion, mothers who had boyfriends after a marriage breakdown, or women otherwise exercising some sexual autonomy were probably subjected to more, and more effective, legal controls in 1900 than a hundred years earlier.[18] (Custody rights, for instance, were always given on the condition that the mother prove her sexual virtue, and were unlikely to be granted if the separated mother did not go to live with her father or brother.)

This uneven development can be seen in the case of the nineteenth-century legal category that gave rise to the most litigation involving women (more than prostitution, and certainly more than rape, which was seldom prosecuted): seduction. Until 1886, seduction was a tort action that had to be initiated by the father of the alleged victim; even when seduction was also incorporated into the criminal code, in 1886, a study of trials shows that the new criminal offence, though not as overtly feudal and patriarchal as the father-centred tort of seduction, was in fact often used to curb women's consensual non-marital activity, not simply to prosecute men.[19] The criminal offence of seduction, unlike its civil counterpart, was of use only to women 'of previously chaste character,' and prosecutions of men often turned into inquisitions into women's moral conduct. (Under civil law, a woman's proven chastity would increase the amount of damages awarded, but fathers of demonstrably 'unchaste girls' could still collect, since the main criterion was their loss of services, not the damage to the woman's body, psyche, or even reputation.) Hence, although the criminalization of seduction could be interpreted as giving women more power to lay charges – as opposed to giving fathers power to sue seducers for causing their pregnant daughters to be less serviceable – this apparent new power was often negated by the 'previously chaste character' clause, as well as, less technically, by the socio-legal construction of women involved in such cases as 'designing women.'

In conclusion, while a large number of women came to enjoy limited legal protection for their independent income and for their relationship with their children, the invidious effects of gender-specific moral regulations (which were often race- and class- and age-specific as well) established sharper divisions both among different groups of women and between women and men. Different aspects of the legal system did not necessarily act in concert with one another. And, further, women as a group were just as likely to be fragmented into subgroups (virtuous versus neglecting mothers, chaste versus unchaste girls) as to be united by a common gender oppression. Gender formation at the legal level, like state-initiated gender formation generally, was thus not a unitary but rather a multidimensional and even contradictory process. Nevertheless, one general question that bears further study is whether the increasing importance of formal legal institutions (as opposed to informal community arrangements) helped to institutionalize and consolidate masculine privilege, insofar as the formal legal apparatus rigidly excluded women throughout the pre-1870 period and for some time afterwards. To put it simply, when lawyers and judges gained in numbers and power, it became more important that these occupations were, though not necessarily open to all men, universally closed to women.

## Schooling and the Regulation of Gender

One of the best-researched areas for examining gender and the British North American state is that of gender and educational reform in Upper Canada. As Bruce Curtis demonstrates in *Building the Educational State: Canada West, 1836–1871*, concepts of gender were embedded in the programs of educational reformers. The Education Acts of the 1830s and 1840s specified that the public officials charged with directing education were to be adult male property-holders elected by other adult male property-holders.[20] Reformers from Charles Duncombe to Egerton Ryerson also appreciated the ways in which education and schools might inculcate appropriate norms of masculinity and femininity, as Houston and Prentice, as well as Curtis, have shown. Although this process was less pronounced at the primary level, as children grew older their education was liable to become increasingly gender-specific.[21] As grammar schools grew in importance and enrolment throughout the century, controversy arose over Ryerson's vision of 'free grammar school tuition for farmers' sons and young men desiring a superior education.'[22] By the 1860s, despite the fact that Ryerson had not 'seen girls in the context of the grammar school,' increased demand by parents meant that coeducational grammar schools and state funding for a curriculum that included the classics for both sexes became increasingly pressing problems for the Department of Education.[23]

If we search for examples of ways in which the state in Upper Canada expressed and attempted to implement certain concepts of gender, the recruitment and training of teachers poses some challenging and complex questions. Duncombe's report of 1836 specifically recommended an improvement in female education, both to produce better mothers and to train future teachers for girls.[24] Certainly the widespread feminization of teaching that occurred in both

Protestant and Catholic schools suggests that, as far as education is concerned, women became an important part of the state.[25] As Curtis's research on the Model Grammar School shows, the training given to these teachers included appropriate morality for men and women, with special emphasis on sexual repression for the latter.[26] Yet the presence of women in the teaching work-force was not especially welcomed by Ryerson and many of his peers, who feared the effect of a female-dominated work-force on salaries and professional standards.[27] The increasingly centralized Upper-Canadian state did incorporate women as workers, but in the process it legitimated a pattern where women's work would be low in status and pay.

## Native Policy

An area that has not yet been extensively reported on in the published literature, and that might provide important insights into the relationship between the state, gender, and race, is Native policy and programs. Under Sir John Colborne, the new policies and structures of Upper Canada's Indian Department in 1830 included plans for agricultural settlement and education that implied a gender-based division of labour within Native societies. To the degree that assimilationist policies were indeed implemented, the duties and prerogatives of women in both hunting-gathering bands and agricultural tribes would surely have been undermined. The government's program was based on the assumption that control of vital food production should be wrested from women and transferred to their husbands. Yet, once again, the state's attempt to order and regulate gender was neither consistent nor independent of other considerations. Inadequate financing hampered Colborne's vision of introducing 'the industrious habits of a civilized life,' and his successor of 1836, Sir Francis Bond Head, repudiated Colborne's ideas. Believing that Colborne's efforts had resulted in disaster and that Indians were doomed to extinction, Bond Head proposed their removal to Manitoulin Island to resume their former way of life.[28]

Although at present it is unclear what effects these policies had on gender organization, we know that government-supported Methodist missions, such as those at the Credit River, Rice Lake, and Grape Island, worked diligently to promote Christian marriages and to eradicate polygamy and extramarital sexuality. From the records left by the Mississauga Methodist missionary Peter Jones, we know that missionary workers were especially concerned with the housekeeping efforts of Native women, insisting that they meet the standards of cleanliness and neatness set by white women. Tidy homes, it seemed, signified both Christian morality and an acculturation that promised the survival of 'the Indian' in Upper Canada. Relationships between the missionaries and the Indian Department were often strained over jurisdictional and financial matters, but there can be little doubt that officials and missionaries were in fundamental agreement where the reform of Native gender relations was concerned.[29] Further research, building on Elizabeth Muir's important study of Methodist missionary women but paying closer attention to gender formation and to the state, is needed.[30]

The state's role in defining and restricting 'Indian' status through-out the 1850s also calls for closer attention. By 1851, such status was determined patrileneally (according to the white governments), and in 1869 the federal government confirmed this practice and pro-ceeded to strip those Indian women who had married non-Indians of their band status.[31] More generally, it seems apparent that govern-ment attempts to formalize relations with Native people tended to disempower women. Officials consistently sought to enhance the au-thority of individual leaders, at least insofar as the 'chiefs' in question proved co-operative. When it came to occasions such as treaty ne-gotiations, there was even a tendency to create authoritative chief-tains, in accordance with government agents' cultural preferences for individual representatives of the larger group. The progressive sub-jection of Indians to bureaucratic control therefore tended to foster new forms of authority within Native societies at the expense of old styles of non-state consensus rule. But of course the 'chiefs' recognized as such by the colonial administration were invariably men. Previ-ously, women had exerted considerable influence over the affairs of the community or tribe; this was the case particularly, though not exclusively, among the Iroquois. As Gretchen Green demonstrates in her study of the women of the Brant family, Mohawk women of the late eighteenth century saw 'the Iroquois traits of complementarity and reciprocity between the sexes ... replaced by far less equal rela-tionships' as a result of greater British political and cultural influ-ence.[32]

The details of the nineteenth-century transformation remain to be explored, but it does seem clear that where 'Indian Affairs' were concerned, racial differentiation, state formation, and gender for-mation went hand in hand. For Native women, the combined result of these three processes amounted to an increase in their political and social marginalization. While it was undoubtedly the white male state that most actively subordinated Native women, through their increased formal differentiation from white women Native women were also prevented from sharing many of the benefits that were later reluctantly granted to white women. Their own gender formation was thus race-specific, as was their relationship to the state. This, in turn, sheds light not only on Native women's lack of interest in many of the issues of first-wave white feminists, but also on the corresponding racial specificity of late-nineteenth-century feminists – the whiteness of the white feminist, so to speak. Thus, our preliminary examination of gender and the state in Native policy shows that, as with development involving child custody, property rights, and divorce, the state's regulation of gender may be mediated by many other factors, making it difficult to point to any one policy on 'gender issues' within the British North American state.

## The Medical Regulation of Gender

Gender formation was also affected in the nineteenth century by activities occurring in the field of medicine. Certainly one of the most significant developments of the period, as already noted in our discussion of the legal regulation of gender, was the elimination of female healers and midwives that accompanied the institutionalization of professionalized medicine. C. Lesley Biggs notes in her article 'The Case of the Missing Midwives: A History of Midwifery in Ontario from 1795–1900' that the drive to professionalize medical practice went hand in hand with the masculinization of the profession, since most of the earliest initiatives in organized medicine centred on the exclusion of women from medical practice.[33] Striving to increase the status and legitimacy of the profession through the monopolization of medical care by licensed practitioners, male physicians waged a protracted struggle in the mid-decades of the nineteenth century to establish the professional structures, the legal frameworks, and the medical institutions necessary for the advancement of professional hegemony.[34] This process of professionalization formally excluded women in a number of ways. Biggs details the ardent political campaign physicians waged against female midwives from the 1820s onwards and the legal prohibitions that were finally entrenched in 1865 to restrict the practice of midwifery to only 'qualified' practitioners.[35] Meanwhile, female students were excluded from the newly formed medical schools, with the insidious result that they were rendered ineligible for registration as qualified practitioners. Professionally controlled systems for the licensing and registration of physicians did not explicitly exclude female candidates, but the prerequisite of formal medical education for registration ensured that women would not qualify. Similarly, lacking the necessary requirements of education and licensing, women were barred from joining professional associations and, more importantly, from employment as practitioners in the new medical institutions that emerged in the mid-nineteenth century – dispensaries, public hospitals, and asylums.[36] All in all, the process of professionalization secured not only the dominance of the medical profession but also the consolidation of male power in a sphere traditionally associated with female lay healing.

The reorganization of gender relations through the professionalization of medicine also had significant implications for women in terms of the gender regulation increasingly incorporated into professionalized medical practice. The regulation of gender by the medical profession constitutes one of the best-researched areas of women's medical history, thanks to the extensive writings of historian Wendy Mitchinson. Examining nineteenth-century medical journals and the reports of asylums for the insane, Mitchinson provides numerous examples of the stereotypical gender concepts embedded in the medical theories promoted by Canadian physicians and of how these perceptions, in turn, influenced the therapeutic practices employed in the medical treatment of women.[37] While the main thrust of Mitchinson's work is an examination of the linkages between gender ideology, medical theory, and the gender-specific therapies developed by medicine and psychiatry, her research nevertheless suggests some of the ways in which gender regulation was incorporated into nineteenth-century medical practice. For example, the evidence she provides on medical advice about reproductive issues indicates how the profession attempted to restrict women's ability to control their own fertility by denying them access to birth-control information.[38] What her work illustrates best is the medical attempt to regulate gender by constructing as pathological any behaviour that deviated from accepted notions of appropriate gender roles for women.[39] As Mitchinson points out, the medical profession went to great lengths to portray activities such as the pursuit of higher education and professional employment, as medically dangerous for women. Moreover, in personal consultations with physicians, women were often cautioned on the litany of ills that could befall them with physical and mental over-exertion, the avoidance of marriage, and the obstruction of 'natural' procreative functions. Depicting a host of activities as potentially damaging to the well-being of both women and their children, the medical view 'coincided very neatly,' as Mitchinson notes, with dominant perceptions of the proper gender role for women. Ultimately, the male medical establishment attempted to circumscribe female activities by imposing not only material but substantial psychological barriers that could make the avoidance of marriage, pregnancy, and motherhood extremely difficult.[40]

While Mitchinson, like many historians, generally interprets the gender-specifics of medical practice as reflective of broader social attitudes towards women, Angus McLaren's work on birth-control and abortion practices in Canada suggests, in fact, quite a different reading of events. McLaren's extensive survey certainly provides some of the most obvious examples of the medical mode of gender regulation and illustrates well how the medical profession strove to change many of the accepted social concepts and practices surrounding reproduction.[41] For example, as McLaren indicates, the medical profession played a crucial role in securing legislation for the criminalization of self-induced abortion before 'quickening' in 1861 and, later in the century, the prohibition of advertisements and sales of birth-control devices and abortifacients.[42] These legal prohibitions significantly restricted women's ability to control both their own fertility and the conditions of birthing by making illegal many of the reproductive procedures previously practised by women. Far from reinforcing traditional gender norms, the medical profession actively campaigned throughout the nineteenth century to instil a number of novel ideas and practices concerning gender and reproduction and, in the process, created a new location for the regulation of gender in Canadian society.

In addition to providing examples of the medical regulation of gender, the studies by Biggs, Mitchinson, and McLaren illustrate the central role played by the state in sanctioning the various goals of the medical profession and, conversely, how gender regulation was transported into the state through the activities of the medical profession. As all three authors show, medical practitioners initially sought to exclude female lay healers and to transform health-care practices strictly through professional measures such as the founding of lying-in facilities, the withholding of contraceptive services, and the promotion of a medical discourse that repeatedly upheld scientific procedures as superior while denigrating women's traditional practices as ignorant, backward, and dangerous. By the 1860s, however, the strategy employed by the profession had shifted noticeably to an increasing reliance on legislative sanctions to enforce professional control over medicine. In doing so, a variety of gender-specific regulatory policies were entrenched within the legal codes of the state. Biggs interprets this shift as emanating largely from the patriarchal and professional self-interests of male practitioners and the difficulties they encountered with enforcement through purely professional means.[43] McLaren's work, however, points to the importance of considering state interests in reforms around gender and, specifically, the way in which reproductive policies stemmed not only from a desire to regulate women *per se* but also from concerns about issues such as the declining Canadian birth rate and fears of 'race suicide.' The legislation governing birth control and abortifacients, as McLaren illustrates, came into place only after Canadians discovered that the decline in the birth rate was primarily an Anglo-Saxon, middle-class phenomenon.[44] While the effects of regulatory policies could often manifest themselves in patriarchal ways, clearly the underlying impetus for legislative reform was also rooted in concerns about the class, racial, and moral make-up of Canadian society.

### Child Welfare and the Regulation of Gender

An area of social regulation that has received considerable attention in the Canadian historiography is child welfare and the various 'child-saving' initiatives of nineteenth-century urban reformers. Historians such as Neil Sutherland, Susan Houston, Joy Parr, Patricia Rooke, R.L. Schnell, Andrew Jones, and Leonard Rutnam have produced a substantial body of literature that traces the evolution of child welfare from the advent in the 1850s and 1860s of juvenile immigration schemes and special institutions for children (orphanages, reformatories, industrial schools, homes for boys and girls, etc.) to the promotion of foster care with the founding of Children's Aid societies in the 1890s.[45] Detailing the class dynamics of child-welfare developments, these studies are useful for analyses of class formation in Canada and point clearly to the close connections between child-centred reform and the social and economic needs of the late-nineteenth-century industrial-capitalist state.[46] Less obvious in this work is the significance of child welfare to the maintenance of patriarchy and the role child saving played in organizing gender and gender relations in Canadian society. At this point a brief discussion of some of the ways in which we might begin to examine the relation between child welfare and gender formation may be helpful for advancing both a gender and a class analysis of the Canadian state.

Joy Parr's excellent study *Labouring Children: British Immigrant Apprentices to Canada, 1869–1924* provides some of the best examples of gender regulation through child welfare and demonstrates how concepts of gender, as well as class, influenced the operation of the juvenile emigration schemes. For example, in detailing the selection procedures for child emigrants, Parr notes how concerns about morality figured more prominently in the case of girls (as opposed to boys) committed to juvenile distribution centres.[47] Similarly, in her discussion of 'philanthropic abduction,' she shows that girls were more likely than boys to be removed from their families and sent to Canada without either the knowledge or the consent of their parents. While Parr does not emphasize the connection of these differences to the gender ideologies supported by the child-saving philanthropists (or the implication of such practices for the regulation of gender in the state), her work does suggest that gender, like class, often interacted with child-welfare concerns in the nineteenth century.

Another book that prompts similar speculation on the significance of gender in child-centred reform is Patricia Rooke's and R.L. Schnell's *Discarding the Asylum: From Child Rescue to the Welfare State in English Canada (1800–1950)*. By outlining the various institutional and foster-care initiatives mounted by Canadian child-savers in the nineteenth century, these authors illustrate that gender concepts were often embedded in the redemptive programs launched to rehabilitate disadvantaged and delinquent youths. For example, child labour, a central feature of the child-saving agenda (designed to instil habits of industry and self-discipline in children through employment in either juvenile institutions or indentured apprenticeships), was rigidly structured according to stereotypical notions of apprenticeship gender roles. Girls received training in domestic service, boys in agricultural and manual labour.[48] Unfortunately, Rooke and Schnell provide few details on the other forms of instruction – religious, moral, and social – that the children received once they were placed in juvenile institutions. Thus, we can only speculate on how deeply concepts of femininity and masculinity were entrenched in the redemption work carried out by the child-savers. Future research in this field may provide a better understanding of the ways in which gender was regulated through child welfare and of the importance of child-centred reform as a new location for the regulation of gender by the state.

A question related to child welfare, and of critical importance to any analysis of gender formation in Canada, is the social construction of motherhood and the changing ideology surrounding child-rearing practices in the nineteenth century. As Neil Sutherland notes in *Children in English-Canadian Society: Framing the Twentieth-Century Consensus*, attitudes towards mothering and appropriate methods of infant and child care changed significantly in the late 1800s, as philanthropists increasingly came to view the improper socialization of children as the root cause of most social problems. Influenced by Froebelian theories regarding the malleability of character, reformers active in the child-saving movement developed a heightened awareness of the importance of mothering in nurturing children through early childhood development. Consequently, reformers organized a number of interventionist strategies in the fields of public health, social welfare, juvenile delinquency, and education to ensure that proper standards were met in the rearing of children.[49] Sutherland's critics have adequately detailed elsewhere the shortcomings of his analysis in terms of class, illustrating how much of the reform effort focused largely on the low-income family and the mothering practices of poor and working-class women.[50] What is missing in the critique of Sutherland's work, however, is an analysis of the primacy child-savers accorded to the working-class woman's role as mother and the significance of this development in terms of late-nineteenth-century industrial capitalism. As feminist writers such as Jane Lewis point out, the promotion of an 'ideology of motherhood' was a central feature of the child-saving campaigns, prompted largely by national concerns regarding the economic, social, moral, and racial stability of Canadian society, as well as by the need to address pressing welfare problems at a minimal cost to the state.[51] While Lewis locates the rise of the 'ideology of motherhood' and ensuing interventionist strategies in the eugenic debates prevalent at the turn of the century, Sutherland's examination of the child-saving activities surrounding juvenile delinquency suggests that the emphasis on the working-class woman's role as mother perhaps has earlier origins in nineteenth-century concerns about the growing presence of 'street waifs' and perceptions of mounting criminal and delinquency problems among urban youths. Again, we can only hope that future research into the gender dynamics of child-welfare practices, the means by which the child-savers attempted to promote an 'ideology of motherhood,' and the ways in which the transmission of this ideology differed along class lines will better pinpoint the shift from viewing woman's primary function as merely biological reproduction to her dominant role as mother and child-rearer.

In addition to the gender ideology embedded in child-welfare practices, Canadian historians also need to examine in more detail the hegemonic status accorded to the model of the nuclear family by the late-nineteenth-century child-savers. Most of the published literature in the field briefly alludes to the heightened importance placed on the family in this period – the distinctions philanthropists increasingly made between the 'good' and the 'problem' family, some of the criteria they used to define the 'problem' family (such as intemperance or sexual licentiousness), and the faith philanthropists eventually placed in the reformative value of a good 'wholesome' family environment for the rehabilitation of disadvantaged and delinquent youths.[52] Absent in these studies, however, is any analysis of the actual type of family organization promoted by the child-saving movement and the implications of this development for both gender and state formation. As British and American feminists have shown, it was not simply vague or over-sentimentalized notions of the family and motherhood that the child-savers promulgated, but very specific ideas of what a proper mother, home, and family should be – ideas predicated on bourgeois norms and the concept of a two-parent household with the adult male as the primary breadwinner.[53] For some women, namely sole-support mothers, this emphasis on the nuclear model had significant repercussions as single parenthood became increasingly viewed as inimical to the proper rearing of children and thus a justifiable location for philanthropic and, later, state intervention. Andrew Jones' and Leonard Rutnam's study *In the Children's Aid: J.J. Kelso and Child Welfare in Ontario* indicates that unwed motherhood was a particular source of concern for those active in the Ontario child-saving movement in the late nineteenth century. Viewing unwed mothers as socially and morally unfit for raising children, the child-savers increasingly advocated the separation of illegitimate children from their mothers and launched an extensive campaign to encourage the adoption of children born out of wedlock.[54] What remains to be examined is how this concern over unwed motherhood related to the heightened emphasis placed on the nuclear model of the family and how, in turn, this emphasis correlated to mounting welfare expenditures in the province. It is perhaps no coincidence that strong familist attitudes and policies emerged during a period when expenditures on social welfare in Ontario nearly tripled within a few decades.[55]

Finally, an area that has received some mention in the child-welfare literature but that certainly requires both further investigation and theorization is the role middle-class women played in the administration of child-saving services in Canada. Most of the published literature in this field notes the preponderance of middle-class women in the child-saving movement and the crucial role they played in the operation of child-emigration schemes, institutions for juveniles, and the various child-centred reform associations formed in the late nineteenth century. Joy Parr's study, for example, shows how some of the earliest initiatives in British child emigration were launched by women like Maria Rye and Annie Macpherson, who channelled their energies into the placement of pauper girls as domestics in Canadian homes.[56] Patricia Rooke's and R.L. Schnell's work, particularly their article 'The Rise and Decline of British North American Protestant Orphans' Homes as Woman's Domain, 1850–1930,' provides examples of similar Canadian initiatives and documents the extensive work undertaken by philanthropic women in the creation and operation of institutions such as orphanages and homes for infants, boys, and girls.[57] These studies are useful for an examination of gender formation in that they highlight the changing socio-economic and ideological conditions that both facilitated and motivated the increased activism of middle-class women in charitable activities – i.e., the growing presence of a leisured group of women with the expansion of the middle-class in Canada, the rise of Protestant evangelicalism, and the increased emphasis on urban amelioration in the second half of the nineteenth century, with immigration and industrialization. Valuable analyses of women's activism in terms of class formation are provided in T.R. Morrison's ' "Their proper Sphere": Feminism, the Family, and Child-Centred Social Reform in Ontario, 1875–1900,' and in several relevant essays in the collection edited by Linda Kealey, 'A Not Unreasonable Claim.'[58] What has yet to be extensively examined or analysed, however, is the relation of women's philanthropism to the formation of the Canadian state. As the following discussion on religion and philanthropy indicates, the boundaries separating public and private domains in the nineteenth century are not as distinct as previously thought.[59] Women's activism in the private sphere, while appearing to exist outside the parameters of the formal state, was nevertheless often deeply and closely connected to the state and certainly laid important foundations for the subsequent development of official welfare institutions.

## Religion and Philanthropy

The question of religion and state formation has received considerable attention in the literature, but gender has generally been absent as an analytical category and organizing principle. Earlier works such as Fred Landon's *Western Ontario and the American Frontier*, S.D. Clark's *Church and Sect in Canada*, John Moir's *Church and State in Canada West*, and Goldwin French's *Parsons and Politics* discussed the church-state relationship in controversies over education, marriage laws, and the clergy reserves. They focused, however, on the denominational and political aspects of these issues.

Much of the work dealing with the social aspects of religious activity in this period emphasizes its private and charitable nature and the desire of those who participated in charitable organizations to exercise control of their group's activities, independent of the state. Allan Greer's 'The Sunday Schools of Upper Canada' points to the significance of this goal in an institution that played an important role in the development of Upper-Canadian literacy. Although some funding was given by the state in the 1820s, generally such schools were established, controlled, operated, and financed by lay members of local communities.[60]

In contrast, the early temperance movement's attitude towards the state changed from a policy of moral suasion to one of prohibitory legislation by the early 1850s; by that time two-thirds of those attending temperance meetings were women and children. Did women play an active part in changing the movement's strategy, pushing it to use the state and emulate the Maine campaign, which won legislation in 1851? F.L. Barron's research on Canadian temperance uncovered strong ties between male political reformers and male anti-drink campaigners, many of whom were criticized for their American connections.[61] Although not focused on gender, his research suggests that the link between temperance and the state came earlier than the 1850s and was forged by men. Could this indicate that Upper-Canadian political activity, even in the cause of social and moral reform, was in this period a masculine activity from which women were excluded? Such was the case, Paula Baker argues, for Jacksonian America. New definitions of the 'republican citizen,' the expansion of the franchise, and a withdrawal of the government from the marketplace led to sharper distinctions between male and female activities, as 'gender, rather than other social or economic distinctions, [became] the most salient political division.' Thus, 'the social,' represented by the home, the family, and motherhood, was increasingly seen as outside politics and as the special domain of women.[62]

Further research must be conducted to determine whether this argument has any relevance for the Upper-Canadian context. Possibly, those who believed in voluntarism and the separation of church and state were motivated by social and moral concerns, as well as political ones. The well-documented antipathy of some Upper-Canadian religious groups to state involvement in religion and their preference for voluntary organization may have sprung from a desire to keep the social realm free of the corruption, violence, and immorality that appeared to permeate political life. Certainly religious writers in the Methodist *Christian Guardian* showed a keen interest in defining codes of masculinity, which, in their insistence upon duty, moral earnestness, and purity, are the antithesis of the rowdiness and violence that often characterized Upper-Canadian politics. Such writers also envisaged a larger and more active role for women in shaping and guiding 'the social' than that foreseen by political leaders, Reform or conservative.[63] As in the United States and Britain, the extra-state social activism of middle-class Canadian Protestant women increased in quantity and quality in the second half of the nineteenth century, a shift that eventually would put pressure on the masculine state to consult women's organizations in its deliberations on social policy. Few women, however, were ever appointed to policy-making positions within the state itself (and those who were seldom spoke for women's interests).

The roots of this turn-of-the-century situation – in which middle-class Anglo-Saxon women purported to speak for all Canada's women, while even this dominant group was confined to social policy and excluded from the 'hard' economic and political issues – can be seen in the pre-1870 period. We have argued that the history of gender and the state in this early period appears to reveal two simultaneous shifts: certain new formal exclusions of women as a group (from politics, from medicine, from reproductive decisions through the criminalization of abortion, and others) went hand in hand with a complex fragmentation of women as a group along racial, class, and moral/sexual lines. The state constituted itself and most of the public sphere as masculine, making it unlikely that anyone would even ask where the mothers of Confederation were as the famous picture of Canada's birth was being painted. Nevertheless, since the state regulation of gender was always criss-crossed with other types of regulation, women were divided against themselves at the same time as they were unified through exclusion. We may be allowed to reach here the possibly presentist conclusion that the legacy of this double movement found in early Canadian state regulation of gender still haunts the women's movement of today.

## NOTES

1 Allan Greer has begun to study the process of masculinization; see his 'Josephte and Jean-Baptiste: Gender in the Lower-Canadian Rebellion of 1837,' unpublished paper delivered to Marxist Institute, Conference on Theory and History, Toronto, January 1989.

2 An important early collection was Linda Kealey, ed., 'A Not Unreasonable Claim': Women and Reform in Canada, 1880s–1920s (Toronto: Women's Press 1979).

3 For an explanation of the distinction between these two, see the first issue of the new journal Gender and History, especially the editorial; see also Joan Scott, 'Women's History,' in her Gender and the Politics of History (New York: Columbia 1988).

4 See, for example, Nicos Poulantzas, State, Power, Socialism (London: Verso 1978); and, from a more post-structuralist perspective, Philip Corrigan and Derek Sayer, The Great Arch: English State Formation as Cultural Revolution (Oxford: Blackwell 1986).

5 For neo-Marxist analyses of the relative autonomy of Canadian state institutions, see Leo Panitch, ed., The Canadian State (Toronto: University of Toronto Press 1977). For feminist analyses, many of which are also neo-Marxist, see the special issue of Resources for Feminist Research, 'Feminist Perspectives on the Canadian State,' 17:3 (Sept. 1988).

6 For example, see J. Dickinson and B. Russell, eds, Family Economy, and State: The Social Reproduction Process under Capitalism (Toronto: Garamond 1986); and A. Moscovitch and J. Albert, eds, The Benevolent State: The Growth of Welfare in Canada (Toronto: Garamond 1987).

7 Jean-Marie Fecteau, 'Régulation sociale et transition au capitalisme: jalons théoriques et méthodologiques pour une analyse du 19e siècle canadien' (Department of History, Université Laval 1986). This is an early report of an ongoing, large-scale project documenting the evolution of the 'mode of regulation' in nineteenth-century Quebec and Canada; we are grateful to J.M. Fecteau for providing a copy of the report.

8 Majorie Cohen, Women's Work, Markets and the Economy in Nineteenth-Century Ontario (Toronto: University of Toronto Press 1988)

9 Jane Ursel, 'The State and the Maintenance of Patriarchy,' in Dickinson and Russell, eds, Family, Economy, and State, 150–91. Ursel uses a version of dual-systems theory to explain the relationship between capitalism and patriarchy, but the analytical potential of this theory is not fully realized because she tends to equate capitalism with production and patriarchy with reproduction, thus obscuring the question of gender domination in the economy and class oppression in the realm of 'personal life.'

10 Ibid., 158

11 This has been argued both within Marxist-feminism and without (from

a radical feminist standpoint). A sampling of both perspectives can be found in Hugh Armstrong, Patricia Connelly, and Angela Miles, *Feminist Marxism or Marxist Feminism: A Debate* (Toronto: Garamond 1985).

12 See Alain Lipietz, 'Reflections on a Tale: The Marxist Foundations of the Concepts of Regulation and Accumulation,' *Studies in Political Economy* 26 (1988), 7–36.

13 Mariana Valverde, *The Age of Light, Soap and Water: Moral Reform in Turn of the Century English Canada* (Toronto: McClelland and Stewart 1991)

14 Constance Backhouse, 'Married Women's Property Law in Nineteenth-Century Canada,' *Law and History Review* 6 (1988), 211–58

15 The first phrase points to the fact that early Married Women's Property Acts were devised not to give women as a group financial autonomy but rather to 'protect' a small group of virtuous women deserted by spendthrift husbands (see Backhouse, 'Married Women's Property Law,' 211–58). The category of girls 'of previously chaste character' was elaborated in the seduction legislation of the 1880s, but it has its roots in earlier rape legislation and case law; see C. Backhouse, 'Nineteenth-Century Canadian Rape Law, 1800–1982,' in D. Flaherty, ed., *Essays in the History of Canadian Law*, vol. 2 (Toronto: Osgoode Society, University of Toronto Press 1983), 200–47. The phrase about prostitutes is taken verbatim from the vagrancy statute applied to women; see C. Backhouse, 'Nineteenth-Century Canadian Prostitution Law,' *Histoire sociale / Social History* 18 (1985), 387–423, and John McLaren, 'Chasing the Social Evil: Moral Fervour and the Evolution of Canada's Prostitution Laws 1867–1917,' *Canadian Journal of Law and Society* 1 (1986), 125–65.

16 C. Backhouse, 'Involuntary Motherhood: Abortion, Birth Control and the Law in Nineteenth-Century Canada,' *Windsor Yearbook of Access to Justice* 3 (1983), 67–71, and S. Gavigan, 'On "Bringing on the Menses": The Criminal Liability of Women and the Therapeutic Exception in Canadian Abortion Law,' *Canadian Journal of Women and the Law* 1 (1986), 279–312

17 C. Backhouse, 'Shifting Patterns in Nineteenth-Century Canadian Custody Law,' in Flaherty, ed., *Essays in the History of Canadian Law*, vol. 1 (1981), 218–48. See also C. Backhouse, 'Desperate Women and Compassionate Courts: Nineteenth-Century Infanticide in Canada,' *University of Toronto Law Journal* 34 (1984), 447–8; and Peter Ward, 'Unwed Mothers in Nineteenth-Century English Canada,' Canadian Historical Association, *Historical Papers*, 1981, 34–56.

18 A similar conclusion is drawn by Graham Parker, 'The Legal Regulation of Sexual Activity and the Protection of Females,' *Osgoode Hall Law Journal* 21 (1983), 187–224.

19 C. Backhouse, 'The Tort of Seduction: Fathers and Daughters in

Nineteenth-Century Canada,' *Dalhousie Law Journal* 10 (1986), 45–80; and K. Dubinsky, 'Maidenly Girls or Designing Women? Prosecutions for Seduction in Ontario, 1880–1929,' paper given at the Canadian Historical Association, Annual Meeting, Quebec City, June 1989

20 Bruce Curtis, *Building the Educational State: Canada West, 1836–1871* (London, Ont.: Althouse 1988), 23–5

21 Susan E. Houston and Alison Prentice, *Schooling and Scholars in Nineteenth-Century Ontario* (Toronto: University of Toronto Press 1988), especially ch. 8

22 Ibid., 328

23 Ibid., 317–30

24 Curtis, *Building the Educational State*, 30–1

25 Ibid., 252–7

26 Ibid., ch. 6

27 Houston and Prentice, *Schooling and Scholars*, 179–84

28 See Elizabeth Graham, *From Medicine-Man to Missionary: Missionaries as Agents of Change among the Indians of Southern Ontario 1784–1867* (Toronto: University of Toronto Press 1975), 23–6.

29 See Donald Smith, *Sacred Feathers: The Reverend Peter Jones (Kahkegaquonaby) and the Mississauga Indians* (Toronto: University of Toronto Press 1987), ch. 11.

30 Elizabeth Muir, 'The Bark Schoolhouse: Methodist Episcopal Missionary Women in Upper Canada,' in J.S. Moir and C.T. McIntire, eds, *Canadian Protestant and Catholic Missions, 1620s–1960s* (New York: Peter Lang 1988), 23–47

31 Collectif Clio, *Quebec Women: A History* (Toronto: Women's Press 1988), 126

32 Gretchen Green, 'Molly Brant, Catharine Brant, and Their Daughters: A Study in Colonial Acculturation,' *Ontario History* 81 (1989), 235

33 C. Lesley Biggs, 'The Case of the Missing Midwives: A History of Midwifery in Ontario from 1795–1900,' *Ontario History* 75 (1983), 21–35

34 R.D. Gidney and W.P. Millar, 'The Origins of Organized Medicine in Ontario, 1850–1869,' in Charles G. Roland, ed., *Health, Disease and Medicine: Essays in Canadian History* (Toronto: Hannah Institute for the History of Medicine 1984), 65–95; Colin D. Howell, 'Elite Doctors and the Development of Scientific Medicine: The Halifax Medical Establishment and 19th Century Medical Professionalism,' in Roland, ed., *Health, Disease and Medicine*, 105–22; Barbara R. Tunis, 'Medical Licensing in Lower Canada: The Dispute over Canada's First Medical Degree,' in S.E.D. Shortt, ed., *Medicine in Canadian Society: Historical Perspectives* (Montreal: McGill-Queen's University Press 1981), 137–63; Kenneth G. Pryke, 'Poor Relief and Health Care in Halifax, 1827–1849,' in Wendy Mitchinson and Janice Dickin McGinnis, eds, *Essays in*

*the History of Canadian Medicine* (Toronto: McClelland and Stewart 1988), 39–61

35 Biggs, 'Case of the Missing Midwives,' 25 and 33

36 For a discussion of the various obstacles confronting women's entry into the medical profession, see Veronica Strong-Boag, 'Canada's Women Doctors: Feminism Constrained,' in Kealey, ed., 'A Not Unreasonable Claim', 109–12, and Carlotta Hacker, *The Indomitable Lady Doctors* (Halifax: Formac Publishing 1984), 17–70. While studies on women's role in pre-institutional forms of health care are sorely wanting for the Canadian context, work by British historians has resulted in some interesting findings. For example, Charlotte Mackenzie finds that prior to the rise of large asylums women played a major role in psychiatric care through the operation of private boarding homes for the mentally ill. If such is the case for Canada, then we need to re-examine asylum formation not only in terms of a transference in psychiatric care from the private to the public sphere but also in terms of a shift in health care from the domain of women to men; see Charlotte Mackenzie, 'Women and Psychiatric Professionalization,' in London Feminist History Group, *The Sexual Dynamics of History: Men's Power, Women's Resistance* (London: Pluto Press 1983), 107 and 116. What also needs to be examined in more detail in the Canadian context is the employment of male practitioners in the hospitals run by religious women. Most of the hospitals initially founded in Canada were organized and operated exclusively by nuns, but studies have yet to document adequately their changing role in providing health-care services. For a discussion of some of the hospitals created by religious women, see: Loretta La Palm, 'The Hôtel-Dieu of Quebec: The First Hospital North of the Rio Grande under Its First Two Superiors,' Canadian Catholic Historical Association, *Study Session* (1974), 53–64; Henry M. Hurd, *The Institutional Care of the Insane in the United States and Canada* 4 vols (Baltimore: Johns Hopkins University Press 1917), 4:274–88.

37 Wendy Mitchinson, 'Historical Attitudes toward Women and Childbirth,' *Atlantis* 4 (1979), 13–34; 'Gynaecological Operations on the Insane,' *Archivaria* 10 (1980), 125–44; 'Gynaecological Operations on Insane Women, London, Ontario, 1895–1901,' *Journal of Social History* 15 (1982), 446–84; 'A Medical Debate in Nineteenth-Century English Canada: Ovariectomies,' *Histoire sociale / Social History* 17 (1984), 133–47; 'Causes of Disease in Women: The Case of Late 19th Century English Canada,' in Roland, ed., *Health, Disease and Medicine*, 381–95; 'The Medical View of Women: The Case of Late Nineteenth-Century Canada,' *Canadian Bulletin of Medical History* 3 (1986), 206–24; 'Hysteria and Insanity: A 19th Century Canadian Perspective,' *Journal of Canadian Studies* 21 (1986), 87–105; 'Medical Perceptions of Healthy

Women: The Case of Late Nineteenth Century Canada,' *Canadian Bulletin of Medical History* 4 (1987), 99–117

38 Mitchinson, 'Causes of Disease in Women,' 390

39 Ibid., 386–90

40 Ibid., 387

41 Angus McLaren, 'Birth Control and Abortion in Canada, 1870–1920,' in Alison Prentice and Susan Mann Trofimenkoff, eds, *The Neglected Majority: Essays in Canadian Women's History* 2 vols (Toronto: McClelland and Stewart 1985), 2:84–101; Angus McLaren and Arlene Tigar McLaren, *The Bedroom and the State: The Changing Practices and Politics of Contraception and Abortion in Canada, 1880–1980* (Toronto: McClelland and Stewart 1986)

42 McLaren, 'Birth Control and Abortion,' 87 and 96

43 Biggs, 'Case of the Missing Midwives,' 33

44 McLaren, 'Birth Control and Abortion,' 99–100

45 Susan E. Houston, 'Victorian Origins of Juvenile Delinquency: A Canadian Experience,' *History of Education Quarterly* 12 (1972), 254–80; Susan E. Houston, 'The "Waifs and Strays" of a Late-Victorian City: Juvenile Delinquents in Toronto,' in Joy Parr, ed., *Childhood and Family in Canadian History* (Toronto: McClelland and Stewart 1983), 129–42; Andrew Jones and Leonard Rutnam, *In the Children's Aid: J.J. Kelso and Child Welfare in Ontario* (Toronto: University of Toronto Press 1981); Joy Parr, *Labouring Children: British Immigrant Apprentices to Canada, 1869–1924* (London: Croom Helm 1980); Patricia T. Rooke and R.L. Schnell, 'Childhood and Charity in Nineteenth-Century British North America,' *Histoire sociale / Social History* 15 (1982), 157–79; Patricia T. Rooke and R.L. Schnell, *Studies in Childhood History: A Canadian Perspective* (Calgary: Detselig Enterprises 1982); Patricia T. Rooke and R.L. Schnell, *Discarding the Asylum: From Child Rescue to the Welfare State in English Canada (1800–1950)* (Lanham, MD: University Press of America 1983); Leonard Rutnam, 'J.J. Kelso and the Development of Child Welfare,' in Moscovitch and Albert, eds, *Benevolent State*; relevant chapters on child welfare also appear in Richard B. Splane, *Social Welfare in Ontario, 1791–1893: A Study of Public Welfare Administration* (Toronto: University of Toronto Press 1965); Neil Sutherland, *Children in English-Canadian Society: Framing the Twentieth-Century Consensus* (Toronto: University of Toronto Press 1978).

46 For a good discussion of the class implications underlying child saving see Craig Heron's excellent review essay 'Saving the Children,' *Acadiensis* 13 (1983), 168–75.

47 Parr, *Labouring Children*, 67.

48 See chapter five in Rooke and Schnell, *Discarding the Asylum*.

49 Sutherland, *Children in English-Canadian Society*, 17–18

50 Sutherland's critics have also convincingly refuted his emphasis on ide-

ological developments as the primary impetus for interventionist approaches in child welfare, arguing instead that late-nineteenth-century child-saving practices are better viewed as a 'tactical escalation' in social reform, emanating from the same philanthropic concerns that motivated earlier educational initiatives. See Heron, 'Saving the Children,' 172, and chapter 1 of Rooke and Schnell, *Discarding the Asylum*, which discusses the evolution of ideologies on childhood.

51 Jane Lewis, 'Motherhood Issues during the Late-Nineteenth and Early Twentieth Centuries: Some Recent Viewpoints,' *Ontario History* 75 (1983), 4–20

52 Sutherland, *Children in English-Canadian Society*, 13–20; Jones and Rutnam, *In the Children's Aid*

53 For example, see: Elizabeth Wilson, *Women and the Welfare State* (London: Tavistock Publications 1977), 130; Michele Barrett and Mary McIntosh, *The Anti-social Family* (London: Verso 1985), 33–4; Linda Gordon, *Heroes of Their Own Lives: The Politics and History of Family Violence* (New York: Viking/Penguin 1988), 113.

54 Jones and Rutnam, *In the Children's Aid*, 155–62

55 Allan Moscovitch and Glenn Drover, 'Social Expenditures and the Welfare State: The Canadian Experience in Historical Perspective,' in Moscovitch and Albert, eds, *Benevolent State*, 19

56 Parr, *Labouring Children*, 29–33

57 Patricia T. Rooke and R.L. Schnell, 'The Rise and Decline of British North American Protestant Orphan's Homes as Woman's Domain, 1850–1930,' *Atlantis* 7 (1982), 21–35

58 T.R. Morrison, ' "Their Proper Sphere": Feminism, the Family, and Child-Centred Social Reform in Ontario, 1875–1900,' *Ontario History* 68 (1976), 45–74

59 Indeed, the boundaries between female 'private' spheres and male 'public' domains become especially fuzzy when the issue of funding for women's charitable institutions is examined. Interesting examples of the blurring of such boundaries can be found in the *Journals of the Legislative Assembly of the United Province of Canada* (hereafter *Journals of the Legislative Assembly*) for the mid-nineteenth century, when women frequently submitted petitions to the government requesting financial assistance for the operation of their juvenile institutions and, in some cases, had the petitions introduced to the legislature by male relatives who were members of the Assembly (*Journals of the Legislative Assembly*, 1850 and 1851).

60 Allan Greer, 'The Sunday Schools of Upper Canada,' *Ontario History* 67 (1975), 161–84

61 F.L. Barron, 'The American Origins of the Temperance Movement,' *The Canadian Review of American Studies* 11 (1980), 131–50

62 Paula Baker, 'The Domestication of Politics: Women and American

Political Society, 1780–1920,' *American Historical Review* 89:3 (1984), 620–47. A parallel argument about the masculinization of republican citizenship is made in Christine Stansell, *City of Women: Sex and Class in New York City 1789–1860* (New York: Knopf 1986). For an argument about the growing identification of 'the social' with the feminine in nineteenth-century Britain, see Denise Riley, *Am I That Name? Feminism and the Category of 'Women' in History* (Minneapolis: University of Minnesota 1988), ch. 3.

63 Cecilia Morgan, 'Evangelical Concepts of Gender, 1829–1850' (MA paper, University of Toronto 1988)

# 7

# Railways and the Development of Canada West, 1850–1870

### DOUGLAS McCALLA

The story of railway development as an aspect of nation building through 'defensive expansionism' is a central element in the case for a distinctive Canadian historical relationship between the state and enterprise.[1] In mid-nineteenth-century Canada, railways were the major collective economic project of leading elements in the provincial business community and of the provincial government, and they were thus a central element in the state-making process. But although their significance has long been recognized, we have much still to learn about them. The substantial international literature of the past twenty-five years on the role of railways in economic development is even now only modestly represented in Canadian historiography. Indeed, Alan Green has noted that, 'for Canada at least, the simple exercise of examining the growth and efficiency of the railway system has not yet been undertaken.'[2] This gap in the literature arises because of the complexity of the issues involved in that 'simple exercise' and because most standard Canadian histories simply assume the importance of railways in the growth of the country and of the state in the development of railways.

This paper derives from a research project that is intended to survey the economic development of Upper Canada / Canada West until 1870. In assessing the latter stages of the province's development, it is necessary to come to terms with railways, both in themselves and for what they say about the state's role and effectiveness in developing the economy. In keeping with that larger project, one of whose objectives is to give a sense of the relative significance of the components of the provincial economy, the emphasis is less on policies than on economic behaviour, seen here through quite simple time series, drawn from quite familiar sources. The objective is to assess the scale, the shape, and something of the economic importance of one of the largest projects of the mid-century era of state making in Canada.

To understand the role of railways in provincial development to 1870, it is necessary to consider the chronology of railway development, the impact of construction, and the significance of early railway operations. To judge the Canadian experience, it is helpful also to consider relevant American evidence. When seen in these contexts, the railway experience in at least Canada West proves to be more positive than standard accounts usually indicate.

### Canada West Enters the Railway Age

Steam technology came to Upper Canada with the steamship, which Upper Canadians quickly adopted. By comparison, the story of railways in the province was much more complex. Except for very short lines, railways entailed substantial indivisible capital investments and could not be built on an incremental basis, as the stock of roads, wagons, and ships was. In the mid-1830s, Upper Canada's two most likely candidates as centres of railway promotion were Toronto and Hamilton. They were small, together numbering less than 15,000 people, and they were well connected by steamers for much of the year. Far from co-operating, as would have been essential for quick provincial action on railways, their local élites were pursuing rival hinterland-development visions. Moreover, there were more attractive uses for the limited resources commanded by local entrepreneurs than direct investment in social-overhead capital.

Thus, major investments were dependent on public funding or on outside investors and, in either case, on the trade cycle. Only in an expansionary investment phase could promising new projects, even in established markets, secure funding. The timing of a quest for funds in Britain for unbuilt, unknown projects on the other side of the Atlantic was a more delicate matter still, as the history of American railway promotion in the period also made clear.[3] Once in existence, companies could sustain investment through retained earnings, the reputation given by current earnings, and their established connections with suppliers, investors, politicians, and financiers.

Canadians first ventured into railways in the 1830s. In Lower Canada, the short Champlain and St Lawrence was built, and in Upper

Canada a number of companies were chartered, including the London and Gore, chartered in 1834 to link London and Hamilton; the City of Toronto and Lake Huron, chartered in 1836; and the Erie and Ontario, chartered in 1835 to join the two lakes.[4] During the 1830s, Upper-Canadian politicians were discovering the techniques of public borrowing as a way to finance desired public works. The province had consolidated its debt and transferred it to London with a £200,000 loan in 1834, while another £400,000 (stg) in debentures was issued in 1835–6, principally for purposes of canal building.[5] Meeting early in 1837, just before the 1830s boom ended in a crash, the provincial Assembly passed dozens of public-works bills (that would collectively have added enormously to the provincial debt) to support a wide range of canals, roads, bridges, and harbours.[6] Quite small sums were provided for the Erie and Ontario and the Cobourg railroads, while up to £200,000 was voted to aid the London and Gore (now renamed the Great Western) and up to £100,000 for the City of Toronto and Lake Huron. These were sums on a scale hitherto expended only on the two main provincial canal projects, the Welland and the St Lawrence. But for a company to secure provincial aid, it first had to raise some capital of its own from shareholders, for only then would the province match the sums raised by issuing debentures to three times that value to the company or directly on the market.[7] Neither company had such funds, and the 1837 crash almost at once ended the companies' chances to secure both private and public funds.

In the extended depression of 1839–43, virtually no North American railway securities could be sold in Britain. Then the English railway boom began to encourage interest in more distant projects, too. In 1845, the Great Western charter was revived, and the St Lawrence and Atlantic was chartered as part of a project to link Portland, Maine, and Montreal, via Sherbrooke. Both sent representatives to London who succeeded in obtaining subscriptions.[8] Unfortunately, far more shares were subscribed for in Britain than could ever have been paid for, the stock boom collapsed, and the Canadians were unable to collect the funds that had been pledged. Physical construction of the Great Western was essentially never begun, though the company was still alive in organizational terms. At the end of the 1840s, about sixty miles of track were in operation in the Canadas, none in Canada West.

By comparison with the United States, where 9,000 miles of track were then in operation, Canada had lagged in the development of the new technology. This lag owed something to the preoccupation of Canadian politicians with completing the St Lawrence canal system in the 1840s. But there were non-official circles in Canada, and urban centres such as Sherbrooke and Hamilton, from which the principal promotions of the 1840s emerged, were not obliged to wait for canals before promoting railways. Even in Montreal, the focal point of the navigation system, there were strong reasons to proceed at once with railways that seemed to complement canal development.[9] The will to adopt the new technology was present in Canada, but not the ability to finance the projects. That inability resulted from the nature of the technology, the availability of more attractive investments on the London market, the American state insolvency and debt repudiation of the 1839–43 period that had severely damaged the reputation of transatlantic securities in London, and the collapse of the speculative English railway boom.

In assessing the early Canadian railway record, it is pertinent that, though most American states had begun to explore railways, a number continued in the 1840s to develop canals as well. The extent of the Canadian lag looks somewhat different, too, when Canada West is seen not as an eastern but as a western region, analogous to Ohio, Michigan, and Indiana rather than to New York and Massachusetts. Only in 1851, when the Erie Railroad reached Lake Erie, were the Great Lakes and a major eastern port joined under one company. By then, all three western states had the beginnings of railway systems, totalling almost 1,000 miles of track. Their lead over Canada West came from their having had a few months' head start in entering the financial markets in 1836–7 – a lead that permitted work to begin – and from the growing interest of eastern American financiers from the mid-forties onward. The states' early ventures into railways were hardly unalloyed successes, however, and Michigan actually sold off its state-owned lines at a loss in the mid-1840s. As for the impact of such projects on economic development, it is not clear how much, if any, ground these states had gained on Canada West by their earlier start in railway construction; it was only in the 1850s that the main interregional trunk lines in the states south and west of Canada West were built and state networks filled out around them.

Canada West finally entered the railway age in the 1850s. By then, the government of the Province of Canada had joined the promotional efforts, through its 1849 Guarantee Act, the 1851 Main Trunk Line of Railway Act, and the 1852 Consolidated Municipal Loan Fund Act.[10] The first two put the provincial government's credit behind approved main-line projects that succeeded in completing half their mileage from private funding; under the last, the province was the ultimate support for any project that could secure sufficient municipal backing and private credit to commence work. If the projects generated sufficient earnings, of course, no government money at all would be required.[11] Necessary though they may have been, the 1849 and 1851 provincial guarantees were not sufficient to get construction underway. Ultimately, cycles in the capital markets and the overall chronology and geographical pattern of North American railway development are at least as important as public policy in explaining the timing of Canada's first railway age.

For the Great Western, Canada West's most successful rail line, a key cyclical factor was the widening premium available in London to investors in bonds of colonial railways by comparison with safe British securities, on which interest rates touched all-time lows in 1851. Late in 1851, the Great Western became one of the first overseas railway companies to use bonds convertible into equity stock on favourable terms to attract British investors. In its approach to them, it was advised and supported by an influential group of London railway brokers and financiers. Almost simultaneously, it was able to raise funds from a powerful American railway interest, the Forbes-Corning alliance, which controlled both the line from Albany to Buffalo that was about to become the New York Central and the Michigan Central from Detroit westward towards Chicago.[12] The Great Western would link the two, especially for passengers, who were only moderately inconvenienced by twice having to change trains at the border, and who valued the time saved by the shorter route west across Canada.

No other Canadian railway was in so favourable a position, but other lines that would benefit under the 1849 Guarantee Act – the St Lawrence and Atlantic and the Toronto-based Ontario, Simcoe and Huron (later Northern) – were well underway in 1852 and would open in 1853. What remained to be put under contract were the links from Toronto to Hamilton (for which the Great Western's British backers were already raising funds) and from Toronto to Montreal, and a second line west from Toronto into Canada West's fertile peninsula. All these were chartered and, T.C. Keefer later argued, would likely have been built because of the way they connected the major trading centres of the province.[13] In alliance with, or led by, Francis Hincks and the Canadian government, British promoters in 1852–3 launched an enormous project, the Grand Trunk Railway of Canada, to fill the gap, and much more. It became at once the central focus of and a major influence on the provincial government's railway and financial policies. It is important to remember, however, that a project of this scale was in no sense the only possibility to complete the core central-Canadian railway system. By the end of the decade, the Grand Trunk supplied more than half the railway mileage in Canada.

The decade's other lines were almost all built in Canada West. The choice to build was made by municipalities whose local boosters could secure municipal approval for funding companies thought essential to local development, either under the Municipal Loan Fund or independently, as Hamilton did. The process was shaped by intercity competition and by the workings of contractors and promoters who quickly learned to use the new rules of funding and of local and provincial responsible government to promote their favourite schemes.[14] When these factors were combined with rosy official expectations of the gains to be derived from railways, a brief and spectacular railway boom resulted, notably in Canada West, where more than two-thirds of the track laid in Canada in the 1850s was located and to which the Municipal Loan Fund initially applied exclusively.

Because it is generally thought that Canada lagged behind the United States and thus required unusually close relations between government and business, it is useful to consider the American experience in these years. In fact, much of the expansion of railways in states to the south occurred at the same time as in Canada West, as the main elements of the trunk line system from the east coast to Chicago and beyond were put into place by 1856. Further, to a degree that Canadians have not always recognized, the United States, too, built at least its early transportation facilities as mixed enterprises. As Harry Scheiber notes, 'local governments contributed nearly half of an estimated 12.8 million dollars invested in Ohio's railroads up to 1850.'[15] Michigan actually built and owned its railways for a time. In Indiana, government and business were linked at the municipal level, albeit on a more modest scale than in Ohio or Canada West.[16] Defensive arguments about faster American progress were important in the rhetoric of Canadian politics, but at times, as in the 1850s, actual developments in Canada West were not so much lagged as simultaneous with and quite similar in institutional character to the southern developments to which they responded.

### The Economic Impact of Railway Construction

From 1852 to 1859, more than 1,400 miles of railway were built in Canada West, almost three-quarters of which were opened between

1853 and 1856 (Table 7:1).* By the end of 1856, all the major urban centres in the province had been linked. By 1860, the railway system of Canada was capitalized at about $100 million, more than half of it represented by the Grand Trunk and almost all the remainder by lines in Canada West, which together reported a capital cost of about $44 million (Table 7:3). Railway capital accounts could be over- or understated by large amounts, depending on the valuations at which companies were taken over, the degree to which securities had been issued at discounts from par value, and the company's practice in distinguishing between capital and operating accounts after a line had opened. In Canada, because there was evident overvaluation in a number of companies, including the Grand Trunk and the Northern, these figures indicate the maximum investment made to open the railways.[17] Of these sums, up to $20 million was furnished under the terms of the Guarantee and Main Trunk acts (plus other aid to the Grand Trunk) and up to $6 million from borrowings by municipalities in Canada West under terms of the Municipal Loan Fund.[18] Most of the money raised under these laws and of the remaining capital was provided by British investors, their willingness to take bonds and stocks depending in varying degrees on state finance. As Scheiber argued regarding Ohio, 'the increased availability of private invest- ment capital, during the recovery of the late 1840s, impelled railroad promoters to redouble their efforts for public aid: all recognized that a tangible expression of support by governmental authorities, in the form of stock subscriptions, loans, or guarantees, would be the most effective lure for foreign or eastern capital.'[19]

The economic impact of these railways was felt initially in their construction. Of the external investment of up to $100 million, most was made in the five years from 1852 to 1856; all was expended by 1859. At least $70 million of the total was invested in Canada West. Thus, in the peak years, more than $10 million per year was being spent on railways there. By provincial standards, this was an enormous sum. In relation to Canada West's 1851 population of almost one million, railway investment amounted to about $10 per person per year, a sum that far exceeded per-capita annual investments from outside the province via formal, recorded channels in any previous year. At a nominal 6 per cent rate of interest, the total capital of $70 million represented an annual cost of $4.2 million to the economy of

---

* Tables referred to in the text appear in the appendix at the end of this essay.

Canada West, equal to $4 per person in 1851 or $3 in terms of the 1861 population of 1.4 million.[20] Expressed in terms of an average household (six persons), the interest charge in 1861 would thus have been $18. As output increased, the relative weight on the economy of such a charge declined. For example, these costs can be related to off-farm sales by farmers in Canada West, which in 1851 averaged $125 per farm and in 1861 $210 (for all farms) or $280 (for farms with marketable surpluses).[21]

These were large investments when viewed in relation to other measures of the scale of the provincial economy on the eve of the railway era. All exports from the Province of Canada combined averaged about $13 million per year in 1850–2, while the only estimate we have for Canadian Gross National Product in the period, by Firestone, gives a figure of $169 million for Canadian GNP in 1851. Thus, at $12.5 million per year in the two Canadas (for the eight years 1852–9), the investment was equivalent to yearly exports in the early 1850s and to more than 7 per cent of 1851 GNP. Firestone's GNP figures are probably too high and embrace the Maritime provinces, too, so it is evident that the investment in Canada West expressed as a percentage of its output alone would have been considerably higher. External investments at or above 8 per cent of GNP also characterized later eras of major railway construction in Canada.[22] From 1851 to 1860, three adjacent American states, Ohio, Michigan, and Indiana, saw gross investment in their railway systems of $171 million, equal to $35,000 per mile of track and $39 per capita in terms of their 1860 populations. Canada West's figures were closer to $51,000 per mile and more than $50 per head (Table 7:6). Any lag as of 1850 had been made up by the decade's end.

Of the British capital invested in Canadian railways, some never left England, being used to pay costs of raising capital, such as commissions and, for later issues, interest on the company's earlier ones. Other capital crossed the ocean as manufactured iron and hardware, steel, machinery, 'railroad iron,' pig-iron, and bars and sheets, imports of which totalled about $3 million per year in 1851–2, surged to $9 million in 1854, then quickly fell back to $5 million from 1855 to 1857, and to 1851–2 levels thereafter. Over the entire construction period, from 1851 to 1859, iron imports, the major capital goods that had to be imported, totalled more than $40 million, of which about half is likely to have been directly attributable to railways (Table 7:11 [a]).[23]

Despite such capital movements, exchange rates held relatively steady.[24] Instead, the capital movements show up as a surge in local prices and in the value of imports of all kinds into Canada, as the Canadian economy rapidly drew in imports (Table 7:11 [b]). By 1854, the value of imports stood at 2.4 times the level of 1850, while exports had gone up 1.8 times, from a lower base.

The total value of imports to the Canadas per year established at the 1854–6 peak was, after the crash of 1857, again attained by 1861–2; and by then the value of exports had caught up. It requires more evidence and analysis than is possible here to estimate how much those later exports were directly or indirectly the consequence of investments spurred by railway construction in the 1850s. But while some of the railway investment flowed immediately out in the purchase of goods for consumption, including some goods formerly supplied domestically, the higher levels of demand in the mid-1850s for many commodities, locally produced as well as imported, should have encouraged investment in farmsteads and other productive facilities beyond what would have occurred in the absence of railways. Additionally, though much of Canada West's productive land was relatively near navigable waterways, some forest and farm products would not have been marketable without railways.

One of the most direct impacts of outside capital was in employment on construction. The provincial work-force has been estimated at about 250,000 in 1851,[25] which provides a scale against which to measure construction demands for labour. Aspects of railway construction called for skill and experience, but other parts of the work entailed relatively unskilled tasks that local residents could certainly have done. Nevertheless, although detailed evidence on railway-construction labour in Canada is not readily available, it is likely that much of the construction work-force consisted of recent immigrants or transient workers drawn by the construction boom.[26] Albert Fishlow suggests that thirty to sixty men were needed per mile of track, the former on some successful American lines, the latter on English lines, where construction was to a higher standard.[27] If, as Fishlow argues, the stock of railways under construction at any time was equivalent to lines opened in that and the next year, 300 to 600 miles per year were underway from 1852 to 1858.

Despite the Grand Trunk's declared intention to build to British standards, contractors in Canada seem at least as likely to have followed North American patterns. In the summer of 1854, the Grand Trunk was said to have 8,000 men at work on the 333 miles of the Montreal-Toronto line. The company's overall peak demand for construction labour is said to have been 15,000 men; with more than 400 miles being built in 1855–6, this number works out to less than 40 workers per mile.[28] Even so, the high, British-based figures are also included in the estimates made here (Table 7:2). Thus, the 300 miles under way in Canada West in 1852 and 1854 would have required between 9,000 and 18,000 workers, and the 600 miles in 1855 would have required 18,000 to 36,000 workers. The last figure would have represented almost 15 per cent of the estimated work-force in Canada West in 1851, or 10 per cent of Pentland's estimate of the 1861 work-force. Even the lowest figure represents a demand for labour on a specific project or set of projects that was quite unprecedented in the province. On the other hand, even at the highest level estimated, more than enough immigrants arrived at Quebec during the period to yield the number required.[29]

These calculations are not meant to suggest that most construction workers were immigrants who came, worked for five or six years as navvies, and then departed. Rather, it is likely that a much larger number of migrants and residents had some experience of the process as labourers or as suppliers of work and services on a contract or sub-contract basis. By permanent and transient immigration and by real-location of labour already within the province, the railways' demand for construction labour was met. The fall in the rate of net immigration for the decade by comparison with all previous decades (to which the evidently considerable emigration of the later 1850s contributed) shows that the economy could not absorb all those drawn to the province by the boom. Railway construction thus seems likely to have had a relatively marginal impact on the process of permanent settlement. On the other hand, the railways did recruit for their operations and maintenance many skilled British workers who entered the work-force at the high end of the working-class wage scale.[30] And by 1860, the railways of Canada West employed between 4,000 and 5,000 workers, a very large number for a single sector of the non-farm labour market (Table 7:3).

The expenditure of so much imported capital in so short a time had an immediate impact on prices.[31] The inflation was not unique to Canada, nor was it all the result of the capital imports for railway construction. Similar forces were at work throughout the western economy from the beginning of the 1850s onward: British prices increased by about one-third in five years from their 1849–51 levels, the lowest in the entire century to that point, and American prices likewise rose rapidly. Still, on the limited basis of produce prices, it

seems that price increases in Canada West were at the high end of
the inflationary scale in the North Atlantic economy. The standard
price index, Michell's, shows a sharp rise in commodity prices at Toronto from 1852 to 1855–7. For virtually all produce items, prices in
Toronto in 1854–6 were at their highest levels since the War of 1812
(see Table 7:10). The problem for the recipient of such higher prices
was to use the money to augment long-term earning power. Those
who paid off debts in the period were ahead of where they would
otherwise have been, as were those who expanded output and sales
without incurring new debt. On the other hand, as the numerous
bankruptcies and widespread liquidity problems that followed the 1857
crisis showed, those who bought land in this period likely paid prices
and incurred debts that would be burdensome when prices later fell,
while those who lent on the basis of higher prices had much difficulty
in securing repayment.[32]

Thus, it is important not to assume that long-term growth was a
consequence of a short period of inflation. We can best see the construction boom, and its particular labour problems,[33] as an essentially
short-term phenomenon whose impact was limited by the involvement
of transient workers, the use of imported inputs, the inflationary effects of capital imports, and the leakage of funds back to metropolitan
centres in the form of sharply rising levels of all imports. Had the
railways not been important in the long term as transportation systems, the construction boom would in retrospect seem almost entirely
ephemeral.

### The Economic Impact of Railway Operations

Railways were a major new technological system that was far from
fully developed anywhere in 1850 or 1860.[34] They made their impact
over an extended time, rather than all at once. As managers would
continue to discover, there was enormous scope for further investment and traffic development, and for improvements in productivity
and reductions in unit costs, through developments within companies
and at the system-wide level, as the railways were increasingly integrated into an international network with standards set by the system
as a whole. The railways' essential role was to provide superior transportation to existing land and water modes for many kinds of freight
and most passengers. In addition, they were a major institutional
innovation in the Canadian economy.

In Canada West there were eleven independent railway companies at the end of the 1850s and nine operating companies in 1870. Tables 7:3 and 7:4, which contain a summary of the data on all companies, provide an overview of the entire system. Table 7:3 focuses on 1860, at the end of the construction era, when traffic had begun to revive after the sharp business contraction of 1857. Table 7:4 is for 1870, just on the eve of additions that would almost double railway mileage in the province.[35] To permit a focus on Canada West, half the Grand Trunk's revenues are arbitrarily assigned to the company's sections in Canada West, from Montreal to Sarnia. Because traffic on the line east of Levis did not even cover operating costs, and the entire 214-mile Eastern Division showed the lowest earnings of the four divisions,[36] this allocation of Grand Trunk revenue and traffic to its western divisions is unlikely to be high.

The main components of the system from the beginning were the Grand Trunk and the Great Western. In 1860, they accounted for more than 80 per cent of railway revenues in Canada West, and in 1870 even more. When the Northern is added, about 88 per cent of 1860 revenues and 92 per cent of 1870 revenues are accounted for. In 1860, only the Great Western, with revenues of $6,400 per mile of track, exceeded the average for Canada West of $3,600 per mile (Table 7:3). In 1870, only the Great Western, by now close of $11,000 per mile, and the Northern exceeded the average of $4,600 per mile. By then, the Grand Trunk had surpassed $5,000, while the others remained at or below $3,000 per mile of track.[37] Annual traffic and revenue data for the three principal companies are provided in tables 7:7, 7:8, and 7:9.

All three companies, like their smaller counterparts, aimed to serve the American market, either for Canadian exports, as in the lines running north from Lake Ontario, or for through traffic from one point in the United States to another, as in the three main companies and the Buffalo and Lake Huron. In the 1860s, the Northern largely abandoned its money-losing quest for through traffic between Georgian Bay and Lake Ontario.[38] For the Grand Trunk, by the mid-1860s through traffic generated about one-fifth of revenues, a figure that did not increase before 1870. The quest for such traffic was integral to the Grand Trunk's long-term strategy, but this business involved intense competition with American routes for a share of the western trade with the eastern seaboard. Its impact on revenues was thus constrained by typically very low rates per ton-mile.[39] The Great Western's figures as given here do not permit consideration of the role of through traffic, despite its importance to the company's strategy, its swift success, and its much higher revenues per mile. For example, through traffic in the first half of 1855 produced 56 per cent of company revenue.[40] But as local traffic developed and new American alternatives appeared, that figure was as likely to decline as to increase. When the three main railways are considered together, there is nothing to suggest that through traffic grew more rapidly than local either in volumes or revenues. Changes in total volumes and revenues therefore indicate at least minimum rates of change in local traffic.

Between 1860 and 1870, revenues for railways in Ontario and Quebec increased at an average rate of 7.1 per cent per year (Table 7:5). Only a few significant segments of the system, of which Great Western passengers are the most important, did not show growth at or above that level. During the 1860s, the physical dimensions of the system grew more slowly than did revenues and traffic, as the system was improved and became more productive. It is unlikely that increased revenues resulted from rising general levels of rates and fares, because freight and passenger volumes generally increased as fast as or faster than revenues. If anything, rate levels were steady or tending to decline in these years.[41] Unfortunately, the data here do not show changes, if any, in average length of passenger journeys and freight hauls.

Not all this traffic growth reflected growth in the provincial economy, for shifts in mode of travel and freight handling from road and water were also included. Within two years of its opening, the Great Western appears to have been hauling at least as much flour and almost as much wheat from the province's western peninsula as the Welland Canal, and to have become the major conduit for more valuable imported merchandise.[42] Water transport scarcely disappeared on the lower Great Lakes in these years; in fact, volumes of lake shipping increased substantially.[43] In 1859, the Grand Trunk noted that it faced competition from twenty-two steamers on the Toronto- or Hamilton-to-Montreal run and equally formidable competition between Montreal and Quebec.[44] In setting rates, the railways had to recognize shippers' ability to use the waterway. For much of Canada West, the combination of lake access and competition by both local and nearby American railways gave highly competitive rates and ensured that the benefits of increased efficiency were passed to shippers and/or consumers. Clearly the growth in traffic was not just a matter of shifting modes, but derived from the continuing expansion and integration of the provincial economy.

In 1870, the revenues of the railways in Ontario and Quebec totalled almost $13 million. When revenues of the railways in Atlantic Canada are included, the total was about $13.7 million, of which, if the attribution of half the Grand Trunk's revenues to its Ontario lines is accurate, Ontario's share was two-thirds. The Canadian total equalled 3.6 per cent of Canadian GNP that year – a large figure for a single industry and technological development.[45] It bears comparison with Fishlow's estimate that the income flow of American railways was equivalent to about 3 per cent of American GNP in 1859.[46]

As systems of transportation and communication, railways had a continuing impact on the location of economic activities, and they fostered the selective growth of some of the leading urban centres. In all of Ontario south of a line from Collingwood to the Ottawa River around Renfrew, there is hardly an urban centre of even 10,000 people today that did not get on a rail line by 1860.[47] But in this pattern, causation was not one way, for the railway map reflected the economic and political power of existing urban centres – that is, development that had already occurred. Railways thus tended to reinforce and extend patterns already taking shape.[48]

As the biggest businesses in Canada, the leading railways represented an important development in the institutional structure of the provincial economy. No other companies had such large fixed capital to maintain and account for; none had such large staffs and complex hierarchies of tasks and skills to organize; none had such large revenues. Railways faced much competition, but were unlike most producers in the oligopolistic characteristics of their markets; hence their frequent efforts to control competition by inter-company rate agreements.[49] Almost no other incorporated companies involved foreign ownership. Additionally, the Grand Trunk and Great Western railways became almost immediately the largest manufacturing enterprises in Canada, as they discovered the economies of internalizing not only the repair and maintenance of their costly plants but the manufacture of their new equipment. In this way they could most effectively use the extensive and relatively highly paid staffs of skilled workers that they had built up.[50]

## Conclusion

Although railways were a principal accomplishment of the mid-nineteenth-century state in Canada, the direct railway legacy of this era has often been seen in very negative terms. For example, Ian Drummond writes: 'By the time of Confederation the railways of Ontario had amassed a dismal financial record. They were in a sorry state, both financially and physically. No one was earning much from railway operation: the Grand Trunk and the Great Western had been kept from bankruptcy only by special intercessory legislation, and few of the locally owned feeder lines were in better shape.'[51] Even if the evidence surveyed here does not fully address either the physical or financial dimensions of the railway story, it is clear that Drummond exaggerates its negative elements and misrepresents the real accomplishments of the first railway era in the province.

If three adjacent states, Ohio, Indiana, and Michigan, are taken somewhat arbitrarily as a standard, the record of Canada West by 1860 was comparable in several respects (Table 7:6). The American average combines Ohio and Michigan, which revenue data suggest were more successful than Canada West, with Indiana, which was much less so. Compared to the average, Canada West built fewer miles of track in proportion to its population, while the track generated more revenue per mile. Indeed, the $3,600 in revenues per mile of track in Canada West in 1860 fell only slightly below the average for the entire United States in 1859, $3,900 per mile.[52] In capitalization, Canada West was clearly higher than its neighbours to the south and west. The higher Canadian figures derive from the Great Western, whose relatively heavy traffic may have justified its higher capital per mile, and from the Grand Trunk, next most heavily capitalized (Table 7:3). If the Grand Trunk was excessively capitalized, that would weigh heavily in the provincial average. Furthermore, 20 per cent of the American mileage had been completed by 1851, at much lower costs per mile than the 1850s price structure allowed. Perhaps, too, the broader Canadian gauge imposed significantly higher costs for roadbed and bridges.[53]

In the next decade, the three leading provincial railways, the Great Western, Grand Trunk, and Northern, all increased revenue and traffic at rates that doubled total amounts in about a decade. Annual data for the three main companies make clear that growth was more or less continuous, and was not simply a phenomenon of the Civil War years (tables 7:7, 7:8, and 7:9). Each company did much better for most or all of the 1860s than it had in the later 1850s by a key measure of performance, the ratio of ordinary working expenses to revenues. There is nothing to suggest that locally owned lines, of which there were few, were in any sense better off than the larger, British-owned ones.

Of the latter, the Great Western remained the best performer. It had reduced fixed charges on its capital by using convertible bonds, which investors converted to common shares in 1855 and 1856. During the 1860s, it replaced most of its original rails and wooden bridges, added a third rail on much of its line to permit movement of standard-gauge cars, and negotiated favourable terms for completion of its payment of sums owed on Canadian government account. In that time, its outlay on account of interest actually declined, and between 1865 and 1870 it paid dividends of 3.5 to 5 per cent per year.[54] These were not enormous payments in terms of the initial visions that railway promoters offered of railway profitability, but they are far removed from the picture painted by Drummond. The company would certainly have been in better financial health still if it had not, at the height of its initial success in the 1850s, made an unfortunate investment in an American extension, the Detroit and Milwaukee. In any case, sub-optimal returns on that part of a railway's capital represented by its common stock were the concern principally of those British common stockholders who had bought their shares at too high a price. As shares turned over, as a great many must have by the 1860s, new shareholders bought in at rates of discount on the par value of shares that reflected past and predicted earnings levels, not those of the original promotional literature. Later, the Great Western proved vulnerable in its heartland to Canadian and American competitors, as the building of increasingly powerful railway systems left smaller companies more and more exposed, but it is anachronistic to stress this problem in the 1860s.

As for the Grand Trunk, it is unlikely that its Ontario sections were the main cause of its problems. Its initial overcapitalization and the politically imposed necessity to build unremunerative lines were both focused in Canada East, where it took over existing companies at excessive valuations and agreed to build an unpromising line to Rivière-du-Loup from Richmond. Its root problem was its initial strategy to seek through American trade, and its excessive scale was dictated by that strategy. Going into bankruptcy or seeking reorganization through a private bill would have been very risky both for its political allies and for its owners. But in avoiding those perils, it also avoided the necessity-cum-opportunity to restructure capital on a more realistic basis. The considerable success in the 1860s of the Northern (which, like the other two major companies, was British owned), owed a good deal to its forced reorganization in the late 1850s.[55] In the 1860s, the Brockville and Ottawa underwent a similar restructuring of capital, and the turn of the Midland came in the 1870s.

During the 1850s, the essential elements of the central-Canadian trunk-railway system were put in place, linking Toronto, Montreal, and all other major Canadian urban centres with one another and, at a number of points, with the United States. To this day the first main lines are major components in the Canadian railway network. At the same time, Canada West fully entered the transition from mainly extensive to intensive growth, as declining rates of population growth, rising output per farm, and other indicators demonstrate. Producers quite quickly adapted to new circumstances, as David Gagan has shown for the farmers of Peel County. By 1870, there was substantially more evidence of industrial development in the leading cities.

It is almost automatic to think of railways as representing a 'move from a commercial to an industrial economy,'[56] but railways were not universally or uniformly associated with the growth of other industries. It is thus unlikely that the shift in the character of Canada West's development at mid-century can be solely attributed to railways, although it occurred during the first provincial railway era and was undoubtedly influenced by the new technology. For example, the demographic pressure that Gagan discusses coincided with the boom but was not a result of it.[57]

Here it may be enough to see railways not as the cause but as a part of the larger development process, playing a role that would continue for decades. They did not exhaust their impact within a few years: they became more productive, their systems developed, they became more fully part of an increasingly integrated American railway network, and the real costs of transport fell, especially between major centres well served by competing modes of transport. As the process continued, they tended to reinforce the power of the most favourably located cities and to foster more internal exchange, wider and more complex markets, and a relatively greater degree of rural integration into markets, all of these being factors in the continuing development of southern Ontario's position as the economic heartland of Canada.

To the extent that 'bureaucratic maturation' is a theme in institutional development in mid-nineteenth-century Canada,[58] further examination of the organizational structures of the principal railways as they consolidated and intensified their activities in the 1860s is very much warranted. As Paul Craven and Tom Traves note, however, until late in the century the railways remained exceptions in the business world, both in the scale and sophistication of their manufacturing operations and in their overall size and complexity.[59] Railways were forerunners of big business in Canada, that is, but they had no immediate imitators.

There is no doubt that railway technology was one critical element in the transformation of Canadian society in the mid-nineteenth century. The state played a major part in the railways' story, especially in facilitating their initial funding, but in a myriad of other ways as well, through the legislature, the law, the actions of politicians and officials, and the efforts of municipalities. In the process, the state itself was much changed, notably in the context of public finance.[60] Of course, there was ample evidence of scandal, inefficiency, and failure. One of the principal vehicles of state activity was the Grand Trunk Railway; as a chosen instrument of public policy,[61] it was weakened by its excessive scale and its inappropriate capitalization. Yet even it generated substantial increases of traffic and revenue in the 1860s. On balance, the railway record in Canada West suggests that failure should not be the essence of the story. Through a complex mix of state and private activity, Canada West acquired and in many ways domesticated a major imported technology at virtually the same time as adjacent states, and in apparently similar quantities. Growth during the 1860s in Canada West suggests the demand for and something of the value of that technology in a progressive economy.

# APPENDIX

All $ figures in the tables that follow are *current* $. Where conversion from sterling is required, the rate used is par of $4.866 = £1 stg.

Abbreviations for Railway Companies

| B&LH | Buffalo and Lake Huron (later leased by GTR) |
| B&O | Brockville and Ottawa |
| C&P | Cobourg and Peterborough |
| E&O | Erie and Ontario (later leased by GWR) |
| GTR | Grand Trunk |
| GWR | Great Western |
| L&PS | London and Port Stanley |
| O&P | Ottawa and Prescott (later St Lawrence and Ottawa) |
| PHL&B | Port Hope, Lindsay and Beaverton (later Midland) |

TABLE 7:1

Railway Construction in Canada West, 1852–60

(All figures are miles of track opened in year.)*

| | 1853 | 1854 | 1855 | 1856 | 1857 | 1858 | 1859 | 1860 | Total |
|---|---|---|---|---|---|---|---|---|---|
| GWR | 229 | 12 | 38 | | 15 | 51 | | | 345 |
| GTR+ (Canada West only) | | | 125 | 297 | | 31 | 70 | 2 | 525 |
| B&LH | | | | 116 | | 45 | | 1 | 162 |
| Northern | 63 | 32 | | | | | | | 95 |
| O&P | | 54 | | | | | | | 54 |
| B&O | | | | | | | 63 | 1 | 64 |
| C&P | | 28** | | | | | | | 28 |
| PHL&B | | | | | 43 | 14 | | | 57 |
| E&O | | 17** | | | | | | | 17 |
| Welland | | | | | | | 25 | | 25 |
| L&PS | | | | 24 | | | | | 24 |
| Other | | | | | 11** | | 4** | | 15 |
| Total | 292 | 143 | 163 | 437 | 69 | 141 | 162 | 4 | 1,411 |

SOURCE: T.C. Keefer, *Philosophy of Railroads and Other Essays*, ed. H.V. Nelles (Toronto: University of Toronto Press 1972), 132–5

\* Lines opened in January credited to previous year

\*\* Lines not in use in 1862

\+ In addition, the GTR had about 500 miles of track in Canada East and the United States. Minor lines in Canada East totalled another 100 miles.

TABLE 7:2

Demand for Construction Labour, Railways in Canada West, 1852–9 (estimated)

| | Miles opened this year | Miles opened next year | Total miles under way | Labour required | |
|---|---|---|---|---|---|
| | | | | @ 30/mile | @ 60/mile |
| 1852 | – | 292 | 292 | 8,760 | 17,520 |
| 1853 | 292 | 143 | 435 | 13,050 | 26,100 |
| 1854 | 143 | 163 | 306 | 9,180 | 18,360 |
| 1855 | 163 | 437 | 600 | 18,000 | 36,000 |
| 1856 | 437 | 69 | 506 | 15,180 | 30,360 |
| 1857 | 69 | 141 | 210 | 6,300 | 12,600 |
| 1858 | 141 | 162 | 303 | 9,090 | 18,180 |
| 1859 | 162 | 4 | 166 | 4,980 | 9,960 |

SOURCE: Data from Table 7:1. Estimate based on Albert Fishlow, *American Railroads and the Transformation of the Ante-Bellum Economy* (Cambridge, Mass.: Harvard University Press 1965), 411.

## TABLE 7:3
### The Railway System of Canada West in 1860

| Company | Miles of track | Capital cost to date ($000,000) | Revenue ($000) | Revenue per mile ($000) | Expense ($000) | Expense as % of revenue | Number of employees | Number of locomotives | Cars (passenger) | Cars (freight) | Capital cost per mile ($000) |
|---|---|---|---|---|---|---|---|---|---|---|---|
| GWR | 345 | 23.0 | 2,198 | 6.4 | 1,121** | 51** | 2,049 | 89 | 127 | 1,269 | 66.7 |
| B&LH | 162 | 6.4 | 316 | 2.0 | 264 | 83 | 458 | 28 | 24 | 255 | 39.5 |
| Northern | 95 | 3.9 | 333 | 3.5 | 260 | 78 | 370 | 17 | 20 | 301 | 41.0 |
| O&P | 54 | 1.4 | 75 | 1.4 | 51 | 68 | 92 | 5 | 8 | 79 | 26.5 |
| B&O | 64 | 1.9 | 54 | 0.8 | 34 | 64 | 74 | 3 | 8 | 79 | 29.7 |
| C&P | 28 | –* | na | – | – | – | na | 4 | 2 | 66 | –* |
| PHL&B | 57 | 5.0* | 54 | 0.9 | 40 | 75 | 66 | 5 | 3 | 65 | 49.0* |
| F&O | 17 | –* | na | – | – | – | na | 1 | 4 | 10 | –* |
| Welland | 25 | 1.3 | 65 | 2.6 | 51 | 79 | 104 | 4 | 4 | 87 | 52.4 |
| L&PS | 24 | 1.0 | 29 | 1.2 | 23 | 78 | 38 | 2 | 2 | 50 | 42.4 |
| Subtotal | 871 | 44.0 | 3,124 | 3.8 | 1,844** | 59** | 3,251 | 158 | 202 | 2,261 | 50.5 |
| GTR | 1,022 | 55.7 | 3,350 | 3.3 | 2,807 | 84 | 3,118 | 217 | 135 | 2,538 | 54.5 |
| Canada total | 1,893 | 99.6 | 6,474 | 3.5 | 4,651** | 72** | 6,369 | 375 | 337 | 4,799 | 52.6 |
| Canada West (incl. ½ of GTR) | 1,396 | 72.0 | 4,800 | 3.6 | 3,227** | 67** | 4,800 | 267 | 270 | 3,530 | 51.5 |

* C&P and F&O not operating in 1860; non-operating mileage is excluded from revenue-per-mile totals.
** See note on source to this table on page 212.

NOTES:

1 No data are given in original source for capitalization of C&P, F&O, and PHL&B. On the basis of Keefer (136), $5 million is assumed to be their combined cost. This may be slightly high, but even so, the error would have only a marginal impact on total figures.

TABLE 7:3 (*continued*)

2  To arrive at full data for Canada West in 1860, it is assumed that the Montreal-to-Sarnia mileage of the GTR (525) should be credited to Upper Canada. Half of GTR revenues are assigned to the province, as this represents half of its mileage.

3  The figure for GWR revenue given here varies slightly (less than 1 per cent) from that in Table 7:7. Different sources are involved in the two tables.

SOURCE: T.C. Keefer, *The Philosophy of Railroads and Other Essays*, 132–7, 156; except that figures marked ** for GWR are from J.M. Trout and E. Trout, *The Railways of Canada for 1870-1* (Toronto 1871, repr. Toronto: Coles 1970), 100. If Keefer is used instead, the following figures for GWR expenses and subsequent totals and percentages would need to be substituted in the table:

|  | Expense | Expense as % of revenue |
|---|---|---|
| GWR | 1,994 | 91 |
| Subtotal | 2,717 | 87 |
| Canada total | 5,524 | 85 |
| Canada West (incl. ½ of GTR) | 4,100 | 85 |

The discrepancy arises because Keefer includes, for the GWR only, expenses for interest payments and rail renewals, neither of which falls properly into the category of 'ordinary working expenses.' For confirmation of expense data used in the table, see Paul Craven and Tom Traves, 'Canadian Railways as Manufacturers, 1850–1880,' Canadian Historical Association, *Historical Papers*, 1983, Table 1.

TABLE 7:4
The Ontario Railway System in 1870

| | Miles of track | Revenue ($000) | Revenue per mile ($000) | Expense ($000) | Expense as % of revenue | Number of locomotives | Cars (passenger) | Cars (freight) |
|---|---|---|---|---|---|---|---|---|
| GWR | 381* | 4,152 | 10.9 | 2,527 | 59 | 133 | 129 | 1,737 |
| Northern | 95 | 734 | 7.7 | 426 | 58 | 24 | 18 | 660 |
| StL&O (ex O&P) | 54 | 129 | 2.4 | 88 | 69 | 7 | 17 | 85 |
| B&O | 90 | 203 | 2.3 | 104 | 51 | 7 | 5 | 138 |
| C&P** | 26 | 21 | 0.8 | 10 | 48 | 4 | 2 | 150 |
| Midland (ex PHL&B) | 79 | 242 | 3.1 | 129 | 53 | 11 | 5 | 382 |
| Welland | 25 | 74 | 3.0 | 76 | 103 | 5 | 3 | 147 |
| L&PS | 24 | 49 | 2.0 | 30 | 61 | 2 | 6 | 44 |
| Subtotal | 774 | 5,604 | 7.2 | 3,390 | 60 | 193 | 185 | 3,343 |
| GTR+ | 1,377 | 7,278 | 5.3 | 4,915 | 68 | 326 | 211 | 3,968 |
| Ontario and Quebec total | 2,151 | 12,882 | 6.0 | 8,305 | 64 | 519 | 396 | 7,311 |
| Ontario (incl. 1/2 of GTR) | 1,443 | 9,243 | 6.4 | 5,847 | 63 | 356 | 290 | 5,327 |

SOURCE: Trout and Trout, *Railways of Canada for 1870–1*, 101, 109, 113, 116, 119–20, 141–3, 145–6, 168, 172

* GWR mileage includes leased branch lines (Erie and Niagara; Galt and Guelph; but not Wellington, Grey and Bruce, the first sections of which were only completed in 1870).

** Cobourg and Peterborough data for 1869

+ GTR includes B&LH; actual GTR mileage in territory from Montreal to Sarnia was 669; for purposes of seeing the entire Ontario system, I have assumed that half of revenues, etc., for the GTR should be assigned to Canada West/Ontario.

Douglas McCalla

TABLE 7:5
Growth of Railway Revenues and Traffic Volumes,
1860–70 (1860 = 100)

|  | Index | Rate of change per annum (%) |
|---|---|---|
| *a. Revenues* | | |
| GWR passengers | 147 | 3.9 |
| freight | 238 | 9.1 |
| combined | 191 | 6.7 |
| GTR combined* | 199 | 7.1 |
| Northern passengers | 193 | 6.8 |
| freight | 226 | 8.5 |
| combined | 220 | 8.2 |
| O&P | 172 | 5.6 |
| B&O | 271 | 10.5** |
| PHL&B | 448 | 16.2** |
| Welland | 114 | 1.3 |
| L&PS | 169 | 5.4 |
| All railways (Ontario and Quebec) | 199 | 7.1 |
| | | |
| *b. Quantities* | | |
| Ontario and Quebec | | |
| miles of track | 114 | 1.3 |
| no. of locomotives | 138 | 3.3 |
| no. of freight cars | 152 | 4.3 |
| no. of passenger cars | 118 | 1.7 |
| GWR | | |
| no. of passengers | 148 | 3.8 |
| tons of freight | 248 | 9.5 |
| Northern | | |
| no. of passengers | 177 | 5.9 |
| tons of freight | 237 | 9.0 |

SOURCE: Tables 7:3, 7:4, and 7:7–7:9
* Base figure includes B&LH, leased by the GTR after 1860.
** These companies had relatively large extensions to their mileage in the decade.

TABLE 7:6

Railways in Canada West in American Context, 1859–60

|  | Ohio | Michigan | Indiana | 3 states | Canada West |
|---|---|---|---|---|---|
| Total railway mileage built | 2,978 | 1,051 | 2,088 | 6,117 | 1,411 |
| Population per mile of track | 786 | 713 | 647 | 726 | 989 |
| Revenue per mile of track | $4,341 | $3,839 | $1,436 | $3,263 | $3,600 |
| Revenue per capita | $5.52 | $5.39 | $2.22 | $4.50 | $3.42 |
| Gross railway investment per mile of track |  |  |  | $31,682 | $51,028 |
| Gross railway investment per capita |  |  |  | $43.66 | $51.58 |

SOURCE: Table 7:3; Albert Fishlow, *American Railroads and the Transformation of the Ante-Bellum Economy* (Cambridge, Mass.: Harvard University Press 1965), 172, 337, 397

NOTES:

1 Canada West data for 1860, U.S. data (except population, from 1860) for 1859. Data in the text (199) for the three states are for railways built from 1851 to 1860 only, while data here are for all railways built in the three states from the beginning. Fishlow does not give investment data by state.

2 In the comparison made here, the difference of a year will tend to favour Canada West, in that, for the three major railways in the province, 1860 revenues were higher than 1859 by more than 16 per cent (see tables 7:7, 7:8, and 7:9). Revenue per mile for the provincial system did not increase as greatly, however, because of additions to mileage during 1859, as the GTR opened its Sarnia extension in Canada West (70 miles) at the end of the year and two smaller roads (totalling 88 miles) also opened during the year.

TABLE 7:7

Great Western Railway Traffic and Revenue Data, 1854–70

| | 1854 | 1855 | 1856 | 1857 | 1858 | 1859 | 1860 | 1861 | 1862 | 1863 | 1864 | 1865 | 1866 | 1867 | 1868 | 1869 | 1870 |
|---|---|---|---|---|---|---|---|---|---|---|---|---|---|---|---|---|---|
| Passengers (000) | 481 | 664 | 861 | 792 | 569 | 495 | 526 | 527 | 573 | 637 | 688 | 714 | 756 | 716 | 745 | 748 | 781 |
| Passenger revenue ($000) | 987 | 1,452 | 1,742 | 1,562 | 1,238 | 1,072 | 1,009 | 899 | 976 | 1,098 | 1,272 | 1,548 | 1,525 | 1,525 | 1,517 | 1,547 | 1,485 |
| Freight (000 tons) | 83 | 176 | 221 | 193 | 177 | 213 | 374 | 442 | 547 | 528 | 476 | 455 | 489 | 582 | 626 | 775 | 926 |
| Freight revenue ($000) | 331 | 783 | 1,151 | 869 | 736 | 737 | 1,071 | 1,333 | 1,644 | 1,714 | 1,689 | 1,582 | 1,610 | 2,008 | 2,138 | 2,267 | 2,554 |
| Total revenue* ($000) | 1,383 | 2,326 | 2,999 | 2,544 | 2,067 | 1,897 | 2,177 | 2,313 | 2,704 | 2,894 | 3,055 | 3,269 | 3,283 | 3,730 | 3,796 | 3,938 | 4,153 |
| Track open (miles) | 241 | 245 | 283 | 290 | 290 | 330 | 345 | 345 | 345 | 345 | 345 | 345 | 345 | 350 | 350 | 350 | 350 |
| Revenue/mile ($000) | 5.74 | 9.49 | 10.60 | 8.77 | 7.13 | 5.74 | 6.31 | 6.70 | 7.84 | 8.39 | 8.86 | 9.48 | 9.52 | 10.66 | 10.85 | 11.25 | 11.87 |
| % revenue from passengers | 71 | 62 | 58 | 61 | 60 | 57 | 46 | 39 | 36 | 38 | 42 | 47 | 46 | 41 | 40 | 39 | 36 |
| Ordinary working expenses as % of total revenue | 49 | 54 | 55 | 57 | 59 | 63 | 51 | 51 | 44 | 43 | 42 | 40 | 45 | 47 | 52 | 57 | 59 |

SOURCE: Trout and Trout, *Railways of Canada for 1870–1*, 99–101. All financial data are converted from £stg at par.
* Total revenue includes express, mail, and sundries, in addition to freight and passengers.

## TABLE 7:8
### Grand Trunk Railway Traffic and Revenue Data, 1857–8 to 1869–70
(Data are for fiscal year ended 30 June.)

| | 1857–8 | 1858–9 | 1859–60 | 1860–1 | 1861–2 | 1862–3 | 1863–4 | 1864–5 | 1865–6 | 1866–7 | 1867–8 | 1868–9 | 1869–70 |
|---|---|---|---|---|---|---|---|---|---|---|---|---|---|
| *Passengers* | | | | | | | | | | | | | |
| Through (000) | | | | | 95 | 114 | na | 264 | 230 | 251 | 231 | 238 | 265 |
| Total (000) | | | | | 768 | 748 | na | 1,434 | 1,423 | 1,416 | 1,413 | 1,461 | 1,593 |
| Revenue, through ($000) | | | | | | | | | 758 | 779 | 718 | 763 | 790 |
| Revenue, total ($000) | | | | | | | | | 2,448 | 2,394 | 2,326 | 2,409 | 2,448 |
| *Freight* | | | | | | | | | | | | | |
| Through (000 tons) | | | | | 87 | 110 | na | 118 | 131 | 141 | 123 | 135 | 183 |
| Local (000 tons) | | | | | 602 | 534 | na | 758 | 815 | 829 | 844 | 863 | 940 |
| Total* (000 tons) | | | c.600 | na | 695 | 665 | na | 939 | 1,021 | 1,014 | 1,033 | 1,078 | 1,225 |
| Revenue, through ($000) | | | | | | | | | 626 | 658 | 586 | 572 | 815 |
| Revenue, total ($000) | | | | | | | | | 3,946 | 3,854 | 4,068 | 4,365 | 4,657 |

TABLE 7:8 (continued)

| | 1857-8 | 1858-9 | 1859-60 | 1860-1 | 1861-2 | 1862-3 | 1863-4 | 1864-5 | 1865-6 | 1866-7 | 1867-8 | 1868-9 | 1869-70 |
|---|---|---|---|---|---|---|---|---|---|---|---|---|---|
| *Total revenue* ($000) | 2,332 | 2,281 | 2,909 | 3,518 | 3,975 | 4,248 | na | | 6,579 | 6,462 | 6,574 | 6,963 | 7,280 |
| % revenue from passengers | | | | | | | | | 37 | 37 | 35 | 35 | 34 |
| % revenue from through freight & passengers | | | | | | | | | 21 | 22 | 20 | 19 | 22 |
| Ordinary working expenses % of total revenue | | 91 | na | 86 | 73 | 62 | 58 | 60 | 59 | 64 | 65 | 64 | 66 |

SOURCE: Trout and Trout, *Railways of Canada for 1870–1*, 83–5; T. Storrow Brown, *A History of the Grand Trunk Railway of Canada, Compiled from Public Documents* (Quebec 1864), NA, Pamphlet 3170, 42-3; and Walter Shanly, *Notes and Corrections to the Report of the Government … [on] the Grand Trunk Railway of Canada* (Toronto 1861), NA, Pamphlet 2925, 22. Financial data are converted from £stg at par.
* Total freight includes some other categories, principally livestock.

## TABLE 7:9
### Northern Railway Traffic and Revenue Data, 1854–70
(1854–6 for fiscal year ending 30 June)

| | 1853–4 | 1854–5 | 1855–6 | 1857 | 1858 | 1859 | 1860 | 1861 | 1862 | 1863 | 1864 | 1865 | 1866 | 1867 | 1868 | 1869 | 1870 |
|---|---|---|---|---|---|---|---|---|---|---|---|---|---|---|---|---|---|
| Passengers (000) | | | | | | | 92 | 101 | 102 | 108 | 104 | 105 | 137 | 129 | 139 | 145 | 163 |
| Passenger revenue ($000) | | | | | | | 89 | 94 | 97 | 102 | 102 | 107 | 124 | 137 | 147 | 151 | 172 |
| Freight (000 tons) | | | | | | | 125 | 146 | 174 | 156 | 189 | 119 | 175 | 201 | 195 | 271 | 296 |
| Timber* (000,000 bd ft) | | | | | | | | 424 | 243 | 280 | 70 | 70 | 69 | 77 | 74 | 116 | 137 |
| Freight revenue local ($000) | | | | | | | 186 | 260 | 209 | 275 | 333 | 341 | 340 | 377 | 364 | 479 | 505 |
| through ($000) | | | | | | | 50 | 48 | 93 | 18 | 15 | 26 | 24 | 22 | 13 | 9 | 28 |
| total ($000) | | | | | | | 236 | 308 | 302 | 293 | 348 | 367 | 364 | 399 | 377 | 488 | 533 |
| Total revenue ($000) | 118 | 213 | 290 | 313 | 262 | 240 | 333 | 411 | 406 | 407 | 467 | 507 | 513 | 561 | 550 | 671 | 734 |
| % revenue from passengers | | | | | | | 27 | 23 | 24 | 25 | 22 | 21 | 24 | 24 | 27 | 23 | 23 |
| Revenue/mile ($000) | | 2.2 | 3.1 | 3.3 | 2.8 | 2.5 | 3.5 | 4.3 | 4.3 | 4.3 | 4.9 | 5.3 | 5.4 | 5.9 | 5.8 | 7.1 | 7.7 |
| Ordinary working expenses as % of total revenue | 75 | 79 | 102 | 80 | 100 | 82 | 78 | 68 | 74 | 54 | 52 | 56 | 60 | 59 | 61 | 50 | 58 |

SOURCE: Trout and Trout, *Railways of Canada for 1870–1*, 111–13. See also Province of Canada, Legislative Assembly, *Sessional Papers*, 1864, no. 15 for one correction to data in Trout volume.

* Square timber converted to board feet by multiplying by 12

TABLE 7:10
Price Rises in the 1850s: Selected Locations, Indexes, Commodities
(1849–51 = 100)

|  | 1854–6 |
| --- | --- |
| *Canada West* | |
| Michell's index of 15 foods, Toronto | 174 |
| Produce at Toronto | |
|   a. Wheat | 199 |
|   b. Oats | 225 |
|   c. Potatoes | 181 |
|   d. Hay | 202 |
|   e. Butter | 153 |
|   f. Beef | 160 |
|   g. Pork | 170 |
| *Canada East* | |
| Wheat at Montreal | 197 |
| Oats at Quebec | 146 |
| *Great Britain* | |
| Wheat | 176 |
| Oats | 154 |
| Rousseaux index of agricultural prices | 129 |
| Rousseaux index of industrial prices | 137 |
| Sauerbeck index of commodity prices | 135 |
| *United States* | |
| Warren-Pearson index, farm products | 135 |
| Warren-Pearson index, all commodities | 130 |
| Bezanson index, Philadelphia, farm crops | 129 |
| Bezanson index, Philadelphia, all items | 124 |
| Berry index, Cincinnati, northern agric. | 145 |
| Berry index, Cincinnati, all items | 140 |

SOURCES: M.C. Urquhart and K.A.H. Buckley, eds, *Historical Statistics of Canada* (Cambridge: Cambridge University Press 1965), 305 (1855–7 are the highest years for the century on this index, which begins in 1848); Douglas McCalla, 'Produce Prices in Upper Canada,' unpublished working paper (Apr. 1987); F. Ouellet, J. Hamelin, and R. Chabot, 'Les prix agricoles dans les villes et les campagnes du Québec d'avant 1850: aperçus quantitatifs,' *Histoire sociale / Social History* 15 (1982), 83–127; B. Mitchell and P. Deane, *Abstract of British Historical Statistics* (Cambridge: Cambridge University Press 1962), 471–4, 488; *Historical Statistics of the United States: Colonial Times to 1970* (Washington: Bureau of the Census 1975), 2: 201–6

TABLE 7:11
Selected Data on Canadian Trade, 1850–66
(a and b $000,000)

| | 1850 | 1851 | 1852 | 1853 | 1854 | 1855 | 1856 | 1857 | 1858 | 1859 | 1860 | 1861 | 1862 | 1863 | 1864–5 | 1865–6 |
|---|---|---|---|---|---|---|---|---|---|---|---|---|---|---|---|---|
| *a. Imports of iron and products* | | | | | | | | | | | | | | | | |
| Manufacturers of iron | | | | | | | | | | | | | | | | |
| and hardware | 1.3 | 1.9 | 1.9 | 2.6 | 3.4 | 2.5 | 2.6 | 2.0 | 1.3 | 1.3 | 1.4 | 1.5 | 1.4 | 1.4 | 1.2 | 1.4 |
| Machinery | 0.1 | 0.2 | 0.2 | 0.4 | 0.9 | 0.6 | 0.5 | 0.3 | 0.1 | 0.1 | 0.2 | 0.2 | 0.2 | 0.2 | 0.2 | 0.3 |
| Iron bars, rods, | | | | | | | | | | | | | | | | |
| sheets | – | 0.5 | 0.3 | 1.2 | 2.0 | 0.6 | 1.0 | 0.9 | 0.8 | 0.9 | 0.8 | 0.8 | 0.8 | 0.9 | 0.8 | 0.9 |
| Pig-iron | – | 0.2 | 0.1 | 0.2 | 0.5 | 0.2 | 0.4 | 0.4 | 0.1 | 0.2 | 0.3 | 0.3 | 0.2 | 0.4 | 0.4 | 0.5 |
| Railroad bars | – | 0.2 | 0.8 | 1.4 | 1.6 | 0.7 | 0.4 | 0.8 | 1.1 | 0.2 | 0.3 | 0.1 | 0.1 | – | 0.3 | 0.1 |
| Wheels, axles, for | | | | | | | | | | | | | | | | |
| railways | – | – | – | – | – | 0.2 | 0.1 | 0.1 | 0.1 | 0.1 | 0.1 | – | – | 0.1 | 0.1 | – |
| Other iron products | – | 0.1 | – | 0.3 | 0.5 | 0.2 | 0.4 | 0.4 | 0.3 | 0.3 | 0.3 | 0.3 | 0.3 | 0.3 | 0.3 | 0.3 |
| Steel | 0.1 | 0.1 | 0.1 | 0.2 | 0.1 | 0.1 | 0.1 | 0.1 | 0.1 | 0.1 | 0.1 | 0.1 | 0.1 | 0.2 | 0.1 | 0.2 |
| Locomotives and | | | | | | | | | | | | | | | | |
| rail cars | – | – | – | – | – | – | – | – | 0.1 | – | 0.1 | – | – | 0.1 | – | – |
| Total | 1.5 | 3.2 | 3.4 | 6.3 | 9.0 | 5.1 | 5.5 | 5.0 | 4.0 | 3.2 | 3.6 | 3.3 | 3.1 | 3.6 | 3.4 | 3.7 |

TABLE 7:11 (continued)

|  | 1850 | 1851 | 1852 | 1853 | 1854 | 1855 | 1856 | 1857 | 1858 | 1859 | 1860 | 1861 | 1862 | 1863 | 1864-5 | 1865-6 |
|---|---|---|---|---|---|---|---|---|---|---|---|---|---|---|---|---|
| *b. Selected imports and total exports* | | | | | | | | | | | | | | | | |
| Cottons | 3.6 | 3.9 | 3.1 | 5.3 | 5.1 | 3.4 | 5.0 | 4.8 | 3.3 | 4.9 | 5.8 | 5.7 | 4.5 | 4.3 | 4.1 | 7.1 |
| Woollens | 2.2 | 2.9 | 3.1 | 5.0 | 5.4 | 3.4 | 4.3 | 3.9 | 2.7 | 3.6 | 4.0 | 4.4 | 4.0 | 4.3 | 6.0 | 7.2 |
| Silks and satins | 0.6 | 0.8 | 0.8 | 1.4 | 1.5 | 0.9 | 1.2 | 1.0 | 0.7 | 0.9 | 0.9 | 0.9 | 0.7 | 0.7 | 0.7 | 1.2 |
| Total iron (from *a* above) | 1.5 | 3.2 | 3.4 | 6.3 | 9.0 | 5.1 | 5.5 | 5.0 | 4.0 | 3.2 | 3.6 | 3.3 | 3.1 | 3.6 | 3.4 | 3.7 |
| Tea | 0.9 | 1.1 | 1.3 | 1.6 | 1.5 | 1.7 | 2.1 | 1.4 | 1.9 | 2.3 | 1.3 | 1.9 | 2.7 | 1.8 | 1.7 | 2.3 |
| Sugar | 0.6 | 0.7 | 0.8 | 1.1 | 1.2 | 1.6 | 2.1 | 1.9 | 1.7 | 1.8 | 1.6 | 1.6 | 1.9 | 1.5 | 1.8 | 1.8 |
| Total dutiable imports | 15.8 | 19.6 | 19.0 | 30.2 | 37.7 | 25.7 | 31.6 | 27.0 | 20.7 | 23.4 | 23.9 | 25.1 | 24.0 | 22.9 | 25.3 | 33.3 |
| Total all imports | 17.0 | 21.4 | 20.3 | 32.0 | 40.5 | 36.1 | 43.6 | 39.4 | 29.1 | 33.6 | 34.4 | 39.8 | 46.0 | 41.3 | 39.9 | 48.6 |
| Total all exports | 12.0 | 13.0 | 14.0 | 22.0 | 21.2 | 24.9 | 29.8 | 25.4 | 22.0 | 23.1 | 32.4 | 34.7 | 31.7 | 37.6 | 37.9 | 47.9 |
| *c. Volume data for tea and sugar* | | | | | | | | | | | | | | | | |
| Sugar (000 cwt) | 128 | 145 | 178 | 235 | 271 | 324 | 302 | 224 | 249 | 280 | 283 | 361 | 388 | 770 | 317 | 334 |
| Tea (000,000 lbs) | 3.5 | 3.7 | 4.5 | 5.3 | 4.9 | 5.6 | 6.7 | 3.8 | 6.0 | 6.8 | 3.7 | 4.7 | 6.6 | 5.0 | 4.9 | 6.8 |

SOURCE: *Journals of the Legislative Assembly of the United Province of Canada*, Tables of Trade and Navigation, relevant years

NOTES:

1 Pig-iron: includes scrap and old iron 1851-2 and pig lead and pig copper after 1858
2 Note that the Reciprocity Treaty came into effect in 1855 and increased the proportion of goods entering duty free.
3 Coin and bullion excluded from import and export data once reported, from 1861
4 'Railroad wheels and axles' also includes 'other articles for railway purposes' from 1861 on.
5 Reporting year changed from 1 July to 30 June beginning in 1864. Thus data here omit first six months of 1864.
6 Because of rounding to nearest 100,000, columns added here may not add to exact totals that can be derived from adding data in source, which are given to last digit.
7 Signifies less than $50,000 or, more commonly, no data

# NOTES

The financial support of the Ontario Historical Studies Series and the research time provided by a Trent University Research Fellowship are gratefully acknowledged. This paper benefited from the opportunity to present a briefer version of its arguments to a seminar at the School of Business, Queen's University. I wish also to thank Peter Wylie for helpful comments.

1 H.G.J. Aitken, 'Defensive Expansionism: The State and Economic Growth in Canada,' in H.G.J. Aitken, ed., *The State and Economic Growth* (New York: Social Science Research Council 1959), 79–114, remains the classic statement. For a revisionist account of how leading politicians saw the future 'national' railway around the time of Confederation, see A.A. Den Otter, 'Nationalism and the Pacific Scandal,' *Canadian Historical Review* 69 (1988), 315–39.
2 Alan Green, 'Growth and Productivity Change in the Canadian Railway Sector, 1871–1926,' in Conference on Research in Income and Wealth, *Long-Term Factors in American Economic Growth*, Studies in Income and Wealth, vol. 51 (Chicago: University of Chicago Press 1986), 798
3 See L.H. Jenks, *The Migration of British Capital to 1875* (New York 1927; repr. London: Thomas Nelson 1963), 75–108; Dorothy Adler, *British Investment in American Railways, 1834–1898* (Charlottesville, Va: University Press of Virginia 1970), 9–15.
4 Others chartered included the Hamilton and Port Dover, the Cobourg, and the Niagara and Detroit Rivers.
5 A convenient source for this material is Peter Baskerville, *The Bank of Upper Canada: A Collection of Documents* (Toronto: Champlain Society 1987), lxxvii.
6 For the list of projects, see Upper Canada, Legislative Assembly, *Journals of the Legislative Assembly of Upper Canada*, 1839, App., First Report of the Finance Committee, 29–35. See also ibid., 128–30, Schedule of Government Debentures.
7 The relevant statutes here were 7 Wm IV cap. 60, 61, 62, 63, 64.
8 The most recent account of the Great Western Railway is D.R. Beer, *Sir Allan Napier MacNab* (Hamilton: Dictionary of Hamilton Biography 1984), 210–25.
9 See, e.g., Peter Baskerville, 'Entrepreneurship and the Family Compact: York-Toronto, 1822–1855,' *Urban History Review* 9:3 (Feb. 1981), 21–3; Gerald Tulchinsky, *The River Barons* (Toronto: University of Toronto Press 1977), 127–47.
10 See Peter Baskerville, 'Transportation, Social Change, and State Formation, Upper Canada, 1841–1864,' 234–5, in this volume.

11 Hence the justification for treating such liabilities as 'indirect debts' in the provincial accounts. See Michael Piva, 'Government Finance and the Development of the Canadian State,' in this volume.

12 See Douglas McCalla, 'Peter Buchanan, London Agent for the Great Western Railway of Canada,' in D.S. Macmillan, ed., *Canadian Business History: Selected Studies, 1497–1971* (Toronto: McClelland and Stewart 1972), 197–216; Peter Baskerville, 'Americans in Britain's Backyard: The Railway Era in Upper Canada, 1850–1880,' *Business History Review* 55 (1981), 315–24; A.M. Johnson and B. Supple, *Boston Capitalists and Western Railroads* (Cambridge, Mass.: Harvard University Press 1967).

13 T.C. Keefer, *Philosophy of Railroads and Other Essays*, ed. H.V. Nelles (Toronto: University of Toronto Press 1972), 145

14 See, e.g., J.K. Johnson, ' "One Bold Operator": Samuel Zimmerman, Niagara Entrepreneur, 1843–1857,' *Ontario History* 74 (1982), 26–44. Although railways were the biggest and most dramatic examples, there were other cases. For the saga of the York Roads see Michael S. Cross, 'The Stormy History of the York Roads, 1833–1865,' *Ontario History* 54 (1962), 1–24. I have discussed a representative figure in the new politics in 'James Beaty,' *Dictionary of Canadian Biography*, vol. 12 (Toronto: University of Toronto Press 1990), 71–4.

15 Harry N. Scheiber, *Ohio Canal Era: A Case Study of Government and the Economy, 1820–61* (Athens, Ohio: Ohio University Press 1969), 286

16 Carter Goodrich, *Government Promotion of American Canals and Railroads 1800–1890* (New York: Columbia University Press 1960), 138–41

17 Kenneth Buckley calculated net capital formation in railway transport and telegraphs in Canada between 1850 and 1860 at $90 million; see M.C. Urquhart and K.A.H. Buckley, eds, *Historical Statistics of Canada*, 1st ed. (Cambridge: Cambridge University Press 1965), 512. From 1851 and 1859, imports exceeded exports by just over $100 million according to data in Table 7:11(b).

Overvaluation arose, for example, when a charter or line was taken over at a value beyond what its earning power justified; when securities were issued below par value (i.e., at an effective rate of interest higher than the nominal rate); and when values were deliberately overstated, as may have occurred in the Northern Railway case, as part of getting more government backing under the Guarantee Act's provisions. See Keefer, *Philosophy of Railroads*, 147–8, 158; and G.R. Stevens, *Canadian National Railways* 2 vols (Toronto: Clarke, Irwin 1960), 1:245.

For the Grand Trunk, fully 20 per cent of total capitalization was said to represent interest during the construction period and discounts on the sale of securities. See A.W. Currie, *The Grand Trunk Railway of Canada* (Toronto: University of Toronto Press 1957), 51. The average for American railways in the 1850s on this account was 14 to 15 per cent of total construction costs; see Albert Fishlow, *American Railroads and the Transformation of the Ante-Bellum Economy* (Cambridge, Mass.: Harvard University Press 1965), 351.

The practice of issuing par-value shares continued to produce nominal overcapitalization. For example, the Great Western in 1859 issued 5 per cent preferred shares for which it received 80 per cent; thus the capital raised was 20 per cent less than stated, and the actual interest rate was 6.25 per cent. See J.M. and E. Trout, *The Railways of Canada for 1870–1* (Toronto 1871, repr. Toronto: Coles 1970), 93.

18 Keefer, *Philosophy of Railroads*, 154–6

19 Scheiber, *Ohio Canal Era*, 284–5

20 It should be noted that many of the Upper-Canadian railways did not even gross 6 per cent on their capital, in 1860 at least (see Table 7:3).

21 See John McCallum, *Unequal Beginnings: Agriculture and Economic Development in Quebec and Ontario until 1870* (Toronto: University of Toronto Press 1980), 127, and Marvin McInnis, 'Marketable Surpluses in Ontario Farming, 1860,' *Social Science History* 8 (1984), repr. in D. McCalla, ed., *Perspectives on Canadian Economic History* (Toronto: Copp Clark Pitman 1987), 45, 48. David Gagan confirms the reasonableness of the assumed household size in *Hopeful Travellers: Families, Land, and Social Change in Mid-Victorian Peel County, Canada West* (Toronto: University of Toronto Press 1981), 64.

22 O.J. Firestone in 'Development of Canada's Economy, 1850–1900,' in Conference on Research in Income and Wealth, *Trends in the American Economy in the Nineteenth Century*, Studies in Income and Wealth, vol. 24 (Princeton: Princeton University Press 1960), 222. Firestone's figure for 1870 was $459 million; the recent work of Alan Green and M.C. Urquhart gives a figure of $383 million for 1870. See their 'New Estimates of Output Growth in Canada: Measurement and Interpretation,' in McCalla, ed., *Perspectives on Canadian Economic History*, 183; they give figures for investment in relation to GNP at 187–8. The highest British figure for railway investment in this era was 6.7 per cent of GNP, in 1847; see François Crouzet, *The Victorian Economy* (London 1982), 299.

23 On American railways in the 1850s, the superstructure represented about 28 per cent of total costs of construction, while iron costs represented 70 per cent of superstructure costs. In addition, equipment represented a further 9 per cent of total costs, and in Canada an unknown but important part of this was imported. On the basis of a total capitalization of *c.* $100 million, these figures suggest that between $24 and $27 million would have been iron's share in the total. If discounts and related costs of capital are excluded, superstructure represented 31 per cent of construction costs and equipment 10 per cent. In Canada, if capitalization minus financing and other costs was *c.* $80 million, the total railway iron figure was likely in the range $20 to $24 million. See Fishlow, *American Railroads*, 350–1, 371.

24 A.B. McCullough, *Money and Exchange in Canada to 1900* (Toronto: Dundurn 1984), 270–1

25 H.C. Pentland, *Labour and Capital in Canada 1650–1860*, ed. P. Phillips (Toronto: Lorimer 1981), 133; the 1851 census showed 280,000 men fifteen years of age and older in Upper Canada, including 184,000 in the twenty to fifty age range.

26 E.g., Stevens, *Canadian National Railways*, 1:260–4; Currie, *Grand Trunk Railway*, 28–9

27 Albert Fishlow, *American Railroads*, 409–13; actually, his British figure is 58, which I have rounded to 60.

28 Stevens, *Canadian National Railways*, 1:260, 265. On Grand Trunk construction standards, see Currie, *Grand Trunk Railway*, 26–8, 53–6; and Keefer, *Philosophy of Railroads*, 149. The Grand Trunk's Victoria Bridge was, however, built to the higher, British standards. See, e.g., Bruce Sinclair, 'Canadian Technology: British Traditions and American Influences,' *Technology and Culture* 20 (1979), 111. It is possible that the severity of the Canadian winter extended construction time beyond two years, but whether it did so as an average for the whole system is not known.

29 Thus, 250,000 immigrants arrived at Quebec between 1850 and 1856; see Helen Cowan, *British Emigration to British North America: The First Hundred Years*, rev. ed. (Toronto: University of Toronto Press 1961), 289. It would be reasonable to assume that at least one-quarter of these immigrants were males of working age. By comparison, the peak demand for canal labourers in the 1840s was never more than 10,000, the maximum occurring some time in the period 1843–5; see Ruth Bleasdale, 'Class Conflict on the Canals of Upper Canada in the 1840s,' *Labour / Le travailleur* 7 (Spring 1981), 11–12.

30 Paul Craven and Tom Traves, 'Dimensions of Paternalism: Discipline and Culture in Canadian Railway Operations in the 1850s,' in Craig Heron and Robert Storey, eds, *On the Job: Confronting the Labour Process in Canada* (Montreal and Kingston: McGill-Queen's University Press 1986), 47–74

31 The implication is that 'cost overruns' (see Peter Baskerville, 'Transportation, Social Change, and State Formation,' 237 and passim) were caused less by inexperienced management and scheming contractors than by macro-economic factors beyond any individual company's control.

32 For the sharp rise and subsequent fall in land prices, see, e.g., David Gagan, *Hopeful Travellers*, 46; see also Edward C. Gray and Barry E. Prentice, 'Exploring the Price of Farmland in Two Ontario Localities since Letters Patenting,' *Canadian Papers in Rural History* 4 (1984), 232–5. On the 1857 crisis and its aftermath, see Douglas McCalla, *The Upper Canada Trade: A Study of the Buchanans' Business, 1834–1872* (To-

ronto: University of Toronto Press 1979), 95–116; and Peter Basker-ville, *The Bank of Upper Canada*, esp. chs D and E.

33 Baskerville, 'Transportation, Social Change, and State Formation,' 238–9

34 See Albert Fishlow, 'Productivity and Technological Change in the Railroad Sector, 1840–1910,' in Conference on Research in Income and Wealth, *Output, Employment and Productivity in the United States after 1800*, Studies in Income and Wealth, vol. 30 (New York: National Bureau of Economic Research 1966), 583–646.

35 Pushed by competition and attracted by new provincial and municipal funding policies, existing and new companies were actively extending tracks in many parts of Ontario. At least 800 miles were underway or about to be in 1870. See Trout, *Railways of Canada*, passim.

36 *Report of Mr. Thomas E. Blackwell ... [on] the Grand Trunk Railway ... 1859* (London 1860), National Archives of Canada (NA), Pamphlet 2872, 8, and App. 6. When this report was prepared, the line was not yet open to Sarnia, but already the lines west of Toronto had, on local traffic only, surpassed the Eastern as a generator of revenue. The situation had not changed a decade later; see Trout, *Railways of Canada*, 79.

37 By comparison, the leading Maritime line, the Nova Scotia Railroad, took in $1,900 per mile in 1870; the European and North American and the New Brunswick and Canada had revenues of around $1,600 per mile. In Upper Canada, they would have ranked behind all but the almost moribund Cobourg and Peterborough. The figure for the New Brunswick and Canada would be only $1,200 if its branches were included. See Trout, *Railways of Canada*, 105, 121–2, 133.

38 Trout, *Railways of Canada*, 110. On the Northern's strategy in this period, see F.H. Armstrong and Peter Baskerville, 'Frederick William Cumberland,' *Dictionary of Canadian Biography* vol. 11 (Toronto: University of Toronto Press 1982), 226–7.

39 *Report of Mr. Thomas E. Blackwell ... 1859* (App. 8–9) gives a through rate of *c.* one cent per ton-mile from west of Toronto to Boston in 1859. Cf Albert Fishlow, *American Railroads*, 65, 339, for contemporary American rate levels. On the rate question in general and the particular competitiveness of the trade with the east coast, see Ken Cruikshank, 'The Transportation Revolution and its Consequences: The Railway Freight Rate Controversy of the Late Nineteenth Century,' Canadian Historical Association, *Historical Papers*, 1987, 121.

40 Great Western Railway Company of Canada, *Report ... for the Half Year ending July 31, 1855* (Hamilton 1855), NA, Pamphlet 2512, 10. For passengers, 61 per cent of revenue was from through travellers, and for freight, 46 per cent of revenue came from through traffic. Contemporary American trunk lines earned 40 to 70 per cent of revenue from through traffic. See Albert Fishlow, *American Railroads*, 64.

41 See Ken Cruikshank, 'The Transportation Revolution and Its Consequences,' passim.

42 The evidence at hand is sketchy but suggestive. In the six months
from 1 Feb. to 31 July 1855, the GWR carried from stations within the
province (i.e., not including Windsor and the Suspension Bridge) as
much flour as the Welland Canal did from British ports in the upper
lakes in all of 1855, and almost 40 per cent as much wheat. Valuable
imports such as cottons, etc., were not separately itemized in freight
reports of either the canal or the railway, but it is safe to assume that
they quickly came to move by rail.

43 The Upper-Canadian lake and river fleet in 1849 consisted of at least
44 steamships and 210 sailing vessels, with a combined tonnage of over
23,000; see *Journals of the Legislative Assembly of the United Province of
Canada*, 1850, App. A, Tables of Trade and Navigation, Statement 17.
By 1874, there were 815 vessels on the Ontario register, totalling
113,000 tons; see Ian Drummond, *Progress without Planning: The Economic History of Ontario from Confederation to the Second World War* (Toronto: University of Toronto Press 1987), 432.

44 See *Report of Mr. Thomas E. Blackwell ... 1859*, App. 10.

45 The Ontario and Quebec figure may also be compared to the value of
two of the principal categories of provincial exports in 1870: John
McCallum, in *Unequal Beginnings*, 128, gives the value of all forest
products and ships at $17.6 million in that year and the value of wheat
and flour exports at $6 million.

46 Fishlow, *American Railroads*, 103.

47 Apart from one or two artificial modern municipalities covering a
number of smaller urban and suburban developments (e.g., East Gwil-
limbury, Nanticoke, Halton Hills) and some suburbs of major centres
such as Markham or Kanata, the exceptions appear to be Dunnville,
Leamington, Milton, Orangeville, Simcoe, Tillsonburg, Stouffville, and
Wallaceburg. Of more northerly centres in this region, Midland, Owen
Sound, and Orillia were beyond the end of tracks in 1860. Virtually all
of the fifty largest urban centres in the region in 1981 were on rail
lines by 1860.

48 Allan Pred, *Urban Growth and City-Systems in the United States, 1840–1860*
(Cambridge, Mass.: Harvard University Press 1980), 166–7, terms such
processes of development 'circular and cumulative growth feedbacks.'

49 E.g., see Trout, *Railways of Canada*, 94, on an 1867 agreement between
the Grand Trunk and Great Western. See also Baskerville, 'Transportation, Social Change and State Formation,' 247–9.

50 Paul Craven and Tom Traves, 'Canadian Railways as Manufacturers,
1850–1880,' Canadian Historical Association, *Historical Papers*, 1983,
254–81

51 Drummond, *Progress without Planning*, 250. See also W. Marr and Don-

ald Paterson, *Canada: An Economic History* (Toronto: Gage 1980), 320, which speaks of 'the sorry plight of Canada's first railways.'

52 Fishlow, *American Railroads*, 337; and *Historical Statistics of the United States: Colonial Times to 1970* (Washington: Bureau of the Census 1975), 2:731

53 I owe this point to Marvin McInnis.

54 Trout, *Railways of Canada*, 92–5, 100–101

55 See Peter Baskerville, 'Transportation, Social Change, and State Formation,' 247.

56 Ibid., 235

57 Gagan, *Hopeful Travellers*, 157, 160

58 Baskerville, 'Transportation, Social Change, and State Formation,' 234

59 Craven and Traves, 'Canadian Railways as Manufacturers,' 280–1

60 Piva, 'Government Finance and the Development of the Canadian State'

61 For this concept, see H.G.J. Aitken, 'Government and Business in Canada: An Interpretation,' *Business History Review* 38 (1964), 5.

# 8

# Transportation, Social Change, and State Formation, Upper Canada, 1841 1864

PETER BASKERVILLE

Nineteenth-century British and American states were, in a variety of ways, instrumental in promoting, financing, and regulating canal and railway development.[1] Explanations for such state intervention in economic affairs vary from emphasizing the influence of Benthamite ideas, to asserting the simple inevitability of a government response to problems that could not be ignored,[2] to engaging in a more systematic appreciation of the social-structural conditions and class interests that facilitate an increase in state activity.

Michael Katz has perhaps generalized most widely from a social-structural perspective concerning the timing and role of an activist state in nineteenth-century North America. In a fifty- to seventy-five-year period in the nineteenth century, Katz discerned a shift away from corporate voluntarism towards state institutionalism. He pointed to the increasingly autonomous role played by the state in social affairs: the creation and management of school systems, prisons, hospitals, and mental asylums, and the growth of 'specialized, expert administration' in place of 'talented generalists' characterized this process. For Katz the impulse underlying this transformation is linked to the changing nature of (North American) capitalism: state formation accompanied and influenced the shift from an era of commercial capitalism to one of industrial capitalism.[3]

A similar wide-ranging depiction of the transformation of the British state has been presented by Philip Corrigan and Derek Sayer. They link the rise of the regulatory state to the emergence of 'bourgeois civilization' and the values that inform that social construct. For

them, as for Katz, these values emerged most clearly as industrialization progressed. For them, as for Katz, bourgeois state policies led
to 'real, painful, harmful restrictions on human capacities.' Finally,
and also as for Katz, their analysis is informed by the concept of ' "long
waves" of revolution in government' waves that presumably swept
everything before them.[4]

While Corrigan and Sayer are careful to note that their work applies only to England and not to its colonies, Katz is less concerned
to differentiate colonial British North America from the United States.
Not to distinguish between the two, however, assumes similar social-
structural conditions, an assumption of dubious validity. At the most
obvious levels the United States enjoyed political autonomy not present in colonial British North America and exhibited a more advanced
industrial economy than did the northern colonies. Yet, despite these
differences, it is nonetheless true, as the sophisticated work of Bruce
Curtis and Brian Young attests, that a bureaucratic and positive state
did exert a profound influence on the lives of many Upper and Lower
Canadians well before 1867.[5] This reality will not be questioned here;
rather, discussion of the role of the Upper-Canadian state in transportation policy will be used to make two points concerning the
emergence of an interventionist state in colonial North America. The
first is simply that the notion of a continuous wave washing all before
it is inappropriate to describe the development of the Upper-Canadian
state. The activist state emerged in a more discontinuous and episodic
manner in Upper Canada than may have been the case in the United
States and England. The explanation for this pattern of discontinuous
development lies in an appreciation of the relatively undeveloped
structure of local social formations in the colony coupled with the
changing nature of colonial-imperial relations.

A second and related point concerns the role of experts in state
formation. Government-employed inspectors are often pointed to as
confirmation of the state's power to regulate routine and standardize
behaviour. The existence and activity of such experts is often used
as an index with which to measure degrees of state activity.[6] The role
of inspectors in the Upper-Canadian context seems most obvious and
sustained in the educational sphere. The temptation is to generalize
from that sphere to the state as a whole. In fact, as the ensuing discussion of transport policy will make clear, inspectors in other spheres
emerged and enjoyed relative power only in periods of crisis.[7] Once
these crises were controlled, colonial politicians, already seeking autonomy vis-à-vis the British Colonial Office, tended to be reluctant to

delegate power to bureaucratic 'experts.' Rather, at least in the case
of railway policy, colonial and, after 1867, Canadian politicians retained direct lines to, although not continuous control of, the private
sector until the early twentieth century. Not only, then, is the transformation of the state in a colonial frame characterized by a process
of episodic development, but also that transformation varied in pace
and perhaps pattern within particular policy sectors. An overall appreciation of state transformation must account for the differentiated
and episodic nature of such change over time. Such an explanation
must be sensitive to the possibility that different forms of regulatory
states emerged at different times and places and for different sets of
reasons.[8]

The circumstances surrounding the formation and operation of 'the
first centralized institution for the construction of public works in
British North America' underline the colonial, dependent context of
the Upper-Canadian state, point to the crisis-driven nature of state
formation in Upper Canada, testify to the tensions and jealousies
between experts and politicians in a colonial frame, and provide support for the notion of discontinuous state formation.[9]

The creation of the Board of Works in 1841 can be seen as a
response to two intersecting pressures.[10] The first, primarily but not
completely local in origin, concerned the crisis occasioned by the
impact of the Erie Canal system on colonial trade. Upper- and Lower-
Canadian merchants had long pushed for the completion of a St Lawrence canal system with which to tap the resources of the North
American interior. By the late 1830s this dream of the Empire of the
St Lawrence was far from being realized. In this context the offer of
a guarantee for a £1.5-million loan by the British government, in
return for Upper-Canadian support for union, seemed a godsend.
Sydenham, the imperially appointed governor general, who wanted
to be known as Lord St Lawrence, was sympathetic to the idea of
using the loan for new construction instead of simply for paying off
accumulated debts.

The system through which previous loans for canal construction
had been expended was extremely decentralized and, as revealed by
a commission of inquiry in the late 1830s, seemed to facilitate the
improper spending of public monies. In order to safeguard the expenditure of the loan, Sydenham pushed the Board of Works bill into
law in 1841. The bill gave to an *expert*, an engineer, Hamilton Killaly,

significant power independent from that of local politicians. The act provided no easy way for the legislature to control Killaly's and the board's activities. Decisions concerning spending, construction, and labour tended to be made by Killaly, initially in consultation with Sydenham, but later, after the latter's death, in virtual isolation.

Sydenham, as Doug Owram and Ian Radforth have shown, was a strong advocate of centralized administrative reform. In fact, he brought with him to the colony a comprehensive program of administrative restructuring that was in tune with current developments in Great Britain. Without his persuasive and powerful influence it is doubtful that a Board of Works along the autonomous and centralized lines created by the 1841 legislation would have appeared. In other words, this important piece of administrative reform emerged in the Canadas due to imperial linkages and pressures rather than simply in response to more purely local concerns. In fact, local politicians soon came to resent, distrust – and dismantle – Sydenham's administrative machinery. Huge cost overruns provided the pretext for the striking of a royal commission, which brought Killaly to heel and led to the board's reorganization in 1846 in a manner that maximized the elected Executive Council's power and minimized that of the board itself.

This first experience by Upper-Canadian politicians with centralized bureaucratic management of important economic activities led to a particular conception of the appropriate structure and form through which activist state intervention could best proceed. From that time onwards, colonial politicians exhibited a marked reluctance to delegate significant power to full-time experts or even to accept advice from the experts they did hire.[11] If in England at this time bureaucratic departments staffed by experts proliferated in the economic sphere, in the Canadas the emerging Executive Council was clearly determined to keep control of the implementation of economic and especially railroad policy firmly in its own hands.[12]

To do so Upper Canada's politicians adopted a twofold strategy. Rather than opt for permanent bureaucratic assistance, the Executive Council relied on short-term, ad hoc, and project-specific appointments in the railway area. While the reorganized Board of Works did maintain some engineers on a full-time basis, its staff at permanent headquarters increased little in the pre-Confederation era.[13] Even more important, the Board of Works did not play an active role in supervising railway development. A body separate from the board was set up with a very small staff to oversee this central area of transport development. At the same time, the government also relied on the judicial process for the enforcement of regulatory legislation, especially in the increasingly contentious area of labour management.[14]

It took a combination of financial and social crises in the mid-1850s before experts re-emerged to potential – and, as it transpired, transitory – positions of influence in this sector of government affairs. As the ensuing detailed examination of government involvement in Upper-Canadian railway affairs demonstrates, the emergence of this particular state form did not prevent the state from effectively acting in different ways towards different social groups. Nor, in the context of literature on state intervention, is this a trivial point. Since the writings of Max Weber, it is often assumed that '[e]ffective state interaction is predicated on the existence of a well-developed bureaucratic apparatus.'[15] The Upper-Canadian state, however, effectively intervened in a central area of economic endeavour at a time of minimal bureaucratic development. That such activity preceded or at best paralleled bureaucratic maturation can be explained by the particular conjuncture of local social-structural characteristics and the nature of colonial-imperial state interaction.

Initially the state played an indirect role in the development of Upper-Canadian railways.[16] Their financing and management were in private entrepreneurial hands, but as a result of both an economic and financial downturn in the late 1840s and weaknesses within that entrepreneurial community, only sixty miles of railway had been constructed by 1849. The state began to take more decisive steps to aid the emerging railway sector. These steps were firmly grounded in past government policies in the economic sphere. The chief political initiators were themselves closely tied to the promotion of one or another Canadian railway. Lawyer-politicians like Allan Napier MacNab from Upper Canada and George-Etienne Cartier from Lower Canada, along with general businessmen-politicians like Francis Hincks and Alexander Galt, pushed for a bill to provide some government backing for railway construction. Hincks, the government's inspector general (or finance minister), argued for a government guarantee of both principal and interest for all major railways, or, as he revealingly referred to them, 'public works.'[17] His cabinet colleagues and the government's London financiers, G.C. Glyn and Baring Brothers, balked at this, pointing to the depressed economy of the late 1840s and the already large public debt, incurred from the financing of canal construction, which weighed heavily on the colonial state. The Guarantee Act of 1849 represented a compromise in that the government guaranteed the interest up to only 6 per cent on all loans for half-completed roads in excess of seventy-five miles in length. Hincks, however, persevered. By 1852 he had legislation in place that allowed municipal governments to provide debenture aid for local railways (aid that seemed to have the backing of the provincial government) and, as part of the Main Trunk Line of Railway Act in 1851, he extended the provincial guarantee to cover the payment of principal as well as interest for the construction of the four largest railways in the Canadas.

The Main Trunk Line act also established a Board of Railway Commissioners to oversee routes, general construction contracts, and the payment of monies under the Guarantee Act. While both the commissioner and assistant commissioner of public works, along with the inspector general, receiver general, and postmaster general, sat on the board, the Public Works Department itself had no role to play in the railway sector. Nor did the board have the right to hire permanent staff for inspection and other duties.[18] Clearly, the government believed that such a board would have only a minimal role to play and that permanent expert help – i.e., the creation of a bureaucracy – was unnecessary. Continuing disputes with the Public Works bureaucracy may also have contributed to the decision to oversee railway development with little staff support. Conflict with experts could thus be precluded.

The state even delegated a significant part of the responsibility and routine for making payments to the Bank of Upper Canada, the oldest Upper-Canadian chartered bank and, since 1850, the government's official bank. The bank provided railways with cash in anticipation of the issuance and sale of railway bonds and, by purchasing municipal bonds, kept the market for such securities at par or better.[19]

By 1852, then, the die was cast. The colonial state had put in place the financial framework within which railways could be constructed and within which the colony could move from a commercial to an industrial economy. Even though Hincks referred to railways as 'public works,' he and his colleagues expected that these enterprises would be promoted, financed, and managed by private entrepreneurs. His goal was to encourage, not to regulate, and certainly not to manage. At the dawn of the industrial era, one could reasonably expect to leave the latter functions to the private domain.

The particular characteristics of those local entrepreneurs most closely involved in railway promotion and management, coupled with pressures from foreign financiers and imperial state interests, soon necessitated more dramatic state intervention. After 1850, local merchants, usually foreign-born and specializing in the import-export sector, dominated the boardrooms of Upper Canada's railways.[20] From a scant 15 per cent of directors between 1845 and 1847, their representation never fell below 42 per cent in the 1850s. Merchant involvement signalled for the first time general acceptance of railways by the local business community. Drawing on skills acquired from the running of their own businesses, merchant directors were adept at cultivating local financial contacts. These links, bolstered by the government's guarantee, provided access to significant banking capital for short-term use by railways. The fact that 75 per cent of the merchant directors were foreign-born and generally involved in import-export functions rather than simply 'local traffic' broadened the network upon which these merchants could draw for resources of all kinds. Using established contacts in England, the merchant directors of many Upper-Canadian railways attracted British and in some cases American capital for local railway development. Using proxies from the foreign investors, many merchants also exercised positions of prominence at the local managerial level.[21]

Yet few merchants invested heavily in local railways. Their primary allegiance continued to rest with their traditional mercantile pursuits.[22] Limited or at best moderate involvement seemed the norm. No merchant had any railway experience prior to the late 1840s. Although such experience did increase as the period progressed, at no time did merchant directors possess the highest average number of years' experience. In fact, high turnover characterized merchant participation: 32 per cent of the merchants left after one year, whereas only 16 per cent of the other directors stayed for less than two years.

The participation pattern of the merchants was of definite importance, since the effective operation of railways presented problems of a magnitude and type never before encountered by this group. Construction problems were foreign to them, as were the intricacies of managing a road in an operative state.[23] Nor could the local economic structure easily generate suitable alternatives to merchant management. The operation of large-scale business enterprises had rarely been confronted in the commercially dominated Upper-Canadian economy. Significant canal construction had taken place, but before the 1840s this had been largely completed by British and American engineers, few of whom stayed in the colony. When the Canadian government took control of the Welland canal in 1841, it let out numerous small contracts; thus, few large contractors emerged within the country.[24] Whereas in the United States the military provided a source of managerial personnel, in Upper Canada, professional military personnel were themselves generally imported from Great Britain. In this context, British and American contractors and engineers wasted little time in taking advantage of the inexperienced local entrepreneurs.[25] To a degree they were aided in their predatory behaviour by politicians of the status of Allan Napier MacNab, John A. Macdonald, Alexander Tilloch Galt, and Luther Holton, who all profited in varying degrees from inside information during construction of the Great Western and/or Grand Trunk railways.[26] Despite the dispatch to the colony, by British investors, of men with some railway managerial experience and the gradual transferral of policy and managerial power from local Canadian boards to British directorates, many major Canadian roads suffered from poor construction and large cost overruns.[27]

The 1851 Main Trunk Line of Railway Act did, of course, give to the government's Board of Railway Commissioners the power to intervene and ensure that costs were in line with work completed. The one case in which this general power led to direct intervention prior to 1857 is instructive. In June 1852 the board, worried by seeming cost overruns on the Northern Railway, decided 'to exercise active supervision' over its construction. In the course of so doing, the specially appointed inspector unearthed faulty construction, pointed to excessive control exerted by the contractor, and for both reasons refused to issue a $500,000 government advance to the road. To requalify for financing the Northern had to upgrade construction and renegotiate the contract, vesting independent control in a full-time chief engineer acceptable to the government. The government's appointee as chief engineer, Frederick Cumberland, devoted more time to his architectural business than to his railway affairs, however; he also accepted a $10,000 under-the-table payment from the road's contractors to turn a blind eye to continued profit taking and slip-shod construction. Because of the ad hoc nature of the government's intervention and general supervisory system, the continuance of this activity went unnoticed.[28]

And so the pattern went. By 1857 the facilitative structure set up by Hincks to advance 'public works' via private endeavour had proven insufficient for the task at hand. By that year the three largest Upper-Canadian railways had petitioned the government for monies to pay the interest on their bonded debt. They also petitioned for the right to raise new capital, under government imprimatur, in order to upgrade construction, procure rolling stock, and extend branch and main lines. The government's local bank was owed £347,000 by the state – seven times what it was under contract to provide – and could not continue to advance railways their required short-term operating capital and hope to maintain solvency. In fact, the bank increasingly became a drain on public resources rather than a support for public enterprise. Municipalities, created in the first place to provide a de-centralized financial system capable of promoting local endeavours, also quickly fell into arrears on debentures issued under the Consol-idated Municipal Loan Fund Act. As early as 1855, twelve were behind in payment.[29]

Mercantile management and permissive state supervision in the railway sector had spawned a full-scale financial crisis by 1857. An incipient social crisis was also fast emerging. This was especially ap-parent in the area of labour relations. Sidney Pollard has called the organization and control of labour 'the central management problem in the industrial revolution.' Certainly early Upper-Canadian railway promoter/managers experienced great difficulty in handling this as-pect of management. During the construction phase of operations, a phase that always overlapped the commencement of passenger and freight service, unskilled railway navvies balked at winter wage re-ductions, excessive working hours, and irregular payments by con-tractors and engaged in a series of disruptive strikes on most railway lines in the early 1850s. This activity reached a climax in Upper Can-ada when in early 1855 an armed battle took place on the Buffalo, Brantford and Goderich railway.[30]

In one sense this behaviour continued a pattern established in the 1840s on the canals. Labour uprisings punctuated the era of canal construction just as they did the era of railway construction. Yet the continuation of this seemingly unrestrained activity had, in the con-text of the railway era, different implications, which were dramatically underlined during the Great Western's first year of carrying freight and passengers. Between mid-December 1853 and the end of October 1854, seventeen separate accidents involving fatalities took place, kill-ing seventy-nine people and injuring seventy. The legislative com-mission appointed to inquire into these accidents concluded that the Great Western's management had, in the case of the six most serious mishaps, failed to ensure that strict adherence to time schedules, reg-ulations, and lines of authority were systematically carried out. '[P]unishments and penalties ... as the matter now stands ... are ar-bitrary, uncertain, partial and ineffective.' Locomotive engineers seemed to think it great sport to run over cattle; track layers and repairers lacked supervision; gravel trains ran on the main line with cavalier disregard of passenger trains' timetables; those higher in the employment hierarchy received less stringent penalties than their subordinates. All these deficiencies derived to a significant extent, the commissioners concluded, from 'a system of management unusual on the continent and ill adapted to the circumstances and magnitude of this enterprise.'[31]

Doggerel in the popular press nicely reflected increased public concern and cynicism. One writer described the overcrowded nature of the coaches and the inevitable accident:

And, crash! right down yon steep incline ...
The crushed and shattered wretches scream
No matter since they pay
Uprouse ye them, my merry Railway men,
And Use them as ye may.

And as another put it: 'such is the rapidity with which distance is annihilated ... that passengers often pass from time into eternity – an *awful distance* – without being aware of it.'[32]

These crises of a social and financial sort led to a restructuring of internal governmental systems and the implementation under government supervision of an increasingly differentiated, specialized, and codified management by experienced and trained professionals in the railway sector. Forced to reinstitute its own financial stability and preserve social stability in the polity over which it governed, the state began to reform its own managerial structures at the same time that it encouraged similar reform within the railway sector.[33] By so doing the state acted as a bridge between the values, attitudes, and behaviours of commercial Upper Canada – typified by its resident entrepreneurs – and the demands of the industrial capitalist world with which Upper Canada was becoming increasingly intertwined.

Such reform, especially of the state's internal operations, was a tricky and complex affair. It would never do, after all, to initiate reform that might lead to the disposal of politicians who had themselves speculated, and thereby in part facilitated the crises of the late 1850s. Thus the appointment by government of an auditor general in 1855, in part to pacify opposition cries of government corruption, was made with only limited enthusiasm; and John Langton, Canada's first auditor general, constantly ran up against political stonewalling as he slowly and methodically regularized the process of government spending, instituted procedural reforms, and tightened and clarified lines of authority. This process, albeit halting and imperfect in execution, led to the passage of a bill in 1864 that represented substantial advance over the informal, decentralized, and casual system within which 'public works' and public financing had operated in the early 1850s.[34]

It made little sense for the government to begin to transform its own managerial system and at the same time allow the largest private business organizations in Upper Canada to undermine such change. The imminent bankruptcy of some of Upper Canada's largest chartered businesses and the deleterious impact that would have on the public accounts, coupled with the restructuring of the state's financial administration, led to increased government concern with the quality and structure of management in the private sector. This concern was heightened by the seemingly uncontrolled behaviour of railway labourers. Following the work of E.P. Thompson, many writers have pointed to the increased discipline and control exercised by management over the labour process in the industrial as compared to the pre-industrial or commercial era of capitalism. The basic issue concerned the culture of the workplace. No longer was it sufficient simply to complete a task. Increasingly, jobs had to be done at a particular time and in a particular way. For obvious reasons this was especially the case with regard to labour in the railway world.[35] The Great Western's early history brought home to the colonial state the necessity for ensuring that a suitable managerial system existed on the Canadas' first railways. As the commissioners realized, the 'character of management' affected not only the state's significant capital investment, but also the lives of citizens; and, when set against the backdrop of labour unrest, inadequate management threatened to undermine the stability of a hierarchically ordered society. Thus the commissioners were 'convinced ... that it is of the greatest importance, *for the proper control of men employed on railroads, as well as for the future safety of the public*, that the Legislature should prescribe rules and regulations for the government of railroads, and of the men employed thereon, any violation of which, should be made a misdemeanour punishable with fine or imprisonment, independent of instant dismissal from the service of the Company.'[36]

The state already had passed legislation that aimed to achieve some of the above. Existing legislation, however, did not provide an adequate means for ensuring the implementation of proper managerial systems. To do this required active state intervention. That intervention took two forms. The first represented an attempt to tighten the power of the judiciary to punish 'Officers and Servants of Railway Companies contravening the By-laws of such Companies, to the danger of person and property.' In addition to allowing companies the right to fine and punish offenders, it re-emphasized the penalties available to the judiciary in the same regard.[37] Most studies have concluded that this means of control was rendered somewhat ineffective because juries tended to side with individuals against the corporation and the state, so that the 'offenders' would often be acquitted. Existing evidence supports this. When, however, these lower-court cases were appealed to the Court of Queen's Bench or the Court of Common Pleas, the state-appointed judges often overruled the jury decisions. The state's will acting through its judicial arm did, then, have a direct impact on disciplinary operations within the Upper-Canadian railway world.[38]

A second form of intervention, much more dramatic, albeit temporary in nature, has received little historiographical comment. This is unfortunate because it can be argued that the second mode of intervention facilitated the transition in the managerial sphere from a predominantly commercially oriented *modus operandi* to a system of operations in tune with the industrial world of the nineteenth century. If one accepts that managerial systems to a great extent heralded how far along the continuum from a commercial to an industrial era a particular society was, then state activity in this area takes on fundamental importance.

In May 1857, the legislature passed an 'Act for the Better Prevention of Accidents on Railways,' which gave to the Board of Railway Commissioners heightened supervisory powers, the right to hire its own secretary, and the right to oversee up to three permanent inspectors of railways appointed by the governor in council and answerable to the Board of Railway Commissioners.[39] For the first time the board could employ a permanent staff of experts with which to inspect and oversee railway matters. Railway inspectors could regularly inspect 'all Railways constructed or in course of construction.' The chief railway inspector, Samuel Keefer, a man with long experience as a Public Works engineer during the canal and railway eras, took his job quite seriously. He considered his mandate to be the inspection of 'everything connected with the construction and management of everyone of the lines.' In sixteen months he travelled upwards of 23,000 miles and inspected twelve railways, usually 'twice and some three and even four times.' Much of his energy and that of his assistant, who followed him to ensure that his written recommendations to the railways were put into force, focused on the quality and safety of the railways' construction. Embankments, ballasting, bridges, viaducts, tunnels, ties, rails, and engines were all inspected from this perspective and on many roads found wanting.[40]

Keefer, however, with the backing of both the Board of Railway Commissioners and the 1857 legislation, followed the exhortation of the commissioners who had investigated the Great Western's accidents and focused on far more than the physical dimension of safety. Invariably, his written reports to railways emphasized the need to institute managerial strategies appropriate to the novel task of running the physically dispersed operations of railways. Concern for devolution of responsibility and regularity of supervision were refrains that ran through most of his reports. In this regard, the railways' Rules and Regulations – books of codified rules – commanded his special attention. Although since 1851 such codes had been required of all railways, Keefer discovered seven companies without published compilations.[41] As he warned the offending Buffalo and Lake Huron's general manager, such books were essential 'in order that every person employed upon the line might have his duty properly defined and made responsible for its faithful performance.' He told the equally negligent Northern Railway to organize under the general supervision of its Engineering Department a regular 'force of carpenters constantly employed making repairs from day to day.' Particular supervision should be in the hands of a full-time inspector 'held responsible for their good order.' He threatened to close operations when railways ignored his recommendations and, backed by the state's power, in several cases did so.[42]

In at least two ways the updating of the published Rules and Regulations by major Upper-Canadian railways reflected state pressure as exerted through the Commission of Inquiry, specific legislation, judicial action, and systematic inspection. The first and most obvious way, as Table 8:1 indicates, was in their simple increase in bulk. The second was in the increased specificity of content: a hierarchical gradation of command, close delineation of responsibilities, and detailed enumeration of punishments attendant on the transgression of such duties. Lack of space forbids a detailed exposition of these points; indeed, the simple increase in the number of rules under each position as indicated in Table 8:1 is probably suggestive enough. One example, however, might suffice to indicate the general trend. The Great Western's 1853 rule book contained four clauses under 'Track Repairers.' The 1854 edition, revised after the commencement of the Commission of Inquiry, not only contained twenty-seven articles that linked responsibilities to chain of command, but was also prefaced by the following stern warning:

> Before any laborer or foreman is engaged by the Inspector, he must be made to understand that the wilful transgression of *any* of the Rules in this Book will be visited by immediate dismissal from the service of the Company, accompanied by a fine of five shillings in the case of a laborer, and fifteen shillings in the case of a foreman. Any insubordination on the part of any man or foreman, drunkenness whilst on duty, being found off his work during working hours, or the commission or omission of any act whereby the passage of Engines or Trains shall or might be endangered – will be punished by fine and dismissal, as above.[43]

These warnings were in addition to the enlarged general-rules section, which itself elaborated at length on possible punishments.

All this, at least on the Great Western, seemed to have a definite impact on the road's managerial structure. The Commission of Inquiry had pointed to the 'disorder and irregularity' of the Great Western's management in the mid-1850s.[44] By 1859, according to Samuel Keefer, this system had been replaced by one that 'has a regularly organized system of every department of its service; from the highest to the lowest. For the care of the track there are competent and experienced Engineers and under them Inspectors, Road Masters and Trackmen in regular gradations who are in constant attendance and faithful in the discharge of their duties.' The Great Western no longer delegated 'its responsibilities to contractors' or subcontractors. In part, under government pressure, the railway's managers had moved from treating labour in the mercantile sense of the 'buying and selling of commodities' to the industrial sense of assuming direct management and 'control over the labour process.'[45] On the Great Western, this process of change was more symbiotic in nature than on some other railways. C.J. Brydges, the Great Western's local general manager, had been for some time engaged in a power struggle with local directors for managerial control. Parts of the commissioners' report and especially their description of the professional policies pursued by Samuel Keefer were welcomed by Brydges. In this sense, the state facilitated the rise to power of professionally oriented managers al-

TABLE 8:1
Railway Rule Books

| Occupation* | Number of Rules | | | | |
| | GW 1853 | GW 1854 | GT 1857 | STL&O 1869 | GT 1885 |
|---|---|---|---|---|---|
| General rules | 5 | 13 | 17 | 17 | 22 |
| Stationmaster | 20 | 20 | 26 | 29 | 32 |
| Switchmen and signalmen | 6 | 8 | 11 | 11 | 13 |
| Police and porters | 4 | 7 | – | – | 15 |
| Enginemen | 31 | 38 | 31 | 24 | 41 |
| Conductors | 12 | 22 | 23 | 15 | 64 |
| Brakesmen | 3 | 6 | – | 3 | 9 |
| Track repairers | 4 | 27 | 26 | 25 | 26 |

* Some occupations have been collapsed as names became increasingly precise reflecting greater precision in task and responsibility. That trend has not been captured in this figure.

ABBREVIATIONS: GW – Great Western; GT – Grand Trunk; STL&O – St Lawrence and Ottawa

ready in place within the railway sector. From the state's point of view, it was, after all, the seeming absence of such well-placed and properly schooled professionals that precipitated the series of crises to which the Upper-Canadian government had to respond.

On other railways, however, even more direct government intervention was required in order to effect this managerial transformation. In a state of 'dilapidation' by 1858 and nearly bankrupt by 1859, the Northern Railway, running out of Toronto, is a case in point.[46] After taking formal control of the road early in 1859, the government negotiated and administered a $1 million restoration of the line's physical plant.[47] The managerial structure created to oversee the actual renovation stands in dramatic contrast to the relatively undifferentiated holistic approach common to the early 1850s. Specialization of task and the delineation of control and responsibility within a hierarchically ordered managerial system characterized the process.

While Cumberland, the road's manager, exercised general supervision over costs and quality of work, he delegated day-to-day control to Sandford Fleming, his chief engineer. As a parallel line of authority, the contractors themselves hired both a general and a day-to-day overseer. In addition, the major subcontractor, Francis Shanly, kept close control over work that he in turn had subcontracted out by the hiring of a 'timekeeper.' The timekeeper made daily visits to work sites and noted the number of workers, the job time and type, and the quantity of materials used. He then compared his weekly notes with those of the subcontractor's timekeeper or foreman.[48] And, finally, of course, the government inspector had the right of ultimate approval (see Figure 8:1).

Quite clearly the worker no longer organized his workplace. Be he mason, pumper, or carpenter, the hired labourer enjoyed almost no job autonomy. Materials, quality specifications, and time constraints were set by others.[49] In fact the greatest managerial problem associated with the Northern's renovation lay not with the hapless worker: the number of direct overseers made it virtually impossible for him to 'scamp' on his work. And equally important, job opportunities for railway construction in Canada were few in the 1860s. In this instance the worker had little option but to obey. How properly to divide authority within the hierarchical managerial structure became the main bone of contention on the Northern. In the course of much, often heated, discussion, lines of authority and responsibility did emerge. In fact it was in an effort to protect authority within this managerial structure that Francis Shanly, the principal subcontractor, hired a professional 'timekeeper' to oversee his workers.[50]

The state had pushed for and helped to create a management system that contained within itself the seeds for further evolution. By the early 1860s the dynamics for change did not rest simply with the desire of one class to dominate another. In this sense, in the world of Upper Canada's railways, a new stage in the development of an industrial managerial class had been reached. Due to a significant extent to the nature of state intervention, by 1860 the managerial class had ceased to be an undifferentiated whole; rather, the thrust for efficiency would now more than ever before emerge from conflict over control within that class.[51]

The state's concern with the manner in which railways controlled and managed their workers related to more than the construction phase of their operations. The codification of the Rules and Regulations concerned both the construction and the running stages of operations, as, indeed, did the focus of the 1854 Commission of Inquiry. Railway inspectors like Samuel Keefer kept close watch over speed, timetables, running arrangements, and signalling systems. While the state does not seem to have maintained the same vigilance over the administrative control of the railways' large locomotive and machine shops, it seems quite reasonable to infer that the pressure for 'a rational and methodical' management in one area would influence arrangements throughout the entire corporation.[52]

Government – A.T. Galt, finance minister
(final say re: details of contract)

Government inspector (final say re:
acceptability of work)

Northern Railway – F.C. Cumberland, managing director
(general supervision)

Chief engineer – Sandford Fleming (specific supervision)

General contractor – Thomas Brassey and Sons,
London, England

Canadian agent – J. Reekie

Contractor's inspector – J. McGrath

Principal subcontractor – Francis Shanly

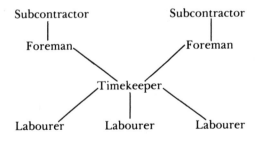

FIGURE 8:1
The Northern's Renovation: Management Structure

The entrepreneurial role exercised by the state in the transformation of railway management under review here might be termed 'low-order' entrepreneurial activity. The intent was not to alter overall goals but rather to establish more effective operating/managing methods for the attainment of those goals. In several ways in the formative period, however, the colonial state also played a role in 'high-order' entrepreneurial decisions, decisions that altered, circumscribed, or conditioned the fundamental orientation of a company's activities.[53]

When the state assumed control of the Northern in 1859, in addition to managing the renovation, it created a financial and operational structure within which the Northern operated for the next twenty years. For the first time British bondholders were given voting and managerial rights. Even more importantly, from Cumberland's perspective as manager, the state through its finance minister, A.T. Galt, extracted the following constrictive concessions. Any aid to steamboats required government approval; all repairs were to be overseen by a government official; and, most significantly, the road's capital account could not be augmented without both parliamentary and shareholder sanction. This meant that any expansion, or, after a necessary renovation, any update of running equipment and general facilities, would either require new legislation or be paid from current earnings. 'We are extremely conservative,' Cumberland admitted to shareholders in 1868, 'in our notions on this road.'[54] This conservatism dated from the state-imposed reconsolidation of 1859–60. Cumberland, throughout the rest of his tenure as manager, had to operate within that environment.

Conditioning activity by the state of an even more dramatic sort took place in the early 1860s. The three largest Canadian railways – the Grand Trunk, the Great Western, and the Buffalo and Lake Huron – had negotiated a tentative agreement that would merge their separate operations into one company. Edward Watkin, newly appointed Grand Trunk president, had hired Brydges from the Great Western in anticipation of the merger and had seen to it that Brydges' successor, Thomas Swinyard, was sympathetic to union. Yet the government refused to pass the Fusion Bill. As a result the Great Western and Grand Trunk continued to fight and weaken one another *vis-à-vis* their larger (due to amalgamations) American competitors. As Swinyard later noted, they were made 'cats paws' of by the larger American through roads.[55] All this occurred within a state-conditioned context.

In the first railway era, the Canadian government did supply funds and act as an ally to the self-serving interests of many railway pro-

moters, financiers, and managers. The state passed legislation that
gave to railway owners and managers and to state-appointed judges
judicial control over the lives of labourers. The state facilitated the
creation of managerial systems designed to control and delimit in a
rigorous fashion past freedoms enjoyed by workers. The politicians
who headed the state often dabbled in railway speculation and constantly safeguarded their own privileged positions in society. In these
senses state activity in the railway sector did lead to 'real, painful,
harmful restrictions on human capacities' and did favour in a differ-
ential way various social groups.

In the course of these actions, the state helped to move Upper
Canada from a predominantly commercial, economic, and social environment to an increasingly industrial-capitalist milieu. Acting to
shield the Canadian public from undue carelessness; to preserve social
stability in the polity over which it ruled; to safeguard its own large
capital investments; to encourage foreign investment; and to protect
its own political future, the Canadian government in the 1850s and
1860s pressured railway corporations to implement managerial reform. Some 'progressive' managers, such as Brydges, used this pressure to help consolidate personal managerial power *vis-à-vis* labourers
and inexperienced merchant directors. In addition to mobilizing and
investing capital, the Canadian state acted as a conduit for the transferral of managerial techniques deemed appropriate for an industrializing economic order. The state borrowed ideas from railway
managers in the United States – the government's Commission of
Inquiry into the Great Western in 1854 had contacted American railway investors and managers to the extent of sending delegates to
Albany, Buffalo, and Detroit for discussions. The state entered into
joint financial and managerial roles with British investors and contractors – as was the case after 1860 on the Northern Railway. By
requiring, through legislation and inspection, the implementation of
new managerial systems, the state exercised an active and interventionist role in Upper Canada's transition from a commercial to an
industrial economic order.

It would be tempting to conclude that state activity in the transportation area heralded the emergence of an institutional bureaucratic state north of the forty-ninth parallel. Yet by 1864 the state
structure created in 1857 and staffed by experts with responsibility
for overseeing railway affairs had been disbanded. Politicians, increasingly involved in a process of disentanglement from direct imperial control, remained reluctant to delegate significant power and

autonomy to permanent experts. Indeed, Samuel Keefer had to submit all reports on all railways to the commissioners for approval prior to sending them to the companies concerned. Also, and especially where the Northern Railway was concerned, many of Keefer's stronger recommendations were vetoed by the board. Clearly Keefer, the 'expert,' was not granted the autonomy he desired. By 1864 the Board of Railway Commissioners no longer employed full-time inspectors. Instead it seconded inspectors from Public Works on an ad hoc 'emergency' basis.[56]

Nor did the board itself exercise a very activist role in railway affairs after 1867. While it had the power to ratify rates, for example, very few of these issues were brought before it in the 1870s.[57] John A. Macdonald kept open a personal line to the executives of the major railways and resisted delegating such a linkage to a permanent bureaucracy throughout his long tenure as Canada's leading politician.[58] He continued to rely on the judicial process to handle those dissatisfied with railway practices.[59] This stood in contrast to the British situation where a stronger commission influenced rate setting, route scheduling, and so on. As a railway executive of a small Ontario company wrote to Macdonald in February 1879,

> a Commission should exist having powers like the English Commission to control in an equitable manner the regulations of all the Railways of the Dominion with one another and with the general public.
>
> If you give the Commission the same powers as its prototype in England possesses you would rid the Government of a great deal of bother in relation to railway questions and you would protect the public ... from ... the Great Railway Corporations.[60]

Despite increased pressure throughout the 1880s and 1890s, Macdonald and his immediate successors did not establish such a commission.

Clearly more was at stake here than jealousy of experts in a bureaucratic setting. John A. Macdonald profited politically by pandering to the desire of large railways to remain free from bureaucratic interference. The Grand Trunk and the Canadian Pacific railways, controlling between them some 80 per cent of mileage in Canada by the late 1880s, delivered votes and jobs on a regular basis to politicians who favoured their interests. As Ken Cruikshank has nicely detailed, it was not until a coalescence of opposed groups that promised to pack equal political clout had emerged at the turn of the century that the national government delegated significant power to a permanent Board of Railway Commissioners staffed by experts.[61] The need for such a board clearly pre-existed its establishment. The social and political power of those who were disadvantaged by its absence was, however, at the time of Confederation and for a generation thereafter, unable to compete against the countervailing influence of Canada's large railway monopolies.

The fact that state intervention in railway affairs did not manifest itself in the form of a continuous wave following the late 1850s should not lead one to minimize the power exercised by the state in the years before Confederation. The point is that that power was exercised in response to a particular series of economic, financial, and social crises. Once these seemed to have been solved, i.e., once a professional managerial system was put in place, the pressure for continued state presence abated. Put simply, the first dramatic examples of state intervention in a major economic area preceded the social and economic milieu necessary for the continuance of such behaviour. The fact that forty years passed before the federal government gave the Board of Railway Commissioners 'almost unlimited power over freight rates'[62] underlines the point that one should be wary of generalizing about a common pattern of state development throughout North America. In the final analysis the social and economic fabric of local polities exercised a major if not determining influence over the timing, degree, and pattern of state intervention in economic and social affairs.

## NOTES

1 For the United States, see H.N. Scheiber, *Ohio Canal Era: A Case Study of Government and the Economy, 1820–1861* (Athens, Ohio: Ohio University Press 1969), and C. Goodrich, *Government Promotion of American Canals and Railroads, 1800–1890* (New York: Columbia University Press 1960). For England, see Henry Parris, *Government and the Railways in Nineteenth-Century Britain* (London: Routledge and Kegan Paul 1965).

2 For the classic statement of the inevitability notion see Oliver MacDonagh, 'The Nineteenth-Century Revolution in Government: A Reappraisal,' *Historical Journal* 1 (1958), 52–67, and for a defence of Benthamism see Jennifer Hart, 'Nineteenth-Century Social Reform: A Tory Interpretation of History,' *Past and Present* 31 (1965), 39–61.

3 Michael Katz, 'The Origins of the Institutional State,' *Marxist Perspectives* (1978), 6–22

4 Philip Corrigan and Derek Sayer, *The Great Arch: English State Forma-*

*tion as Cultural Revolution* (Oxford: Blackwell 1985), 1–13

5 See Brian J. Young, 'Positive Law, Positive State: Class Realignment and the Transformation of Lower Canada, 1815–66,' and Bruce Curtis, 'Class Culture and Administration: Educational Inspection in Canada West,' both in this volume, and Bruce W. Curtis, *Building the Educational State: Canada West, 1836–1871* (London, Ont.: Althouse 1987); Brian J. Young and John A. Dickinson, *A Short History of Quebec: A Socio-Economic Perspective* (Toronto: Copp Clark Pitman 1988).

6 Roy M. MacLeod, ed., *Government and Expertise: Specialists, Administrators and Professionals, 1860–1919* (Cambridge: Cambridge University Press 1988).

7 On the importance of crisis and the nature of disjuncture in state development see Roy MacLeod, 'Introduction,' in MacLeod, ed., *Government and Expertise*, 22, and Theda Skocpol, 'Bringing the State Back In: Strategies of Analysis in Current Research,' in P.B. Evans, D. Rueschemeyer, and T. Skocpol, *Bringing the State Back In* (Cambridge: Cambridge University Press 1985), 14.

8 On the necessity of emphasizing local circumstance and looking with caution on broad theorizing see P.B. Evans, D. Rueschemeyer, and T. Skocpol, 'On the Road toward a More Adequate Understanding of the State,' in Evans, et al., *Bringing the State Back In*, 351, 363. For a strong statement of the same point in a slightly different context see Chad Gaffield and Gerard Bouchard, 'Literacy, Schooling and Family Reproduction in Rural Ontario and Quebec,' *Historical Studies in Education*, 1:2 (1989), 103–20.

9 Doug Owram, ' "Management by Enthusiasm": The First Board of Works of the Province of Canada, 1841–1846,' *Ontario History* 70:2 (1978)

10 The discussion in the next three paragraphs is based on information in Owram, ' "Management by Enthusiasm," ' Ian Radforth, 'Sydenham and Utilitarian Reform,' in this volume, and J.E. Hodgetts, *Pioneer Public Service: An Administrative History of the United Canadas, 1841–67* (Toronto: University of Toronto Press 1955), 176–204.

11 For a discussion of the ongoing tension between the Board of Works bureaucracy and elected politicians see Hodgetts, *Pioneer Public Service*, ch. 12.

12 MacLeod, ed., *Government and Expertise*, passim

13 On the part-time nature of the board's field-staff see Hodgetts, *Pioneer Public Service*, 42.

14 See Ruth Bleasdale, 'Class Conflict on the Canals of Upper Canada in the 1840s,' *Labour / Le travailleur* 7 (1981), 9–39, and Paul Craven, 'The Law of Master and Servant in Mid-Nineteenth Century Ontario,' in D. Flaherty, ed., *Essays in the History of Canadian Law*, vol. 1 (To-

ronto: Osgoode Society, University of Toronto Press 1981), 175–211, for early examples of judicial power.

15 D. Rueschemeyer and P.B. Evans, 'The State and Economic Transformation: Toward an Analysis of the Conditions Underlying Effective Intervention,' in Evans, et al., *Bringing the State Back In*, 59

16 For a more detailed discussion of the state and Upper-Canadian railways covering some of the material presented here but from a different perspective, see Peter Baskerville, 'Railways in Upper Canada/ Ontario: The State, Entrepreneurship and the Transition from a Commercial to an Industrial Economy,' *Zeitschrift der Gesellshaft für Kanada-Studien* 12 (1987), 19–40.

17 The best overview of this early policy is Michael Piva, 'Continuity and Crisis: Francis Hincks and Canadian Economic Policy,' *Canadian Historical Review* 66 (1985), 185–210.

18 14 and 15 Vic. cap. 73, sect. 17

19 Peter Baskerville, *The Bank of Upper Canada: A Collection of Documents* (Toronto: Champlain Society 1987), cv–cxxvii

20 Statistical backing for the analysis of merchant presence on railway boards can be found in P. Baskerville, 'The Boardroom and Beyond: Aspects of the Upper Canadian Railroad Community' (Unpublished PH D diss., Queen's University 1973), 295–356.

21 W.P. Glad, 'Approaches to a Theory of Entrepreneurial Formation,' *Explorations in Entrepreneurial History*, 2nd ser. 4 (1967), 253, stresses the importance of birthplace. Peter Baskerville, 'Americans in Britain's Backyard: The Railway Era in Upper Canada, 1850–1880,' *Business History Review* 55 (1981), 314–36; D. McCalla, *The Upper Canada Trade: A Study of the Buchanans' Business, 1834–72* (Toronto: University of Toronto Press 1979); F.N. Walker, ed., *Daylight through the Mountain: Letters and Labours of Civil Engineers Walter and Francis Shanly* (Montreal: Engineering Institute of Canada 1957), 243, 265, provide evidence of merchant success in raising capital.

22 National Archives of Canada (NA), John Young Papers, LB4, Harris and Young to T.C. Street, 1850 and 1851; NA, Buchanan Papers, 14, P. Buchanan to I. Buchanan

23 Walker, ed., *Daylight through the Mountain*, 197, 207, 231, 243

24 Bleasdale, 'Class Conflict on the Canals,' 9–39; Owram, ' "Management by Enthusiasm," ' 171–88; Baskerville, 'Americans in Britain's Backyard,' 324–30

25 Peter Baskerville, 'Professional vs. Proprietor: Power Distribution in the Railroad World of Upper Canada/Ontario, 1850–1881,' *Historical Papers* (1978), 49–50

26 Henry C. Klassen, 'Luther Holton: Mid-Century Montreal Railwayman,' *Revue de l'Université d'Ottawa / University of Ottawa Quarterly* 52:3

(1981), 316–39; Peter Baskerville, 'Sir Allan Napier MacNab,' *Dictionary of Canadian Biography* vol. 9 (1976), 519–27

27 For the role played by foreign appointed managers see Baskerville, 'Professional vs. Proprietor'

28 NA, Department of Public Works (DPW), RG11, 802, S. Keefer to Commissioner, 15 June 1852

29 See Baskerville, *The Bank of Upper Canada*, sections C, D.

30 Sidney Pollard, *The Genesis of Modern Management: A Study of the Industrial Revolution* (London: Edward Arnold 1965), 160. Paul Appelton, 'The Sunshine and the Shade: Labour Activism in Central Canada, 1850–60' (MA thesis, University of Calgary 1974).

31 *Journals of the Legislative Assembly of the United Province of Canada*, Reports of the Commissioners Appointed to Inquire into a Series of Accidents and Detentions of the Great Western Railway, Canada West, 3 Nov. 1854 (hereafter Commission of Inquiry), 18 Vic., App. YY np

32 *British Colonist* (Toronto), 12 Sept. 1851; *Leader* (Toronto), 17 Aug. 1854

33 For a similar notion of 'symbiosis' in managerial development see Samuel P. Hays, 'Political Choice in Regulatory Administration,' in Thomas K. McCraw, ed., *Regulation in Perspective: Historical Essays* (Boston: Division of Research, Graduate School of Business Administration, Harvard University 1981), 135.

34 H.R. Balls, 'John Langton and the Canadian Audit Office,' *Canadian Historical Review* (1940), 150–76; W.A. Langton, *Early Days in Upper Canada, Letters of John Langton* (Toronto: Macmillan 1926); NA, RG58, Auditor General Papers 1855–64; J.E. Hodgetts, *Pioneer Public Service*

35 E.P. Thompson, 'Time, Work-Discipline and Industrial Capitalism,' *Past and Present* 38 (1967); J.V. Barkans, 'Labour, Capital and the State: Canadian Railroads and Emergent Social Relations of Production, 1850–1870' (MA thesis, McMaster University 1976); Paul Craven and Tom Traves, 'Dimensions of Paternalism: Discipline and Culture in Canadian Railway Operations in the 1850s,' in Craig Heron and Robert Storey, eds, *On the Job: Confronting the Labour Process in Canada* (Kingston, Ont.: McGill-Queen's University Press 1986), 48–9

36 Commission of Inquiry (my emphasis)

37 19 Vic., cap. 11

38 Craven and Traves, 'Dimensions of Paternalism,' 51–2; Brian Cheffins, 'Ontario Railways and Tort Law, 1850–1875; An Examination of the Subsidy and Law and Economics Theories of Tort Law,' unpublished paper, University of Victoria 1984

39 20 Vic., cap. 12, sect. 1 and 2

40 20 Vic., cap. 12, sect. 2; Archives of Ontario (AO), Box 27(c), Samuel Keefer, 'Inspector of Railways Report for 1858,' 8–10. See NA, DPW, RG11, 134 and 142, for numerous reports.

41 14 and 15 Vic., cap. 73; NA, DPW, RG11, 142 passim

42 NA, DPW, RG11, 134, Keefer to MacKirdy, 11 Nov. 1858, Keefer to Beatty, 16 Nov. 1857, 17 Apr., 4 Aug. 1858. He delayed the opening of the Port Hope and Lindsay and Preston and Berlin, closed the Cobourg and Peterborough, and recommended the closure of the Northern but was overruled by the commissioners; see ibid., 134 and 142 under respective headings.

43 The 1853 and 1854 Rules and Regulations are included in Commission of Inquiry, Evidence.

44 Commission of Inquiry; Alan Wilson and R.A. Hotchkiss, 'Charles John Brydges,' Dictionary of Canadian Biography, vol. 11 (Toronto: University of Toronto Press 1982), 121–5; Baskerville, 'Professional vs. Proprietor'

45 NA, DPW, RG11, 134, Keefer to Galt, 25 Mar. 1859; Harry Braverman, Labor and Monopoly Capital: The Degradation of Work in the Twentieth Century (New York: Monthly Review Press 1974), 62–3

46 NA, Fleming Papers, A. Brunel, memo. on Northern Railway, 1857 (Private and Confidential); NA, DPW, RG11, 134, S. Keefer to Beattie, 4 Aug., 13 Dec. 1858; ibid., S. Keefer to Galt, 18 Dec. 1858; Metropolitan Toronto Library (MTL), Northern Railway Company, Annual Reports 15 Feb. 1857, 7–10; Report of the Select Committee on the Affairs of the Northern Railroad and Northern Extension Railroad, Canadian House of Commons, Journals, 1877, Appendix 5 (NR), 27, 91.

47 The negotiations can be traced in the following: NA, Baring Papers, A835, Blackwell to T. Baring 21 Feb. 1859; NA, Department of Finance, RG19, E1(A), 3368, Cumberland to Galt, 11 Mar. 1859, H. Jackson to Galt, 23 Mar. 1859; NA Inspector General Papers, RG7, G14, 48, A. Galt, Report on Northern Railway, 1859; MTL, Northern Railway Company, Annual Reports, Report of Executive Council, 11 May 1859, and Order in Council, 12 May 1859; NA, RG46, 778, Cumberland to Board of Railway Commissioners, 26 May 1860.

48 AO, F. Shanly, Letterbook, 1860–4, Shanly to Worthington, 3, 11 May 1861

49 AO, F. Shanly Papers, 34, J. McGrath to Shanly, 7 May 1861; J. Reekie to Shanly, 13 June 1861; Letterbook, 1860–4, Shanly to Worthington, 11 May 1861

50 Note the pressure by McGrath, AO, Shanly Papers, 34, J. McGrath to Shanly, 2, 7 May 1861, and Shanly's response, Letterbook, 1860–4, Shanly to Worthington, 3, 11, 16 May 1861; Shanly to McGrath, 8, 13 May 1861.

51 For an example of this general point see AO, F. Shanly Papers, 34, J. Reekie to Shanly, 13 May 1861; S. Fleming to Shanly, 31 Jan. 1862; Letterbook, 1860–4, Shanly to McGrath, 17 Apr., 8 May 1861.

52 For two excellent studies of this aspect of early railway management

see Paul Craven and Tom Traves, 'Dimensions of Paternalism,' and their 'Canadian Railways as Manufacturers, 1850–1880,' Canadian Historical Association, *Historical Papers* 1983, 254–81.

53 This characterization is plausible when looked at from the perspective of long-term corporate ends. When viewed, however, from the perspective of labour, the alterations effected are much more dramatic in nature. Workplace control, whether maintained by the rigorous application of penalties, as promised in the Rules and Regulations, or by paternalistic/deferential policies, or by a combination of both, shifted from the worker to an increasingly differentiated managerial class. On 'low-order' and 'high-order' entrepreneurial activity, see Charles E. Harvey, 'Business History and the Problem of Entrepreneurship: The Case of the Rio Tinto Company, 1873–1939,' *Business History* 21 (1979), 3–22; Geoffrey Channon, 'A.D. Chandler's "Visible Hand" in Transport History,' *Journal of Transport History* 2 (1981), 53–64.

54 *Globe* (Toronto), 14 Feb. 1868

55 NA, RG30, 7, no. 1660; vol. 1003, Watkin to Brydges, 13 Dec. 1861; NA, Baring Papers, 3, F. Head to Baring, 30 Jan. 1862, J. Rose to Baring, 10 Mar. 1862; Baring Papers, C1369, Watkin to Baring, 5, 19 Apr. 1862; Watkin to Glyn, 28 Mar. 1862; NA, J.A. Macdonald Papers, 297, Brydges to Macdonald, 2 May 1862; University of Western Ontario (UWO), Thomas Swinyard Papers, 1870–83, Swinyard to Watkin, 17 Nov. 1875, LB1870 ff, Swinyard to Harris, 2 May 1883.

56 The disagreements over the Northern came to a head when Keefer told A.T. Galt, the chairman of the Board of Railway Commissioners, that if the road stayed open it was Galt's responsibility, not Keefer's. NA, RG11, V134, Keefer to Galt, 18 Dec. 1858. For the disbanding of the board's staff, see NA, RG46, V778, 15 Jan. 1863 (quote from here), 15 Mar. 1864.

57 NA, RG46, V778, passim

58 NA, J.A. Macdonald Papers, C.J. Brydges correspondence; J. Hickson correspondence; G. Stephen correspondence; and W. Van Horne correspondence

59 Paul Craven, 'The Meaning of Misadventure: The Baptiste Creek Railway Disaster of 1854 and Its Aftermath,' in Roger Hall, William Westfall, and Laurel Sefton MacDowell, eds, *Patterns of the Past: Interpreting Ontario's History* (Toronto: Dundurn 1988), 108–29; Ken Cruikshank, ' "Law" vs. "Common Sense": Railways, Shippers and Judicial Regulation, 1850–1903,' paper presented to Legal History Conference, Ottawa 1986. It should be noted, too, that Judge J.C. Morrison, past president of the Northern Railway, and Judge Thomas Galt, brother of A.T. Galt, both found for the railway sector in important cases.

60 NA, J.A. Macdonald Papers, V355, G. Laidlaw to J.A. Macdonald, 3 Feb. 1879

61 Ken Cruikshank, 'The Transportation Revolution and Its Consequences: The Railway Freight Rate Controversy in the Late Nineteenth Century,' *Historical Papers* (1987), 112–37
62 Ibid., 136

# 9

# Government Finance and the Development of the Canadian State

MICHAEL J. PIVA

In 1840 when Britain 'reunited' Lower and Upper Canada, the colony was still very much a frontier society whose civil institutions remained simple if not primitive. The political and administrative structures in place in Upper and Lower Canada bore little resemblance to modern parliamentary practices. Although both provinces had enjoyed representative government for half a century, real political power lay outside the elected assemblies. Governors sought the advice of an appointed Executive Council and the administrative assistance of a small provincial bureaucracy. Clear lines of authority, however, often remained diffuse. In theory all government officials acted on behalf of the governor; in practice many officials enjoyed considerable autonomy. Nowhere was this diffuse administrative system more apparent than in government finance. Such a situation was understandable in the context of the 1790s and early 1800s; it became intolerable during the Union period.

The Province of Canada grew rapidly following the Act of Union. The 1840s witnessed the completion of the St Lawrence canal system, and immigration increased rapidly, particularly at the end of the decade. The first years of the 1850s brought another round of intense and dynamic growth fuelled by a railway-construction boom. Between 1851 and 1861 the population grew from 2.4 to 3.2 million.[1] The value of Canadian imports increased from $21.4 million to $43.1 million while the value of exports increased from $13 million to $34.7 million.[2] This spectacular growth in population and economic activity placed new pressures and demands upon the Canadian state, demands that stretched to the limit the financial resources of the young province.

Economic policies in nineteenth-century Canada presumed that development could best be ensured by improving the colony's infrastructure. In time most businessmen and government officials came to believe that an improved infrastructure required the active intervention of the imperial and colonial states. As commitments grew, the governments faced a series of fiscal crises – in 1837–9, 1847–9, and 1857–9. Financial administration, as a result, involved exercises in crisis management; as often as not it was an exercise in damage control. Government officials reacted to financial problems; they rarely anticipated developments. Each crisis, however, led to a series of reform initiatives the final product of which was the creation of a relatively modern administrative system for managing government finance. This paper will briefly review the response to the 1837 and 1847 crises and then examine in more detail the final stages of the reform process that followed the 1857 depression.

Although the financial issue was by no means the only one being addressed, the Union itself represented a response to Upper Canada's financial difficulties. Part of those difficulties revolved around the inadequacy of the administrative controls that was revealed when the province came close to defaulting on debt-service charges in 1837.[3] A union of the two Canadas provided one solution: debt-ridden Upper Canada, with its more limited financial resources, would join relatively debt-free Lower Canada with its greater financial resources. As neither Canadian province was keen on the union, an additional incentive had to be provided to the Upper-Canadian Assembly; Britain promised to guarantee the interest on a new £1.5-million loan. Even this limited assistance was made 'discretionary on the part of the Governor-General and only to be used in order to obtain the consent of the Provinces to what may be deemed by him a final and satisfactory settlement.'[4] Before there would be any loans, however, Governor Sydenham would revamp the administrative structures of the Canadian government.

Too many unsupervised civil servants had been running government departments. Members of the Executive Council, meanwhile, carried no clear administrative duties. Sydenham intended to solve both problems:

it has appeared to me absolutely necessary, that on the one hand, the Governor should be able to rely upon the zeal and attention of the

Heads of Departments not merely to act under his immediate directions upon every minute point, but also to feel themselves really responsible for their conduct of their different offices, and on the other hand, their being members of one or the other House of Parliament, the public would possess a wholesome control over their acts, and the security would be obtained for the general administration of affairs being in accordance with the wishes of the legislature.[5]

Members of the Executive Council would be drawn from the ranks of the legislature. As members of the council they would help formulate policy and assume specific administrative duties as heads of their respective departments. They would also explain and defend government policy in the Assembly.[6] Although the receiver general became a member of the Executive Council, Sydenham's administrative scheme ensured that this office remained a purely administrative position with no policy component. Sydenham chose instead to upgrade the Office of the Inspector General appointing John Macaulay, a strong personality and someone he trusted, to head the new office.[7]

The administrative reforms introduced by Lord Sydenham provided the prerequisite for responsible government. The Executive Council under Sydenham now had the means to administer government policy as well as a mandate to contribute to policy formation. Expected to contribute to policy formation and to defend government policy in the legislature, the council would, with time, come to dominate the decision-making process. Greater political and administrative controls, however, did not prevent the province from spending its way into another crisis by the end of the decade.

Coincident with the final achievement of responsible government, the province faced another short but severe financial crisis. Francis Hincks, the new inspector general, attacked these renewed problems by first articulating an overall strategy and then adopting a number of new initiatives to achieve these objectives. He presented his program to the Executive Council in December 1848:[8] what is remarkable about this document is not its originally but its comprehensiveness.

Hincks began with the frank admission that the St Lawrence canals would not generate sufficient revenue for their maintenance let alone the revenue needed to pay interest and principal on debts incurred for their construction. This severely restricted prospects for further public-works spending; yet, like his predecessors, Hincks believed that rapid economic growth depended upon immigration and additional transportation improvements. Hincks would link the problems of immigration, settlement, and railways in a novel way: he proposed to capitalize Crown lands as a security for the public debt. According to the inspector general, £600,000 had been raised by the sale of but a third of the Clergy Reserve lands. Another sixteen million acres of Crown land lay within fifteen miles of seigneuries or townships in Canada East and the Huron Tract and the Ottawa Valley in Canada West. These lands would produce an estimated income of £2 million and 'their value would be increased materially by the construction of the public works in the Province.' Land sales would create an 'efficient Sinking Fund for the repayment of any loan.'9

The linkage between Hincks' various proposals came with the notion that Crown land sales would provide a capital fund that could be used to purchase outstanding provincial debentures. This required rapid immigration, which would increase trade as well as bring vacant land into production. Immigration could best be stimulated by improving transportation and communications, improvements that in turn might require an increase in the public debt to supplement the canals with railways. This construction would not only open new areas to agricultural settlement, but would also provide immigrants with construction jobs that allowed them in turn to earn and save enough to buy Crown lands. The essential task, then, was the development of 'public-works' projects.

The debt was already large, and financial pressures ensured that it could not be increased beyond the new loan of £500,000 (stg) then being negotiated to meet existing commitments. In order to avoid a further increase in the debt, Hincks proposed the creation of local municipal institutions with the power to tax and borrow. Local authorities would then be in a position to promote local improvements. Larger provincial projects, such as trunk railways, would be encouraged by provincial assistance to private entrepreneurs attempting to raise capital. In 1849 Hincks and the Reform government passed the Municipal Corporations Act and the Guarantee Act to accomplish these ends. These initiatives did not work quite as intended; neither the municipalities nor the railways were able to raise money on their own credit, even with, in the latter case, a government guarantee on interest payments. As the financial crisis eased after 1850 Hincks moved to amend his original proposals.

To aid municipalities Hincks created the Consolidated Municipal Loan Fund Act for Upper Canada in 1852.10 A total of £1.5 million (stg) 'Provincial' debentures paying 6 per cent interest were to be issued against a special fund created and administered by the province.

Municipalities borrowed against this fund to support transportation improvements, usually railways, but also roads and bridges. They would pay 8 per cent interest to cover costs and help build an effective sinking fund. Although the province interposed itself between the municipalities and creditors, these debentures were not secured by the Consolidated Revenue Fund and thus did not, technically, represent an increase in the public debt. As Etienne-Pascal Taché advised Baring and Glyn, 'you will exercise your own judgment regarding them ... as there is no liability on the Provincial Revenue for such issues.'[11] Although the Municipal Corporations Act applied only to Canada West, most of the larger centres in Canada East were already incorporated. To aid them the Consolidated Municipal Loan Fund Act for Lower Canada provided another £1.5 million (stg).

Hincks also increased the assistance offered to provincial railways. The Guarantee Act of 1849 covered only 'the interest on loans to be raised by any Company chartered by the Legislature of this Province for the construction of a Line of Rail-way not less than seventy-five miles in extent' up to 6 per cent. Railways could qualify for the guarantee as soon as they completed half the proposed line.[12] The policy, however, did not work as intended, as the St Lawrence and Atlantic, the first to qualify for the guarantee, could not sell its bonds in London at acceptable prices.[13] Against the advice of his London agents Hincks decided to substitute provincial for railway bonds.[14]

Although not repealing the Guarantee Act, the Assembly passed the Main Trunk Line of Railway Act in August 1851.[15] Intended primarily to promote the much-discussed intercolonial railway, Section 23 guaranteed 'the payment of the principal ... as well as ... the payment of the interest thereon' and authorized the government to issue 'Provincial Debentures for the amount to be guaranteed, or any part thereof.' The government attempted to limit its liabilities by restricting the guarantee to the Grand Trunk, the St Lawrence and Atlantic, the Great Western, and the Ontario, Simcoe and Huron railways. As government bonds sold quickly and at relatively high prices, the 'indirect' debt exploded. By mid-1855 outstanding debentures issued as part of the government's guarantee for railway loans totaled £3.5 million (stg), and an additional £900,000 (stg) would be added to the total by the year's end.[16]

Although better administrative controls introduced by the Sydenham reforms combined with a more integrated approach to economic and financial policy provided a marked improvement over the somewhat haphazard administrative and policy programs of the pre-Union period, much remained to be done. Administrative controls remained relatively lax, as the case of Upper Canada's school inspector illustrates. Appropriated funds were often advanced to government officials, who kept the money 'in any Bank they chose, and drew for it as they chose.' In Egerton Ryerson's case, such advances involved large balances of 'upwards of £20,000.' Ryerson made no distinction between these funds and his private accounts. Between 1851 and 1855 the Bank of Upper Canada paid interest on this money to Ryerson who 'felt myself no more obligated to account for any allowance the Bank was pleased to make on such deposits than to account for any other private money.' Ryerson considered interest paid to be 'compensation' for his acting as 'treasurer and paymaster' for large sums disbursed by his office; he regarded interest paid on government funds 'as my own.'[17] More significant in its impact on public finance were the compounding 'indirect' debts that followed Hincks' various initiatives. Throughout the 1850s the government maintained the fiction of 'direct' and 'indirect' debts and considered only the former in its fiscal calculations. Even here the government failed to take full advantage of the opportunities presented by prosperity to reduce its 'direct' liabilities.

The commercial depression ended in 1850; between 1849 and 1856 revenue increased by nearly 200 per cent (see Table 9:1). Expenditure grew by a similar amount, although annual budgetary surpluses on the Consolidated Revenue Fund varied considerably. With a cumulative surplus of over £1.2 million (cy) during these years the government was clearly in a position to reduce significantly its liabilities. Those liabilities were not, however, reduced; they increased. The debt position of the Canadian government deteriorated steadily during these years (see Table 9:2). This in itself indicates that the Public Accounts provide a highly misleading view of the government's real financial situation.

Unable to negotiate a new loan of £500,000 (stg), the province had faced severe financial difficulties throughout 1848 and 1849. The government, which was short of cash, issued small-denomination, short-term debentures to pay its various accounts. Originally adopted in 1848 to pay canal contracts, by mid-1848 these 6 per cent debentures were being used 'in lieu of money' to pay most government accounts, including the salaries of civil servants. These debentures, in turn, were to be accepted by the government in payment of all accounts, including customs. In May 1850 the government finally completed its new £500,000 (stg) loan and immediately called in and redeemed all

TABLE 9:1
Revenue and Expenditure, Consolidated Revenue Fund, Canada, 1848–56 (£000 cy)

| Year | Total revenue | Customs revenue | Total expenditure | Interest on public debt | Balance |
|------|------|------|------|------|------|
| 1848 | £ 379.7 | £ 304.4 | £ 474.5 | £169.2 | £( 94.8) |
| 1849 | 513.4 | 412.6 | 477.2 | 182.7 | 36.2 |
| 1850 | 704.2 | 583.5 | 541.8 | 202.1 | 162.4 |
| 1851 | 842.2 | 703.7 | 647.4 | 225.4 | 194.8 |
| 1852 | 880.4 | 705.5 | 810.9 | 215.4 | 69.5 |
| 1853 | 1,195.1 | 986.6 | 777.5 | 227.4 | 417.6 |
| 1854 | 1,369.3. | 1,168.0 | 954.9 | 226.1 | 414.4 |
| 1855 | 1,019.0 | 813.8 | 1,111.7 | 219.5 | ( 92.7) |
| 1856 | 1,238.7 | 1,028.9 | 1,105.2 | 225.2 | 133.5 |

SOURCE: 'Public Accounts of the Province of Canada for the Year 1857,' App. 4, *Appendix to the Journals of the Legislative Assembly*, 1858. All calculations are my own.[18]

the outstanding small-denomination issues.[19] What remained of the 1850 loan was deposited with a number of banks to be used to redeem maturing debentures. Redemptions in 1854 and 1855, together with losses incurred in ill-advised speculation,[20] ensured that by 1856 the government would again be short of cash. Indeed, in that year the government borrowed funds to meet interest payments on its public debt. The direct debt, meanwhile, had become but a third of the total debt. In order to promote railways, an additional £3.5 million in provincial debentures had been issued by mid-1855. To this could be added another £3 million raised through the sale of Municipal Loan Fund debentures.

In 1840 a debt crisis had been one factor promoting the Union; at the time the total debt of the two Canadas had been but £1.44 million (cy). Fifteen years later the province had managed to increase its liabilities nearly twelve times during a period of unprecedented prosperity, economic growth, and reported budgetary surpluses. The next financial crisis was already in the making even before the next economic depression became manifest.

On 1 January 1856 the Ontario, Simcoe and Huron Railway defaulted on interest payments due on its government-guaranteed debts. In July 1856 the government advanced to the Grand Trunk Railway £101,328.15 (cy) to meet interest due on its own bonds in London and another £25,000 (stg) to meet interest due in Boston and New

TABLE 9:2
Public Debt of Canada, 1849–56 (£000,000 cy)

| Year | Direct debt | Indirect debt | Total | Debentures redeemed |
|------|-------------|---------------|-------|---------------------|
| 1849 | £4.09       |               |       | £.02                |
| 1850 | 3.75        | £( .19)       | £ 4.70| .09                 |
| 1851 | 4.45        | .67           | 5.12  | .07                 |
| 1852 | 4.67        | .92           | 5.59  | .02                 |
| 1853 | 4.62        | 2.86          | 7.48  | .33                 |
| 1854 | 4.35        | 5.36          | 9.71  | .31                 |
| 1855 | 4.31        | 7.15          | 11.46 | .68                 |
| 1856 | 4.70        | 7.49          | 12.19 | .12                 |

SOURCE: National Archives of Canada (NA), Finance, RG19, vol. 3368, 'Memo of Public Debt of Canada,' Jan. 1859; 'Statement of the Public Debt from the Year 1851 to 1860,' Sessional Paper 3, *Sessional Papers*, 1861; 'Statement of Debentures Redeemed under Authority of Act 12 Vic., cap. 5, to 31 January 1854,' App. D, *Appendix to the Journals of the Legislative Assembly*, 1854; App. D, *Appendix*, 1855; App. 30, *Appendix*, 1856; App. 4, *Appendix*, 1857

York. Two other advances followed in September for £14,888.13.4 (cy) and £12,500 (cy) to meet interest payments. The Great Western Railway, having already defaulted on its payment to the Sinking Fund in September 1855, now defaulted on its interest payments, due 1 January 1857.[21] By the end of 1855 Upper Canada's municipalities were £36,000 and £24,300 (cy) in arrears on the Consolidated Municipal Loan Fund for interest and payments to the Sinking Fund respectively.[22] Like it or not, the government was liable for these 'indirect' debts. As T.C. Baring would later observe,

> The interest on these Municipal Loan Fund Bonds is as you know guaranteed by the Province, though the guarantee is worded in so ambiguous a manner as to leave it in doubt whether the Province could be legally compelled to pay. Of course more than half the Municipalities find themselves unwilling or unable (for many of those in Upper Canada are very hard up) to provide their own interest, and consequently one of the heavy items in Galt's financial statement this year [1859] was the amount required to meet this difficulty.[23]

The depression of 1857 ensured that neither the municipalities nor the railways would be in a position to meet their obligations. The government would have to bear the burden of both the direct and the indirect debt when its own revenues were falling dramatically.

Canada now faced its most serious financial crisis, in circumstances in which room to manoeuvre had nearly disappeared. Easy solutions were no longer available; this time there could be no quick fix.

Reform involved a number of general and specific questions. To begin with, the government needed to revamp its administrative system. In particular the antiquated accounting practices of the pre-Union period had become utterly inadequate. Public accounts that reported both budgetary surpluses and rapidly increasing debts obviously disguised more than they illuminated. Between 1855 and 1859 the government adopted a number of measures, beginning with the appointment of an auditor general and culminating with the revamping of the Office of the Inspector General, a measure that substantially improved administrative practices.

The accounting and administrative practices of the provincial government were both archaic and confused. The receiver general received public monies, dispensed all cheques, issued and kept records for all debentures, and kept accounts of these various transactions. The inspector general kept a second set of books, but used a sufficiently different system that the two, in the words of the Standing Committee on Public Accounts, did not 'assimilate.'[24] At the end of the fiscal year the receiver general submitted accounts to the inspector general, who reviewed them before submitting the Public Accounts to the legislature. This review did not constitute an audit in the usual sense of the term, nor did the submission of accounts to the legislature provide budgetary estimates or allow effective budgetary control over government spending. In 1845, Charles Metcalfe ordered the deputy inspector general to carry out an audit of the Public Accounts, but his review proved superficial. No single set of financial statements, meanwhile, provided a general picture of the government's financial position. The Consolidated Revenue Fund, although the most important, was by no means the only fund managed by the government. Beginning in 1855 the government would first create the Office of the Auditor General and modernize accounting practices, and finally create a Department of Finance complete with the usual mechanisms of control, including the formal submission of budgetary estimates to the legislature.

In 1855, John Langton became auditor general; as he explained to his brother, 'I expected to find a mess but the reality exceeded my expectations, especially as I have only yet got into the threshold of the dirtiest stall in the Augean stable – the Board of Works.'[25] By the time he settled into his duties the collapse of trade in 1857 had created a fiscal crisis. As revenues plunged, Langton reported that it was impossible to make reasonable estimates of either income or expenditures given the chaotic state of the Public Accounts. As he later explained: 'In former years these statements embraced only such payments and such revenues as belonged to the Consolidated Fund, and there was nearly an equal amount scattered through the separate statements of Special Funds, or which did not appear in detail at all, and could only be imperfectly gathered in the aggregate, from a comparison of the several items in the statement of Affairs of the year under consideration with those of the previous year.'[26] To correct this situation the government instituted a series of accounting reforms in 1858. Langton produced comparative statements for 1857 and 1858 to illustrate just how dramatically the old system understated revenues, expenditures, and annual balances (see Table 9:3). The budgetary deficit in 1857 proved to be more than 500 per cent larger than originally reported in the Public Accounts. Henceforth the legislature would be provided with general statements on income and expenditures and assets and liabilities that clearly indicated the actual financial state of the province. These would complement a number of detailed accounts on particular aspects of government operations that continued to form parts of the inspector general's report.

No sooner had the new accounting system been put into place than the government reorganized the Office of the Inspector General, eventually renaming it the Department of Finance. To the old responsibilities of keeping accounts, ensuring their accuracy, and advising the Executive Council on both financial and economic policy, the new minister added the responsibility of supervising and controlling departmental spending. The first step was to eliminate the spending autonomy of departments. After 1857 all revenues collected by departments, including Crown Lands, Public Works, and Customs, were to be paid to the receiver general; henceforth 'the practice of Permitting Collecting Officers to deduct their Salaries or Fees has been disallowed.'[27] In addition, the Bank of Upper Canada would no longer by allowed to advance money to departmental officials on the credit of the province. This eliminated the ability of a department to overdraw amounts placed at its disposal.[28] Each department would also have to submit budgetary estimates to the minister for general review and possible amendment. The minister then prepared a budget to be submitted to the legislature. Such procedures introduced an element of financial planning and eliminated the spending autonomy

TABLE 9:3

Income and Expenditures, 1857–8 ($000)

|  | 1857 | 1858 |
|---|---|---|
| *Old Accounting Practice* | | |
| Revenues | $ 5,353 | $ 5,061 |
| Expenditures | 5,693 | 6,143 |
| Balance | (340) | (1,082) |
| | | |
| *New Accounting Practice* | | |
| Revenues | 10,583 | 10,271 |
| Expenditures | 12,688　. | 11,403 |
| Balance | (2,106) | (1,132) |

SOURCE: 'Comparative Statement of the Expenditure and Revenue Applicable to the Consolidated Fund, for the Years 1857 and 1858, Upon the Principle of Statement No. 3, of the Public Accounts of 1857,' and 'Comparative Statement of the Entire Payments and Receipts of the Province in the Years 1857 and 1858, Upon the Principles of Statement No. 3, in the Public Accounts of 1858,' in 'Public Accounts for the Province of Canada for the Year 1858,' App. 5, *Appendix to the Journals of the Legislative Assembly*, 1859. All calculations are my own.

of many departments. No longer could departments such as the Board of Works spend on their own initiative, leaving the inspector general to deal with the consequences. This process culminated in the Audit Act of 1864, which provided the auditor with comptroller powers.[29]

The provincial government had little choice but to adopt such reforms. The hot-house atmosphere of rapid economic growth that characterized the first fifteen years of the Union period had helped gloss over administrative inadequacies. By 1857, however, the limits of frontier agricultural expansion had been reached; as economic growth slowed the province could no longer afford the lavish spending program of the past. Modern accounting practices provided the essential financial information that made budgetary control and realistic planning possible. By 1860 the reforms in the Department of Finance ensured that Canada's antiquated system had been completely abandoned, replaced by a modern system of financial management. The more restrictive economic environment of the late 1850s made other reforms equally desirable.

The economy, for example, needed a real currency. The province used pound currency for accounts, but there was no legal tender in this currency. Although most banks and some private merchants issued penny and half-penny tokens as well as notes, coins of all kinds circulated.[30] Each variety had to be rated through legislation, yet the actual rates of exchange varied considerably.[31] The problems encountered by customs collectors such as Thomas Parke illustrate the difficulties inherent in such a system.

Importers paid taxes and tolls with all manner of notes, coins, and token; collectors like Parke were required to establish reasonable equivalents of value. They were also required to deposit all monies collected each day in the government account at the Bank of Upper Canada. As Parke discovered in August 1856, the bank sometimes refused to accept these deposits. Parke was bewildered that the bank could perpetrate this 'harassing system' by refusing 'good money.' It turned out, however, that this was not all 'good money.' Parke had, for example, collected £300 in notes from the Bank of Stanstead. The Bank of Upper Canada refused to accept these, as, the previous spring, they 'could find no such Bank.' Gold coins collected by Parke turned out to have been the private production of a San Francisco merchant who used inferior gold and minted the coins with less than the standard weight.[32] Such a chaotic system was perhaps inevitable in a colonial frontier economy, but by the late 1850s the more developed province required a more modern system.

To deal with this problem the province introduced new legislation making the dollar the currency of account. The government also introduced an appropriate coinage. By April 1859 $356,000 in bronze and silver coins was put in circulation through the banks, each receiving amounts proportionate to its paid-up capital.[33] Eventually, $45 million worth of coins minted in 1858 and 1859 would be placed in circulation.

More difficult to correct was the problem of the public debt. Despite the fiction of 'direct' and 'indirect' debts, the government was liable not only for provincial issues marketed through its own agents but for all provincial debentures turned over to railways. There was also the problem of debentures issued on the Municipal Loan Fund. The government could ill afford to default on any of these liabilities.

If the government was to assume direct responsibility for its huge 'indirect' debt, Galt intended at least to reduce the cost of servicing that debt. As he explained to Thomas Baring, he intended 'to redeem the outstanding Municipal Loan Fund Debentures, and the Currency Debentures held in this Country, all bearing six % [sic] and saleable under par. To this extent I should wish to issue Consols, and also for such Sterling Debentures, as may be converted at favourable rates. There are upwards of Two Millions Sterling falling due within six years, which may probably be dealt with.'[34] New debentures used to convert or redeem old issues would pay 5 rather than 6 per cent interest. Galt anticipated that an annual saving of £100,000 (cy) in debt-service charges would result from this conversion. In early 1859 the first £350,000 (stg) worth of new 5 per cent twenty-year debentures were sent to Britain. The proceeds of these bonds helped cover budgetary deficits for 1858.[35] Then, in July 1859 the Bank of Upper Canada exchanged £150,000 (stg) worth of Municipal Loan Fund debentures for an equal amount of the new bonds.[36]

Not until 1860, however, did activity in Britain pick up. By December 1860 Baring and Glyn reported that £2.3 million (stg) worth of 6 per cent bonds had been cancelled.[37] On 1 January 1861 the government began paying only 5 per cent interest on outstanding Municipal Loan Fund debentures, and announced that it would continue to purchase at par or exchange these holdings for other provincial 5 per cent debentures until 31 December 1861.[38] To finance these purchases the government issued an initial £2.8 million (stg) in new 'Consolidated Loan' 5 per cent debentures.[39] Although dated 1 January 1860, these bonds were all shipped to Britain during May and June.[40] An additional £2.9 million worth were forwarded between July and September 1860,[41] followed by another batch of new bonds in 1861.[42] As Galt had exclaimed earlier in the year: 'It is a big figure I want ... It will be a capital operation, much the best we have ever attempted.'[43] Between 1859 and 1861 the province sold $35.6 million worth of new debentures and redeemed $21.5 million worth.[44]

The government also altered its relationship with the Grand Trunk Railway. In addition to straining relations between the government and the railway, the financial problems of the Grand Trunk also complicated relations between the province and its London agents. Baring and Glyn had been handling all government business in Britain since the failure of Thomas Wilson and Company back in 1837, and had been named joint agents in 1848. This connection led in the case of Baring to an increasingly large involvement in the affairs of the Grand Trunk. Glyn, meanwhile, were the London agents for the Bank of Upper Canada, the holders of the provincial account after 1849. When the bank entered a period of decline at the end of the 1850s Glyn eventually took over its claims on the Grand Trunk as payment for its own claims against the bank.[45] Both Baring and Glyn were heavily committed to the Grand Trunk, whose voracious appetite for capital created a tangled web of financial dealings among the government, its London agents, and domestic banks.[46] As government agents, Baring and Glyn enjoyed privileged access to the minister of finance, upon whom they pressed the claims of the railway.

The railway was in constant financial difficulties, which only grew worse as the initial stage of construction drew to a close. Poor construction standards and the earlier decision to build a wider-gauge system ensured that new capital would be needed to rebuild the only recently opened line.[47] A proposal to issue £100,000 in new preferential bonds in 1858,[48] however, had produced little revenue; Glyn observed that, 'It is vain attempting to raise money for the Company under existing circumstances.'[49] The provincial government was sympathetic, but with capital markets tight and revenues declining, no further aid, in either subsidies or loan guarantees, would be provided.

Under the terms of the 1856 Grand Trunk Relief Act the government placed the holders of new preferential bonds ahead of their own claims against the company. Then in 1857 a new act removed government appointees from the railway's board of directors and deferred all claims, including interest on provincial debentures issued on behalf of the railway, until some unspecified future date when the railway became profitable.[50] These acts established an arms-length relationship between the two. The railway continued to pressure the government for additional relief, particularly in 1859.[51] Galt politely but emphatically refused: 'it is quite unnecessary to say that if a crisis occur, no possible assistance can be looked for from this side.'[52] During his first term as minister of finance Galt held to this position despite intense lobbying from both Baring and Glyn.

Evidence of a more sophisticated and integrated approach to financial and economic policy, meanwhile, can be found in tariff policy.[53] Although the provincial government came under increased pressure from protectionists demanding 'Security in investments for Manufacturing purposes, as would materially encourage home Industry,'[54] the fiscal demands proved even more pressing. When Galt became inspector general in 1858 he believed that the worst of the depression was behind him and that he could look forward to 'a speedy revival of Trade.' Increased trade together with the recently adopted Cayley tariffs would, he hoped, eliminate the budgetary deficit.[55] Avoiding another deficit, however, was insufficient if Galt were to succeed in his debt-conversion program. By the end of the year it became clear that these hopes were not going to materialize.

The Cayley tariff did not produce the expected increase in government revenues (see Table 9:4). The value of non-reciprocity imports fell dramatically in 1858 to only $22.5 million. Even with higher import duties, revenue from customs collections fell to only $3.4 million. Galt could expect only a modest increase in imports for 1859; he needed much more revenue than the Cayley tariff could provide. In January 1859 he began canvassing opinions both within and outside the government on proposed changes in tariff policy. Galt had little choice but to introduce a revenue tariff, yet he clearly toyed with protectionist notions.[56]

Although usually considered a policy designed to protect domestic manufacturers, Galt's new tariffs were far more complicated than this aim alone required. He also intended to protect import merchants in Canada East, as well as the Grand Trunk Railway. His new tariffs substituted *ad valorem* rates for most of the old specific duties. As R. Spence observed:

Several merchants admitted to me today that it would to a great extent facilitate business, and the only objection I heard, with a single exception, was 'that it favoured Montreal more than Upper Canada' in other words that it would drive the New Yorker out of the Canada market. To this I think there can be no objections if the UC Merchant can buy as well at Montreal as at New York. It is time we had a Canada Policy – and if there are no other or stronger reactions than those adduced [*sic*] by persons in favor of buying at New York – the true promoters of Canadian interests will support your views.[57]

Certainly the Montreal Board of Trade recognized that *ad valorem* duties were 'better calculated to promote trade through our own Channels,' as did many other observers.[58] Protecting importers along the St Lawrence system protected other commercial interests as well. George Carr Glyn, for one, recognized the benefits for his primary Canadian asset: 'It strikes us that your new Tariff will help the traffic of the St. Lawrence and the G. [*sic*] Trunk. I congratulate you on your success in parliament.'[59]

There is some evidence to suggest that the tariff did indeed favour the St Lawrence route. To the degree that most reciprocity products from the United States entered the country upriver, the effect of the Galt Tariff seems to have been to encourage a larger share of non-reciprocity products to arrive via the St Lawrence from countries other than the United States. As trade recovered, the value of all imports increased by 67.1 per cent between 1858 and 1862.[60] The sharp rise in reciprocity imports accounts for the bulk of this increase;

TABLE 9:4
Customs Revenue, 1857–61 ($000)

| | Value of Imports | | |
| | Reciprocity goods | Non-reciprocity goods | Revenue |
|---|---|---|---|
| 1857 | $ 9,667 | $29,765 | $3,596 |
| 1858 | 6,601 | 22,477 | 3,368 |
| 1859 | 8,530 | 25,025 | 4,456 |
| 1860 | 8,476 | 25,970 | 4,757 |
| 1861 | 11,297 | 31,670 | 4,775 |

SOURCE: Canada, *Trade and Navigation Reports,* cited in L.H. Officer and L.B. Smith, 'The Canadian-American Reciprocity Treaty of 1855 to 1866,' *Journal of Economic History* 28 (1968), 600; and 'Public Accounts of the Province of Canada for the Year 1857,' App. 4, *Appendix to the Journals of the Legislative Assembly,* 1858; App. 5, *Appendix,* 1859; Sessional Paper 1, *Sessional Papers,* 1860; Sessional Paper 3, *Sessional Papers,* 1861; Sessional Paper 4, *Sessional Papers,* 1862. All calculations are my own. Pound currency was converted into dollars in 1857 at the rate of four to one.

reciprocity goods imported from the United States increased by 160 per cent, while reciprocity goods imported from all other countries increased by 64.1 per cent. Non-reciprocity imports from the United States, commodities affected by Galt's tariff, increased only 6.7 per cent, while such imports from other countries increased by 75.1 per cent. Imports of all commodities entering Canada by sea via the St Lawrence system, meanwhile, increased by 67.6 per cent during these years, roughly the equivalent of the total increase in all imports.

Although protecting the traditional commercial interests of the St Lawrence system, the Galt tariff attempted to recognize the needs of domestic manufacturers as well. In January 1859 Galt had sent a circular letter asking for comments on his proposed tariff revisions. Nearly all the business organizations and private individuals who responded recognized and approved the protectionist elements in the new tariff proposals.[61]

Galt consulted and listened to protectionists and their arguments, yet his primary concerns remained the fiscal needs of the province. Already committed to £350,000 (stg) debenture issue in 1859 to cover past deficits and another £3 million issue in 1859 and 1860 to finance his conversion of outstanding 6 per cent debentures, Galt had to improve the fiscal position of the government. As he explained to Baring and Glyn in March 1859, he intended to avoid 'any resort to the money market for new funds, unless it be in payment of the advances made by your respective firms.' His 'whole policy,' was 'framed with a view to avoid any further demand on the London market.'[62]

Despite political difficulties in Upper Canada[63] and protests in Britain, by the end of the year Galt had reason to congratulate himself. Whatever protectionism might have been built into the tariff, it certainly was not preventing imports. A rapid recovery in trade, in both imports and exports, combined with the higher duties ensured that revenue from customs duties rose from $3.4 to $4.5 million between 1858 and 1859. As Cayley observed in October 1859, 'The Revenue is running up I am glad to see ... Times are mending with us but getting in old arrears is always a slow process.'[64]

An indication of Galt's original intentions can be gleaned from his subsequent budgets. By the end of 1861 the fiscal pressure on the province had eased. Although budgetary deficits remained, the economy had improved and the conversion of outstanding 6 per cent debentures, including the Municipal Loan Fund, had been carried through successfully. In the circumstances Galt proposed to rework Canada's tariff structure. He proposed raising $1.5 million in additional revenues with higher specific duties on tea, sugar, molasses, and coffee.[65] This would allow him to lower the general rates. To George Carr Glyn he commented, 'I will not conceal from you that adopting this course I feel that I shall encounter the most serious opposition as being somewhat in advance of the intelligence of the country, but now that the American Tariff has afforded me the means of doing so, I can no longer [consent] to be the apparent advocate of a system to which my own judgment is wholly opposed.'[66] To Thomas Baring he added: 'The measures proposed by the Government will I trust give satisfaction in England, and remove the complaint made against our Tariff as Protective.'[67] The ministry, however, fell before the legislature could implement Galt's proposed tariff changes. His successors believed that the fiscal needs of the government would not allow tariff reductions.

Galt is best known for his 1859 tariff reforms, which provoked a contemporary and subsequent historical debate about its protectionist elements. Ministers of finance design policies to solve problems: Galt faced a fiscal crisis, not a trade crisis. He provided the best assessment of his tariff: his was a revenue tariff that provided some incidental protection.[68] Therein lies its significance; what made Galt unique was his consideration of both the trade and revenue implications of his tariff proposals. He designed a revenue tariff that provided as much protection as possible consistent with the fiscal needs of the government.[69]

The Province of Canada had come a long way since that February day in 1840 when the blare of cannon announced the union of Upper and Lower Canada to the colony's unenthusiastic citizens. This had been a shotgun wedding forced on a defeated Lower Canada and a financially strapped Upper Canada. Among other things the Union represented an administrative response to Upper Canada's financial difficulties. Sydenham introduced administrative structures essential to the establishment of modern cabinet government. These new administrative structures ensured that greater political control could be exerted over the day-to-day business of government finance. This in turn made it inevitable that the provincial administration would exert greater control over policy formation. The process culminated, following a new economic crisis in 1847–8, in a reassessment of all programs and policies by the Reform inspector general, Francis Hincks.

Hincks' programs remained consistent with established policy objectives and orientations. Rather than new directions, Hincks provided a more integrated economic strategy accompanied by a range of specific tactical initiatives. These strategies, however, remained relatively crude and unsophisticated. A new financial crisis in the wake of the depression of 1857 forced another re-evaluation of policies and programs.

As in 1848–9 there would be few startling new initiatives. Rather there would be modifications more consistent with existing financial and fiscal limits. Precisely because financial options were more limited, there would have to be better administrative control as well as a more effective employment of a wider range of economic levers available to the government. Alexander Tilloch Galt and his Liberal-Conservative colleagues would also develop a better understanding of the interrelationship among fiscal, economic, and commercial policies. Financial difficulties continued to plague the province, but after 1862 the government addressed these questions with a more sophisticated appreciation of the complexities of financial management and more effective administrative structures that allowed them to exert more control over their own destinies.

## NOTES

1 Series A2/14, Population of Canada, in M.C. Urquhart and K.A.H. Buckley, eds, *Historical Statistics of Canada*, 2nd ed. (Ottawa: Statistics Canada 1983)

2 Canada, *Trade and Navigation Reports*, cited in L.H. Officer and L.B. Smith, 'The Canadian-American Reciprocity Treaty of 1855 to 1866,' *Journal of Economic History* 28 (1968), 600

3 These issues are pursued in Michael J. Piva, 'Financial Crisis, the Union of the Canadas, and Canadian Autonomy, 1837–1845,' Symposium in Canadian Economic History, University of Ottawa, Ottawa, Ontario, 14 Nov. 1986, and Piva, 'Financing the Union: The Upper Canadian Debt and Financial Administration in the Canadas, 1837–1845,' *Journal of Canadian Studies* 25 (1990–1), 82–98.

4 'Memorandum,' cited in Paul Knaplund, ed., *Letters from Lord Sydenham, Governor-General of Canada, 1839–1841, to Lord John Russell* (Cliffton, NJ: A.M. Kelley 1973), 25n6

5 National Archives of Canada (NA), Governor-General's Office (GGO), RG7, G12, vol. 57, 289–94, cited in J.E. Hodgetts, *Pioneer Public Service: An Administrative History of the United Canadas, 1841–1867* (Toronto: University of Toronto Press 1955), 27

6 The real difference between this and 'cabinet government' as usually understood concerned lines of responsibility. Because Sydenham insisted that each minister was responsible to the governor, his council lacked a sense of collective responsibility. It did, however, create the essential preconditions for responsible government. 'Administrative reforms meant to head it [responsible government] off,' as J.M.S. Careless observes, 'all unintentionally, helped instead to bring it on within the decade.' J.M.S. Careless, 'The Place, the Office, the Times, and the Men,' in J.M.S. Careless, ed., *The Pre-Confederation Premiers: Ontario Government Leaders, 1841–1867* (Toronto: University of Toronto Press 1980), 7

7 See Charles Sanderson, ed., *The Arthur Papers* 3 vols (Toronto: Toronto Public Libraries and University of Toronto Press 1959), 'Private,' Lord Sydenham to Sir George Arthur, 1 Nov. 1840, 3:167–8. Also see *Arthur Papers*, 'Private and Confidential,' Arthur to Sydenham, 7 Nov. 1840, 3:172–4.

8 NA, Executive Council Office (ECO), State Book 1, vol. 71, Inspector General [F. Hincks], 'Memorandum on Immigration and on Public Works as connected therewith,' 20 Dec. 1848, 400–19 (hereinafter cited as 'Memorandum on Immigration').

9 Ibid., 418–19

10 'An Act to Establish a Consolidated Municipal Loan Fund for Upper Canada,' 16 Vic., cap. 22, *Provincial Statutes of Canada* 1852–3. See Albert Faucher, 'Le fonde d'emprunt municipal dans le Haut-Canada,

1852–1867,' in his *Histoire économique et unité canadienne* (Montreal: Fides 1970), 83–106, and Michael J. Piva, 'Continuity and Crisis: Francis Hincks and Canadian Economic Policy,' *Canadian Historical Review* 66 (1985), 198–200.

11 NA, Department of Finance, RG19, B2(b), vol. 1161, E.-P. Taché, Receiver General, to Baring Brothers and Company and Glyn, Hallifax, Mills and Company, 14 Jan. 1853

12 'An Act for Affording the Guarantee of the Province to the Bonds of Rail-way Companies on Certain Conditions, and for Rendering Assistance in the Construction of the Halifax and Quebec Railway,' 12 Vic., cap. 29, *Provincial Statutes of Canada*, 1849

13 NA, Glyn Mills Papers, MG24, D36 (A/540), Baring and Glyn to Francis Hincks, Inspector General, 10 Jan. 1851

14 Ibid., Baring and Glyn to Hincks, 10 Jan. 1851, and Glyn and Baring to Hincks, 23 May 1851

15 'An Act to Make Provision for the Construction of a Main Trunk Line of Railway throughout the Whole Length of This Province,' 14–15 Vic., cap. 73, *Provincial Statutes of Canada*, 1851

16 See NA, Finance, RG19, vol. 1162 [C.E. Anderson, deputy receiver general], 'Memorandum of Provincial Guarantee to Various Railway Companies – Sterling,' 25 July 1955.

17 Select Standing Committee on Public Accounts, 'Minutes and Proceedings of the Committee,' 18 May 1858 and 28 May 1858, App. 4, *Appendix to the Journals of the Legislative Assembly of the United Province of Canada* (hereafter *Appendix to the Journals of the Legislative Assembly*), 1858. The appointment of John Langton as auditor general led to the discovery of this practice, and eventually Ryerson refunded nearly £1,400 to the province.

18 The Public Accounts for 1857 included summary tables covering the years 1842 to 1857. Although these tables do not always agree with figures published yearly in the Public Accounts, the differences are small and result from improved accounting practices. The 1857 summary tables are also preferred because individual items and headings changed a number of times during these years. Comparison over time is thus extremely difficult using the yearly public accounts.

19 Piva, 'Continuity and Crisis,' 196–7

20 See Michael J. Piva, 'The Canadian Public Debt, 1848–1856,' Annual Meeting of the Canadian Historical Association, Montreal, Quebec, June 1980. On 1 Apr. 1854, £200,000 (stg) worth of provincial debentures were due to mature, and as the date drew near E.-P. Taché ordered Baring and Glyn to purchase £260,000 (stg) worth of Consols 'on the best terms that can be procured.' According to the Receiver General, 'the intention of said investment was in the first instance for the

purpose of reselling in the month of April next and redeeming the proceeds of some £20,000 of 5 pCt [sic] Provincial Bonds due in London.' NA, Finance, RG19, vol. 1161, Taché to Baring, 8 Oct. 1853, and Taché, 'Memo,' 16 Mar. 1854. No sooner did the province complete its purchases of Consols than the price fell. Rather than take a loss on its Consols, Canada negotiated short-term loans from Baring and Glyn to cover debenture redemptions of £200,000 (stg) in 1854 and another £400,000 (stg) in 1855. Eventually the government sold most of its Consols at a considerable loss. In addition to this loss the government had to pay 2.5 per cent interest on the 1854 and 1855 short-term loans as well as the usual commission and brokerage fees on all these transactions. See NA, Finance, RG19, vol. 1161, Taché to Baring, 23 Jan. 1855, and ibid., vol. 1162, Taché to Glyn, 28 Apr. 1855, Taché to Glyn, 11 June 1855, Anderson to Glyn, 30 July 1855, Anderson to Baring, 30 July 1855, Taché, 'Memorandum,' 27 Dec. 1855, Taché to Glyn, 31 Dec. 1855, Taché to Baring, 31 Dec. 1855, Taché to C.E. Trevelyan, Secretary, HM Treasurer, 31 Dec. 1855, Taché to Matthew Marshall, Chief Cashier, Bank of England, 31 Dec. 1855, Taché to Glyn, 28 Jan. 1856, Taché to Baring, 18 Feb. 1856, and Taché to Glyn, 18 Feb. 1856.

21 See NA, Finance, RG19, vol. 1162, Taché to George-Etienne Cartier, Provincial Secretary, 20 Feb. 1856, and Anderson, 'Statement showing the Obligation or Debt to the Government of the Ontario, Simcoe, and Huron Railroad Company in detail, also the payments they have made etc, etc, being the Return asked for by The Hon. The Provincial Secretary in his letter of 8th May for the Information of the Legislative Assembly,' 12 May 1856, J.C. Morrison, Receiver General, to Glyn, 14 July 1856, Morrison to Baring, 14 July 1856, Morrison to Glyn, 22 Sept. 1856, Anderson to Jno M. Grant, Secretary, Grand Trunk Railway, 22 Sept. 1856, and CEA [Anderson], 'Memorandum of Advances to Grand Trunk Railway Co. since 1st April 1856,' 23 Oct. 1856, Morrison to T.L. Terrill, Provincial Secretary, 28 Feb. 1857, Anderson to Brydges, 10 Mar. 1857, and Anderson to C.J. Brydges, 22 May 1857.

22 NA, Finance, RG19, vol. 1162, Taché, 'Memorandum,' 22 Nov. 1855. Also see ibid., Taché to J.A. Macdonald, 16 Nov. 1855.

23 NA, Baring Papers, MG24, D21, vol. 3, T.C. Baring to Thomas Baring, 16 Apr. 1859, 1204–1207

24 'Second Report of Standing Committee on Public Accounts,' *Journals of the Legislative Assembly of the United Province of Canada*, 1854–5. Also see J.E. Hodgetts, *Pioneer Public Service*, 99–108.

25 John Langton to William Langton, Toronto, 17 Apr. 1856, in W.A. Langton, ed., *Early Days in Upper Canada, Letters of John Langton* (To-

ronto 1926), 242–57, cited in Peter Baskerville, *The Bank of Upper Canada: A Collection of Documents* (Toronto: Champlain Society 1987), 196

26 John Langton, Auditor General, 'Public Accounts of the Province of Canada for the Year 1858,' App. 5, *Appendix to the Journals of the Legislative Assembly* 1859

27 'Public Accounts of the Province of Canada for the Year 1857,' App. 4, *Appendix to the Journals of the Legislative Assembly*, 1858

28 Board of Audit Report, 'Public Accounts of the Province of Canada for the Year 1857,' App. 4, *Appendix to the Journals of the Legislative Assembly*, 1858. An exception was made in the case of the monthly pay lists.

29 'An Act to Amend the Law Respecting the Public Accounts, and the Board of Audit,' 27–28 Vic., cap. 5, *Provincial Statutes of Canada*, 1864

30 See Adam Shortt, 'History of Canadian Metallic Currency,' in E.P. Neufeld, ed., *Money and Banking in Canada* (Toronto: McClelland and Stewart 1964), 116–31. Also see Angela Redish, 'Why Was Specie Scarce in Colonial Economies? An Analysis of the Canadian Currency, 1796–1830,' *Journal of Economic History* 64 (1984), 713–28.

31 A.B. McCullough provides the best general account of exchange rates in the nineteenth century. See A.B. McCullough, *Money and Exchange in Canada to 1900* (Toronto: Dundurn 1984).

32 See NA, Finance, RG19, F1(a), vol. 3366, Thomas Parke, Collector (Welland Canal, Port Colburne), to William Cayley, Inspector General, 4 Aug. 1856, and Thomas G. Ridout, Bank of Upper Canada, to Anderson, 8 Aug. 1856. The Bank of Stanstead had recently opened, but Ridout reported that its notes were circulating without the signature of any officer at the inspector general's office. The bank would accept the gold coins at a 2 per cent discount.

33 See NA, Finance, RG19, vol. 1163, T.D. Harington, Deputy Receiver General to the Cashier, Banque du Peuple, 27 Dec. 1858. Similar letters were sent to eleven other banks. Also see Harington to Thomas Graham, Royal Mint, 4 Apr. 1859.

34 NA, Alexander Tilloch Galt Papers, MG27, 1 D8, vol. 1, 'Private,' A.T. Galt to Thomas Baring, 16 Aug. 1858

35 See NA, Finance, RG19, vol. 3376, Galt to Glyn, 10 Jan. 1859, Galt to Baring, 10 Jan. 1859, Galt to Baring and Glyn, 7 Feb. 1859, Galt to Glyn, 14 Feb. 1859, Galt to Baring, 14 Feb. 1859, and Galt to Baring and Glyn, 14 July 1859. Baskerville points out that the Bank of Upper Canada was in severe financial difficulties, and Galt wanted to avoid a forced sale of these bonds on the London market.

36 NA, Finance, RG19, vol. 3376, Galt to Baring and Glyn, 14 July 1859. Also see Baskerville, *Bank of Upper Canada*, cxxxii.

37 NA, Finance, RG19, vol. 1164, George Reiffenstein, Clerk, Receiver General's Office, to [Dickenson], 8 Jan. 1861

38 See NA, Finance, RG19, vol. 1164, Harington to J.D. Nutter, Agent, Provincial Bank of Canada, Montreal, 25 Jan. 1861, and Harington to U.I. Tessier, President, La Banque Nationale, 9 June 1861. The government extended its offer into 1862. See NA, ECO, RG1, E1, State Book X, vol. 86, 'Minutes,' 3 Feb. 1862, 38.

39 NA, ECO, RG1, E1, State Book V, vol. 84, 'Minutes,' 16 May 1860, 146–7

40 NA, Finance, RG19, vol. 1164, George Sherwood, Receiver General, to Baring, 5 May 1860, Sherwood to Glyn, 5 May 1860, Sherwood to Baring, 22 June 1860, and Sherwood to Glyn, 22 June 1860

41 See ibid., Harington to Glyn, 14 Sept. 1860.

42 In October 1860 the government ordered another £2.2 million worth of bonds printed. NA, Finance, RG19, vol. 1164, Harington to George Mathews, Engraver, Mtl, 15 Oct. 1860. Also see vol. 1165, Harington to Glyn, 9 Aug. 1861, Harington to Baring, 9 Aug. 1861, Harington to Glyn, 1 Nov. 1861, Harington to Baring, 1 Nov. 1861, Harington to Glyn, 8 Nov. 1861, Harington to Baring, 8 Nov. 1861, Harington to Glyn, 22 Nov. 1861, Harington to Baring, 22 Nov. 1861, Harington to Glyn, 27 Dec. 1861, and Harington to Baring, 27 Dec. 1861.

43 NA, Galt Papers, MG27, 1 D8, vol. 2, Galt to [S.] Smith, Friday Night [Jan. 1860]

44 See 'Public Accounts of the Province of Canada, 1859,' Sessional Paper 1, *Sessional Papers*, 1860; 'Public Accounts of the Province of Canada, 1860,' Sessional Paper 3, *Sessional Papers*, 1861; and 'Public Accounts of the Province of Canada, 1861,' Sessional Paper 4, *Sessional Papers*, 1862. All calculations are my own.

45 As a result of this the bank was able to reduce its debt to Glyn by $890,000. See Baskerville, *Bank of Upper Canada*, cxliii.

46 The best analysis of the convoluted dealings among the Bank of Upper Canada, the government, the railway, and Baring and Glyn can be found in Baskerville, *Bank of Upper Canada*, particularly cxxxii–cxliii.

47 See A.W. Currie, *The Grand Trunk Railway of Canada* (Toronto: University of Toronto Press 1957), 54–6.

48 Under the terms of the original Guarantee Act confirmed in the Main Trunk Line of Railway Act the provincial government held the first mortgage and a lien on the Grand Trunk. The Grand Trunk Relief Act of 1856 authorized the issue of £2 million (stg) 'preferential' stock, which provided the first claim on the railway ahead of the provincial lien. Specific sections of the line would receive specific amounts of the preferential bonds and had to be completed at specific dates. See 'An Act to Grant Additional Aid to the Grand Trunk Railway Company of Canada,' 19–20 Vic., cap. 111, *Provincial Statutes of Canada*, 1856. After first rejecting the proposals from the Grand Trunk for the release of £100,000 (stg) to repay bank loans as inconsistent with the requirements of the act, the cabinet reconsidered the matter and authorized

the sales on 12 Apr. 1858. See NA, ECO, RG1, E1, State Book S, vol. 81,
Minutes, 3 Apr. 1858, and 12 Apr. 1858, 466–7, 504–7. Also see NA,
Finance, RG19, vol. 1163, Anderson to Glyn, 19 Apr. 1858. Earlier, a
new act allowed the company to draw the proceeds of the preferential
bonds for any purpose so long as amounts specified for particular sections were completed on time, although the deadline for completion
was extended by one year. 'An Act to Dispense with Government Directors in the Grand Trunk Railway Company of Canada, and to Facilitate the Completion of the Company's Works from Riviere du Loup
to Sarnia,' 20 Vic., cap. 11, *Provincial Statutes of Canada, 1857*. In July
1858 new legislation allowed the railway, by a two-thirds vote of shareholders, to raise new capital by preferential bonds without restriction.
See 'An Act to Amend the Acts Relating to the Grand Trunk Railway
Company of Canada,' 22 Vic., cap. 52, *Provincial Statutes of Canada*,
1858.
49 NA, Glyn Mills Papers, MG24, D36 (A-540), George Carr Glyn to Galt,
23 Nov. 1857. The release of the preferential bonds had originally
been authorized in early October 1857. See NA, Finance, RG19, B2(b),
Morrison, to Sir C.P. Roney, Secretary, Grand Trunk Railway, 7 Oct.
1857.
50 'An Act to Dispense with Government Directors in the Grand Trunk
Railway Company of Canada, and to Facilitate the Completion of the
Company's Works from Riviere du Loup to Sarnia,' 20 Vic., cap. 11,
*Provincial Statutes of Canada*, 1857. Individual members of the government, such as John Ross, remained closely connected to the Grand
Trunk. Peter Baskerville suggests that the unpopularity of the Grand
Trunk forced the government to find other ways of aiding the ailing
line. Politically it was easier to aid the Bank of Upper Canada and
through the bank indirectly aid the Grand Trunk. 'The government
and the London agents,' Baskerville argues, 'came to the bank's aid for
one primary reason: in prolonging the bank's existence they saw a last
opportunity to save the Grand Trunk and protect their immense investments.' Baskerville, *Bank of Upper Canada*, cxxxviii
51 NA, Galt Papers, MG27, 1 D8, vol. 1, 'Private,' Jno Ross to [Galt], 19
Aug. 1859; 'Confidential' George Carr Glyn to Galt, 23 Aug. 1859;
Thomas Baring to Galt, 23 Aug. 1859; 'Private and Confidential,' Ross
to Galt, 23 Aug. 1859; 'Private,' Ross to Galt, 25 Aug. 1859; 'Private,'
Galt to Ross, 9 Sept. 1859; 'Private,' Ross to Galt, 13 Sept. 1859;
George Carr Glyn to Galt, 20 Sept. 1859; 'Private,' Ross to Galt, 24
Sept. 1859; 'Private,' Ross to Galt, 27 Sept. 1859; Baring to Galt, 30
Sept. 1859; 'Private,' Galt to Ross, 3 Oct. 1859; vol. 10, 'Confidential,'
Galt to George Carr Glyn, 9 Sept. 1859; 'Confidential,' Galt to
Thomas Baring, 9 Sept. 1859; 'Confidential,' Galt to George Carr

Glyn, 3 Oct. 1859; and 'Confidential,' Galt to Thomas Baring, 10 Oct. 1859

52 NA, Galt Papers, MG27, 1 D8, vol. 10, 'Private,' Galt to George Carr Glyn, 1 Mar. 1860; and 'Private,' Galt to Thomas Baring, 1 Mar. 1860

53 The Cayley and Galt tariffs have been the subject of an extensive historical literature. Until recently, most but not all historians emphasized the revenue aspects of the tariff, including Oscar Douglas Skelton, *The Life and Times of Alexander Tilloch Galt*, ed. and intro. Guy MacLean (Toronto: McClelland and Stewart 1966), W.T. Easterbrook and H.G.H. Aitken, *Canadian Economic History* (Toronto: Macmillan of Canada 1956), and Gordon Blake, *Customs Administration in Canada: An Essay in Tariff Technology* (Toronto: University of Toronto Press 1957). More recently both Tom Naylor, *The History of Canadian Business, 1867–1914*, 2 vols, vol. 1, *The Banks and Finance Capital* (Toronto: Lorimer 1975) and William L. Marr and Donald G. Paterson, *Canada: An Economic History* (Toronto: Macmillan of Canada 1980) argue that the tariff was for revenue. Traditional arguments that the tariff was protectionist include Edward Porritt, *Sixty Years of Protection in Canada, 1846–1907: Where Industry Leans on the Politician* (London: Macmillan 1908). Recent literature has renewed the debate and insists that the Galt tariff provided effective protection for manufacturers. See in particular D.F. Barnett, 'The Galt Tariff: Incidental or Effective Protection?' *Canadian Journal of Economics* 9 (1976), 389–407, Gregory S. Kealey, *Toronto Workers Respond to Industrial Capitalism, 1867–1887* (Toronto: University of Toronto Press 1980), and A.A. Den Otter, 'Alexander Galt, the 1859 Tariff, and Canadian Economic Nationalism,' *Canadian Historical Review* 63 (1982), 151–78. Ben Forster provides the best recent assessment of the tariff in *A Conjunction of Interests: Business, Politics, and Tariffs, 1825–1879* (Toronto: University of Toronto Press 1986). Forster is concerned in the main with the rise of protectionism in Canada but recognizes the divisions within the business community. He argues that the Cayley and Galt tariffs were designed primarily as revenue tariffs to solve the pressing financial difficulties facing the government. Galt, however, tried to balance conflicting protectionist interests, giving as much protection as possible consistent with the revenue needs of the government. This paper supports the Forster interpretation.

54 NA, Finance, RG19, E1(a), vol. 3367, petition from 'The Manufacturers and Mechanics of Montreal' [1857]

55 NA, Galt Papers, MG27, 1 D8, vol. 1, 'Private,' Galt to Thomas Baring, 16 Aug. 1858

56 NA, Finance, RG19, E1(a), vol. 3368, 'Political Economy,' [Jan. 1859]. This note, although undated and unsigned, appears to be in Galt's

hand and clearly articulates most protectionist arguments. Forster attributes this note to Galt. Forster, *Conjunction of Interests*, 44n52

57 NA, Finance, RG19, E1(a), vol. 3368, R. Spence to Inspector General, Saturday [Jan. 1859]

58 Ibid., John G. Dinning, Secretary, Montreal Board of Trade, to Galt, 19 Jan. 1859. Also see G.B. Forsyth, Chairman, Quebec Board of Trade, to Galt, 31 Jan. 1859, Charles Robertson, Secretary, Toronto Board of Trade, to Galt, 3 Feb. 1859, and Jasper Silkison to Galt, 21 Mar. 1859. Also see Forster, *Conjunction of Interests*, particularly 43–4, 47–8.

59 NA, Glyn Mills Papers, MG24, D36 (A-540), 'Private,' George Carr Glyn to Galt, 15 Apr. 1859

60 The following information is drawn from 'Tables of the Trade and Navigation of the Province of Canada for the Year 1858,' App. 6, *Appendix to the Journals of the Legislative Assembly*, 1859, 'Tables of the Trade and Navigation of the Province of Canada for the Year 1860,' Sessional Paper 2, *Sessional Papers*, 1861, 'Tables of the Trade and Navigation of the Province of Canada for the Year 1862,' Sessional Paper 2, *Sessional Papers*, 1863. All calculations are my own.

61 See NA, Finance, RG19, E1(a), vol. 3368, Dinning to Galt, 19 Jan. 1859, James Shannon, Secretary, Kingston Board of Trade, to Galt, 27 Jan. 1859, and Forsyth to Galt, 31 Jan. 1859. Not everyone believed, however, that Galt's tariff would provide real protection. All protectionists agreed that the 'lowest possible rate' should be charged on raw materials in order to 'encourage the industry of the Province.' Galt, however, was raising the duty on many imported raw materials and processed products from 2.5 and 5 per cent to 10 per cent. The increased cost of such imports would negate any additional protection that might have been gained by tariff increases on finished products. The Kingston Board of Trade wanted all items on the 5 and 10 per cent list gradually reduced until all were on the free list by 1862. See NA, Finance, RG19, E1(a), vol. 3368, 'Memorial of the Undersigned Merchants and Manufacturers of the City of Montreal,' Frothingham and Workman, et al., to Galt, 11 Mar. 1859 (forty-one signatures appeared on this Memorial), William Rodden to John Rose, 7 Feb. 1859, George Peck to Galt, 7 Mar. 1859, W.S. Macdonald to Galt, 17 Mar. 1859, and Edward Berry, President, Kingston Board of Trade, to Galt, 15 Mar. 1859. As Forster points out, many protectionist manufacturers protested against Galt's tariff as finally implemented. Indeed, Isaac Buchanan led the opposition attack in the legislature. See Forster, *Conjunction of Interests*, 46–8.

62 NA, Finance, RG19, vol. 3376, Galt to Baring and Glyn, 7 Mar. 1859

63 T.C. Baring reported to Thomas Baring that Galt's tariff had been received so badly in Upper Canada that there was talk of a 'political cri-

sis and change of Ministry.' See NA, Baring Papers, MG24, D21, vol. 3,
T.C. Baring to Thomas Baring, 17 Mar. 1859.

64 NA, Finance, RG19, F1(a), vol. 3369, Cayley to Galt, 20 Oct. 1859

65 NA, Galt Papers, MG27, 1 D8, vol. 10, 'Private,' Galt to George Carr
Glyn, 7 Feb. 1862. Galt believed that recent increases in the American
tariffs on these items allowed him to raise the Canadian rate without
tempting smugglers. He went on to comment that 'I do not intend to
increase the rates on goods, in the first place, because I consider them
high enough for revenue, and secondly because my doing so would
cause unpleasant feeling in England when we desire to avoid any cause
of offense.'

66 Ibid., 'Private,' Galt to George Carr Glyn, 19 May 1862

67 NA, Baring Papers, MG24, D21, vol. 3, Galt to Thomas Baring, 19 May
1862, 1549–52

68 In his original budget speech outlining his tariff proposals Galt listed
three objectives: revenue, to create a system favourable to the St Lawrence route, and to provide incidental protection to manufacturers.
See *Globe* (Toronto), 12 and 14 Mar. 1859. Throughout the controversies that raged over his tariff proposals he never deviated from this explanation of his purposes. To manufacturers upset that the tariff
provided too little protection Galt proved, in the words of the Hamilton *Spectator*, 'obdurate.' He repeated that 'revenue must be had' and
duties would be set accordingly. See *Spectator* (Hamilton) 12 Mar. 1859.
He repeated these same arguments to the British government when
they forwarded complaints that the tariff provided too much protection.

69 Forster portrays Galt in more Machiavellian terms. Various business
groups were divided both within the manufacturing community and
between manufacturing and commercial interests. As a member of a
relatively weak government Galt attempted, according to Forster, to
'divide and conquer' with his tariff. Forster, *Conjunction of Interests*, 49

# 10

# Ideology, Society, and State in the Maritime Colonies of British North America, 1840–1860

## GRAEME WYNN

By North American standards, the three colonies that came to be called the Canadian Maritime provinces are – and were – small. New Brunswick, approximately 73,000 square kilometres in area, is less extensive than Maine and South Carolina; Nova Scotia (55,000 square kilometres) does not match West Virginia in area and is barely double the size of Maryland; among all the states and provinces of North America, only Rhode Island is smaller than Prince Edward Island, which at less than 6,000 square kilometres is approximately the area of Delaware. Together, the three colonies are substantially smaller than the New England states, and in the mid-nineteenth century the area of the united Canadas was more than six times theirs. So, too, in population. In 1851, the three Maritime colonies had 534,000 inhabitants (Nova Scotia 276,000; New Brunswick 194,000; Prince Edward Island 64,000), little more than half the total in Canada West, and some 50,000 fewer than in the neighbouring state of Maine. Ten years later, when the six states of New England had more than 3 million inhabitants, the population of the Maritimes was 682,000; Montreal, a city of 100,000, had 20,000 more residents than Prince Edward Island.[1]

Perceived from afar as a unit – in the early nineteenth century they were often described collectively as the Lower Provinces, and participants in the Confederation debates of the 1860s sometimes referred to them as the Maritime Provinces – these colonies were deeply divided in politics, economy, ethnicity, and religion. Separate jurisdictions, in 1840 and 1860, each had its own lieutenant-governor, council, and assembly. Commercially, they generally looked east and south, with strong links to Britain, the British West Indies, and the northern States. But within this matrix, economies cross-cut political boundaries. Most of New Brunswick's people lived in the St John–Fundy catchment and looked to Saint John as their commercial capital (as indeed did many settlements on the Nova Scotian side of the Bay of Fundy); on the northern (gulf) shore of New Brunswick, and in Prince Edward Island, however, Halifax held greater commercial sway than Saint John. Across the colonies, fishing, shipbuilding, lumbering, and farming underpinned local life, but the first three were, largely, separate spheres that gave markedly different casts to landscapes, economies, and societies in those areas in which they dominated. Further, although perhaps eight of every nine inhabitants of the Maritimes in 1860 were native-born, most identified strongly with the ethnic, religious, and other traditions of their forbears, who in the process of settlement had made the colonies a patchwork quilt of different 'allegiances' – Acadian, Loyalist, pre-Loyalist, Palatinate, Yankee, Scots, Irish, English – fragmented by adherence to one or another of a dozen different religions.[2]

Reflecting these patterns, diversity, complexity, fragmentation, and heterogeneity have become the *leitmotivs* of scholarly reflection upon the region. For all its modest size, it is commonly portrayed as a place without a 'unifying configuration of physical features,' a world of 'islands, peninsulas, and river valleys' marked by particularism, small-scale competition, and cross-purposes. Within provincial bounds 'local interests were thoroughly schooled to grudge ambitions to others'; considered as a whole, and compared to territories of similar or greater size elsewhere, this region appears 'unusually divided against itself.' Even the surrounding sea – which some have seen as a unifying influence, if only by implying that Maritimers are people who 'smell of salt to the Prairie' – 'provides a matrix rather than a focus.'[3]

Faced with this mountain of regional complexity, it is surely wiser to contemplate it at some remove – to describe its peaks and vales, corries and couloirs as they diversify and give shape to its formidable bulk – than to attempt an assay of its every grain and crystal. From the vantage of distance, light and shadow, pattern and form can be picked out and interpreted against the backdrop of the whole; with skill and appropriate emphases, diversity and dissimilarity can be rendered intelligible, labyrinthine reality can be ordered and understood. By contrast, the assay-master stands to be overwhelmed by the sheer magnitude of his task. Yet in the end we cannot rest content – with

Charles G.D. Roberts, looking again over the marshes of Tantramar – to 'Muse and recall far off.' The poet, fostering memories and the comforting vision of an unchanging landscape, might well stay his steps, 'lest on too close sight' he 'Spy at their task ... the hands of chance and change.' But if we would truly grapple with the multi-faceted complexity of the Maritimes, we cannot afford 'not [to] go down to the marshland,' across the hillsides, along the roads, through the towns, and into the villages of the region, to observe the actions, chart the ideas, and explore something of the everyday lives of its people, and to assess the imprint of those ever-busy hands of chance and change upon its fabric.[4]

The pages that follow are intended to carry us on just such a journey. Comprising a series of discrete vignettes, drawn from many corners of the three provinces, they provide a varied parade of scenes from the rich tapestry of two decades of regional life.[5] Adits driven into the mountain of regional complexity, they seek to reveal more of the area's nooks, crannies, strata, and structure than it is possible to espy from the vantage of distance without burying comprehension beneath the endless detail of the everyday. Like most travel itineraries, these vignettes offer only glimpses of a wider picture, and they share – with the encounters and experiences of almost any adventurous exploration of new territory – a random or markedly kaleidoscopic quality that belies their interconnected, reflexive character.[6] Just as the cumulative impressions of alert travel provide the basis for height-ened understanding of the country through which one has passed, however, these vignettes offer evidence for reflection upon the par-ticular conjuncture of ideology, society, and state in the mid-nine-teenth-century Maritime colonies. The final third of the paper is given to focusing these reflections, to teasing order and interpretation from the hues, shapes, interpenetration, and arrangement of the several kaleidoscopic fragments of the preceding pages.

## Glimpses of a Troubled City

Encompassing three parishes in the mid-1850s, the city of Saint John was a bustling commercial and manufacturing centre with more than 30,000 residents.[7] The major city of its province, the hub of the Bay of Fundy, and the leading centre of the timber trade in southern New Brunswick, it was a place of compact neighbourhoods, many of them densely built up with three-storey tenements and two-storey duplexes on the narrow lots that were characteristic of the settlement. The fact that approximately three-quarters of Saint John's 4,200 family heads had been born in the British Isles reflected the rapid growth of the city in the nineteenth century and its position at the western end of an active transatlantic trading system. Native New Brunswickers, descendants of the city's Loyalist founders or migrants from the colonial countryside, made up most of the remaining population. Almost two-thirds of the inhabitants of this urban area lived in the peninsular parish of St John; slightly more than 10,000 people occupied the neighbouring parishes of Carleton (across the harbour) and Portland (north and west of St John parish). On the peninsula that formed the heart of the urban area almost three of every five households were headed by men (or women) of Irish birth, and well over a third of all residents in Saint John and Portland had been born in the Emerald Isle. A clear majority of these had lived in the city for a decade or more. Participants in the steady exodus from Ireland that brought tens of thousands of Irish men, women, and children to British North America before 1840, they were mainly artisans and tenant farmers from the northern counties, strongly Protestant in religion and generally sympathetic to the British monarchy. By 1850, a substantial number of them were employed in white-collar, artisanal, and semi-skilled jobs. If relatively few lived in the city's better neighbourhoods – near the business district and on the Courtenay Bay side of the peninsula – they were otherwise widely scattered through the town. In contrast, the significant minority of Saint John's Irish households headed by Catholics included a disproportionate number of unskilled workers. Recent arrivals, refugees from the Irish famines of the 1840s, they were crowded into substandard housing in two small areas of the city: York Point in the northwestern corner of the peninsula, and the wharf area of Portland, which lay in the shadow of Fort Howe, directly across the Mill Pond (and Portland Bridge) from York Point.

The decade that produced this distinctive, divided ethnic geography was a tumultuous one for the residents of Saint John. A quickening tide of immigration turned into a flood between 1845 and 1849 when more than 30,000 newcomers, almost all of them Irish, disembarked in the port. Heavily tied to the timber trade, the economy of the city was buffeted during the 1840s by recurrent crises of confidence, price instability, and fluctuating demand precipitated by the British government's decision to dismantle the system of preferential tariffs under which the colonial timber trade had grown up. Prophecies of economic collapse were common. With the abolition of old imperial trading policies culminating in the repeal of the Navigation

Acts in 1849, barriers to trade with the United States fell; artisans and farmers who produced for local markets saw their livelihoods jeopardized. Between 1840 and 1842, the number of tailors in the city fell by 85 per cent, the number of shoemakers by almost the same proportion. In the middle of the decade the newly formed Provincial Association carried a monster petition (with 2,500 signatures) to the colonial legislature, requesting protection for the farmers, fishermen, and manufacturers of New Brunswick. Tariffs of 10 and 20 per cent were levied on a range of manufactured goods, but did little to stave off depression at the end of the decade; hundreds of artisans and labourers were reported to have left Saint John, some of them for the distant – and doubtful – prospects of California gold.

At the same time the city was deeply divided by a series of increasingly violent confrontations among its citizens.[8] In both 1841 and 1842, Irish Catholics clashed with members of the Orange lodges (which had begun to proliferate in city and colony) in the streets of Saint John. The first was a minor skirmish precipitated by the erection of a commemorative arch by the Orange Order; the second degenerated into a riot on 12 July, when several hundred Catholics gathered to jeer outside a house flying an orange-beribboned Union Jack. A year later, to the day, Catholics and Protestants clashed again, although there was no official parade to mark King William's victory at the Boyne. In 1844, Squire Manks, a prominent local Orangeman, shot and killed a Catholic Irishman in York Point, and nine months later the year ended with a week of disturbances in which Catholics and Orangemen picked fights with 'certain ... obnoxious individuals.' On the following St Patrick's Day, celebrating Catholics were fired upon by Orangemen, and general rioting ensued. Two years of 'calm' hardly broke the pattern. Through the 1840s, poverty and privation spurred robberies and assaults that the city's magistrates and watchmen were powerless to control. Then, on 12 July 1847, Orangemen followed a band playing sectarian songs into York Point. They were met with sticks and stones and driven back across the bridge to Portland. Adding firearms to their numerical reinforcements, they marched again into the Catholic ghetto. Shots broke out and the ensuing general mêlée ceased only with the calling out of the military at midnight. Through the weeks that followed, vengeance assaults and murders occurred in Saint John. In July 1848 the city was quiet as Orangemen celebrated the anniversary of their 1847 victory in Fredericton; but in 1849 violence erupted again, when Saint John Orangemen invited their provincial brethren to the city for a massive procession. Early on 12 July, heavily armed Orangemen from the parishes of Portland and St John gathered to meet Carleton lodge members disembarking from the harbour ferry. Together they marched through York Point to Indiantown where they would greet brethren from the St John Valley. Outnumbered by a jeering Catholic crowd, they suffered the humiliation of dipping their banners beneath a pine-bough arch at the foot of Mill Street. After the arrival of the valley men, however, they returned 600 strong to York Point despite the entreaties of city officials. Five hundred Catholics lay in wait. In a hail of bullets and bricks, possibly a dozen or more people were killed and hundreds wounded before the Orangemen emerged from York Point to continue their march through the city while troops, stationed in Market Square earlier in the day, moved in to seal off the Catholic ghetto and prevent further skirmishes.

Back of these confrontations lay a complex changing grid of sentiment, affiliation, and power in the rapidly expanding Irish population of Saint John. Earlier, secular organizations that sought to advance the interests of all those of Irish descent in the city (such as the St Patrick's Society established in 1819) were challenged by new, more aggressive, and increasingly partisan representatives of sectoral interests. Early in the 1840s the Saint John Sons of Erin supported Daniel O'Connell's vision of a Catholic Irish state, and there was an active Repeal Association in the city; a decade before, the Sons had celebrated St Patrick's Day before a 'harp surrounded by shamrocks and orange lilies entwined to form the motto United We Stand: Divided We Fall.'[9] At the same time, Saint John Catholicism became more self-conscious with the consecration of New Brunswick's first Catholic bishop and the growth of ultramontanism in the province. On the Protestant side, the Orange Order expanded in tandem. As late as 1840, prominent citizens filled leadership roles in both the Sons of Erin and the emerging Orange movement. Two years later, the so-called Protestant Conservative Association claimed to have enrolled 600 men at a single meeting. By 1846 the city had ten active Orange lodges, some with more than 100 members. For those who refused to join the secret, quasi-military Orange organization or to take a pew in St Malachi's Church, newspapers provided a ready source of partisan opinion. The *Mirror* favoured recourse to violence if that were necessary to repeal the Union of Great Britain and Ireland; The *Liberator* denounced those Catholics who questioned clerical authority; and the *Loyalist* defended and promoted the Orange cause with skill and vigour.

With lawlessness, violence, and confrontation seemingly endemic in the 1840s, the Common Council of Saint John sought ways to control the city. At the beginning of the decade an eleven- or twelve-man 'watch' was charged with keeping the city's night-time peace. There was no equivalent in Portland. Employed by the Common Council, but underpaid, understaffed, and overwhelmingly Irish Protestant, the Saint John watch was described by the Grand Jury as 'lamentably inefficient either for the preservation of good order or the prevention of crime.'[10] Nor, some claimed, were the elected aldermen who served as magistrates for their wards, and their constables, much more effective in policing the city and apprehending criminals. Lamenting the dangers of being abroad at night, the editor of a leading city newspaper suggested that citizens follow the lead of New Orleans' residents, and carry weapons if they ventured out in the dark.[11] By the end of 1841, 400 or so of the city's freeholders (or their sons) had joined the Saint John Mutual Protection Association to patrol the streets. Through the following years the question of how best to police the city was hotly debated. Few doubted the need for improvements, but tough decisions about the distribution of power and control had to be made. At least the watch might be increased in size without infringing upon traditional prerogatives. But this posed its own problems. As the mayor recognized, recruits would have to be drawn from 'classes whose feelings, sympathies and prejudices all make them partisans on one side or the other, and so increase in place of putting down the agitation.'[12] There were proposals to appoint stipendiary police magistrates and police forces responsible to the province's Executive Council – but these foundered on the reluctance of the Saint John Common Council to relinquish powers. Other possibilities were mooted and rejected. Crime and violence continued. Then in 1847 the lieutenant-governor moved to secure establishment of a permanent police force under a stipendiary magistrate in Portland. Soon thereafter the Saint John council doubled the size of the watch. By 1849 a stipendiary magistrate with administrative responsibility for the police force had been appointed in Saint John. Constables' salaries were raised, and their number increased. Uniformed, armed, and accorded new status as part of a professional bureaucracy, they succeeded in bringing order to the city's streets in the 1850s, as the economy improved and the influx of immigrants waned.

## A Colonial Parable

When he wrote to the printer of the *St. Andrews Standard* in March 1840, Patrick Medley described himself as a settler in southwestern

New Brunswick whose aim was to depict life in his neighbourhood 'way back near the Bailey Settlement.'[13] His was a neatly conceived tale. 'Dennis Snug' and 'Slouch' were its protagonists. The former was a diligent farmer who worked hard on his land, took care of his stock, and lived in comfort. 'Slouch' was also a farmer – of sorts. Not content with devoting his every effort to the productivity of his back-country acres, he spent his winters 'trivin away at all kinds of lum-berin.' To feed his oxen engaged in the heavy work of getting out timber, the hay from Slouch's farm was taken to the woods, while the cattle at home starved. 'Between hauling provisions and river drivin, and the likes of that,' there was precious little time to attend to the farmer's winter chores. 'Nothin [was] done about fences except maybe putin up the old rotten poles.' When spring came, very little seed was put in the ground. Overworked in the woods, Slouch's oxen were too weak to plough, so Slouch had to 'wait till Dennis Snug got his work all done before he could borrow his oxen to plough a place for to rase a few prataes on, and then there was little or no manuer, and to tell the truth how could there be! for the poor starvin critters of cattle got nothin to ate but a trifle mornin and evenin and then turned out of doors in the cauld.' To make matters worse, when the surveyor came to measure Slouch's logs, he found one was small, another 'shakey,' the next rotten; together they amounted to very little. Provisions consumed in the woods also turned out to be more costly than anticipated. At the end of the day Slouch had to sell some of his land to pay his debts.

## A Pamphlet on Agriculture

Anxious for guidance, many an 'improving farmer' of the mid-nine-teenth-century Maritime colonies turned to one or more of the several texts on agriculture that circulated in the region before Confedera-tion. In the libraries of local agricultural of scientific societies, or on the shelves of like-minded friends, there was plenty of choice. Many classics from abroad circulated in the colonies, among them the works of the renowned agricultural chemist J.F.W. Johnston (who paid an extended visit to New Brunswick in 1849), Henry Stephens, William Youatt, and Arthur Young. From the United States came Jesse Buel's *Farmer's Companion* and *Farmer's Instructor*, as well as several books by Johnston's student John P. Norton. For those who preferred home-grown instruction there were, of course, John Young's *Letters of Agri-cola* – published in Halifax in 1822, yet full, according to J.F.W. John-ston a quarter of a century later, of 'sound knowledge,' 'honest common sense,' and 'warm but prudent zeal' – and James Dawson's *Contributions toward the Improvement of Agriculture in Nova Scotia*, which shared (with Agricola's letters and similar works) the derivative quality reflected in its subtitle: *Compiled from Youatt, Johnston, Young, Peters, Stephens &c.* Less voluminous, but in its way no less important, there was also James Ross's *Remarks and Suggestions on the Agriculture of Nova Scotia.*[14]

Published by James Bowes and Sons of Halifax in 1855, this pamphlet claimed distinction. Its author was a practical farmer, the occupant of Faddan Farm on the flanks of the Rawdon Hills, east of Windsor, some fifty kilometres from the provincial capital. His remarks and suggestions, he was at pains to point out, were 'not the fanciful productions of fireside speculation, but the sober conclusions at which ... [he] had arrived, during a moderately long life entirely spent in the laborious pursuits of Agriculture.' Critical of the gentlemen farmers enthused by Agricola, who conducted their farms with 'ruinously profuse' expenditures, as well as of 'imported knowledge' advanced without local experience, Ross sought to redeem Nova Scotia's agricultural reputation and to provide useful guidance for ordinary settlers who depended upon their farms for their livings.

Not surprisingly, much of his booklet offered very specific advice. On new farms, 'fields should never exceed ... four acres each,' the beginning farmer should establish a seven-field rotation as soon as possible, and then extend it to nine to give him thirty-six acres under cultivation. Because manure would be scarce initially, it should be applied to the potatoes, turnips, and other green crops; later, as stock numbers were increased, fields should be fertilized in sequence, with carefully collected barnyard manure applied at the rate of fifty-five cartloads per acre. With similarly detailed discussions of drainage techniques, of the range and value of labour-saving implements available to Nova Scotian farmers, and of the variety and productivity of the different types of land in the colony, this was a manual to which farmers with a bent for improvement, settlers perplexed by the challenges before them, and colonists in need of basic information might turn for help.

Those who did so would quickly recognize that Ross's intentions were larger than the simple provisions of facts. His booklet sought to set the earnest farmer on a distinct and demanding course. Ross was firmly against display. Show was not evidence of prosperity. Economy in farming was a great virtue. 'He who acts judiciously,' he wrote, 'will prefer commodious barns and stables for his crops and cattle to a fine house.' More than this, Ross was critical of those archetypal Nova Scotian jacks-of-all-trades who divided their attentions among several pursuits as whim or weather dictated. Recognizing that necessity obliged the settlers of young countries to turn their hands to 'a great variety of labour,' and that this both encouraged the 'versatility which is naturally inherent in man' and called 'many of his best energies into action,' he nonetheless insisted that such multifaceted activity was a 'misallocation of energy' in most parts of mid-nineteenth-century Nova Scotia. In his mind there was no question that the 'skillful farmer will ... allot his time' and complete the jobs assigned to a particular period on schedule. On Ross's favoured farm, years and days were divided into three. As the seasons turned there came times for sowing, for cultivating, and for harvesting. This everyone knew; but Ross would allocate specific numbers of days to these tasks: planting should be done by the tenth or twelfth of June; no more than three weeks should be given to making hay; two weeks were sufficient for the grain harvest. So, too, it was important to observe the divisions of the day with undeviating attention, never permitting 'the labours of one part to interfere with those of another.' The various small jobs that demanded attention on every farm should be taken care of before 8:00 a.m.; between 9:00 and 1:00 and 2:00 and 6:00 the plough or cart should be yoked, and an acre of land ploughed or a certain quantity of manure carried to the fields. The evenings were for care of the stock and 'those numerous small pieces of labour of which every careful farmer will find abundance in a well-regulated establishment.' Holding himself as a model, Ross concluded: 'Unless on very extraordinary occasions I never permit any thing to interrupt the completion of work so arranged ... Knowing that there is a reasonable time for every part of my work, I never say, if I can get this or that done, but having made my arrangements, I endeavour to put them in execution in their proper season, and the man unaccustomed to systematic effort can scarcely form an accurate conception of the amount of labour which can thus be done, even by an individual.'

## A Year at New Rhynie

Snowing
The End of 1853
The end of the year 1853
Three times I say this is the End of
the year 1853

So wrote John Murray in the journal of New Rhynie farm in the late evening of Saturday, 31 December 1853, after a day spent cutting firewood and cobbling shoes.[15] Day by day, without fail through the year, he had recorded the business of life on his 112-acre farm fronting on Haliburton Stream a mile or so from the town of Pictou. Home to a substantial family of six children ranging in age from fifteen-year-old James to toddler William, New Rhynie was one of the better farms in its county. Valued at £700 in the census of 1851, it had approximately sixty acres under the plough, its stock included twenty-two cattle, twenty-five sheep, and a couple of horses, and its occupants lived in a large new house some twenty or thirty yards back from the road that led from Pictou to River John and on to New Brunswick.

A native of Aberdeenshire in his sixtieth year, John Murray was a man of some standing in his community. Departing Scotland in his early twenties, he had spent two years in Halifax before migrating again to 'Dominica' in the West Indies. Fourteen years later he had returned to Nova Scotia to purchase the Pictou property that he named after the parish of his birth and on which, in 1853, he had lived for almost two decades. Two years after his arrival in the county he married Scottish-born Jane Irving of Mount Thom, who was twenty years his junior, and three years later the first of their five sons was born. John Murray quickly began to play a significant part in local affairs. One of the overseers responsible for the deployment of statute labour on county roads during the late 1830s, he was also, in 1837, a founding member of the Pictou Agricultural Society, and a member of its committee of management in 1839. Through the next several years he played an active role in the affairs of the society, judging its ploughing matches, purchasing small quantities of the new seed wheats imported by the society, and taking several premiums for stock at its annual exhibitions. Late in the 1840s, Murray began to participate more fully in the life of Pictou's First Presbyterian Church, where he and Jane had been married; less than two years after he thrice bade farewell to 1853, Murray was elected an elder of the congregation and would discharge the duties of that office 'with exemplary fidelity and conscientious devotedness' until his death in 1873. A neighbour of long-serving county sheriff John Harris, and an associate in church and agricultural society of many of Pictou's leading citizens, including merchants J.D.B. Fraser, William Matheson, John Yorston, James Fogo, sometime provincial superintendent of education James W. Dawson, and others such as Israel Stiles, James Purvis, Henry Lowden, and E.M. McDonald, Murray was by wealth and connection among the loosely defined élite of the mid-nineteenth-century Pictou countryside.

With a productive farm and easy access to Pictou, John Murray made frequent trips to town, to sell his produce, to purchase the services of a blacksmith, or to acquire necessities and luxuries for his household. Trips to local mills and to neighbouring farms also provided opportunities for sales of small quantities of eggs, butter, potatoes, and so on. On average through the year such off-farm journeys occurred better than twice a week (although their incidence was highly variable and clearly seasonal). Not every such trip brought a sale or purchase. On occasions Murray went to town to assess the state of the market (before deciding, for example, to slaughter one of his animals); on others he returned home with the goods he had hoped to sell. In the meticulous accounts of 'Articals Bought' and 'Articals Sold' that Murray kept in addition to his journal in 1853, however, sales are recorded on almost 100 days of the year; purchases of goods were just as frequent. In total, farm sales for the year amounted to almost £70, two-thirds of which was accounted for by butter (300 lbs), meat (three carcasses of beef, eleven of pork, and twelve and a half of lamb), hides, skins, and flour. Total recorded expenditures, which amounted to less than £46, included the 'Parsons Stypends,' a stud fee for 'Jets mare,' school fees and supplies for the older children, taxes of £1.1.4, wages for servants Christy Ann (who left for Canada in May), 'Ellonar Jane Carmicle,' and May 'Mattall' (each of whom stayed approximately a month in the late summer and early fall), and various sums for spinning, weaving, and the use of a threshing machine.

Omitted from the accounts, but just as central to the operation of New Rhynie farm, were the reciprocal exchanges that enmeshed John Murray and his family in a web of mutual interdependence and more or less formal obligations. Some of these were straightforward enough – simple payments in kind to neighbours in return for certain goods or assistance with a specific task. Thus on 6 June, Murray gave two bushels of oats to John Curry for his help in killing a pig. Some were acts of neighbourly charity, as for example when Murray took oats and wheat to the mill 'for Alexander McKay that got his house burnt fully.' Communal responsibilities – the three days of statute labour on the roads required of John Murray in June, or the less formal 'breaking of roads' after major snowstorms – formed a third category of obligations. Others ensued from complex, continuing relationships, built perhaps on proximity and friendship, whose rich nuances it is now impossible to uncover. Favours were done, favours were returned; in a loose way there may have been some informal reckoning of the balance of obligation; but in the end it was the mutual identification of a general equilibrium of give and take (and perhaps in the case of youthful labour simply the chance of change and company) rather than the strict tally of shillings and pence that defined these associations. So 'Elicksonder' Young helped the Murrays with their hay harvest on at least two late July days; two and a half months later, Murray's sons James and Mercer (aged thirteen) were across the line fence that marked the western boundary of New Rhynie 'with the Ponie assisting J.W. Harres Shurref at Threshing.'

Far more intricate, because it was close and continuing, was the Murrays' relationship with the mason, James Dawson. Dawson was a relatively frequent visitor to New Rhynie. On several occasions he came to borrow the Murrays' pony; in February he was on hand to help with the slaughtering of an ox; and in April he put his special skills to use in building a chimney on the east end of the Murrays' house. A few days after the chimney was finished, Murray got four loads of manure from Dawson, and took him one and a half bushels of potatoes. In June and September there was more manure from Dawson's stable for New Rhynie's fields. In rough return, Murray hauled several loads of sand for the mason, and in October delivered a load of cabbages to him. None of this figured in John Murray's accounts. But several years later his son John D. would marry James Dawson's daughter Jane.

For Jane (Irving) Murray, life on New Rhynie farm followed a rhythm very different from that of her husband during 1853. Because the New Rhynie journal is generally silent about the activities of the sabbath, we might assume that she and her children joined John in the family pew of the Prince Street church on most Sundays of the year. We might also assume that she accompanied her husband on a few of his numerous trips into Pictou and that she probably attended the funerals of Christopher Underwood and Jane Curry at his side. But in the journal record of market visits, trips to the mill, and the incessant round of work in the fields and barns, the only three references to Jane Murray note her absence from New Rhynie: in March when she went to Cariboo; in mid-September when she, James, and Mercer visited New Glasgow; and later that month when she and John and six-year-old Charles visited her family in Mount Thom. By implication her place was in the home.

Although she had more help around the house than most of her rural counterparts, and was thus relieved of the chores of spinning and weaving, thirty-nine-year-old Jane Murray's days were full. With four children under the age of eight, the family had added a female servant to their household since the census of 1851, but on the departure of Christy Ann they were unable, for whatever reason, to retain regular help. Jane's mother came from Mount Thom for extended stays, through most of May and most of July. There were nevertheless innumerable chores to which Jane must have turned her daily attention, from cooking and washing to churning butter, tending the hens, ducks, and turkeys, caring for the garden, and putting up provisions. In the fall there were the additional demands of the harvest, with its long days, large appetites, and extra mouths to feed. Occasional visits from Mount Thom relatives broke the routine and brought news, as, presumably, did the enforced overnight stay of five travellers on their way to New Brunswick who were marooned by a heavy mid-April snowstorm. Still, Jane's was likely a life of closely circumscribed horizons, an existence structured (as was John Murray's) by a demanding routine of work, but lived within much narrower spatial limits and devoid (by contrast) of opportunities for casual social intercourse.

## Mounts of Hope

Rambling among the Bluenoses in the summer of 1862, Andrew Learmont Spedon of Chateauguay County, Canada East, remarked upon the progress of Saint John, a 'once dirty, insignificant hamlet' now 'swallowed up by the magnificent city, whose wealthy and elegant edifices, designed by the lights of science and projected by the hand of industry ... [stood] as the unmistakable evidence of ... wealth and prosperity.'[16] Especially worth remark were the 600-foot-long suspension bridge spanning the river just below the falls and, beyond it, in the parish of Lancaster on the West bank of the St John, the Provincial Lunatic Asylum – 'a splendid building, having a front 300 feet in length with two wings projecting from the main body, each 160 feet long ...' set amid forty acres of well-cultivated ground. Completed fourteen years earlier, on a site that was 'a mere waste,' it possessed, observed Spedon, 'a commanding position, and a fine view of the city and surrounding country.'

Six years before, Halifax's natal day had fallen into American humourist Frederic S. Cozzens' *Month with the Blue Noses*.[17] Special because it included a ceremony to mark the return of the 62nd and

63rd regiments to Halifax from the Crimea, this day of celebration
in 1856 also saw a great procession with a particular and unusual
purpose. As Cozzens described the 'luckless pilgrimage,' upon which
'the jolly old rain poured down': 'There were the "Virgins" of Ma-
sonic Lodge No.–, the Army Masons, in scarlet; the African Masons,
in ivory and black; the Scotch-piper Mason, with his legs in enormous
plaid trowsers ... the Clerical Mason in shovel hat, the municipal artillery; the Sons of Temperance, and the band. Away they marched,
with drum and banner, key and compasses, BIBLE and sword, to Dart-
mouth, in a great feather, for the eyes of Halifax were upon them.'
Their purpose was to lay 'the corner stone of a Lunatic Asylum,' a
feat accomplished by Lieutenant-Governor LeMarchant with the assistance of Alexander Keith, provincial grand master of Freemasons
in Nova Scotia, New Brunswick, Prince Edward Island, and New-
foundland (who had participated in a similar ceremony in Lancaster,
New Brunswick, in 1847) and framed by artillery salutes. Built on an
eighty-five-acre site, the asylum, like the New Brunswick institution
and the asylum and house of industry erected at Brighton on the
York River a mile and a quarter from Charlottetown in the late 1840s,
had a picturesque situation a short remove from the province's major
city.[18] The building, occupied in 1857, though not completed for
some years, was just as impressive as its Lancaster counterpart. Built
of brick in the Georgian style, its central four-storey structure was
flanked by wings of two and three storeys. Called Mount Hope, it
stood on rising ground with noble views of village, farm, wood, and
harbour. Its grounds, surrounded by a hawthorn hedge, included
lawns, grain fields, a garden, and a nursery of trees and shrubs. Altogether it offered 'very decided proof of provincial advance' and
was a 'credit to the country.'

The similarities of site, situation, and structure among the lunatic
asylums of the three colonies were not accidental. Although construction of these institutions spanned a decade and more, each was intended to provide a carefully designed and closely controlled
environment in which the minds of the afflicted could be coaxed back
to sanity. Advocates of new facilities for the accommodation of the
insane in the colonies after 1835 borrowed heavily from the doctrines
of American reformers that depended, in turn, upon the pioneering
works and writings of William Tuke in England and Philippe Pinel
in France. By these lights, the location of hospitals for the insane
'should not be near a large city, nor within half a mile of any street
which is, or will likely become, a populous part of the town.' The site

'should be so elevated as to command a full view of the surrounding country.' The asylum should be situated 'where the scenery is varied and delightful.' At best it should command views of 'a navigable river bearing on its basin a variety of water craft, public roads thronged with the evidences of life and business, but not so near as to be exciting, [and] a populated and cultivated country.' And its buildings, surrounded by ornamented grounds, 'should be in parallel lines and as nearly in a right line as they can be.'

According to current wisdom, both the external appearance and the internal economy of the asylum exerted an important corrective influence on its occupants. Work, play, and worship were the cornerstones of life in the institutions, but of these work was the most vital. It occupied the mind and stayed the patients' morbid, melancholy inclinations. It taught industry and fostered useful skills. And it drained the excess energy that produced frenzied behaviour. Field and dairy, threshing floor and woodpile, workshop and sewing room were 'as indispensable as the strong rooms have been for the refractory in times past.' But work was most useful if closely integrated into a highly organized routine. Authorities held little hope of improvement for the insane outside the asylum; 'without system there ... [would not] be success,' reported the Nova Scotia commissioners appointed to consider construction of an asylum in 1846. But it was confidently anticipated that appropriately designed, located, and managed institutions offering 'the most humane and enlightened treatment' would reduce 'the numbers of Insane in proportion to the population.'

## Of Acadians and 'People of Colour'

Two pictures open Frederic Cozzens' *Month with the Blue Noses*. These, asserts the author, are 'the first, the only real likenesses of the real Evangelines of Acadia.'[19] Travelling with the lines of Longfellow's poetry firmly in mind, and seeking to write an 'Evangeliad,' Cozzens was disappointed by his first glimpse of Chezzetcook, the largest Acadian settlement in the vicinity of mid-nineteenth-century Halifax. Its cottages were 'not the Acadian houses of the poem, "with thatched roofs and dormer windows projecting"' but comfortable homely looking buildings of modern shapes, shingled and unweathercocked. There were 'no cattle visible, no ploughs, nor horses,' but the boat builders and coopers who worked on the shore – very poor people with no milk, ale, or brandy for thirsty travellers – were 'simple, honest, and good tempered enough.'

At daybreak, a few women from Chezzetcook might be seen, fleetingly, in Halifax – the two who provided the frontispieces for Cozzens' book were among them, though, he took great pains to explain, it was no easy task to capture them on daguerrotypes, for 'as soon as the sun is up [they] vanish like the dew.' 'A basket of fresh eggs, a brace or two of worsted socks, a bottle of fir-balsam,' these things comprised 'their simple commerce.' To sell them, they walked the twenty-two miles from Chezzetcook, and then returned on foot. This journey was 'no trifle' agreed Cozzens, 'but Gabriel and Evangeline perform it cheerfully, and when the knitting-needle and the poultry shall have replenished their slender stock; off again they will start on their midnight pilgrimage, that they may reach the great city of Halifax before daybreak.'

Expressing surprise that a 'mere handful' of Acadians should live so near the colonial capital, yet remain so isolated that their 'village of a few hundred should retain its customs and language, intact, for generation after generation,' Cozzens was quickly given an explanation for what he considered unaccountable. The reason was 'because they stick to their own settlement; never see anything of the world except Halifax early in the morning; never marry out of their own set; never read – I do not believe [said his informant, that] one of them can read or write – and are in fact *so slow*, so destitute of enterprise, so much behind the age ...'


'I went into the jury court,' wrote J.F.W. Johnston in Halifax at the beginning of his North American tour in 1850, 'where the author of *Sam Slick* was the presiding judge, and I was both surprised and pleased to see a perfectly black man sitting there in the box as a juror.'[20] For Johnston this was evidence enough that in British North America 'people of colour' enjoyed 'the same political privileges as are possessed by other classes of her Majesty's subjects.' Some of them, descendants of eighteenth-century immigrants to Nova Scotia reported Johnston, were industrious owners of small farms. Yet most of those the traveller saw in the streets of Halifax were 'acting as porters and in other humble employments.' Generally they were spoken of 'as indolent, as hanging about the towns and as suffering much from the severity of the winter.' Had Johnston done as other commentators of the period did and crossed the harbour to travel north and east along the Nova Scotian coast, he might have added detail to these fleeting impressions. 'We saw,' recorded one who passed this way in 1856,

> a log house perched on a bare bone of granite that stood out on a ragged hillside, and presently another cabin of the same kind came in view. Then other scare crow edifices wheeled in sight as we drove along; all forlorn all patched with mud, all perched on barren knolls or gigantic bars of granite, high up like rugged redoubts of poverty, armed at every window with a formidable artillery of old hats, rolls of rags, quilts, carpets and indescribable bundles, or barricaded with boards to keep out the air and sunshine.[21]

This was 'a Negro settlement' inhabited, explained the traveller's guide, by 'a miserable set of devils' who would not work. During most of the year, he continued, 'they are in a state of abject want, and then they are very humble. But in strawberry season they make a little money and while it lasts are fat and saucy enough. We can't do anything with them; they won't work. There they are in their cabins, just as you see them, a poor woe-begone set of vagabonds; a burden upon the community; of no use to themselves, nor to anybody else.'

### Taking a Census

When on 9 April 1860, the legislature of New Brunswick passed 'An Act to provide for taking a Census' (23 Vic. cap. 49), it followed a relatively well-worn path. Decennial censuses had been taken (by rather different methods) in the United States since 1790, and in England and Wales since 1801; increasingly detailed enumerations of New Brunswick had been conducted in 1824, 1834, 1840, and 1851; and there was growing conviction, in the middle of the statistical nineteenth century, that such exercises were valuable: census returns, readers of the Saint John *Morning Freeman* were informed 'afford much useful information, dispel many erroneous ideas, and form the basis of most important legislation.'[22] Yet in April 1860 the precise nature of this 'useful information' remained to be decided. According to the enabling act, the taking of the census meant 'the taking an account of the Population and such other inquiries relative thereto, or relative to the Agricultural, Mechanical, Lumbering or other resources, or such other Statistics as the Governor in Council shall prescribe.' Much remained to be done in deciding upon the categories of enumeration and in establishing the means by which data were to be collected. At minimum, appropriate geographical divisions had to be established, enumerators chosen and appointed, and rules and regulations and schedules drawn up, before the enumeration could be conducted and the results tabulated. Recognizing as much, the legislature provided that 23 Vic. cap. 49 should come into effect on 1 January 1861. Still, it was March 1862, almost two full years after passage of the census act, before the results of that vaguely defined initiative were presented to the Assembly.

By the end of February 1861, the 'schedule of enquiries' had been finalized. The census was to elicit information in six broad categories: population, buildings, agriculture, manufactures, minerals, and fisheries. The first and second schedules each included sixteen questions, the last a mere five; manufacturers were listed, according to their product, in a dozen subcategories and, as with minerals (of which six and a catch-all 'other' were identified in the schedule), the name of the producer and the number of hands employed were to be recorded. Agriculture was by far the most complex category: because both the yields and acreages of crops were sought, a nominal thirty-five questions might entail, at maximum, forty-eight entries per farmer. Taken as a whole, this was a concerted effort to identify salient characteristics of the developing colony, far more ambitious than its 1851 predecessor. Still, the emphasis of this enumeration was economic. Schedule I sought information about religious adherence and 'race,' and listed the numbers of 'sick and infirm,' 'deaf and dumb,' 'blind,' and 'lunatic and idiotic,' as well as the births, marriages, and deaths of the preceding year. Schoolhouses and places of worship were counted in Schedule II, but in essence this census documented production.

In July, the provincial secretary began to appoint his census enumerators, one for each of the 160 census districts into which the province was divided. Paid at the rate of ten shillings per day, these were desirable appointments; unsolicited applications for the position of census taker began to reach the governor in council in September 1860, almost a year before the census would be taken, and a further three dozen were received in the next ten months. But the great majority of appointments were by recommendation; hard on the heels of the New Brunswick election in June, the provincial secretary asked members of the Assembly for nominations from their districts. Hardly surprisingly, relatives, friends, and supporters were prominent among those whose names were forwarded. So, for example, Samuel Freeze and S. Nelson Freeze were appointed census-takers in Norton and Sussex parishes on the recommendation of George Ryan, MLA for

Kings, who had married Miriam Freeze three decades earlier, and John Farris, MLA for neighbouring Queens, left no room for ambiguity in suggesting his brother-in-law, among others, to the provincial secretary: 'I wish to inform you the men that I want appointed to take the census of the county ... these are the men that I want appointed and please appoint the same.'

According to the instructions given to the enumerators, the census was to be taken 'with the least possible delay' and should 'represent the state of the country as it existed on the 15th August.' Yet there were delays and complications from the start. The enumerator for Upper Queensbury, twenty-five kilometres upriver from Fredericton, was not appointed until 3 September; in at least one instance, an enumerator's blank schedules were sent to the wrong post office, where they lay for weeks; other census-takers found themselves without blanks of one or more schedules well into September; and at least three enumerators failed to realize that Schedule VI was on the back of Schedule V. Even when appointments were made and schedules provided on time, the enumeration was sometimes slowed by the difficulties of travel, illness, and the absence of people from their homes. One enumerator did not begin work until 20 November. Although slightly more than half the returns reached Fredericton by the end of October, eight remained outstanding at the beginning of the new year, and the last was not received until 23 January 1862. Generally, enumerators spent between twenty and forty working days at their task, but it required a full two and a half months for W.L. Prince to enumerate the inhabitants of Moncton. Such a protracted process clearly jeopardized the accuracy of the census: how many could recall, accurately, the state of their farms on 15 August, two or three months after that date? How many simply assumed the date of this enumeration to be the point of reference in reporting the number of births or deaths in the preceding year?

There were also problems in the formulation of census categories. Schedule III required a return of 'Pork, slaughtered, pounds,' but enumerators were not informed whether they should enter 'the quantity to be slaughtered [in] the fall of 1861 or what ... [they found to] have been slaughtered on the 15th of August ... or what ... [had] been slaughtered in the fall of 1860.' Similarly, there was ambiguity in the 'Hands Employed' column of the agricultural schedule: did it mean 'Hired Laborer or all belonging to the Family able to work'? Those enumerators who sought clarification were instructed to enter their own estimates of 'the number of males and females that could do the work if steadily/continuously employed.' When the returns were finally compiled, many essentially arbitrary decisions had to be made. The numerous farmer-lumberman and fishermen-farmers of the 'Rank or occupation' columns had to be shoe-horned into one of the compilers' broad occupational categories: Professional, Trade and Commerce, Agricultural, Mechanics and Handicraft, Mariners and Fishermen, Miners, Labourers, and Miscellaneous. So inconsistent were the returns on 'race' that this categorization was omitted from the printed tabulation. And the picture was little clearer in respect to religious affiliation. 'Owing to misconception on the part of a large number of Enumerators,' explained compilers Charles Everett and James Beek, 'it became necessary in the abstract to include the Baptists and Free Christian Baptists in one body and the adherents of the Church of Scotland, Free Presbyterian Church and Presbyterian Church of New Brunswick in another body.' By chance (or more confusion), Samuel Freeze of Kings County appeared on two enumerators' returns, his own and A.B. Smith's. The returns were completed a month apart, Freeze's at the end of December, Smith's in January. Both, of course, should have referred to the state of Freeze's household and farm on 15 August. By Freeze's own account he was an Episcopalian tavern-keeper with 30 improved acres on a 200–acre farm valued at $2,000, whose household included a servant, Matilda Hoggins, and two labourers, Richard Bigelow and John Golding. According to Smith, Freeze was an innkeeper and farmer and a member of the Free Baptist Congregation; 40 of his 200 acres were improved and his farm was worth $2,400; his servant was Emily Driscoll, he had only one labourer, Bigelow, and one of his sons, aged three by Freeze's count, was now four. Well might Everett and Beek have reflected at the end of their task on the fact that it was 'without doubt, extremely difficult to devise such forms of schedule as will tend to procure accurate accounts of the several matters which it may be considered advisable to embrace in the Census Returns.'

### Greeting a Prince

On the morning of 30 July 1860, the weather in Halifax was 'anything but agreeable;' 'drizzling showers' fell from a grey sky. Yet almost all Haligonians were out of doors. In buoyant spirits they crowded the waterfront and lifted their voices in 'thrilling and vociferous cheers which rang loud and long' as the Royal Squadron bearing His Royal Highness, Albert Edward, Prince of Wales, anchored in front of the city. Once ashore, the prince was mounted upon a 'fine high-mettled charger' to take his place in a procession that included the Union Engine and Axe fire companies; the North British and Highland societies; the Charitable Irish Society; the St George's Society; the Carpenter's Charitable Society; the African Society; the Sons of Temperance; the Volunteer Artillery and Rifle companies; and representatives of Her Majesty's forces. Through streets lined with soldiers and volunteers, thronged by thousands, and decorated with at least seventeen arches, as well as 'transparencies,' flags, banners, and evergreens, the parade followed the firemen, who bore 'a trophy fifty feet high, surmounted by a colossal figure holding a hose-pipe,' as 'thirty five hundred school children, dressed in white and blue ... sang the National Anthem.' In the next three days, His Royal Highness reviewed troops, witnessed Indian Games (where he laughed 'heartily at the ludicrous scene' presented by a war dance), mingled with zest at a grand ball attended by 3,000, watched displays of fireworks, and (it was said) 'sat on his horse nobly and never flinched' when drenched by a sudden shower.[23]

Through early August, the Prince's grand progress continued, to Saint John, to Fredericton, and then to Charlottetown, before he took ship from the island on the eleventh, bound for Quebec. In detail, the royal itinerary differed from day to day, but the general pattern of community responses to the Prince's visit was as constant as the weather was miserable. There were levees, balls, and formal presentations of addresses; 'National and Trade Societies and Volunteers' – of which there were – 'great number' and whose members were invariably pronounced 'a fine-looking body of men' – paraded; streets were decked with bunting and whole cities beautifully illuminated; bonfires were built, bells rung, and guns fired; 'people cheered and cannon roared'; enthusiasm and joy knew no bounds, even when planned fireworks displays 'were completely destroyed by the immense deluge of rain.'

Testaments to colonial loyalty were everywhere. At the grand ball in the Provincial Building in Charlottetown, one of the 'many beautiful devices 'that graced the scene carried the message:

Thy grandsire's name distinguishes this isle;
We love thy mother's sway and court her smile.

In Saint John, 5,000 'fancifully dressed' and flower-bedecked school

children added three verses to their rousing rendition of 'God Save
the Queen,' ending:

Hail, Prince of Brunswick's line,
New Brunswick shall be thine;
Firm has she been
Still loyal, true, and brave
Here England's flag shall wave
And Britons pray to save
A nation's heir.

And on 7 August, when His Highness returned to the mouth of the
St John River en route to Windsor, Pictou, and Charlottetown, 'a
party of stalwart though gentle firemen' unharnessed the horse from
his carriage and pulled ' "their dear little prince" as they delighted
to call him,' across the Suspension Bridge to the wharf.

Even Bishop Medley (who excused his decision to preach a sten-
torian sermon on the text of Romans 14, verse 12 – 'So, then everyone
of us shall give an account of himself to God' – to those who crowded
into Fredericton's Christchurch Cathedral with the Prince on 5 August by claiming that he had 'a higher mission to discharge' than
simply to voice the 'language of congratulation') could not entirely
avoid the spirit of loyal adulation that gripped his fellow colonials.
'When we look round among the nations of the earth and consider
the past and present conditions of countries favoured with a fruitful
soil and a more genial climate than our own' intoned the Bishop in
the middle of a sermon full of eloquent warnings of the awful power
of God's judgment,

how inestimable is the price of our manly, rational, and constitutional
freedom, how deeply should we cherish, how diligently should we guard
and preserve, the integrity of our limited monarchy, the nice balance
of our respective estates and realms, the just and merciful administration of our laws and the various expressions of freedom and safe-guards
against license with which a gracious Providence has endowed us. Our
monarchy, our language, our religion are rich in all the associations
of the past ... Our sufferings and our joys are the common property
of the empire. One year our bosoms throb with fear and sorrow at the
massacre of Cawnpore, in another we hail the coming of a Prince, not,
like his great ancestor reaping his youthful harvest of renown and blood
inflicted upon a foreign land, but sent forth by the love of the Mother

of our country, to consolidate the affection of a distant empire and to bring nearer in loyalty, love, and friendship the claims which science and commercial action have already united.

Little wonder that the young prince claimed to leave the lower provinces with 'an endearing regard and sympathy' for their inhabitants in whom he found 'the love of freedom ... combined with a deep-rooted attachment to the mother country, and the institutions in which we have all been nurtured.'

## Reflections

Good geographers, it has been said, have stout boots. By this simple maxim, those who lack these essential pieces of research equipment are, at best, pretenders to the proud title 'geographer,' 'armchair' scholars bound to the comforts and limited horizons of their studies; at worst they are traitors to the traditions of their discipline, men and women of blinkered vision whose understanding is sorely compromised by their failure to range over reality in all its complex, interconnected variety. Now there is much to be said for field-work; no map, document, or census table can adequately convey the look of the land, neither computer tapes nor dusty library stacks can illuminate the patterns and processes that shape places in quite the way that the physical exploration of a territory may do. But good boots do nothing to ensure good thoughts. Just as the traveller who embarks without information and curiosity is likely to arrive broadened in the beam rather than the mind, so the geographer who goes into the field without careful preparation – and thus unable to formulate well-grounded, if still tentative, explanatory hypotheses to account for what is seen – is likely to reap little intellectual reward from the effort. Whether cosseted tourist, wild rover, or well-shod field-geographer, in short, the strict empiricist is destined to return far richer in observations than understanding.[24]

By the same token, we cannot come to grips with the past simply by retrieving fragments of it. The facts do not speak very eloquently for themselves. Many and various as they are, the vignettes that comprise the bulk of this paper provide a terribly incomplete rendering of the diversity of land and life, economy and society in the mid-nineteenth-century Maritime colonies. Taken on their own they form a rather incongruent assortment of snapshots – so many grains of sand, as it were, arrayed on the page. True, their number could be multiplied, almost endlessly. But in the end such proliferation would only exacerbate the sense of discord, and bring us closer to the assay-master's dilemma. Still, none of this justifies retreat from our en-gagement with the variety, nuances, and textures of life as it was lived, for it is just such intricate, multifaceted reality that we must seek to grasp if we would justify and sustain the vitality of our in-quiries. The challenge, for those who would make sense of places – be they travellers, geographers, or historians – is surely to confront complexity in ways that can heighten understanding instead of simply adding to our store of factual knowledge.[25]

In the broadest and most ambitious of terms this means approach-ing the places and people in whom we are interested with a curiosity honed on the whetstones of contextual understanding, pertinent com-parison, and theoretical insight, in an effort to locate them on those 'grand maps of history' that promise to illuminate and explain how the world came to be as it is.[26] In more concrete, mundane, and certainly more circumspect vein, it means approaching the vignettes that comprise the body of this paper not as so many unconnected word pictures of a hopelessly disparate realm, but as a series of eth-nographic jottings, each and all of which capture something of the assumptions, aspirations, and attitudes, the classifications and regu-lations, the constructions and constraints that gave shape and meaning to life in the settings that they encapsulate. Perceived thus, woven back into the rich contextual fabric of provincial existence from which they are drawn as so many threads, and considered against recent discussions of the sources of social power, the processes of state for-mation, and the development of modernity, these vignettes reveal much about ideology, society, and state in the mid-nineteenth-century Maritimes.[27]

In reviewing them in this light we recognize first the pervasiveness of what Max Weber called the ethos of modern Western capitalism – calculating, rational, 'sober bourgeois capitalism' – in the rhetoric of the colonies.[28] In its emphases on time discipline and the division and specialization of labour, James Ross's pamphlet on agriculture embodies the confidence of the Victorian age in the benefits of system and the possibilities of improvement. In rural Nova Scotia, the doc-trines of Adam Smith and the practices of English factory owners would redeem both the productivity and reputation of the colony's most important industry. With farmers committed to unwavering, persevering, and above all systematic effort, with their energies no longer dissipated by want of calculation and design, individual profits and colonial prosperity were regarded as certain. Doubters need only consider the plight of Nova Scotia's negro settlers, a plight produced, according to prevailing views, by the failure of these 'vagabonds' to work as industriously as they ought. Nor was it incidental that work and system were touted as cures for insanity. That the judicious application of labour and capital to the myriad activities of the farm required careful assessment of inputs, outputs, expenditures, and returns escaped mention in Ross's pamphlet, but was well understood by other leading agricultural improvers of the period. Through books, newspapers, and county agricultural societies the importance of system and science, and with it the importance of detailed record keeping of the sort practised by John Murray of New Rhynie, was driven home to those colonial farmers who would listen.

Patrick Medley's parable of 'Snug' and 'Slouch' spoke in different tones to much the same project. At base its message was simple: those who 'cleared land, developed their farms and lived on them were the real producers.' Farming was a stable enduring occupation; the well-managed farm was a 'permanent enterprise oriented to constantly renewed profit.' Lumbering was a precarious, adventitious speculation, a lottery attractive for its promise of 'spectacular ad hoc killings.' As 'O'Leary,' a stereotypical Irish ex-lumberman who appeared in a series of letters from Paul Jones to the *New Brunswick Courier* had it, the lumber industry was 'a game of haphazard.'[29] Those who engaged in it might prosper temporarily, but in the end they would find 'their farms mortgaged [and] their houses ... tumbling down wid hardly a light of glass in them but stuffed wid ould rags hats and straw.' By contrast, the settler who invested in 'the bank of earth' would dwell in a 'neat and smart' house, and his 'ould wife' would always have ' "siller" in her pouch.'

By the middle decades of the nineteenth century these were well-established themes in the formal discourse of colonial life. Given full and self-conscious expression in Thomas McCulloch's 'Letters of Mephibosheth Stepsure' early in the 1820s, they were reiterated time and again in vice-regal pronouncements, in the columns of the provincial press, in the apological observations of travellers, and in the reports and injunctions of the provincial and local agricultural societies whose formation and continued activity rested upon the fiscal support of the three colonial governments.

Closely associated with these rhetorical and administrative attempts to influence the construction of aspirations and to entrench the ethos of rational capitalism in the colonies was a moral agenda. Here farmers and lumberers again found themselves the metaphorical centrepieces of a wider tableau. They were 'as unlike each other *professionally* as ... the black Ethiopian and the White European *personally*.' Lumberers lived a 'toilsome and semi-savage life'; they were men of 'spendthrift habits and villainous and vagabond principles,' strangers 'to every rational enjoyment'; their work was demoralizing and debilitating, they 'spent their winters in the woods and their summers lounging about the towns.' 'Happy' farmers, by contrast, followed 'a pursuit of innocence and peace,' derived their pedigree from the patriarchs, and stopped to no man; their characteristically neat cottages surrounded by rich and cultivated land betokened their elect status. Farmers were snug by virtue of their sober and industrious characters; profane, sabbath-breaking, gambling lumberers were poor, indifferent, lazy, idle, loutish, and slovenly fellows – slouches indeed.

That these were thoroughly derivative arguments drawn from the ancients and the agricultural literature of Renaissance Europe mattered not a whit. Nor was it of much moment to those who used them that they caricatured – rather than characterized – the colonial scene. Their purpose was to cajole, not to describe. They sought to define a moral universe, to encourage particular forms of behaviour by portraying them as normal, appropriate, and acceptable, and to discourage others by representing them as inept and repugnant. Nor were they the only vehicles for the promotion of a sober, industrious, bourgeois mentality. The temperance movement, which flourished in the region during the 1840s and 1850s, was directed to similar ends.[30] Teas, picnics, processions, and excursions brought the sons, daughters, and cadets of temperance together, developed a sense of camaraderie among them, and heightened the visibility of their cause. In 1852, 9,000 people petitioned the New Brunswick Assembly for a ban on the import of alcoholic beverages; passed into law, their resolution imposed official prohibition on the colony through 1853, but quickly proved unworkable. 'Conceived in tyranny,' as Attorney-General Lemuel Allen Wilmot recognized, it soon led to 'fanaticism and violence,' and was rescinded in 1854.[31] Still, the temperance movement had revealed its political power and its moral authority in 'urg[ing] upon other men, as good, such lines of conduct as are good for them, whether good or evil to the other people.'[32]

Nowhere were the contours of the emerging social order more clearly revealed than in mid-nineteenth-century Saint John. Here the endemic disorder and ethnic rioting – and the responses of city officials to both – reflected and helped to frame prevailing convictions about the nature of colonial society. Orangemen in New Brunswick shared with their brothers on both sides of the Atlantic, an unswerving loyalty to the Crown and a fervent belief in the superiority of Protestantism. Irish famine immigration was resisted because it was seen as one part of a massive campaign to establish the authority of the Vatican around the globe: 'A great ... conflict is at hand,' warned the Saint John *Church Witness* in September 1853, 'between Protestant Truth and Popery leagued with Infidelity.'³³ And 'Popery,' it was alleged, had formidable troops on its side: 'no one can deny,' claimed the *Loyalist and Conservative Advocate*, 'that the lower orders of the Roman Catholic Irish are a quarrelsome, headstrong, turbulent, fierce, vindictive people.' One might as well attempt to 'wash the Ethiope White' as to 'tame and civilize' the native of Connaught and Munster. Time and again, editorials in the 'Orange' press played on these themes. Almost every contemporary newspaper carried anecdotes and 'Irish jokes' that mocked the Celtic newcomers as barbaric or ignorant of both. When economic arguments were added to these ethnic (or racial) slurs – for the destitute immigrants formed a large pool of cheap labour in direct competition with unemployed native labourers during the 'hungry forties' – they formed a powerful goad to Protestant nativism. Fully half of New Brunswick's mid-nineteenth-century Orangemen were born in the colony; their membership in the Ulster-based organization was a measure of its attraction as a defender of Protestantism and British hegemony.

When Orange fervour spilled over into vigilante action and the provocation of conflict by ceremonial invasions of Catholic areas of the city, the processes of colonial justice generally ensured more lenient treatment of Protestant than Catholic participants. When the worshipful master of the Wellington Orange Lodge shot a Catholic Irishman in 1844, he was placed in protective custody rather than arrested and was quickly exonerated of any crime – on the claim of self-defence – by city magistrates. After riots in 1842, an all-Protestant force of special constables arrested several Irish Catholics who were subsequently convicted of rioting. Three years later, both Orangemen and Irish Catholics were arrested after fierce fighting in the streets, but the all-Protestant Grand Jury refused to bring their co-religionists to trial. And in 1849, when the clash of Orange and Green forces was widely anticipated, and the route of the Orangemen's approach to York Point was clear well in advance, garrison troops were deployed not to ward off conflict by barring entrance to the Catholic district, but to seal off the riot once the Orange parade had moved through the area, and thus to allow the procession to continue, un-molested, through the core of the city. Here the sentiments and con-victions of Saint John's powerful majority were made clear: Irish Catholics were rejected for their cultural and religious differences; disparaged in the vigorous rhetoric of the day, they became legitimate targets of attack as the authorities turned myopic eyes on the pro-vocative actions of vehement nativist Protestants.

Elsewhere, anti-Catholic ideology also ran strongly during the 1840s and 1850s. In Prince Edward Island, 'Romanism' became an issue in the elections of the late 1850s, campaigns that turned on 'a serious and most unaccountable misunderstanding' over the place of the Bible in the educational system and that produced an all-Protestant admin-istration in a colony whose population was almost half Roman Cath-olic.[34] In Nova Scotia, 'Popery' was seen as a threat to established values, denounced for undermining colonial attachments to Britain, and criticized as an obstacle to colonial improvement.[35] 'The Popery of the [D]ark [A]ges ... [was] the Popery of the present generation.' Catholic countries published fewer books and had fewer miles of rail-way than Protestant ones; thus 'Protestant areas nourished "progress" while Catholic lands promoted ignorance and lethargy.' As Scottish-born, Free Church minister the Reverend A. King told a Halifax audience, and readers of his pamphlet *The Papacy: A Conspiracy against Civil and Religious Liberty* (1859), Catholic priests nipped 'in the bud in the first appearance of ... that assertion of liberty to think and act for himself, which belongs to man as a moral and accountable being.' Little wonder, in this view, that the Acadians of Chezzetcook were '*so slow*, so destitute of enterprise, so much behind the age.'

Beyond all this lay various, more or less explicit, 'official' initiatives and strategies that worked to shape and confirm social and political identities in the three Maritime colonies. When colonial governments embarked on the construction of asylums for the insane, their actions implied more than the simple provision of facilities for the unfortu-nate. The new institutions were trophies in the landscape, placed there with appropriate fanfare to symbolize the progressiveness of their creators. They reflected the growing embrace of the asylum for treat-ment and correction, and were but single – if important – pieces in a larger mosaic of corrective institutions. By 1860, Halifax had a handful of penitentiaries, homes for juvenile delinquents, and rescue homes for prostitutes, as well as a poor's asylum and Mount Hope.[36] Saint John likewise, in the dozen years or so before the opening of its institution for the insane, built a cholera hospital, a county gaol/

house of correction, an almshouse-workhouse-infirmary, and an emigrant orphan asylum. Nor did these developments lack significance as colonial initiatives. In 1845 the erection of a combined asylum for the three provinces was mooted but came to naught in the face of perceived 'difficulties' and the conviction that 'separate establishments for each of the provinces would be more desirable.'

By the mid-nineteenth century, there was a growing consciousness, among their élites, of Nova Scotia, New Brunswick, and Prince Edward Island as separate communities. Peter Fisher published the first *History of New Brunswick* as early as 1825, and (according to D.C. Harvey, at least) Nova Scotians *as such* had begun to emerge between 1812 and 1835, when the record of literary achievement shows them 'rubbing the sleep out of their eyes and facing their own problems, in various ways, but with discernment and energy.'[37] Certainly there is no gainsaying the importance of T.C. Haliburton's writings, with their portrayal of the Nova Scotian as half-Yankee, half-English, the best product of his race.[38] And of Prince Edward Islanders, it was proclaimed in 1853: 'removed as they are from all intercourse with the world, these narrow-minded Provincials really fancy themselves *par excellence* THE people of British North America.'[39]

To a degree such identifications were fostered by the legislatures, sessions, courts, and grand juries that formed the essential infrastructure of these mid-nineteenth-century colonial 'states.'[40] Communities returned representatives to provincial assemblies and by and large were administered through courts of session composed of justices of the peace (appointed by the governor and council) who served, on paper, to extend the influence of central government into local affairs. Although the Common Council of Saint John, established in 1785, held legislative, executive, and judicial powers, and a few other towns and cities in the region gained autonomy through incorporation after 1840 – viz Halifax (1841), Fredericton (1848), and Moncton, Charlottetown, and Sydney (1855) – local government by sessions was the norm in both Nova Scotia and New Brunswick until the late 1870s. Moreover, many local officials – such as the supervisors of New Brunswick's great roads and the firewardens of Fredericton – were appointed by the lieutenant-governor in council.

That these officials and institutions were tentacles of the 'state' is indubitable, but their strength in that capacity should not be overestimated. Technically subject to central control, most justices enjoyed a great deal of freedom in their conduct of local business; many indeed fell sorely short of the demands of their offices. Furthermore, proposals for municipal incorporation in the 1840s were rejected as 'encroach[ments] upon the liberties of the people.' Colonial politics revolved, for the most part, around the local distribution of government largesse rather than the development of a coherent political ideology at the centre and its implementation on the periphery. For all the social importance of politics and its undoubted role in shaping the channels of power in individual communities, in the 1860s as in the 1830s it was essentially about local patriotism. As Joseph Howe noted in the 1840s, the central administrative duty of the government lay in 'dispensing the patronage of the County'; the fact that assemblymen were consulted about the appointment of justices of the peace was 'a substantial concession from the Crown to the People.'[41] New Brunswick lawyer and assemblyman George S. Hill voiced similar conclusions more colourfully in arguing that 'The Russians under Peter the Great thought the privilege of wearing long beards the essence of liberty – our people judge it to consist in the right of sending members to the Fredericton legislature to get their by-road and school money – all beyond is a *terra incognita*, which they have no curiosity to explore.'[42]

The role of the colonial 'state' in staking out a cognitive territory with which its citizens could identify and the severe limits to its effective authority were clearly revealed by New Brunswick's attempt to count its people in 1861. By mounting a census of the colony, the legislature instantiated conceptions of New Brunswick as a distinct and, in some sense, unitary territory; by establishing – whether *de jure* or *de facto* – the categories of that enumeration, it defined, however implicitly, those things that it held to be important; and, inadvertently or no, it served to blur distinctions (between Baptists and Free Christian Baptists, for example) that others held dear. Yet the fumbling, bumbling manner in which the census was conducted was a stark testament to the limits of central power. Without a professional bureaucracy to conduct the work, New Brunswick's authorities fell back upon traditional channels of patronage in selecting their census-takers; among the motley crew of enumerators that this produced, few, apparently, were cowed by instructions to complete their work with 'the least possible delay.' In its many confusions and inaccuracies the census of 1861 stands as a measure of the very real constraints limiting the totalizing power of the 'state' in the mid-nineteenth-century Maritime colonies.

This is not to suggest that progress towards the development of more powerful and effective instruments of government was absent during the early nineteenth century. In both Nova Scotia and New Brunswick, the widespread disregard of statutes intended to control access to both land and timber was gradually restricted by refinement of both the relevant regulations and the means of their enforcement. So 'squatters' and 'trespassers' – official descriptions of those who claimed natural or moral rights of access to the abundant resources of the colonies – were evicted and fined, and provincials were increasingly forced to acknowledge the property rights legitimized by the state and to conform to the terms of lease and sale that it established for them.[43] So, too, the development of a uniformed, bureaucratic police force in mid-century Saint John marked a significant extension of the effective range of control by centralized authority. But always there remained, through the mid-century decades, large segments of colonial life that lay, to all intents and purposes, beyond the effective everyday sway of the colonial 'state.'

To throw these patterns into bolder relief, it is useful to consider the mid-nineteenth-century Maritime colonies against the framework of societal types outlined in the writings of Anthony Giddens.[44] Primarily concerned to provide a perspective on the novel world of the late twentieth century, Giddens identifies several salient contrasts between traditional (so-called class-divided) and modern states. Foremost among them are those related to the range over and intensity with which economic and political power can be exercised. In traditional states, Giddens avers, 'the administrative reach of the political centre is low'; in modern ones it is extensive. So, traditional states have frontiers, modern ones borders. In the former, most people live lives shaped by the rhythms of the seasons, structured by personal contact, and bounded by the limits of domestic production; they occupy relatively closed pockets of local order that combine to make of any more extensive territory a cellular, segmented space within which ruling groups – concentrated in the cities – are generally unable to influence the day-to-day lives of their subjects, although they utilize their control of 'authoritative resources' (generally military power) to pacify and extract surplus production from the people. In the latter, new technological and organizational means of overcoming the barriers of time and space allow for interaction and the co-ordination of activities without face-to-face contact; here control over 'allocative' (economic) resources is critical; there is a high level of internal order; government is polyarchic, in the sense that it is responsive to the preferences of the people; codes of conduct tend to be spatially extensive, patterns of production are highly integrated, and administrators characteristically have an enormous capacity to shape even the most intimate features of their subjects' daily activities. Fundamental to this transformation has been the growing power to bridge distances: by the development of writing and, later, other forms of information storage (which opened out the possibilities of social interaction beyond those provided by the evanescent spoken word and heightened the prospects of central surveillance); by the acceptance of money (which enlarged the radius of exchange beyond that possible in a barter economy and led eventually to the commodification of everyday life); and by improvements in the transportation/communication system that produced time-space convergence (or a reduction in the friction of distance – measured in terms of time or cost – between places) and thus facilitated system integration.

At base, this conceptualization rests upon an essential distinction between 'the state' as an instrument of government or power and 'the state' as 'the overall social system subject to that government or power,' or, in other words, between the state as an administrative apparatus and the wider 'civil society' of which it is a part. Recognizing as much, we can associate the contrasts between traditional and modern societies sketched above with a decisive shift in the ability of the state, as instrument, to penetrate the civil realm. In traditional societies, substantial spheres of life 'retain their independent character in spite of the rise of the state apparatus.' Thus the classic contrast between city and countryside – markedly distinct places despite their interdependence. With the rise of the modern (nation-)state (as an administrative organ), however, the distinction blurs then disappears; few areas or spheres of life survive beyond the administrative reach of the state, and those that do 'cannot be understood as institutions which remain unabsorbed by ... [it].'

Against this backdrop – barely and inadequately sketched as it is here – the contours of Maritime distinctiveness begin to stand out. On the face of it, the mid-nineteenth-century colonies embodied elements of both 'traditional' and 'modern' archetypes. There were close and finite limits to the administrative state's ability to penetrate and organize the colonial countryside; the provinces were a patchwork of social, ethnic, and religious fragments; relationships built on barter and reciprocity integrated people into local worlds; many colonists remained remote from central authority, unaware of many of its dictates, and prepared in many cases to transgress against others with scant fear of detection. Colonial administrators, on the other hand, sought to shape and circumscribe the lives of colonial residents by

defining property rights, requiring road work, and administering justice. They took account of the colonists and their production. And
they brought some of them under even more continuous surveillance
in the asylums, prisons, and rescue homes that were built during these
years. These colonies were, moreover, territories with clearly identified boundaries, capitalist societies without limitations on the alien-
ability of property, and places in which steam trains and steamships
had begun to revolutionize transport by 1840.

Yet it would be a mistake simply to classify the colonies, on this
evidence, as 'transitional.' Rather than standing at some intermediate
point in this conjectural framework, they form a special variant of
the models identified by Giddens. Outliers of empire, they were neither modern states nor traditional 'class-divided' societies. Shaped by
the encounter of post-Enlightenment Europe with a remote and essentially undeveloped wilderness, they were peculiar hybrids. They
exhibited many of the forms of the modern administrative state, but
lacked final sovereignty and were poorly integrated, by virtue of their
colonial status and the difficulties of communication and time-space
co-ordination across their territories. Janus-like, they present different appearances to our gaze. Viewed from their political centres –
Halifax, Fredericton, and Charlottetown – these small, and recent,
colonial societies reveal many characteristics of the modern state and
its substantial administrative apparatus. Courts and assembly cham-
bers provided forums for the defence and advancement of civil and
political rights; restrictions on the (male) individual's freedom to join
organizations, express opinions, hold public office, and vote were few;
newspapers offered several alternative sources of opinion, provided
readers with a steady flow of 'decontextualized' information, and
broadened the sense of membership in a political community; political
leaders competed for support; and elections determined the composition of governments. Statutes applied colony-wide; surveyors of
land and timber were appointed far and near to administer regulations
framed in the capitals; institutions were created to adjust 'deviants'
– criminal or insane – to the norms of 'acceptable behaviour'; public
accounts were subject to scrutiny; and colonial census statistics began
to provide the basis of that 'reflexive self-regulation' so essential to
the administrative power of the state. Official documents, reports,
and correspondence reveal much about these aspects of colonial
administration. Their real effects upon the rank and file of colonists
are considerably harder to assess, however.

It is clear, nonetheless, that to view these societies from their pe-

ripheries – from the fields, camps, dories, and kitchens of their predominantly rural populations – is to see them in a very different guise.
Through most of the region, the sanctions of religion and the local
community were more important than formal policing in maintaining
'order';[45] among people dispersed upon their farms, working in the
woods in small, informal groups, or fishing in crews of one or two,
there could be little surveillance over production. Although the colonies were defined and bounded spaces, they were hardly 'conceptual
communities'; their people spoke different languages (the Gaelic, reported mid-nineteenth-century visitors to Cape Breton, was more
common there than in Scotland; French was the language of Acadian
areas; Lunenburgers clung to their German, and so on); and they
worshipped in different churches; in these relatively new-settled places
there was little shared history (or, yet, symbolic historicity of the sort
that would be provided by celebrations of the Loyalist centenary in
the 1880s).[46] Even colonial government – the central structure of the
administrative state – failed to override the profoundly fragmented
and local character of colonial life; late in the 1850s, Lieutenant-
Governor Sir Edmund Head of New Brunswick lamented the absence
of 'public' (communal rather than individual, colonial rather than
parochial) interest among the assemblymen of his province.[47] However impressive in the colonial capitals, many tentacles of the administrative state reached but weakly into the provincial hinterlands.
Distance – the formidable time and cost of movement in this new
world – was a significant barrier to integration of the corners of
colonial life with the centre.[48] Elaborated and refined through the
first half of the century, the administrative apparatuses of these colonial states (which owed much to the model of the developing English
nation-state) cast longer, more solid shadows in 1860 than in 1800 or
1830, but their penumbras were wide, and they clearly failed to blan-
ket several facets of colonial life.

All of this leaves us, finally, with an important and infinitely elusive
question: how was the world made sense of by inhabitants of these
three colonies? If there is an easy yet broadly accurate answer it is,
simply, differently. Consider, for example, the black juror in a Halifax
courtroom noted by J.F.W. Johnston. To Johnston, and no doubt to
many leading citizens of the province, his presence suggested the
equality of political privileges in British North America. But the reality of circumstances in those nearby 'redoubts of poverty' – described
by other travellers – that were home to many of the colony's black
residents surely conveyed a different message to those who lived in

them. In the end we can do no more than allude to the range of this diversity and recognize its complex manifestations. Yet in doing so we demonstrate, again, the magnificent, messy complexity of this 'naughty world' that can be illuminated but neither entirely boxed in nor completely explained by our theories of it.[49]

Consider first John and Jane Murray. In a very real sense, John Murray lived in several worlds. He was a colonial Briton, a resident of Nova Scotia subject to its statutes (which were themselves subject to disallowance in London), and entitled to participate in the election of a representative from his county to the House of Assembly in Halifax. But quite how strongly he felt his provincial identity, and whether it was as important to him as his identification with Pictou, Hardwood Hill, the small cluster of people who lived between Haliburton Stream and the harbour, or the larger congregation of First Presbyterian Church, we will never know. Certain it is, though, that as a prosperous, improving farmer, John Murray was a participant in the agricultural enlightenment, rational, observant, and calculating in the operation of his farm. A devout Presbyterian, he gave a significant part of his time to the affairs of his church. A Scot in Pictou, he found his religious identity reinforced by his ethnic allegiance. Sometime overseer of district roads, prizewinner, judge, and committee member in the local agricultural society, he was both recipient and (indirectly) dispenser of small sums of provincial-government largesse. Connected firmly to the market, he was also enmeshed in a web of local exchange and mutual interdependence. For Murray these, surely, were not separable spheres. Life involved a complex set of obligations, involvements, decisions, and actions. It was centred on New Rhynie and essentially local, despite the wider economic, political, and intellectual horizons to which many of Murray's contacts ultimately led. And how much more decisively was this true of Jane Murray. If the state impinged little on the everyday existence of her husband, its presence was almost entirely absent from hers. She was not, of course, entirely removed from its orbit. In denying her a vote because she was a woman, the statutes of Nova Scotia limited her participation in political life and circumscribed her ability to influence the exercise of political power in her society. In ascertaining how much butter and homespun she made in the course of a year, provincial authority 'invaded' her home – but it did so in the person of a neighbour, and then only once a decade. So far as we can judge, and on balance, in short, 'state activities, forms, routines and rituals' neither greatly affected the conduct of life nor played much part in the constitution of Jane Murray's identity (or that of countless other mid-century Maritime colonists).

Recognizing as much, we are drawn to conclude that religion was a far more powerful influence upon everyday life in these mid-century colonies than was the influence of the provincial 'state.' Consider, in support of this contention, Bishop Medley (who on 5 August 1860, at least, was inclined to give credit to 'gracious Providence' for the constitutional freedom enjoyed by New Brunswickers). Or contemplate those who marched behind Orange banners through the streets of Saint John in the 1840s. Remember those Catholic Irish who resisted Protestant incursions into their districts of the city. Recall those Presbyterians who objected to the failure of provincial census-takers to record accurately the nuances of their sectarian subdivisions. And bring to mind those Acadians of Chezzetcook whose houses clustered around their chapel. Generally closely associated with the tragic myths on which each of the ethnic/immigrant groups of the region built cohesion out of their pasts, religion was in some important sense the substance of the region's several mid-nineteenth-century cultures, the means of social integration through which collective memories were organized and constructed to form a far more effective basis for definitions of 'us' and 'other' than was provided by the still relatively feeble fabric of the colonial state.[50] Colonial politics in the mid-nineteenth-century Maritimes were what W.L. Morton described twenty years ago as 'limited politics': for most people they were secondary to the more compelling preoccupations of religion, ethnicity, business, and survival.[51]

None of this is to deny the existence of what might broadly be called a 'political culture' in the Maritimes. But as Greg Marquis has argued recently, this was a culture with its roots firmly planted across the Atlantic.[52] Editorial and other contributions to the provincial press and speeches made in councils and assemblies leave no doubt that 'the plain language of [Maritime colonial] politics ... came from English history.' In relatively recently settled colonies, whose people were deeply divided by religion, ethnicity, and experience; whose economies were equally fragmented into distinct sectors (with different needs and interests); and which lacked the communications infrastructure to integrate scattered peoples into a single community, reference to an English past (and all that heritage stood for in terms of industrial ascendancy, imperial achievement, and political tradition) provided a ready symbolic touchstone for the majority of the region's peoples. They were – as they never tired of reiterating in protest at the reduction of British preferential tariffs or tenancy in Prince Edward Island – British *subjects*, their rights, implicitly, those secured by the Glorious Revolution of 1688, rather than the 'rights of man' due 'citizens'.[53] Guard and cherish and preserve the integrity of 'our limited monarchy,' the 'nice balance' of 'our respective estates and realms,' urged Bishop Medley. 'Our sufferings and our joys are the common property of the empire.'

Time and again, colonials looked to developments in seventeenth-century England to give meaning to their circumstances. For Orangemen the references were specific and the images vivid. Ritual, songs, and parades celebrated the Protestant Succession, revered William III, and commemorated the Battle of the Boyne. In lodge after lodge, members of the order learned a particular version of the past that made much of loyalty to the Crown and the need for eternal vigilance against popish intrigue. For others, the lessons of history were framed in less explicit and extreme terms, but they were nonetheless important. If the tenants of Prince Edward Island were downtrodden, they could find hope in 'acquaintance with English history,' which revealed 'the historic tendency of the race to throw off oppression.' When, in 1868, Canadian initiatives were seen to threaten Nova-Scotian liberties, they were compared to the rule of the Stuarts. And seventeenth-century 'Country Party' rhetoric, suspicious of centralized government, opposed to taxation, and attached to local custom, echoed through the pre-Confederation Maritimes.[54]

Of all this there was no better symbol than the monarchy, and there is no better indication of its significance in the Maritimes than the events surrounding the visit of the Prince of Wales to the region in 1860. Although Halifax publisher William Annand made available a collection of Joseph Howe's letters and speeches in 1858 – and in the next decade or so the 'discontinuity' of (impending) Confederation spurred publication of documents pertaining to the early-eighteenth-century history of Nova Scotia, a new, political, history of New Brunswick, and other reflections of a developing awareness of provincial distinctiveness – through the mid-century decades, 'loyal, true, and brave' Maritimers courted Victoria's smile.[55] To the degree that they did so, the 'colonial state' remained in some important sense a limited state.

And so, in the end, there is perhaps no better way of making sense of this kaleidoscopic picture than with a simile. Recognizing with historical sociologist Michael Mann that social life is built upon the overlapping skeletons of state, culture, and economy, but that these are very rarely congruent, we might conceptualize the frameworks that gave pattern to life in the mid-nineteenth-century Maritimes as the parts of a wheel.[56] In this view, London appears as the ideological and emotional hub of the 'political culture' of the Maritimes; the colonial state becomes the rim, linking people together and exercising certain authority over them, but generally in a weak and provisional way – peripherally; and religion, ethnicity, and locality, coupled with those quintessentially Victorian doctrines of system, sobriety, thrift, and toil (especially on the land), assume the position of spokes, giving shape and form and structure to the everyday lives and identities of most colonists.

## NOTES

This paper represents a first effort to bring to bear on the Maritimes some of the literature and ideas that have been the focus of discussion among human geographers at the University of British Columbia for some time now. I am indebted to that group – especially Trevor Barnes, Derek Gregory, Cole Harris, Dan Hiebert, David Ley, and Gerry Pratt – for the lively, challenging, but always pleasant and thought-provoking exchanges we have shared. Although I gladly give credit for the stimulus I have derived from these fine colleagues, I also absolve them of responsibility for the particular interpretive paths I have chosen. My debt to the Killam Program of the Canada Council is substantial. Their award of a 1988–90 Research Fellowship provided the vital freedom to read and think that lies behind this essentially experimental paper. I also thank Marlene Shore and Ramsay Cook for their comments; and I am grateful to Greg Marquis for providing me with a copy of his unpublished paper 'In Defence of Liberty.'

1 For more extended comment on the development of the region see: G. Wynn, *Timber Colony: A Historical Geography of Early Nineteenth Century New Brunswick* (Toronto: University of Toronto Press 1981); W.S. MacNutt, *The Atlantic Provinces. The Emergence of Colonial Society, 1712–1857* (Toronto: McClelland and Stewart 1965), 213–70; and W.M. Whitelaw, *The Maritimes and Canada before Confederation* (Toronto: Oxford University Press 1934), 7–37. J. Gwyn, ' "A Little Province Like This": The Economy of Nova Scotia under Stress, 1812–1853,' *Canadian Papers in Rural History* 6 (1988), 192–225, is the most important recent work.

2 Some of these cleavages were explored, for example, in A.H. Clark, 'Old World Origins and Religious Adherence in Nova Scotia,' *Geo-*

graphical Review 50 (1960), 54–72; A.H. Clark, Three Centuries and the Island (Toronto: University of Toronto Press 1959). For a general review of the ethnic-diversity theme see G. Wynn, 'Ethnic Migrations and Atlantic Canada: Geographical Perspectives,' Canadian Ethnic Studies / Etudes Ethniques au Canada 18 (1986), 1–15.

3 The point is evident in almost all general surveys of the region's history and/or geography. In addition to the works noted above, see G. Wynn, 'The Maritimes: The Geography of Fragmentation and Underdevelopment,' in L.D. McCann, ed., Heartland and Hinterland: A Geography of Canada (Scarborough, Ont.: Prentice-Hall 1987), 174–246; J.G. Reid, Six Crucial Decades: Times of Change in the History of the Maritimes (Halifax: Nimbus Publishing 1987). For quotations in this paragraph see: A.G. Bailey, 'Creative Moments in the Culture of the Maritime Provinces,' in his Culture and Nationality: Essays by A.G. Bailey (Toronto: McClelland and Stewart 1972), 49; R.C. Harris and J. Warkentin, Canada before Confederation (Toronto: Oxford University Press 1974), 169; MacNutt, Atlantic Provinces 268; C. Bruce, 'Words Are Never Enough,' in R. Cockburn and R. Gibbs, eds, Ninety Seasons: Modern Poems from the Maritimes (Toronto: McClelland and Stewart 1974), 62. See also on this theme G.A. Rawlyk, ed., Historical Essays on the Atlantic Provinces (Toronto; McClelland and Stewart 1967), 1; D.C. Harvey, 'The Heritage of the Maritimes,' Dalhousie Review 14 (1934), 29; J.M. Beck, 'The Maritimes: A Region or Three Provinces?' Transactions Royal Society of Canada, Series IV, 15 (1977), 301–13.

4 C.G.D. Roberts, 'Tantramar Revisited,' in D. Pacey, ed., The Collected Poems of Sir Charles G.D. Roberts (Wolfville, NS: Wombat Press 1987), 78–9

5 That the focus of what follows is more heavily upon New Brunswick and Nova Scotia than Prince Edward Island reflects my own disproportionate knowledge of the mid-nineteenth-century Maritime colonies as much as the relative thinness of good work on the island (which the researches of Ian Ross Robertson, in particular, are at long last beginning to overcome). Throughout, I have kept footnoting to the major works upon which particular sections of my discussion depend; fuller details of the sources of quotations are generally available in these works.

6 Rather than proclaim a renowned model or deep philosophical roots in justification of the rather idiosyncratic organization of this paper, I trust that the point of this structure, and the travel/exploration metaphor – neither of which is entirely irrelevant to the wider purposes of this essay – will become evident in its conclusion. If any single piece of writing shaped my initial experimentation with this form it was perhaps my recollection of K.S. Inglis, 'Ceremonies in a Capital Landscape: Scenes in the Making of Canberra,' Daedalus (Winter 1985),

85–126, although a second reading of it, after I had embarked on my own piece, left me disappointed that it fell short in the task of interpretation.

7 T.W. Acheson, *Saint John: The Making of a Colonial Urban Community, 1815–1860* (Toronto: University of Toronto Press 1985) offers a full and careful treatment of most of the material summarized here; as elsewhere in this essay, emphases and arguments are not necessarily those of the works from which information is drawn.

8 Acheson, *Saint John*, 92–114, is complemented here by S.W. See, 'The Orange Order and Social Violence in Mid-Nineteenth-Century Saint John,' *Acadiensis* 13 (1983), 68–92.

9 Acheson, *Saint John*, 100

10 Ibid., 219

11 *New Brunswick Courier* (Saint John), 9 Jan. 1841

12 Acheson, *Saint John*, 224

13 This tale can be found in the *St Andrews Standard*, 14 and 21 Mar. 1840, in the form of two letters from Patrick Medley to the Printer.

14 J. Ross, *Remarks and Suggestions on the Agriculture of Nova Scotia* (Halifax 1855); further discussion of this literature and its place in the agricultural improvement movement can be found in my 'Exciting a Spirit of Emulation among the "Plodholes": Agricultural Reform in Pre-Confederation Nova Scotia,' *Acadiensis* 20:1 (1990), 5–51.

15 J. Murray, 'New Rhynie' Farm Diary and Accounts, 1853. Public Archives of Nova Scotia, MG100, vol. 194, no. 16

16 A.L. Spedon, *Rambles among the Bluenoses; Or, Reminiscences of a Tour through New Brunswick and Nova Scotia* (Montreal: J. Lovell 1863), 59–65

17 F.S. Cozzens, *Acadia: Or a Month with the Blue Noses* (New York: Derby and Jackson 1859), 33

18 The fullest treatment of the development of these asylums is in H.M. Hurd, ed., *The Institutional Care of the Insane in the United States and Canada* 4 vols (Baltimore: Johns Hopkins University Press 1916–17), 1:427–97; 4:37–119, 203–18. D. Francis has summarized much of this material in his 'The Development of the Lunatic Asylum in the Maritime Provinces,' *Acadiensis* 6 (1977), 23–38.

19 Cozzens, *Acadia*, iv

20 J.F.W. Johnston, *Notes on North America, Agricultural, Economical and Social* 2 vols (Edinburgh: Blackwood 1851), 1:7

21 Cozzens, *Acadia*, 40–1

22 This discussion derives in large part from A.A. Brookes, ' "Doing the Best I Can": The Taking of the 1861 New Brunswick Census,' *Histoire Sociale / Social History* 9 (May 1976), 70–91

23 Details of the royal progress can be found in the appropriate provincial newspapers, but there is a full and effective summary in *The Tour of H.R.H. The Prince of Wales through British America and the United*

*States, by a British Canadian* (Montreal: J. Lovell 1860), 25–51, from which most of this discussion is derived.

24 I think back here to one of the distant roots of my discipline, to the work of Grove Karl Gilbert, geologist and explorer of the American West who argued over a century ago (in 'The Inculcation of Scientific Method by Example,' *American Journal of Science*, 3rd ser., 31 [1886], 286–7) that 'The great investigator is primarily and pre-eminently a man who is rich in hypotheses'; that 'A phenomenon having been observed, or a group of phenomena established by empiric classification, the investigator invents an hypothesis in explanation'; and that 'In the testing of hypotheses lies the prime difference between the investigator and the theorist. The one seeks diligently for the facts that may overthrow his tentative theory, the other closes his eyes to these and searches only for those which will sustain it.' For more on Gilbert, see R.J. Chorley, A.J. Dunn, and R.P. Beckinsale, *The History of the Study of Landforms; Or the Development of Geomorphology*, vol. 1 (New York: J. Wiley and Sons 1964), 546–72.

25 The arguments of this paragraph have, of course, been well made several times; for examples old and new see M. Bloch, *The Historian's Craft* (New York: Vintage Books 1953) and B. Bailyn, 'The Challenge of Modern Historiography,' *American Historical Review* 87 (1982), 1–24.

26 I borrow the 'grand maps' phrase from D. Gregory, who has used it in his forthcoming ' "Grand Maps of History": Structuration Theory and Social Change.' As Gregory points out, it was used originally by Theda Skocpol to refer to the recovery of sociology's historical imagination.

27 The essential books in the rapidly growing literature against which the vignettes are considered in the pages that follow are: M. Mann, *The Sources of Social Power* vol. 1, *A History of Power from the Beginning to* A.D. *1760* (Cambridge: Cambridge University Press 1986); P. Corrigan and D. Sayer, *The Great Arch: English State Formation as Cultural Revolution* (Oxford: Blackwell 1985); A. Giddens, *The Constitution of Society: Outline of the Theory of Structuration* (Cambridge: Polity Press 1984); A. Giddens, *A Contemporary Critique of Historical Materialism*, 2 vols, vol. 1, *Power, Property and the State* (London: Macmillan: 1981); vol. 2, *The Nation State and Violence* (Berkeley: University of California Press 1987). Here, I trust, some of the reasons for the travel metaphor around which this paper is built begin to come into focus. In a sense this essay is intentionally double-edged. Its first purpose is to look at the Maritimes through the lenses provided by the above-mentioned literature; this, so to speak, involves a certain 'rummaging in the hold of history' in an effort to rearrange some of the cargo borne by Clio's large Maritime fleet. Its second is to respond to the challenge of 'evolving an appropriate style, a mode of discourse' capable of wedding evidence and theory, of transcending the dualism between 'analytic' and 'narrative'

history, and of dealing coherently with space, time, agency, and structure; on this challenge see P. Abrams, 'History, Sociology, Historical Sociology,' *Past and Present* 87 (1980), 3–16. It may well be that I hit neither target squarely here, but it does seem important that the effort to ground Giddens' ideas (in particular) be made, because in much of his writing 'particular contexts are used more as passive illustrations than as active explanations,' N. Thrift, 'Bear and Mouse or Bear and Tree? Anthony Giddens's Reconstitution of Social Theory,' *Sociology* 19 (1985), 621.

28 M. Weber, *Economy and Society* (Berkeley: University of California Press 1978), 1:100–5; Corrigan and Sayer, *Great Arch*, 'Afterthoughts,' 182–5; Giddens, *Nation State and Violence*, 123–33. Through this first section of the conclusion, I attempt to realize, in a way, Giddens' claim that theoretical concepts (such as those of structuration theory) are 'sensitizing devices,' and that being theoretically informed does not mean 'always operating with a welter of abstract concepts.' Thus such 'theorizing' as there is here is deliberately unobtrusive; given the focus of the workshop for which this paper was written, it draws most explicitly from Corrigan and Sayer, *Great Arch*.

29 Paul Jones to the Editors, *New Brunswick Courier*, 5, 12, and 26 Jan., 2, 9, and 16 Feb., 2 Mar. 1850. This item and several of those discussed below are considered at greater length in my ' "Deplorably Dark and Demoralized Lumberers": Rhetoric and Reality in Early Nineteenth Century New Brunswick,' *Journal of Forest History* 24 (1980), 168–87.

30 The temperance movement is treated in J.K. Chapman, 'The Mid-Nineteenth-Century Temperance Movement in New Brunswick and Maine,' *Canadian Historical Review* 35 (1954), 43–60, and in E.J. Dick, 'From Temperance to Prohibition in 19th Century Nova Scotia,' *Dalhousie Review* 61 (1981), 530–52.

31 W.S. MacNutt, *New Brunswick, a History: 1784–1867* (Toronto: Macmillan 1963), 351. Further thought on this general theme is provoked by J. Fingard, 'The Relief of the Unemployed Poor in Saint John, Halifax, and St. John's, 1815–1860,' *Acadiensis* 5 (1975), 32–53.

32 J.S. Mill, cited in Corrigan and Sayer, *Great Arch*, 129

33 See, 'Orange Order,' 79–80.

34 I.R. Robertson, 'The Bible Question in Prince Edward Island from 1856 to 1860,' *Acadiensis* 5 (1976), 3–25; see also his 'Party Politics and Religious Controversialism in Prince Edward Island from 1860 to 1863,' *Acadiensis* 7 (1978), 29–59.

35 A.J.B. Johnston, 'Popery and Progress: Anti-Catholicism in Mid-Nineteenth Century Nova Scotia,' *Dalhousie Review* 64 (1984), 146–53

36 J. Fingard, 'Jailbirds in Victorian Halifax,' in P.B. Waite, S. Oxner, and T.G. Barnes, eds, *Law in a Colonial Society: The Nova Scotia Experience* (Toronto: Carswell 1984), 89–102

37 D.C. Harvey, 'The Intellectual Awakening of Nova Scotia,' *Dalhousie Review* 13 (1933), 1–22

38 T.C. Haliburton, *The Clockmaker; Or the Sayings and Doings of Samuel Slick of Slickville*, 1st-3rd Ser. (London: R. Bentley 1839–40); nor indeed should the role of Joseph Howe be overlooked: see J.M. Beck, *Joseph Howe* (Kingston: McGill-Queen's University Press 1982), vol. 1, *Conservative Reformer, 1804–48* and vol. 2, *The Briton Becomes Canadian, 1848–73*.

39 Robertson, 'Bible Question,' 3

40 S. Oxner, 'The Evolution of the Lower Court of Nova Scotia,' in Waite, et al., eds, *Law in a Colonial Society*, 59–80. J.M. Beck, *The Evolution of Municipal Government in Nova Scotia, 1749–1973* (Halifax 1973). H. Whalen, *The Development of Local Government in New Brunswick* (Fredericton 1973), 11–39

41 J. Howe, *Lord Falkland's Government* (Halifax 1842), 2–7

42 Cited in G. Marquis, 'In Defence of Liberty: 17th-Century England and 19th-Century Maritime Political Culture,' paper delivered at the Atlantic Canada Studies Conference, Edinburgh 1988, 9

43 For examples see G. Wynn, 'Administration in Adversity: The Deputy Surveyors and Control of the New Brunswick Crown Forest before 1844,' *Acadiensis* 7 (1977), 49–65; S.J. Hornsby, 'An Historical Geography of Cape Breton Island in the Nineteenth Century' (PH D diss., University of British Columbia 1986), 82–91.

44 Sorely limited though it is, this discussion attempts to edge towards an exploration of the 'fundamental *reciprocity* between theoretical constructs and empirical materials,' an approach that some have found wanting in Giddens' writing; see, for example, N. Gregson, 'Structuration Theory: Some Thoughts on the Possibilities for Empirical Research,' *Environment and Planning* D 5 (1987), 73–91; for the reciprocity quote see D. Gregory, 'Thoughts on Theory,' *Environment and Planning* D 3 (1985), 387. The most relevant of Giddens' writings to the discussion that follows is *Nation State and Violence*, but see also *Power, Property and the State* and *Constitution of Society*. The extensive literature commenting on Giddens' project is also useful in explicating its evolving pattern; in a mountain of material see, for example, A. Callinicos, 'Anthony Giddens: A Contemporary Critique,' *Theory and Society* 14 (1985), 133–66; H.F. Dickie-Clark, 'Anthony Giddens's Theory of Structuration,' *Canadian Journal of Political and Social Theory* 8 (1984), 92–110; D. Gregory, 'Space, Time and Politics in Social Theory; An interview with Anthony Giddens,' *Environment and Planning* D 2 (1984), 123–32; *Theory, Culture and Society* 1 (1982), 63–113, a 'symposium' on Giddens; and D. Held and J.B. Thompson, eds, *Social Theory of Modern Societies: Anthony Giddens and His Critics* (Cambridge: Cambridge University Press [1989]).

45 For another variant, see J. Fingard, 'Masters, and Friends, Crimps and

Abstainers: Agents of Control in 19th Century Sailortown,' *Acadiensis* 8 (1978), 22–46.

46 M. Barkley, 'The Loyalist Tradition in New Brunswick: The Growth and Evolution of an Historical Myth,' *Acadiensis* 4 (1975), 3–45

47 A.R. Stewart, 'Sir Edmund Head's Memorandum of 1857 on Maritime Union: A Lost Confederation Document,' *Canadian Historical Review* 26 (1945), 406–19

48 For some discussion of the geography of movement in the region during these years see J.S. Martell, 'Intercolonial Communications, 1840–1867,' Canadian Historical Association, *Report* (1938), 41–61, and G. Wynn, 'Moving Goods and People in Mid-Nineteenth Century New Brunswick,' *Canadian Papers in Rural History* 6 (1988), 226–39.

49 The allusions here are to M. Mann's observation that 'societies are much messier than our theories of them,' in *Sources of Social Power*, 4, and B. Kennedy's critique of rigid explanatory frameworks especially those derived from physics in 'A Naughty World,' *Transactions of the Institute of British Geographers* NS4 (1979), 550–8.

50 For further comment on this idea see S.F. Wise, 'God's Peculiar Peoples,' in W.L. Morton, ed., *The Shield of Achilles: Aspects of Canada in the Victorian Age* (Toronto: McClelland and Stewart 1968), 36–61.

51 W.L. Morton, 'Victorian Canada,' in *Shield of Achilles*, 311

52 Marquis, 'In Defence of Liberty'

53 Or, to provide another, earlier, example on the same lines, Joseph Howe's trial in 1835 is seen to have convinced him that 'his countrymen would not secure the rights of Englishmen ... through newspaper writing alone.' J.M. Beck, ' "A Fool for a Client": The Trial of Joseph Howe,' *Acadiensis* 3 (1974), 27–44

54 Marquis, 'In Defence of Liberty,' has more on these matters; any serious sampling of the contemporary press throws up examples.

55 W. Annand, *The Speeches and Public Letters of the Honorable Joseph Howe* 2 vols (Boston 1858); T.B. Akins, *Selections from the Public Documents of Nova Scotia* (Halifax 1869)

56 Mann, *Sources of Social Power*, ch. 1